chairman mao
meets the
apostle paul

chairman mao meets the apostle paul

Christianity, Communism, and the Hope of China

K. K. YEO
(YEO KHIOK-KHNG)

Brazos Press

A Division of Baker Book House Co
Grand Rapids, Michigan 49516

Published by Brazos Press
a division of Baker Book House Company
P.O. Box 6287, Grand Rapids, MI 49516-6287

Printed in the United States of America

Library of Congress Cataloging-in-Publication Data is on file at the Library of Congress, Washington, D.C.

For current information about all releases from Brazos Press, visit our web site:
http://www.brazospress.com

Faith, hope, love abide,

but the greatest of these is hope!

contents

acknowledgments

I wish to express my heartfelt gratitude to those who blessed me with grants and resources that made the research for this book possible. The following grants and libraries have been instrumental in this research project: Lilly Faculty Research Grant (1999–2000) from the Association of Theological Schools in the United States and Canada; sabbatical leave and leave of absence (July 1999–March 2000), as well as research funding, from Garrett-Evangelical Theological Seminary (Evanston, Ill.); American Academy of Religion Small Grant (1999); Society of Biblical Literature Research Grant (1999); the Three-Self Library (Shanghai); the Library of Congress (Washington, D.C.); the United Library of Garrett-Evangelical Theological Seminary and Seabury-Western Theological Seminary (Evanston, Ill.); the Skokie Public Library (Skokie, Ill.); and the libraries of Northwestern University (Evanston, Ill.), the Lutheran School of Theology (Chicago), the University of Chicago, Trinity International University (Deerfield, Ill.), Wheaton College (Wheaton, Ill.), and Princeton Theological Seminary (Princeton, N.J.).

The following scholars and friends were supportive and helpful to me in this research. Drs. Steven Long, Brook Ziporyn, and Kurt Richardson critically read the first draft and made numerous constructive suggestions. Lilly Faculty Fellows—Drs. Ronald Thiemann, Sang Hyun Lee, Edward Roslof, Thomas Buckley, Richard Lischer, Kathleen McVey, Jean-Marc Laporte—offered an interdisciplinary review of the project. Nancy Poling and Jana Bennett proofread the manuscript with care and speed. The Covenant Group (Steve Long, Ed Phillips, Phil Meadows, Julie Duncan) to which I belong at Garrett-Evangelical think, argue, and pray with me. Dr. Robert Jewett kept pushing me to my limit, passed along newspaper clippings and scholarly papers, and introduced me to two movies (*The Red Violin* and *Emperor and the Assassin*) relevant to the work. Drs. Donald Alexander, Philip Chia, Lo Lungkwong, Neal Fisher, and Jack Seymour were also instrumental in their leadership positions. I wish to acknowledge all the others who have helped me, even though I cannot mention all of their names here. Any errors or discrepancies are entirely mine. I also wish to thank Lau Kung-siu, Timothy, Joseph, and Phoebe Yeo for their understanding and kind spirits. I appreciate Rodney Clapp and Rebecca Cooper of Brazos Press for their professional help throughout the publication process.

Theological research and writing have always been redemptive to my soul. Particularly in this project, christological and apocalyptic eschatologies have sustained my effort to wrestle with theodicy in Chinese history. Bauckham explains it much better than I can: "Only eschatological transcendence can keep the theodicy question open, refusing to forget the dead and the victims in hope of their resurrection and glorification in the transcendent future which is the future of all history."[1] I want to acknowledge the presence of my relatives in Teocheow, Shantou. It was a great joy for me to meet my relatives at a small village for the first time during the summer of 1999. Following my visit, my father was able to return to his birthplace for the first time since he left for Sarawak (Malaysia) sixty-five years ago. I have heard of many tragedies and hopes they experienced prior to, during, and after Mao's era. To the great spirits of my ancestors and relatives in China, may they find faith, hope, and love!

This book is dedicated to Drs. Donald Alexander and Robert Jewett, whose mentoring spirits have nurtured me to be a Chinese Christian. Their friendship encourages me to be truthful, critical, and charitable to both the Chinese and Christian traditions, from which I find immeasureable resources for faith and hope. To Professors Alexander and Jewett, I am grateful.

Epiphany 2000

a note on style

The writing style of this book follows that of *Journal of Biblical Literature* and *Chicago Manual of Style*, two of the most accepted guides in the guild of biblical scholarship. However, since I list all bibliographical data in full in the bibliography at the end of the book, I have simply supplied the last names and the shortened titles of the article or book in the notes.

The most difficult stylistic issue concerns the spelling of Chinese words. Romanization of Chinese characters is quite simple, but several systems have been used up to now. The two most popular systems are Wade-Giles (traditional) and pinyin (recent). As much as possible, I have used the pinyin system because it is a more accurate rendition and a widely accepted system by Chinese worldwide and in the United Nations.[1] Thus, for example, I have used Beijing for Peking, Guangzhou for Canton, Mao Zedong for Mao Tse-tung. I do not change the words of scholars in quoted material, so readers will note some inconsistencies. Furthermore, names popularly referred to in the past but not in the pinyin system will remain as they were written in the past—thus Sun Yat-sen (Sun Zhongshan),[2] Bishop K. H. Ting (Ding Guangxun), Y. T. Wu (Wu Yaozong), T. C. Chao (Chao Zichen), Watchman Nee (Nee Tuosheng), Kuomingtan (KMT, Guomindang, Nationalist Party), and *Tien Fung* (rather than the correctly romanized *Tian Feng*). To be completely consistent, one would use Hsiangkang and Jiang Jieshi, but few readers would know that these refer to Hong Kong and Chiang Kai-shek respectively, so I have retained the more popular spelling. In some cases, I provide traditional spelling in parentheses, such as Meng Zi (Mencius), Yangtze (Yangzi), and Cai Hesen (Tsai Ho-sen).

One last point on writing Chinese names: I have decided to respect the Chinese propriety of putting the family name (Westerners call this the last name but to the Chinese this is the "source" name in which the genealogy is traced) first and the personal name last. It is not only wrong but also culturally improper (thus insulting) to refer to Tse-tung Mao or Guangxun Ding. Of course, if a Western format is adopted, such as

K. H. Ting, then one is not bound within Chinese culture to write Ting K. H.; in fact I think it is improper to write Ting K. H. Thus, my name is written as K. K. Yeo or Yeo Khiok-khng but not Yeo K. K. or Khiok-khng Yeo.

Words in original languages are transliterated and will be put in parentheses for readers who find greater affinities, thus richness in the nuances of meanings, with original languages.

introduction

Theological Politics and Utopian Studies

China is a mystical and changing dragon, a symbol that offers hope and happiness to the Chinese people. Westerners are intrigued by this dragon, especially its political and theological convictions, which often differ from our own. Of course, we read current events related to this mystical dragon based on our own ideologies or convictions, which explains in large measure why our position on certain issues differs from that of the Chinese. For example, should there be one China or two—the People's Republic of China (mainland) and the Republic of China, Taiwan—and what role should the United States of America play in shaping relations between China and Taiwan? With respect to human rights, the exiled Tibetan Buddhist leader, Dalai Lama, has long enjoyed respect and sympathy from many Westerners who often question the human-rights record in China. Thus it is no surprise that many American friends tell me that the Chinese government's crackdown on Li Hongzhi's Falun Gong (Falun Dafa is a syncretistic form of Buddhist meditation and *qi-gong* exercise whereby energy flow is regulated toward healing and gaining supernatural power) violates human rights as well as religious and political freedom. Similarly, though it is a silent topic in China, many wish to know more about the prodemocracy movement culminating in the Tiananmen Square incident.

Other events likewise reveal how one's convictions influence one's view of current events. For example, recently the Taiwanese-born scientist Li Wunho was charged and acquitted of stealing and passing to the Chinese government the blueprints of American nuclear technology at the Los Alamos nuclear facility. Although Li was shackled and put in solitary confinement, his unfair treatment by the American government never gained public attention in the States. Yet week after week *Yazhou Zhoukan* (*Asian Newsweek*) published articles of outcry and protest. In addition, the 2000 Nobel Prize in Literature was awarded to a mainland Chinese now residing in Paris. Could it be that Mr. Gao, whose most widely known work is the novel *Soul Mountain,* won the prize because of his reflection on the political reality of China, in addition to his literary excellence? Most recently (April 2001) an American spy plane flying over the Chinese airspace at Hainan Island was shot down by the Chinese. Already tense Sino-American relations were strained even more over the rhetoric of President Bush's apology: he used the word "regret," while China demanded the word "sorry." In all these cases, the real cause of tension is perhaps the ideological differences between the United States and China.

The examples given above suggest two points. First, since Mao's China came into existence in 1949, this dragon has mystified many of us. Many fear and distrust China because of what Mao has done. We will do better in relating to China and understanding the complex situation in China if we know how Mao has shaped China's political and theological convictions. Since Mao interjected his views and values into the old Chinese worldview and ethos, this book will focus on the impact of politics and theology (from Marx) on Chinese tradition and culture.

The second point we can learn from the examples given above is that, though Mao is dead, Maoism is not. This changing and creative dragon has a discernible personality and behavior. The New China founded by Mao appears to be another kind of animal—communists rule, but the rulers of New China continue to be divinized as the sons of heaven. Chinese politics (government) and theological claims (divinity) are interrelated, and this relationship has not changed in Chinese history. Even in the post-Mao China, with all the modernizations now taking place, the thought of Mao ("Maoism" in Chinese) is ingrained in the Chinese way of life.

"Chairman Mao Meets the Apostle Paul" is not a commercial cliché; it is an interpretive history of how Chinese communism and Chinese Christianity met and clashed during Mao's regime. My interest is to allow Paul to engage Mao in matters of politics and theology, eschatology and utopianism. This book will focus on eschatology (Marxist, Maoist, and Christian) because Maoism allows Chinese culture to meet Christian theology through Marxism.

This book does not seek primarily to describe the historical facts. Rather, it attempts to offer a critical interpretation of historical events under Mao's regime. Although the Cultural Revolution is a past event, the human spirit's quest for an ideal society and hope for happiness is always a present reality. Even the Chinese government has reflected critically on the Cultural Revolution, admitting Mao's "gross mistakes" but concluding that his "merits outweighed his errors." I too will reflect on the Cultural Revolution, however, I will do so through a critical engagement of this event with certain Pauline writings. Thus, "Chairman Mao Meets the Apostle Paul" is a hermeneutical motif allowing Pauline eschatology critically to engage Maoist utopianism. This meeting between Mao and Paul will illumine the end (purpose, goal, meaning, termination, extermination) and process (sovereignty and freedom, time and space, secular and sacred, will and violence, transcendence and salvation) of history.

Mao and Paul meet again and again in the lives of Chinese Christians,[1] Chinese religionists, and theologians, especially those who have read the Bible and the Little Red Book. Even though I am a Chinese Christian too young to have struggled with the complex reality of social, political, and religious issues during Mao's regime in China, I am a Chinese theologian and a diaspora Chinese Christian committed to making sense of Maoist thought and Pauline theology. Mao and Paul met in my reading of the letters of Paul to the Thessalonians many years ago when I first became a student of the Bible and the thought of those Christians in China who lived under Mao's regime. The main impetus for juxtaposing Thessalonians and Chinese Christianity, as well as Paul and Mao, was the continuous flash of images that overlap in the two seemingly disconnected epochs of history: the similar religious experience of those Christians in Thessalonica under the Roman regime and the experience of Christians in China under Mao, especially in the political context of considerable restriction of freedom; the context of suffering and violence and the eschatological and utopian ideologies of Mao and Paul; the search for meaning in the histories of Maoism and Paulinism; and the parallels in the ways scriptural study and liturgical forms have been fervently used to worship Mao and Christ.

As a Chinese biblical scholar who works with crosscultural hermeneutics, I take it as my goal and methodology to bring the Bible, Chinese culture, and contemporary theological concerns together.[2] On one plane the proposed research is a triangular hermeneutic between Chinese Christians, biblical texts (especially the Thessalonian correspondence), and Maoist ideology; on another plane it is a triangular hermeneutic between Christians today, biblical texts, and our concerns about the new millennium.

Thesis: The "Theological Politics" of Paul and Mao

Hope in Theological Virtues and Anagogical Interpretation

Since this project focuses on the theological politics of Paul and Mao with regard to their different views of history, the fourfold interpretation/sense of the precritical model provides insights into the form and content of theological politics.[3] The *literal* meaning of a scriptural text (whether a writing of Paul or Mao) contains the historical or the immediate extralinguistic referent. The *allegorical* meaning contains the interpretive code for metaphorization. A *tropological* meaning is a psychological or ethical reading for the community. Finally, the *anagogical* interpretation involves a political reading concerning the meaning of history.[4]

The literal provides the basis for the other three levels of interpretation. In the medieval period the last three senses or meanings corresponded to the three theological virtues of faith, love, and hope, a distinctively Pauline formula. Yet history does not exhaust the meaning of an event. Consequently, theology provides Christians with the springboard for their metaphorical interpretation. Their Christian experience allows them to imagine in the allegorical meaning what the church is and teaches regarding trusting and believing in Christ. An allegorical meaning corresponds to the virtue of faith. Theology, however, is not an end in itself. It will lead to doxology or ethics or to an awesome response to God's grace. Thus, a tropological meaning teaches believers to live as God's people, that is, to practice the virtue of love (of God and neighbors). Yet this is not all, for theology is not concerned primarily with anthropology; theology is concerned with God and God's activities in the cosmos and history. Consequently, an anagogical meaning teaches the cosmos that all are under God's dominion and that they are to *expect* God's future of perfection—the virtue of hope.[5] Methodologically speaking, the study will be carried out on three levels: literary, crosscultural and dialogical, and critically constructive.[6]

This meeting between Paul and Mao is theologically revealing and methodologically legitimate because Pauline theology is political and Maoist politics is theological.[7] Moreover, the perspective of this volume on Mao and Paul is *perspectival*.[8] It is not a balanced and comprehensive study about the lives of Mao and Paul; it is about the theological thinking of both men with respect to their views of history. Paul, being a Christian theologian and apostle, explains his distinctive religious life and theological thinking. Does Mao have his religious or theological perception and worldview? The answer is affirmative. While one might find a theological inquiry into Mao suspect, since he was a politician, I am convinced that attention to millenarian and utopian language allows us to see the religious and theological aspects of his thinking in their sociopolitical praxis. One should not assume that one who does not have an explicitly professed religious lifestyle does not have a religion or theology. I will show that Mao had a profound religious conviction and worldview. I want to take Mao's political theory and practice seriously, but I want also to situate Maoism in the context of the Chinese utopian tra-

16

dition and worldview and then to observe how Chinese Christians living under Mao's regime understood (or did not understand) his religious thinking.

Finally, an interdisciplinary study of theology and politics is a realistic and comprehensive enterprise, because political theology and theological politics were the respective essences of Paul and Mao's thinking. By that I do not mean that every theology, such as that of Paul, will form a state and assume governmental power.[9] Nor do I mean that every political form, such as that of Mao, when packaged in religious language and form, denotes a mature understanding of God. I mean that in reality the spheres of influence in theology and politics always interact with each other. Consequently, any theology or political ideology that intentionally interacts with the other constitutes a more responsible movement in society.

Theology and Politics: Where Boundaries Meet

Maoist authoritarian utopianism for the sake of Chinese nationalism and the Christian reading of Pauline eschatology into Western omnipotence reflect the same imperial hermeneutics whose "political unconscious"[10] is the centralization of power by means of dominating the periphery. Thus, a reading of Mao's and Paul's texts is not an objective, detached, absolute enterprise, for Paul's and Mao's ideologies are political theology.[11]

But what is *theology* and what is *politics?* Theology is concerned with the redemptive and creative activities of God in the world through the divine agents of the Messiah (Immanuel), the church (the body of Christ), the sacraments (re-presentation of divine future and grace in the present brokenness), as well as the cosmic movement of the Holy Spirit.[12] Politics is concerned with the government of a state or a society for the common good through an exercise of power in defense (sovereignty, law, and order), economy (distribution of resources and contribution of abilities), education (aspiration and transformation of human beings), and so forth. Theology and politics share the common concerns of hoping to construct an ideal society of goodness, order, and prosperity vis-à-vis a utopian society. In other words, all forms of Christian theologies and all forms of politics are acts of imagining (in the classical sense of poetics and *mythos* and not in the modern sense of unreality or wild fantasy) a better world. Imagination works in metaphorization as human interpreters reimagine and redescribe reality.[13] The *mythos* or imagination of theology and politics is the hermeneutical coding and ideological presupposition that differentiates theology from politics, even though they are distinguishable.[14] Pauline eschatology and Maoist utopianism have similar aspirations to imagine a better world.

The thesis I intend to demonstrate is as follows: The *mythos* of Paul's apocalyptic eschatology is the coming God whose crucified and resurrected Son defines for humanity the end of history—end as both *finis* and *telos*. At the end (*finis*) of time is the new beginning (*telos*) of heaven and earth. God's redemptive purpose at the *finis* of history defines for history its *telos*. God's eschatology does not give in to *finis*; it transcends it.

Paul's apocalyptic eschatology may look dualistic in differentiating the secular and the sacred, the earthly and the heavenly, but in fact it seeks to overcome the myth that sacred and secular realms are two separate realities. In fact, the future of the coming God "intrudes into" the world of violence, lostness, and chaos. God's future breaks into history to bring about wholeness (*shalom*), life superabundant, and meaning despite possible destruction at the end of the world. In Pauline Christology especially, the significant point is not the incarnation or the infancy story; it is Christ's crucifixion and resurrection. The end of the crucified Christ was his true beginning. "Christian eschatology follows this christological pattern in all its personal, historical, and cosmic dimensions: *in the end is the beginning*."[15] There is hope amidst all historical ambiguities because God's future transcends history and God is the actor in history. The death of Jesus reveals the hypostatic union of God and humanity that points to the intimate involvement of God in history.

I use words and phrases such as "interruption," "intrusion," and "breaking into" to describe God's involvement in history. As Jürgen Moltmann rightly points out, "intrusion" and "interruption" do not in and of themselves define an eschatological category such as dualism.[16] Rather, my use of such words reflects the *seemingly* dualistic view of apocalypticism. That is, "interruption" and a dualistic worldview may seem to imply that God and the world exist in an alienated relationship, but of all the views of history, apocalyptic eschatology describes most forcefully God's indwelling of the world. Apocalypticism's cosmic dualism does not assume alienation between God and the world, it portrays the radical engagement and conversion of the earthly by the transcendental realm.

Apocalypticism's cosmic dualism arises from its countercultural theologizing, for apocalypticism emerges always as a sharp critique to a dominant ideology that holds to a *pax Romana* (will to power) or a holy empire (divine monarchy). The emphasis of Paul's apocalyptic eschatology is a critical response to these ideologies of de-eschatology, a response that shows God's radical and dynamic involvement in the world. That God is scarce, distant, or absent in human history could be said to be the thesis of Marxism and Maoism, the kind of thesis that Pauline eschatology would critique.

Marxism and Maoism's *mythos* has a secular, thus anti-God, political theology. I read the Pauline interpretation of the "antichrist" in 2 Thessalonians 2 as a critique of Mao. The "antichrist" is a political or religious leader who claims to be God, one who thus assumes hegemonic power and brings about an extremely violent lawlessness. Maoism accepts a Marxist view of historical materialism that is devoid of God's future and involvement; it is a complete distortion of Christian eschatology. The result of Maoism's adaptation of the Chinese cyclical view of time to Marxist materialism is the secular utopianism of "permanent revolution." Furthermore, when Maoism combines its Confucian patriarchal consolidation of power with the Marxist insistence on class struggle and the Chinese Legalist maneuver of power by means of militarism, the result is the personality cult of a "divine emperor." In short, Mao lives in a utopian dream by prolonging the historical present and reigning with violence.

In the "divine emperor" of Maoist theological politics, the *mythos* of politics and that of theology become one and the same, with de-eschatology as the view of history. Inevitably, this secular *mythos* would first reduce Christian theology and God's church to a fragment of social life that is termed "sacred" (theology is no more the comprehensive view of God's redemptive activities in the world), then replace theology with its own secular vision of salvation, hope, and progress.[17] As I will show, the "secular" *mythos* does not mean that Marxism and Maoism are ignorant of transcendence. In fact, as in both Marxism and Maoism, the secular *mythos* is a critique and replacement of the Christian *mythos*. Pauline eschatology points to the "in-breaking" reign of God in the world by means of "sacralization"—desecularization by means of incarnation—that is, "a deeper and deeper saturation of the world with the spirit of God."[18]

Agenda and Outline

To delineate the above thesis in the critical dialogue between Paul and Mao, I center the discussion around their view of history: (de-)eschatology, (anti-)utopia, and millenarian hope(lessness). Chapters 1 and 2 provide background material concerning various views of history from the Bible and China in the context of a pursuit of utopia that engenders hope or hopelessness for any community facing violence, suffering, and meaninglessness. These chapters preview the landscape of both Mao's and Paul's thought with regard to the *ideal society* and the spatial-temporal *process of history*. I do not intend to survey comprehensively all views of history and utopian thought. My purpose, rather, is to trace the rise of eschatological, apocalyptic, and utopian views of history in their particular cultural contexts. My primary thesis, that the hope for an ideal society is a theological move to transform cultural ambiguity, will be clearly seen in the history both of the East and of the West.

Chapters 3 and 4 begin a dialogue about utopian views of history between the East and the West, with the Marxist view playing a key role. These chapters analyze how Maoism reappropriates or rejects both Marxist and Chinese views of history, especially their eschatological and utopian motifs. The thesis throughout these chapters is that one's view of history can bring about hope or hopelessness. The Marxist view of historical materialism attempts to create a communist utopia that will bring economic justice and proletarian empowerment to the working class. But the Marxist secular view of history ("philosophy of history") is devoid of God's radical involvement in class history; worse yet, its belief in "Promethean Revolution" rather than christological eschatology results in a historical process without either the *finis* of violence or the *telos* of the consummated *shalom*.

Chapters 5 and 6 work out the critical dialogue between Mao and Paul with regard to a utopian view of history and eschatological hope. I begin by tracing the rise of Maoism, focusing on the millenarian ideology of Mao and the rise of Chinese Christianity in response to the peculiar political and religious ideologies of the motherland. Mao's attitude toward religion is a wholesale import of Marx and Feuerbach, thus a secularization of the traditional Chinese worldview that includes "gods and ghosts" (chapter 5). The Marxist view of historical materialism creates for Mao, in his adaptation of a traditional cyclical worldview, a "philosophy of history" that is contradictory and permanently revolutionary. Mao is known for his political thought of *contradiction* and *permanent revolution*. Marxism has taught Maoism to eliminate the *finis* and *telos* of history, that is, both the ending of catastrophes and the goal of salvation. There is no christological eschatology in Marxism and Maoism. Marxism has also taught Maoism to replace theological politics with political philosophy. Since "God" is humanity's creation, a tool used by the powerful to enslave the working class, religion must be eliminated. But in rejecting God and God's activities in history, Marxism and Maoism trust in historical forces, revolutions of the proletariats. Maoism takes this a step further and divinizes the masses as god. The people acknowledge Mao as their national savior and worship him as god. In an attempt to separate politics from theology, Mao has created a new theology in his personality cult.

Chapters 7 and 8 focus on the utopianism of Maoism as it critically dialogues with Pauline eschatology. These chapters juxtapose Paul's eschatological critiques with the Maoist material, focusing on issues such as power, leadership, ideology, eschatology, utopianism, and millenarian hope. It has shocked me to discover that Mao's view of history and that of the Christian West are the same; both subscribe to a modern view of time as a linear progression. The scientific calculation of time creates a myth that time is merely a linear progression of past, present, and future. The past is taken to mean the passing of the present, the future is the prolongation of the present, and the present is the only possession one has. The realized eschatology of Mao and the Christian West places all their emphasis on the present.

The biblical and Pauline understanding of eschatology is radically different from the Maoist or Western view. From a biblical perspective, past, present, and future are not tenses but modes of existence and aspects of action.[19] In other words, God's narrative in human historical time is what Christian eschatology is all about. *Present* describes our spontaneous and continuous experience of the holy despite our current historical ambiguity and despair. *Past* refers to the realized acts of God in history. *Future* is the coming (advent or *parousia*) of God's radically new creation, which is assured by the past and to be realized in the present. Pauline eschatology is about the end of the catastrophic world and the beginning of God's kingdom. The manifest destiny of history is God's new creation toward wholeness.

Caught between the Christian West and Maoism, the Chinese church faced multiple challenges. Given the power differentiation between the Communist Party and the Chinese churches, one needs to be sympathetic to the Christian community's need to survive. My intent is not to describe Chinese Christianity as the perfect movement but to theologize about how Chinese Christians have understood (1) the eschatological hope of Pauline theology and (2) themselves to be called bearers of the holy. As God's community, the Chinese *ekklesia* knew of their beloved status in the divine election. They were called faithfully to bear witness to God's future arrival on Chinese soil.

Chapter 9 is a triangular dialogue among Mao, Paul, and Chinese Christianity. However, two interrelated themes are always in view throughout the last five chapters: one's view of history and the use of power. To complete the metaphorization process of this work, chapter 9 continues what the previous chapters have done: reimaging reality for the *Sitz im Leben* of our world today. It suggests the hermeneutical implications of this study for post-Paul Christians and post-Mao Chinese. These implications are significant because contemporary utopian and millenarian thoughts are pervasive. On the one hand, we witness a continuation of secular messianic movements in science and technology. Universal hope for the ideal society will persist in human history. And some speak of the end of history as worldwide peace and prosperity. On the other hand, we continue to witness apocalyptic terrorism and nihilism, fearful visions of extermination and termination without the kingdom of God.

There is no guarantee that hope will not disappoint us. In retrospect, we call such hope "false." But the theological performance of christological-eschatological hope is precisely that believers live out God's eschatology and allow God's manifest destiny for the world to be realized again and again. In other words, hope may disappoint us, but it can also be born again and again. We may not know how the historical future is going to unfold, but we have confidence that the future and its end are in God's hands—and that God's future already sustains us in his new creation. Because we do not know how the world is going to end, we need all the more to trust that God's new beginning will find us, amaze us, and raise us to new life.

Utopian Studies

Before going further, it is necessary to clarify a few terms used in this book: eschatology, apocalypse and apocalypticism, millenarianism, and utopianism. In a nutshell, *eschatology* is a theological term referring to the end and goal of history, *apocalypse* is a literary term (the documents or literary products can be traced back to second century B.C.E. of the Jewish exilic crisis), and *millenarian* is a sociological term referring to a community's hope for deliverance (traceable as far back as the Israelite deliverance from Egypt in the thirteenth century B.C.E.).

Eschatology has at least three meanings. First, it can refer to the study of the end time or end things, such as the final states, heaven and hell, the end of the world, or the second coming of Christ. Second, eschatology can refer to a teleology of history, that is, history's final goal and ultimate purpose. Since the Christian understanding of history's teleology is defined in terms of God's ultimate redemptive activities and God's future, eschatology is sometimes called a "theology of history." A third meaning is referred to as "radical eschatology" because "its tendency is to radically question *every* 'thing.'" Sauter explains: "The intent of radical eschatology is to be *theo*logy from its very roots (hence 'radical'). It talks about God by looking only to God and proclaiming God as 'the Coming One,' by becoming itself a sign of hope in everything it tries to say."[20] All three meanings play a part in biblical eschatology. Thus, since biblical eschatology envisions not only the end of the world but also the beginning of the new order, it can be said that eschatology is concerned with "last things" and "first things."[21] Christian eschatology sees in the end of the world the beginning of the new Jerusalem vis-à-vis the boundaryless, transcendent city of God that is constructed by the Lamb of God. In biblical theology, eschatology encompasses the three meanings above, and I will use the term as such in this volume as well.

The second term, *apocalypse,* means "revelation." It may refer to any literary work (e.g., the book of Revelation) that describes the end of the world, usually involving visions of transcendent realities, angelic intermediaries, and a cataclysmic battle between good and evil. Both eschatological and apocalyptic worldviews see history as under the control of God despite the destructive reign of evil in the present time.

Eschatology is similar to apocalypse except that the eschatological ending of history does not necessarily envision a violent destruction or contain a visionary description of the historical process. Furthermore, apocalyptic literature is closely associated with an "end-time" messianism.[22] While *apocalypse* is a literary genre (form), *apocalyptic eschatology* is a particular worldview (content). Related to these two is *apocalypticism,* which is the socioreligious movement (function) of those holding to apocalyptic theology.[23] Because of confusion in differentiating apocalypse, apocalyptic, and apocalypticism, as well as the value judgments that come with definitions of apocalypticism, most social scientists prefer the word *millenarianism* to *apocalyptic* when referring to movements.[24] My task in this work is to understand the theology and function of apocalypticism, that is, the worldview and activities of the millenarian community.

My use of the apocalyptic worldview in this volume focuses on the revealing acts of God in history. My thesis is that God's interruption in human history as seen in the death and resurrection of Christ allows us to discern the meaning and intended goal of history. God's involvement in history is apocalyptic in the sense that the Christ event is the meta-narrative and *mythos* by which we decipher meaning out of chaos, redemption out of violence.

Sociologists (whether social scientists or social historians) and anthropologists use the terms *millennial* and *millenarian* to refer to apocalyptic/eschatological groups. Related terms used by social scientists include millenarism, millennialism, millenarianism, chiliasm (from the Greek word meaning "thousand"), nativistic movements (the uprising of native groups against oppressive colonizers), revitalization movements (in which some golden age of the past is longed for), messianic movements (appearance of a charismatic savior), and crisis cults (radical religions that emerge in times of cultural crisis). A millennial expectation often involves certain charismatic manifestations, such as the extreme enthusiasm of the group.[25]

Millenarian language is neither religious nor antireligious; it is a sociological language that could describe any social movement, whether religious or political. Thus, to seek a common ground between Maoism and Christianity, I attempt to use the common language of sociology, the language of millenarian movements and utopian seekers, to refer to Maoist or Pauline communities. The sociological language allows each group to be itself as both meet and critically interact with one another. It is true, no doubt, that all sociopolitical language is also theological.[26] That is why speaking of the "theological politics" of Mao and Paul is methodologically valid.

The last central term to be defined is *utopia*, which is often understood to bear two meanings. The first meaning reflects the Greek compound *ou* plus *topos* ("no place"), while the second is based on the Greek *eu* plus *topos* ("good place"). If one takes the word to have a twofold meaning, then a better way to write the word would be "e/outopia."[27] Such forms of writing express the ambiguity and tension of the word: the hope of a good place somewhere *and* the ready acceptance of not reaching it, either because there is no such place or because one is not able to realize it.

Ernst Bloch in *The Principle of Hope* expounds the basic human consciousness of daydreaming in which the "Not-Yet-Existent" and the "Not-Yet-Conscious" anticipate the "Real-Possible."[28] Daydreaming is different from "mere fantasizing." Utopian hope is not merely a waking dream or wishful thinking; it is a willful thinking of the *summum bonum* (highest good).[29] Without the highest good, the perfect place envisioned is merely wishful thinking. When the wishful thinking of something that could be and will be becomes a conviction that present reality, especially evil reality, can be transformed, a vision of a better and possible future becomes a willful pursuit. It is the *tension* between the hope of striving for it and the understanding that one might not attain it that constitutes healthy human existence. Historically, there might have been no such place, but morally, imaging a good place is necessary because it offers hope and meaning to our existence as an individual, a society, a nation, or a world.[30]

The ideal, perfect, and good place is a transhistorical moral yearning and existential hope that provides history with a *telos*. Or vice versa, the *telos* provides history with the possibility of hope. History is a movement of time through space; thus the end speaks of goal and purpose. In the movement of time, purpose is a goal. The e/outopia gives history a future (*telos* as end), a meaning (*telos* as purpose), and a consummation (*telos* as goal).[31]

Conclusion

Even though utopian and millenarian thought can be characteristic of any religious or secular movement, the observation that utopia is the secular equivalent of millennium and that millennium is a religious form of utopia is certainly valid.[32] The utopian and millenarian perspectives are differentiated by their views of history, whether eschatologically oriented in goal and hope or controlled by God. Thus, the diverse millenarian views of history need to be differentiated in the next few chapters. Kumar argues, "If utopia is a serious speculation about the possibility of human betterment, it is the millennium that supplies the ingredient of hope without which such speculation becomes an idle fancy or an intellectual game."[33]

We will relate the discussion to the views of history held by Marxism and Maoism in the following chapters. The task for us is to observe how political and theological convictions of various systems bring about violence and devastation or hope and salvation.

1

utopian views of history from the bible

Eschatology, Apocalyptic Thought, and Millenarianism

Paulinism and Maoism are not simply theological or political ideas. They are various *praxes* of community striving to live in a less-than-perfect reality with courage and vision. The same can be said of the Jewish communities and the early Christian communities in the Bible. The process of theologization (the pursuit of and living in *summum bonum*) continues to be the human task as humans hope for utopia despite the harsh reality they are in. Whereas Marxism and Maoism secularize and replace Christian theology with a philosophy of history in reaction to the dominant political theology of Christian millenarian reign on earth, we will witness in this chapter an opposite theologizing process. The Jewish and Christian communities attempted to sacralize and replace the dominant secular politics of the day with a theology of history as they critiqued the Babylonian and Roman empires. Apocalyptic and millenarian eschatology feeds hope to these oppressed groups. In tracing the emergence of various strains of utopianism in Jewish and Christian communities, we will see the countercultural spirit of their theologies.

A Millenarian View of History in the Old Testament: From Paradise to Apocalyptic Eschatology

The Garden of Eden: Paradise Past and Future

Almost all primitive paradise narratives depict ideal settings found in pristine, pre-fall civilizations with rustic rivers and a fruitful garden. These settings are ideal conditions for human bliss because human toil does not yet exist. Simplicity and contentment are the characteristics of such bliss. Like other paradise narratives, the Genesis 2 account of the Garden of Eden is a utopian narrative, but it uniquely seeks to give a theological interpretation of paradise.

The Genesis story of this terrestrial paradise is different from paradise myths in other cultures in several ways. First, the Genesis account is theocentric; that is, the biblical paradise myth points to God's sovereignty in creation and God's triumph over evil as well as the human fall. This is clear if we read the paradise account in the narrative flow of the creation accounts. In contrast to the Babylonian belief that creation was the result of both divine coupling (birth of the gods) and divine conflict (creation of heaven, earth, and humans), Genesis 1 portrays God creating "the generation (*toledot*) of the heavens and the earth" (2:4a) by means of his word.[1] God is at work in creation and history, but God transcends creation and history. Lohfink writes: "History is not added to creation as something alien to it; creation is from the beginning so designed by God that it will unfold itself as history."[2] It was God's intention to create humans and to have them live in paradise. Even after the fall, since the paradise narrative is a post-fall theologization, God is perceived to be in full control of history.

Second, God's intention to bless human beings living in paradise is maintained only when they live in communion with God. This point is clear if we read the seventh day's Sabbath as not merely God ceasing to create but more precisely as God resting from work and enjoying the self-communion within the Godhead. Moreover, the Sabbath rest was divinely given to human beings to enter into as a day of rest (cessation from work) and blessedness (in communion with God).[3] Paradise is not returning human beings to themselves (secularism); paradise is the Creator's invitation of human beings back to God (doxological theology). Lohfink explains: "Through this day of rest that cuts periodically into life God draws the people out of its work every week anew, so that it cannot lose itself in world and work. It is to shape the world through its work, of course, but not to enslave itself to the world and its gods."[4]

Genesis 1 already narrates "the surplus of created things"[5] in God's creation. In Genesis 2, God further showers Adam and Eve with indefinite freedom and the power to rule the earth to the extent that it will be paradise. This gift of freedom is not for the sake of violent domination but rather for intimate communion with God (Sabbath), each other ("bone of my bones and flesh of my flesh" in 2:23), and God's creatures (the power of naming so that animals exist in a certain relationship with humanity).

Third, the paradise account, if read in juxtaposition to the fall narrative, portrays the means to maintain a blissful place, namely, living in a trusting relationship with God by means of God's word (or commandment). God's gift of freedom to humanity is guaranteed not anthropocentrically, by human will or delight, but theocentrically, by God's creative word. The creation accounts already highlight God's word as the medium of creation ("God says: 'Let there be . . .' " in 1:3, 6, 9, 11, 14, 15, 20, 24, 26). God also spoke to humanity (2:16–17), asking it by means of trusting in God's word not to eat the fruit from the tree of knowledge of good and evil. The description continues to say that the first sin came about when a tempter swayed Eve and Adam's trust in God's word (3:1–5). They doubted, distrusted, and then disobeyed God's word by eating the forbidden fruit (3:6). Only the first sin of Adam and Eve matters in accounting for the human fall, and the first sin of humanity is a theological one (trusting God or not), not a moral one (doing something right or not). Paradise is lost when humanity trusts the tempter more than the Creator. Thus, this Jewish-Christian paradise account explains reality theologically, not morally. The violent act of the tempter against the integrity and creativity of God's word leads to violence in history when Adam and Eve will their own destiny rather than turn to the God of plentitude and *summum bonum* in trust. Violence—such as the story of Cain and Abel—limits human freedom and enslaves humanity in fear, jealousy, and evil.[6]

Fourth, the first biblical description of paradise is similar to the golden age of other cultures, but the biblical description believes that this paradise will not only be restored to its original state but will also be transformed to a greater and consummated form. Here the hermeneutical appropriation of the first paradisaical hope is again and again read against the historical contexts of the later readers. Even though some religions are concerned with other worlds and utopias are concerned with social transformations, Judeo-Christian traditions are also concerned with transcendental issues. The historical rootedness of Christianity makes its religiosity historical and prophetic, and the prior emphasis on God's sovereignty in its theology makes its utopian visions transcendental. The Garden of Eden account portrays the earth, as problematic as it is, as once having been an ideal place of bliss, a garden in the East (Gen. 2:8).[7]

Fifth, as early as this first Judeo-Christian text about the Garden of Eden, human history was placed in a dynamic historical-transcendent time with the possibility of a new beginning. It shows that God, not the world, is God and that God is an actor in history who also transcends history. Lohfink writes: "Israel learned that God stands in contrast to the nations and history—not as their own profound center, but over against them as the ruler of history."[8] This also explains how during the later periods of oppression Jewish and Christian believers reworked their millenarian vision with an eschatological projection. This world-view is different from the cyclical worldview of other cultures.[9] The cyclical worldview is influenced by the movement and change of nature; time and the calendar are measured by planets and constellations, the powers that subjugated humanity: day and night, moon and sun, and the seasons. The annual recurrence of festive celebration is centered around the movement of nature: New Year as Harvest Festival, Moon Festival, Saturnalus, or the Sun God. The linear, historical worldview of the biblical tradition, however, seeks to overcome the cyclical worldview of pagan culture for several reasons: (1) Pantheism's belief in a cyclical worldview confuses Creator with creatures, God with humanity. The linear worldview differentiates *and* relates Creator and humanity through the notion that humanity has been created in the "image of God." (2) Human consciousness of time in the undifferentiated relationship of God and humanity closes off the transcendence and interruption of another realm. In the linear and historical movement of time consciousness, people begin to articulate how God is working in history. God's transcendence "breaks into" human history for the purpose of redemption.

Sixth, the authors of the Genesis account are concerned with placing the divine Torah at the center of Jewish community, thus portraying God's sovereignty in God's creation and the necessity of keeping Sabbath as well as obeying God's word. The Garden of Eden account is not just reminiscent of the paradise forever lost; it seeks to explain the origin of evil, suffering, struggle, and the possibility of living in and through all these ambiguities. Thus, human trust and obedience are held in dynamic tension with the sovereign will of God in history.[10]

This paradisaical hope emerged within the context of Jewish diaspora, when Jews hoped for national restoration and deliverance from the foreign governments of Babylonia, Greece, and Rome. Below we will trace how this paradisaical/utopian hope began to have its millenarian tone when the hope of a messiah and the arrival of a new order for Israel—the people of God—were called forth.[11]

Different Interpretations of National History in the Old Testament

The Jewish view of history is not monolithic. As early as the Jewish exile, at least three different traditions interpreted their experience. All three traditions have various degrees of millenarian emphases, since the common concern of the "lostness" of the exilic experience and the "saving acts" of the God of hope preoccupy the three main interpretations of the national history of the Jewish people in the Hebrew Scriptures.

The first interpretation is the Priestly tradition (P), which believes that cultic propriety (i.e., sacrificial rites and liturgical purity) constitutes a right relationship between God and his people. In sharp contrast to the Babylonian view of nature as divine and Babylonia as sacred, this tradition views Yahweh as the sovereign Creator of the cosmos and Lord of history. For example, the ancient Table of Nations in Genesis 10 does not include Israel because Israel is not cosmologically or naturally sacred. In light of the disappearance of her identity as a nation while in exile, Israel is the unique creation of God and has God as her King. Israel is different from the nation states. The Priestly tradition seems not to emphasize the Abrahamic or Mosaic covenants but uniquely highlights the Adamic and Noahic covenants of God with humanity. The theological implication of this is that history has a Creator who willed a beginning for a group of people who, having had no identity previously, will have a sacred identity in history. This sacred identity is established by means of cultic propriety and liturgical purity as they maintain their relationship to the Creator God. Thus, God's providence in history is neither an assumed natural consequence nor a matter of luck. History can be sacred and meaningful. But the role of Israel is not read arrogantly as a dominating one in world history. Rather, the providence shown to Israel is read against the universal history of the Adamites and Noahites. The periodization of human history is then traced back to the initial point of God's creation of the cosmos and of Adam as the primeval epoch, back to the Israelite patriarch as the chosen of God, and to the exilic experience as the continuation of the sacramental history under the lordship of God.

The second interpretation, which focuses on Zion and David, views the David-Solomon period of theocracy as the ideal state model for Israel. The God of Israel promised David, "Your house and your kingdom shall be made sure forever before me; your throne shall be established forever" (2 Sam. 7:16 NRSV). The exilic generation, wrestling with destruction and suffering in exile, envisioned the prosperity of a dynasty and the glory of a holy city as the consummated revelation of God in Zion (Isa. 52:1–10). Although the new world order, the new saving history, is

31

centered in Zion, God—not Israel—is vindicated in Deutero-Isaiah (chs. 40–55). Zion is to be inhabited by those who are despised and rejected by the nations of the world. The exile motif in Babylonia is compared with the exodus experience in Egypt (41:17–18; 43:2; 50:2), and the exodus/exile motif is linked to the creation account in Genesis 1, which stresses God's uniqueness and sovereignty (cf. Isa. 43:11–13) over Egypt, Babylonia, and Persia (at the time of the interpreters). The creation account is a revision of the Babylonian myth in which Marduk struggled against Tiamat the dragon. In other words, God's creation results in the emergence of order out of chaos, rest out of struggle, and sovereignty of a beginning of an eschatological-teleological history over against the nature-cyclical worldview of world culture.

The third interpretation, the Deuteronomist tradition (D), sees Torah obedience, prophetic urgency, and covenantal loyalty as the hope of national restoration.[12] Deuteronomists attempted to revive the old Yahwist tradition of the northern kingdom and the centrality of Jerusalem. The Josianic (640–609 B.C.E.) discovery of an ancient document provided a possible means of revival for the Israelites then (622 B.C.E.) and later (597 and 587 B.C.E.). However, Josiah's reform failed, and his military force was crushed by the Egyptians because the sins of his grandfather Manasseh had incurred the judgment of God upon Judah (2 Kings 23:25–27). Yet the Deuteronomistic plan of Torah obedience and covenantal faithfulness projected hope for the exilic generations. The creation of the Pentateuch for the exilic generation, which did not have Scripture, presupposed God's acts in history. The meaning of history is not self-evident, and history's ambiguities invite people to pose questions to themselves and ultimately to God and, in the case of the exilic generation, to search for national restoration. Deuteronomist theology understands history as a periodization of kingdom and exile, suffering and restoration. It looks to the Sinai covenant and the wilderness experience as the golden age of Israelite history.

The exilic crisis in Babylon and even the cultural genocide perpetrated against the Jews by Antiochus IV in the second century B.C.E. provided occasions for Israel to envision the ideal future when God would surely vindicate his people. This utopian hope was anchored in the three traditions and reinterpreted by the exilic generation as it looked to the future and searched for the meaning of history. All the traditions sought concrete historical experience to support their theological interpretation of their history and future; therefore, the three traditions were not merely a speculative theology of history. All three traditions attempted to view history as a single whole, not disjointed and broken into national or religious pieces.

The Exilic Experience: The Messianic Hope of Restoration

Jewish millennialism can be traced to the Israelite religious and political experience as early as the sixth century B.C.E. (597 and 587), when the Jews were in exile in Babylon. Jewish reaction to the surrounding Middle Eastern culture and its nature-cyclical views of history (the totality of the cosmos as divine, the representation of gods in hierarchy of beings) slowly formed the Jewish millenarian view of history. In contrast to the dominating, established world culture of the Babylonians, Israel looked back at its history to interpret the present crisis and came up with a book of remembrance (Mal. 3:16)[13] as well as messianic hope of restoration.[14] The book was to help the exilic community serve the Lord in memory of and hope in God's sovereign love. The canon of Scripture thus formed followed in its main points the "historical credo of Israel" identified by Gerhard von Rad (cf. Deut. 26:5–9).[15] Probably at the time of the exilic period, the Deuteronomic community began to collect sacred books in their traditions to look backward (memory) and forward (hope) for meaning and direction in history. A few distinctive theologies emerged out of this exilic experience.

First to emerge was a theology of monotheism with a concomitant self-understanding that Israel was the elect of God. Israel was not a primal people-group but an elect or called people of this unique God ("God is One" not as monotheism but as uniqueness of Yahweh from other gods) to be God's love and instrument in history. Olson writes,

> Israel was a people created in time by a deliberate act of God's will in history. . . . Canaanite and cultural Hebrew nature-cycle festivals were historicized in the Hebrew scriptures and brought within the one story of a willed beginning, of covenant peoplehood, and of a still open and linear future.[16]

Thus the early Jewish theology of God and God's people in the drama of history does not point to the gods' representation, evolution of nature, or the cyclical coincidence of historical events but to divine providence, intention, and action in history for the sake of humanity. Furthermore, while the exilic experience theologizes this theocratic and divine-interventionist (not yet incarnational) worldview, it also interprets exile as God's judgment on his people for their sins of idolatry and apostasy.

Second, in response to the shock and pain of migration and alienation, the Jews developed a millenarian vision of a complete transformation of land, people, religion, and temple. This is especially vivid with Ezekiel's visions (see also Isa. 1–39; 44–46). His apocalyptic vision of God defeating the world-class enemies in the battle of Gog and Magog (representing the gentile world) stresses God's sovereignty over Israel and the nations. (Ezek. 39:21: "I will display my glory among the nations, and all the nations will see the punishment I inflict and the hand I lay upon them.") In Jeremiah God's faithfulness and everlasting love that will never quit suggests that eventually God will be worshiped. In other words, God's glory will prevail over the injustice, wars, exiles, and idolatry of the world (see Jer. 23:1–8).[17] Further, Jeremiah 23:5–6 proclaims: " 'The days are coming,' says Yahweh, 'when I will raise up for David a righteous branch, and he shall reign as king, and he shall be wise and shall execute justice and righteousness in the land.' "[18]

Third, there also emerges during this time a remnant theology that emphasizes the redemptive acts of God in history. This theology points to God's sovereign will to use a minority of the chosen to realize God's will. In other words, two interrelated ideas of a righteous remnant and the purification of suffering seek to interpret the sovereign will of God in human history. The remnant theology believes (1) that, despite evil in the world and the unfaithfulness of God's people, God will keep a remnant of his people faithful and pure and (2) that God will purify his people via the suffering they go through so that evil will be used as a means of purification rather than for the destructive end of history. Another prominent motif is the suffering of the righteous remnant; this is a theology of suffering for others. Thus the Servant Songs in Deutero-Isaiah portray Isaiah as one who is to suffer for the nations vicariously. In other words, a monotheistic belief (God is One) and a nationalistic faith (Holy One of Israel) in the exilic theology is expanded to include Gentiles and nations in a grand narrative of human history under the sovereign Creator God. As Isaiah 56:7b testifies, "My house shall be called a house of prayer for all people." The instrumental role of God's elect in history to realize God's salvific intention is significant. Olson summarizes:

> But the Exile in turn was seen—as break, expiation, or preparation—to open the way to the climax of the drama, which will follow the Exile. History has now been organized, on the basis of this periodization, into a single dramatic whole. Jerusalem will be the centre of mankind's attention; Yahweh will be acknowledged everywhere. This new age will not annul the past: the ten lost tribes are to be restored in some fashion. And those most concerned to set Yahweh's action and thus Israel's significance on the widest stage could contemplate opening the holy community to gentiles. The last age thus answers finally the fall of all men recounted in Genesis, where no solution is found. God will now vindicate all his actions throughout the course of the drama.[19]

Finally, a fourth theology emerges (as evident in the scroll of Isaiah) with the millenarian theology of holistically viewing God's acts in history; it includes the recurring themes of promise *and* fulfillment, judgment *and* redemption, warning *and* comfort, suffering *and* reigning. The literary reading of Wolfgang Roth on the scroll of Isaiah as "the vision of the whole" (29:11) convincingly analyzes the theology of Isaiah in light of the deserted city (1:2–4:6) and Israel's future as well as the peaceable mountain (Zion; 5:1–27:13), Assyria's withdrawal and Jerusalem's rescue (28:1–37:38), Babylon's fall and Zion's restoration (38:1–55:13), and the presence of Zion's future (56:1–66:24).[20]

The Periodization of History in Daniel

The periodization of history in Daniel theologized God's redemptive acts in history. After the collapse of the Persian Empire in the late fourth century B.C.E., Jerusalem was hellenized in the Macedonian-Egyptian Empire of the Ptolemies and the Macedonian-Syrian Empire of the Seleucids. Antiochus III (223–187 B.C.E.), a Seleucid of Syria, granted Jews their cultural autonomy, but Antiochus IV Epiphanes forced an acute hellenization campaign in Palestine. The degradation of the temple by hellenizers and Seleucids, followed by its desecration in 168–167 B.C.E., resulted in the Jewish revolt led by Judas Maccabeus in 166. The temple was rededicated in 164. Most scholars believe that the book of Daniel was written during this period; its distinctive Jewish millenarian theology was expressed in the apocalyptic genre.

The periodization of history in Daniel 2 and 7 viewed the four world empires (Babylonian, Median, Persian, and Greek) as idols and beasts becoming world-dominating cultures. Daniel's response to these superpowers' expansionism, imperialism, hegemonism, and ultimately antitheocracy was to assert Yahweh's rule over his people and the world. It is important to view Daniel in the context of the anti-Jewish and anti-God campaigns of Antiochus the "Divine-Manifest" and their corresponding Jewish revolts.

Daniel's periodization of history placed the Greeks as the last of the worldly empires. Thus Antiochus IV was the culmination of evil against God and God's people (the Jews). The Greek period of Antiochus was to be "different from the former ones" (Dan. 7:24) in that it was a period of the little horn with eyes like the eyes of a human and a mouth speaking great things (7:8, 11, 20). As had been the case with the Babylonian and later with the Greek hegemony, political and cultural imperialism was rooted in an idolatry of replacing God and God's salvation history with the ruler's decree that he be adored by his subjects (in the case of the Babylonian king in 3:7, an image of gold was to be worshiped) as well as his claim that he was god manifest (*epiphanes* in the case of Antiochus, meaning "manifestation" or "appearance"). Antiochus's campaign was the culmination (8:23: "when the transgressions shall have reached their full measure") of God being replaced by a human-made divinity, of truth being replaced by boastful claims, and of salvific history being replaced by military might and destruction (see 8:12, 24). Antiochus's empire "grew great, even up to the host of heaven; and some of the host of the stars it cast down to the ground and trampled upon them" (8:10). The intense conflicts and historical duality of millenarian theology in the book of Daniel (see 8:25; 11:45; 12:1) was partially the result of reading the world events theologically; thus, historical dualism and conflicts portrayed the violence of the world empires against reality, God, and the salvation of his people. Millenarian theology critiqued these rival world empires.

Many Jewish responses, such as military revolt, revolutionary uprisings (11:14), cultic purifications (1:8–19), and Torah observances (Ezraic programs that failed to achieve their purpose), began to emerge during this period of history. However, Daniel's understanding of history was informed by the Deutero-Isaiah theology of God's sovereignty and self-vindication through God's remnant, the holy community of God. Daniel believed that "by no human hand shall he [Antiochus] be broken" (8:25). Daniel's hermeneutic looked back to Israel's history of the previous exilic generation under the Babylonian and Persian empires. Daniel learned from the Jewish tradition that a military confrontation with the superpower was a display of distrust against Yahweh (cf. Isa. 20:4–6; Jer. 37:5–10).[21] God's sovereignty in history was displayed not in his vindication of his people but in God's own vindication. The devastation cast by the rival powerful empire on God's chosen people was ultimately a declaration of war against God. But God's people were not to use military might to challenge their enemies; God's millenarian kingdom would be ushered in by God himself in a *kairotic* (appropriate or ripe) moment. The duty of God's people was to understand salvation history under the sovereignty of God and to trust and be faithful to God as the holy community of God. Hellenization and imperialism could not be resisted by revolutionary wars; it could only be resisted, in Daniel's vision, by means of Yahwistic piety. Thus the "son of man" in Daniel 7:13–14 (also the vision of 7:15–27) was depicted in contrast to Antiochus. The son of man judged and defeated Antiochus (7:26), and because of his piety the son of man inherited the kingdom of God.

An Eschatological View of History in the New Testament: Messianic and Millenarian Hope

The Long Legacy of Jewish Messianic Hope Reinterpreted in Christian Theology

The utopian hope began to adopt its millenarian tone when Israel was looking for a messiah while in exile. The hope for a messiah was initially a hope for the anointed one, historically identified as the king whose reign was consecrated by the power from on high. The greatest king was David, for his kingdom was the pinnacle of all Jewish kings.[22] This messianic hope was especially visible during the destruction of the First Temple and the Babylonian exile. Thus from Amos down to *Enoch*, a long history of Jewish prophecies interpreted suffering and trial as judgments brought on by national apostasy, and they predicted the day of the Lord as the end of judgment, purification, and deliverance. Jewish people hoped for the restoration of Israel by an ideal and able king, of which King David was the paradigm.

The book of Isaiah contains many well-known utopian prophecies, which are vivid descriptions of paradise on earth: "The wolf shall also dwell with the lamb, and the leopard shall lie down with the kid, the calf and the young lion and the fatling together" (Isa. 11:6). "Nations shall beat their swords into plowshares and their spears into pruning hooks; nation shall not lift up sword against nation, neither shall they learn war any more" (Isa. 2:4). "The ransomed of the Lord shall return and come to Zion with songs and everlasting joy upon their heads; they shall obtain joy and gladness, and sorrow and sighing shall flee away" (Isa. 35:10). The realistic (not escapist) nature of this utopian hope made the struggling and suffering Jewish people hopeful. It was not a hope to reach a world beyond this one; rather, "the eyes of the blind shall be opened, and the ears of the deaf shall be unstopped" (Isa. 35:5), "the desert shall rejoice and blossom as the rose" (Isa. 35:1), and "the parched ground shall become a pool, and the thirsty land springs of water" (Isa. 35:7). Paradise was the promised land of Canaan on earth; the new Jerusalem was the old Jerusalem restored to God's glory; heaven was God's throne inhabited with God's people.[23]

Not only did the messianic hope of "the mighty God, the everlasting Father, the Prince of Peace" (Isa. 9:6) go unrealized; Jewish (and Christian) people were also severely persecuted later by Seleucid kings of Syria and then by Roman emperors, following the destruction of Jerusalem and the Second Temple. It was during this period that the apocalyptic genre surfaced in Jewish religious literature (Daniel, intertestamental literature such as *Enoch,* Qumran literature, and parts of the New Testament). Torah provided an important divine principle for the people to live by in the present as they hoped for a coming millenarian reign of God on earth.

Christian millenarian ideas, however, adapted Jewish apocalyptic and millenarian ideas in the political context of the Roman Empire, and some of these reinterpretations spiritualized the utopian and prophetic traditions of Judaism. However, apocalyptic and eschatological thoughts remained perennial motifs in Christian theology. The significance of apocalyptic thought was so essential in early Christian doctrine that Ernst Käsemann claims that "apocalyptic was the mother of all Christian theology."[24] Thus, scholars such as Johannes Weiss, Martin Kähler, and Albert Schweitzer interpreted early Christian movements as either apocalyptic or eschatological.[25] Some theologians see an apolitical nature in early Christian theology, thus replacing eschatology with ethics,[26] but contemporary scholars have begun to appreciate the political nature of biblical apocalypticism and eschatology.[27]

Christian Apocalyptic Eschatology and the Reign of God in the Gospels

To understand Christian apocalyptic eschatology, one must begin with the reign of God in the Gospels. Of course, trying to understand Jesus and the reign of God in the Gospels in this age of the conflicting findings of "Jesus Seminars" and various historical searches for Jesus is fraught with difficulties. Luke Timothy Johnson writes humorously but revealingly:

> To list only a few [portraits] that have emerged [in the contemporary quest for the historical Jesus]: Jesus as romantic visionary (Renan), as eschatological prophet (Schweitzer, Wright), as wicked priest from Qumran (Thiering), as husband of Mary Magdalen (Spong), as revolutionary zealot (S. F. G. Brandon), as agrarian reformer (Yoder), as revitalization movement founder and charismatic (Borg), as gay magician (Smith), as cynic sage (Downing), as peasant thaumaturge (Crossan), as peasant poet (Bailey), and as guru of oceanic bliss (Mitchell). The common element seems still to be the ideal self-image of the researcher.[28]

My intention is not to enter the historical-critical debate of the Third Quest for Jesus. Rather, in this section I wish to discuss the basic thrust of the eschatological motifs in the works and teachings of Jesus based on the four New Testament Gospels. Even then the discussion must be limited because of space and for the reason that this volume is on Paul's interpretation of Jesus rather than the Gospels' interpretation. Thus, I will briefly focus on Jesus as the Jewish Messiah and the eschatological prophet of God. (For more, see the sources cited in the notes.)

Jesus' self-perception as a prophet is found in the Gospels (Mark 6:4; 8:27–30; Luke 13:33) and widely accepted by scholars.[29] However, this prophet was concerned not only with the arrival of a transcendental kingdom, either to restore Israel or to redefine hope and salvation for Israel, but also with the social transformation of the entire society.[30] If the temple is interpreted to have been "an instrument of imperial legitimation and control of a subjected people,"[31] the eschatological prophet proclaimed not a political revolution of toppling the existing regime but a theological-political movement of transforming existing power structures as people trusted in God's eschatological reign. The eschatological vision of Jesus was one of egalitarian justice and inclusive love for the world, where patriarchy (in familial and societal structures), hierarchy (in institutional power structures), imperialism (in Roman, Herodian, and even priestly politics), oppression (between the ruling elite and marginalized peasants), and colonialism (in racial tension and immigration situations) resulted in violence—socially, politically, and religiously. For Jesus, theology and politics were not two separate, independent realms. "Jesus was political in the same way the pre-exilic prophets in general were political: He believed that God's blessing of the people depended on their manifesting in the political sphere the justice God required of covenant people."[32] Kaylor points out the political dimension of Jesus' theology in the Beatitudes (Matt. 5:3–12; Luke 6:20–23), the Lord's Prayer (Matt. 6:9–15; Luke 11:2–4), and the parables. Hallowing God's name in the prophetic tradition was to eliminate injustice and to usher in the just love of God in concrete sociopolitical situations. Provision of the eschatological bread was to remind people of God's future and to sustain their present bodily needs. Forgiveness of debts and deliverance from the evil of violence were related to God's coming kingdom.

Apocalypticism "was the distinctive cultural form taken by imagination in late second Temple Jewish society."[33] Horsley argues that the creative imagination of this Jewish apocalypticism enabled God's people to imagine God's promises of blessings to the people in time of dissonance: "Seemingly illusory fantasies of 'new heavens and a new earth' in fact expressed the knowledge that life could again be human, that God, who willed human values such as justice and freedom from oppression, was still ultimately in control of history and faithful to the historic promises."[34] Similarly, in the context of Roman oppression, which rejected the early Christian movement as illicit superstition, Jesus and his early disciples reinterpreted previous Jewish apocalyptic material (e.g., Isaiah, Daniel, Ezekiel, etc.) in order to discern God's intention in the imminent consummation of history after its possible catastrophic end.

Despite the disobedience of his own people and the resistance of world empires, God will bring his saving will to history. In Matthew, Christ climaxes the genealogy, thus fulfilling the hope of Israel. The age of fulfillment is dawning with the birth of the expected Messiah. This Christ is also descended from David, the great king in Israel's history (2 Sam. 7:12–17). But the Babylonian exile mentioned in the genealogy means that disaster might overcome Israel's hope, since the Davidic kingdom had been smashed. However, the new David will set up a new reign of God, which is not a nationalistic and geographically bound kingdom. The people of God do not constitute a "holy empire." The *ekklesia* (church) cannot be the "imperial church." The key characteristic of the people of God, whether Israel or the re-creation of Israel through the Jesus movement, is the inclusive justice and lavish grace of God. His reign is characterized by the superabundant life of his Son.

Thus right from its opening chapter the New Testament portrays the inclusion of women in the genealogy, which suggests the possibility of the newness of God's salvific work. In the ancient world, descent was traced through the male, yet four women aside from Mary are named in Matthew 1: Tamar (1:3), Rahab and Ruth (1:5), and the wife of Uriah (1:6). Moreover, these are unusual women in origin and morality. Tamar disguised herself as a harlot to seduce her father-in-law, Judah, so that she could bear children, Perez and Zerah (Gen. 38). Rahab, a harlot in Jericho, saved Joshua's two spies (Josh. 2; 6). Bathsheba, the wife of Uriah, became the wife of David (2 Sam. 11–12). All were foreigners (Gentiles), yet all were candidates to become part of God's people. Unlike the law of the worldly empires, God's kingdom works on the principle of plentitude and extravagant love, not on the "rightful" positions that culture assigns to people.

The Jesus movement continues this eschatological working of God, first in his beloved Son, Jesus the Messiah, and then through the gathering (*ekklesia*) of God's people (the twelve, the seventy, then the body of Christ in different locales). The four Gospels often look back to the Old Testament because the *New* Testament is a fulfillment of the Old. The God of the Bible does not throw dice; God is not programmed by historical forces. God is the God of history. In God's sovereign act of "intruding" in history, humanity can rest assured that God's future will not lead to destruction.

The distinctive Christian view of history is its central event, which focuses on the person of the God-Human Jesus Christ, who defines the end (purpose, goal, and fulfillment) of history. Jesus clarifies the ambiguities of the historical past and future. Jesus infuses history with mean-ing, redeeming and consummating history. As such, reading history according to a biblical perspective involves a proleptical process of back-ward and forward movements. This backward and forward reading of history occurs throughout the life of Jesus[35] and in the two culminating points in history: the death and resurrection of Christ, and the escha-ton (final point) of history.

The Christian view of history is essentially salvation history centered on the person and work of Jesus Christ. At the first point, the death and resurrection of Christ stretches back to the beginning of creation and makes clear that God has not ceased creating, despite the fall, sin, evil, suffering, wars, injustice, and the like. In other words, what is prom-ised and implicit in God's initial creation to accomplish what is good continues to be the will of God in history. This central event, the death and resurrection of Jesus, also projects to the second point, thus stretch-ing history forward, transcending the ambiguities of the past and pres-ent, and engendering hope in a future that guarantees resurrection (from death) as well as a new heaven and a new earth (in transformation of the present heaven and earth). Along these same lines, Eliade writes: "Messianism hardly succeeds in accomplishing the eschatological val-orization of time: the future will regenerate time; that is, will restore its original purity and integrity. Thus, *in illo tempore* is situated not only at the beginning of time but also at its end."[36] The end of history is not the termination, the conclusion, the finishing point of time and space. Rather, it is the ultimate goal and thus the ultimate meaning of history. Again, the eschatological perspective's view of history is centered in per-son and community (who, i.e., Jesus Christ), not in an idea (what, e.g., freedom) or chronological time (when, e.g., 2000) or place (where, e.g., utopia). Cullmann observes that "what really begins with the appear-ance of Jesus Christ is not a new epoch of secular history, called 'Chris-tian,' but *the beginning of an end*. The Christian times are Christian only in so far as they are the last time."[37] Christians place their hope in Jesus Christ, their Messiah, who has died and been resurrected and who will come again at the end to usher in the new age in its fullness.

Christian millenarian theology, whether traceable to Judaic and Mesopotamian archaic beliefs or views that arose later, is similar to its various religious-philosophical and secular utopian versions. Even among the Christian movement there are different strands of utopian visions. Moreover, we see how early Christian millenarian movements readapted earlier strands within their social-political contexts. For exam-ple, on one hand we have Jesus' statement that "my kingdom is not of this world" (John 18:36), while on the other hand we have the Lord's Prayer: "Your kingdom come. Your will be done on earth as it is in heaven. Give us this day our bread of tomorrow" (Matt. 6:10–11). This explains the sometimes diverging, sometimes confluent strands in the New Testament, where social-political utopias (such as Luke, James, Hebrews, Romans, 1 Corinthians), pacific utopia (1 and 2 Thessalonians), or even apocalyptic utopia (Revelation) are found.

Except for extreme apocalyptic texts (e.g., where the earth will be destroyed), most apocalyptic and eschatological texts foresee the restoration of the earth after its destruction by evil forces. In other words, the New Testament's utopian and millenarian visions rarely advocate withdrawal and escapism (if so, they probably belong to the extreme strand of apocalypticism), because the dominant prophetic and utopian theologies of Judaism continued to be influential in New Testament eschatology.

The Millenarian Theology of Paul in 1 and 2 Thessalonians

Thessalonians is the part of Christian millenarian thought in which Paul expressed his belief that the last day will be characterized by conflicts of good and evil, war and struggle, suffering and persecution. But during this period of cataclysmic strife, believers must be hopeful and faithful because Christ will defeat the Antichrist, good will triumph over evil, oppressors will be judged, and believers of God will be delivered, raised to meet Jesus, and live with God forever. The second coming of Christ, a cosmic event that is socially reforming and politically subversive, will usher in a new millennium.

1 Thessalonians: A Theology of Hope, Faith, and Love

The Thessalonian Christians whom Paul addressed in his two letters faced a number of problems, not the least of which were hopelessness and suffering. The former problem lies in the background of Paul's first letter to the Thessalonians, the latter in the background of his second letter. The problem of hopelessness for the Thessalonian Christians was doubly compounded by the absence of Christ (the benefactor) and Paul (the benefactor's agent). Paul addressed this absence problem in at least four ways. First, the end time was reinterpreted as the "already but not yet" event. Second, certain emissaries—Timothy in the case of Paul's absence, the apostles in the case of Christ's absence—are presented in order to re-present the epiphany of Paul and Christ. Third, Paul explains the dynamic and transcendent working of the Spirit as the power of God among the believers. The Holy Spirit also signifies the dawning of the new age of salvation and hope, when Christ is coming. The Holy Spirit represents the presence of the eschatological reality, the eschatological gift that inspires joy. The eschatological gift of God through the Holy Spirit has nurtured their faith in Christ and the hope of God's imminent triumph. Fourth, the writing of the epistle (in the absence of Paul) and the proclamation of the gospel or traditions (in the absence of Christ on earth) are seen as keeping intact the flow of authority and clarity of teaching. In other words, the problem of absence does not necessarily have to be solved by full presence. Rather, a substitution, replacement, or reinterpretation of presence will suffice to generate the rhetoric of hope.

Paul's theology of hope points to the presence of the living God as elusiveness (3:9; 4:8, 17). The living God is nevertheless ineffably present. J. G. van der Watt speaks of God as "consciously present":

> The way in which God is "consciously present" is a godly way, a true way. His actions resulting from this "presence" will reflect the quality and nature expected of the true God! Being God, this life is, for one thing, absolute. God is (present participle) the living God; he does not derive his life from elsewhere. As the living God, he can also give life, as was evidenced for instance, in his raising of Christ.[38]

Indeed, God is the Father who chooses (1:4), calls (2:12), gives the Spirit to (4:8), wills the sanctification of (4:3), and makes perfectly holy (5:23) each believer. Such is the loving parent God who is active in their lives; such is the living and true God they are going to serve. Being the divine agent of the loving parent, Christ has died and been raised for the sake of the Thessalonian congregation (1:10; 4:14; 5:10). He is destined to be the salvific and sanctifying agent (5:9, 18), the deliverer from divine wrath and giver of peace for believers (1:10; 5:28). Christ is also the source of the Thessalonians' hope as they wait for his return (1:3, 10; 4:15; 5:23).

The theology of hope in 1 Thessalonians portrays the rightness of the favored people and the damnation of the enemies. Congregational imitation of Paul and Christ (1:6–10) indicates the ground of hope operative among the audience; clarification of the apostolic example (2:1–12) posits the "rightness" of the apostle and the "wrongness" of the hinderers. Paul's repeated and determined effort to revisit the Thessalonians (2:17–20) reinforces the conviction of his confidence in the congregation: they were his hope, joy, crown, boasting, and glory.

The theology of 1 Thessalonians focuses on the bilateral themes of suffering and *parousia*-hope, with the assurance that God will wholly sanctify believers until the *parousia* of Christ. The letter's rhetoric of hope focuses on the *parousia*-hope, not the resurrection-hope. Although New Testament writers use *kyrios* (Lord) to refer both to God and to the resurrected and coming Christ, most (if not all) of the twenty-four occurrences of the term in 1 Thessalonians refer to Jesus. More important, none of these uses refers to Christ's resurrection, while a number of them explicitly mention his *parousia* (2:19; 3:13; 4:15, 16, 17; 5:2). Likewise, even the reference to Jesus as God's Son highlights the importance of Christ's *parousia* as the basis of the Thessalonians' hope ("wait for his [God's] Son from heaven," 1:10).

In 1 Thessalonians 5:2, Christ has replaced God as the eschatological Lord-Judge. The wrath of the Lord-Judge is yet to arrive, and all persons will be subjected to it. Christians can take courage not because of their virtue but because of the other divine attribute—wrath. God has destined them not for wrath but to obtain salvation. In the Hebrew Bible the "day of the Lord" traditionally described the visitation of the Lord to reign in power. On that day the Lord will bring salvation to the chosen ones, the righteous, but judgment on the unrighteous. The moral connotation of that day is significant to Paul. "Indeed the future reign of God whose wrath-filled dimension already impinges upon the present to punish sinners (1 Thess. 2:16) likewise impinges upon the present insofar as believers are constituted in a state of holiness which is the first experience of future salvation."[39] Following the prophetic tradition of Judaism, Paul speaks of the day as both salvation and judgment.[40] But this day is not the last day of historical time: "This last day in time is at once the present of eternity to all times. This 'last day' is 'the day of days.' There is no way of thinking of the day of resurrection. In content it is defined as 'the day of the Lord,' to which all times are simultaneous."[41]

First Thessalonians encourages a hopeful living that leads one to live a life worthy of the gospel (2:12; 4:1), that is, a life of sanctification (4:3, 4, 7; 5:23) and blamelessness (3:13; 5:23) rather than a life of *porneia* (4:3), transgression (4:6), and wrath (5:8–9). The word *Lord* appears frequently in the exhortation section (3:11, 12; 4:1, 2, 6; 5:27), indicating the tight connection between *parousia*-hope and ethical living. While waiting for the *parousia*, believers serve a living and true God (1:9). Thus a Christian ethic is informed and motivated by eschatology, unlike an eschatologyless theology that has no sense of ethical lifestyle. The rhetoric of hope assures the validity of traditional ethics.

The interactive relationship of faith, love, and hope is crucial. By trusting in God (rather than in the political propaganda of 5:3) through the salvific gospel (5:9) of the death and resurrection of Jesus Christ (4:14), believers are called and taught a dynamic faith (1:3, 4, 7; 4:9) that manifests love (1:3; 3:6; 4:9, 10; 5:8) and hope (1:3; 2:19; 4:13; 5:8).

Faith without love results in fornication and transgression, both of which incur God's wrath (4:3–6). Faith without love is like a noisy gong (cf. 1 Cor. 13:1). For the Thessalonians faith will manifest itself in love because they are elected by God and called as the beloved community of faith (1 Thess. 1:4). Love is a harmonious, joyful, interactive relationship among the Thessalonians as well as between the called community and the calling God. The Holy Spirit is the divine agent in whom God's love and joy have been given to the Thessalonians (1:6; 4:8). They are the corporate "in Christ" community (2:14; 3:8; 4:1, 16; 5:12, 18). As they are taught by God to love one another (4:9), Paul exhorts them to actualize the gift of love in their lives more and more (4:10, 12).

Faith without hope results in fear and uneasiness of mind. Faith without hope is like an exhausted engine, a car out of gas. The problem in 1 Thessalonians is neither faith nor love but hope, or the breakdown and lack of hope in the triad formula. Like a telescope, hope enables one to anticipate beyond present suffering the transcendent reality of possibility. Hope enables one to see the *parousia* (5:9) beyond the death and resurrection of Christ (4:14, the content of faith). Hope grants Paul the reason to be joyful and proud of the Thessalonian believers (2:19). In times of affliction, hope energizes believers by giving them the joy and assurance of God's love, a purpose in life, and a calling they can follow. Pauline theology is one of *parousia*-hope, a way to reach holistic faith, love, and hope, signified by the God of *shalom* who has called them to be whole in body, spirit, and soul. The whole reality of salvation we find in Christ is promised in the death and resurrection of Christ but fulfilled and consummated in the *parousia* that is now anticipated by believers.

Paul's use of honor language in 1 Thessalonians intends to relocate honor not in the temporal eye of the present but in the eschatological eye of the ultimate, that is, the imminent day of the Lord. If God is the absolute norm of honor, it makes sense to Paul that the temporal-spatial present is partial and even delusive at times. Does death now mean termination? Does suffering now mean woe and curse? Does the absence of Christ now mean betrayal or a fraudulent faith? The answer is given by the honor language of Paul in the style of boasting: "For what is our hope or joy or crown of boasting before the Lord Jesus at his coming? Is it not you? For you are our glory and joy" (2:19–20). It is honorable to turn from idols to serve a living and true God, so also to wait for God's Son from heaven, whom God raised from the dead, Jesus who delivers us from the wrath to come (1:9–10). It is honorable to lead a life worthy of God, who calls us into God's own kingdom and glory (2:11–12). It is honorable to belong to our God and Father, who establishes our hearts unblamable in holiness at the coming of our Lord Jesus with all his holy ones (3:12–13). It is honorable to have the destiny of obtaining salvation rather than wrath (5:9). And it is honorable to trust in hope that the God of wholeness will make us whole and blameless at the coming of our Lord Jesus Christ (5:23). In the tension of the present and the future, the Thessalonians are asked to live honorably as children of the Great Benefactor, as children of God's favor (grace). They are asked also to be benefactors to all. In other words, in the "todayness" of God's future, they are God's channels of blessing.

2 THESSALONIANS: APOCALYPTIC HOPE AND THE JUSTICE OF GOD

Paul attempts to correct the Thessalonians' problem of suffering by appealing to the sovereignty of the Lord (of the day). Paul corrects their wrong assumption about the realized *parousia* by contrasting the false and real Messiah, *parousia*, hope, and ethic. Paul corrects the overly enthusiastic eschatology of the *ataktoi* (disorderly ones) by teaching a work ethic informed by a balanced and tensioned eschatology: works as doing good toward oneself and others. The major exhortation of the epistle concerns moral integrity (1:11; 2:16–17; 3:1–3, 5, 16) and love of truth. Thus Paul's rhetoric in 2 Thessalonians is one of wholeness of faith, love, and hope, rooted in the grace of God's love and lordship in the eschatological Christ.

The appearance of the word *charis* (grace) in 2 Thessalonians is significant, occurring in the prescript and in the closing (1:2; 3:18; cf. 1:12; 2:16). Both in the beginning and the closing, grace is associated with peace. Jewett argues that "the underlying theological matrix of the letter is thus an apocalyptic theology of grace and wrath in which Christ is the primary actor."[42] The common benefaction language in Greco-Roman culture would provide the semantic domain for the use of *grace* in the letter.[43] The lordship of the eschatological Christ and the judgment of God are prominent themes in 2 Thessalonians.

God's justice is the prominent theological motif in 2 Thessalonians.[44] God has called the Thessalonians, and they suffer as a demonstration of God's just judgment (1:5). The justice of God will be shown when their suffering is vindicated and rewarded and their persecutors punished. God is the executor of justice, the apocalyptic Judge, and Christ is the agent. Jesus is the power, the end-time Judge; his role parallels God's role in the *parousia*. Jesus' earthly life is not mentioned at all in this letter; his birth, baptism, and death seem to play no significant part in Christian life, nor do they seem to serve as a basis of christological salvation. Rather, Jesus the Lord, the final Judge of the coming *parousia*, the powerful Judge, will de-energize the man of lawlessness by the breath of his mouth (2:8). He will punish the persecutors (1:9). His *parousia* will be evidenced by power and flaming fire (1:7–8). Consequently, Christian hope and salvation rests not only in their present baptism but in the future arrival of the Lord, when they will gather before him (2:1).

The Lord "will protect and establish them from the evil one" (3:3). "Jesus's future role is the measure of 'doing good' (2 Thess. 3:13), 'standing fast' (2 Thess. 2:15), and 'approving the good and doing the work of faith' (2 Thess. 1:12)."[45]

The judgment of God falls on those who "do not obey the gospel of our Lord Jesus" (1:8). *Gospel* is a term that becomes significant in the letter's thanksgiving (1:8) and second proof (2:14), in which the truth concerning the *parousia* of Christ makes up the essential content. This content is the essential basis of salvation and a community lifestyle. The proclaimed gospel for the purpose of "obtaining the glory of our Lord Jesus Christ" (2:14) is the central motif found in the second proof of the epistle. God's call is effective through the preaching of Paul, Silvanus, and Timothy. The Thessalonians' "belief in the truth" (2:13) is significant also, since it is found in the same proof. In short, one's present response to the gospel will determine one's future destiny.[46] For example, persecutors who do not obey the gospel of Christ (1:8) and who refuse to love the truth (2:10) will experience God's eschatological wrath. Christians are called "through belief in the truth" (2:13), and they will obtain the glory of Jesus Christ (2:14).

The realized eschatology of the readers of 2 Thessalonians produced an antiworks ethic. Faith is fidelity, without which ethical behavior becomes human boasting. God is the Faithful One (1 Thess. 5:24; 2 Thess. 3:3) to whom believers faithfully relate and respond through ethical living. Their faith is a response to God's faithfulness so that they can attain a holistic ethical life. Their faith is grounded in the faithfulness of God and in the belief that "Jesus Christ died and was raised" (1 Thess. 4:14). Since the faithfulness of God entails God's bringing in of the eschatological reign, the belief that Jesus died and was raised is rooted in the tension of the two Christ-events: Easter and the *parousia*. Ethical living may be hindered or destroyed by the hopelessness produced by persecution and death. Hope granted the Thessalonians confidence in the faithfulness of God, strength in enduring suffering, and joy in living a holy life before God and people. So a faithful and hopeful Christian could not help but live a life of love as an expression of his or her faith and hope. Such ethical living is far from an interim ethic, which means that the pursuit of holy living is for the sake of the preparedness of the coming Messiah. Ethical living is for the sake of God, not for self-boasting. An eschatologically informed ethic calls believers to live their faith in love, yet it also calls into question their security and perfectionism. Paul is sure of the coming of the *parousia*. He never pinpoints the "times and seasons"; he is assuredly open to the time. As such, he is confidently open to the world in which the Lord-Judge will come. Paul's faith in the eschatological hope keeps his work and ethic intact.

47

The realized eschatology of the audience is also an anti-Spirit eschatology. The prophecy of realized eschatology comes from a false spirit who, so it is claimed, no longer needs to learn truth from God. However, Paul links "sanctification by the Spirit" and "belief in the truth" (2 Thess. 2:13), indicating the need of rhetorical transcendence by means of the Spirit.

PAUL'S RESPONSE TO THE REALIZED ESCHATOLOGY OF THE *ATAKTOI*

Paul's teaching in 1 Thessalonians that the eschaton would arrive shortly was understood by some Thessalonian Christians to mean that the millennial kingdom of God had already come. Whether the imminent, surprising arrival of the Lord was unclear or misunderstood by the audience cannot be ascertained from the text. It is more likely that the audience, convinced of the millennial, ideological expectancy, felt that the end had come. It may also be that the urge that it should come was so strong that they engaged in preparing for it, some even trying to bring about its coming.

Second Thessalonians rebuts the claim that the day of the Lord had come.[47] Paul first denies the false teaching concerning the presence of the *parousia* and the status of believers in 2:2. The two proofs that follow in 2:3–12 and 2:13–3:5 argue that a series of signs must precede the coming of the *parousia* and that believers can have assurance that they will prevail until that time, provided they stand firm in the Pauline teachings and example. What signs must precede the *parousia?* In 2 Thessalonians 2:1–12 Paul explains that the *parousia* will not come until there is a widespread rebellion against God. This rebellion will be led by the one who is the very embodiment of lawlessness, the one who will usurp the throne of God and claim divine honors for himself. But since this rebellion had not occurred, Paul's readers could rest assured that the day of the Lord had not come.

COMPARING THE ESCHATOLOGICAL VIEWPOINTS OF 1 AND 2 THESSALONIANS

Pauline eschatology in 1 Thessalonians stresses the imminent *parousia*, whereas in 2 Thessalonians the expectation of the *parousia* is delayed. To solve the problem of Christian suffering, 2 Thessalonians not only insists on God's election (as does 1 Thessalonians) but also stresses the need for Christians to be faithful to the truth so that they will receive the future glory of our Lord Jesus Christ (2:14). Second Thessalonians encourages abiding in the tradition Paul and his colleagues taught and imparted to them in 1 Thessalonians.

The idea of wholeness is frequently expressed by terms related to sanctification in 1 Thessalonians (*hagiosyne* in 3:13; *hagiasmos* in 4:3, 4, 7; *hagiazo* in 5:23) but only once in 2 Thessalonians (2:13, *hagiasmos*). In 1 Thessalonians Paul is helping his readers to be whole in faith in the midst of conflicting and persecuted circumstances. In 2 Thessalonians his mission is to help them not to be overly enthusiastic about the Lord's coming. A person who has a realized eschatology is a person who has no eschatology, because such a one is overconfident in matters of suffering and of a work ethic. Paul's rhetorical strategy in 2 Thessalonians is to help this group of people extend the eschatological scheme further into the future.

Whereas 1 Thessalonians portrays God the Father and Jesus the *parousia*-hope as the benefactors of grace for the holistic salvation and sanctification of the Thessalonians, 2 Thessalonians portrays God the Judge and Jesus the apocalyptic agent as the Lord of the day (appointed time), Lord over the lawless one, and the Master responsible for the community's well-being. God is the just Judge[48] for both the suffering and the oppressors, the afflicted and the afflicters. God's just judgment will result in reward, salvation, and rest for the persecuted and in punishment, damnation, and wrath for the persecutors.

Thus the two epistles to the Thessalonians have different eschatological viewpoints. Since 1 Thessalonians deals with eschatological confusion, Paul clarifies the "times and seasons" of the *parousia*. While one cannot know the "date," one is to watch and hope for the coming. Paul's response gives the encouragement of "imminence" of the *parousia*. The rapid return of the Messiah Paul has predicted is in line with early church tradition, the Jewish apocalyptic tradition, and the Qumran community. But Paul's eschatology is not just a philosophical clarification; it is an emotional response to a church that has gone through much affliction. Paul's response creates among the congregation the impression of the beloved awaiting the lover.

Revelation: The Roman Empire and the Lamb of God in a Christian Theology of History

The book of Revelation does not set forth stages of world history but rather a Christian theology of history with a heavy orientation on eschatology. Elizabeth Schüssler Fiorenza's survey of various approaches to viewing history is helpful to our understanding of Revelation's theology of history. Schüssler Fiorenza points out that interpretations from both the *geschichtstheologische* (theology of history) approach and the *heilsgeschichtliche* (salvation history) approach emphasize eschatology as

49

the fundamental principle of interpretation.[49] Thus the eschatological interpretation is the proper horizon for understanding Revelation. Eschatology involves "future history." The "breaking-in" of God's kingdom and the destruction of evil forces at the end time confirm for believers their present reality that violence will be "conquered" (by the Lamb of God). The present is subordinated to the future and confirmed by the past; the present receives its significance from the future. The book of Revelation is a Christian theology of history in terms of the Christ-event, which defines the meaning of history in terms of eschatology.

The two main characteristics of apocalyptic literature are interrelated and relevant to the present thesis, since apocalyptic literature presents a theology of history and is itself literature created in the midst of crisis with the "purpose of exhortation and/or consolation by means of divine authority."[50] Concerning the latter, Schüssler Fiorenza observes, "In contrast to some Jewish apocalyptic writings, Revelation attempts to give meaning to the present suffering of the community not with reference to a divine plan of history, but with an understanding of the present from the horizon of the future, that is, from the coming kingdom of God."[51] John presents a theology of history in which the historical process is completely under God's control.[52] For John, both the present and the final period (*Endgeschichte*) are under the lordship of the glorified Christ. In other words, the present belongs to the future, and the latter is experienced now. In unveiling the eschatological reality for his audience, John claims that the fulfillment of the promise in the future can be seen and experienced now.

The question that troubles the biblical writer and his audience is not so much the meaning of history (though that is partially the issue) but the meaning and termination of suffering in history. To convey the meaning in suffering, John offers a particular view of history. He does not narrate the *whole* of world history from the beginning to the eschatological end. Rather, as Schüssler Fiorenza points out, "Revelation consists of pieces or mosaic stones arranged in a certain design, which climaxes in a description of the final eschatological event. The goal and high point of the composition of the whole book, as of the individual 'little apocalypses,' is the final judgment and the eschatological salvation."[53] If our interpretation here is correct, we can say that John attempts to stretch human finitude beyond the present to the historical past (Jesus' death and resurrection) and to the futuristic end of time (eschatological hope), thus granting humanity a vision of the past, present, and future. The future and present overwhelm John's concern for the past. That is, the reality of the future can envelop (extend backward to) the past and the present and save believers from being lost or ambiguous, thereby claiming them as belonging to the absolute future of history, which is God.

From a literary point of view, then, we would say that the genre of Revelation falls within the scope of Jewish apocalypse. From a theological point of view, however, it is a Christian apocalypse. Revelation depicts the religious, cultural, economic, and political struggles of Christians at the end of the first century, probably during the reign of the Roman emperor Domitian.

In ancient mythology the highest god possessed plates or scrolls that contained the destiny of the whole world, just as here Jesus is depicted as the eschatological ruler of the world and its destiny. The scroll in Revelation 5 is similar to the scroll of the law that contains God's will or judgment on the future day (Isa. 8:16; 29:11; Dan. 12:4). The scroll also resembles the heavenly tablets containing the gods' decisions about the future (*1 Enoch* 81:1–3).[54] It is also pertinent that, according to Roman law, certain documents were required to be sealed by seven witnesses. John was surely aware of this Roman legal tradition. Sealing, too, has its significance. In Daniel 8:26 the prophet is told to "seal up the vision, for it pertains to many days from now" (cf. Isa. 29:11). The Jewish apocalyptic "heavenly tablets" contained "all the deeds of men . . . that will be upon the earth to the remotest generations."[55]

Clearly John believes that the faith of his audience depends on holding a particular view of history, that is, knowing the end. Present faith is objectified when it is linked to the end of history. That faith is assured in its linkage when it is connected to the christological definition of the end. Revelation of the yet-to-come Hidden One in the present defines for present faith the ultimate purpose and victory of God's activities in history. The power of apocalyptic rhetoric in Revelation, as A. Y. Collins has pointed out, resides in the power of catharsis in crisis. Often two sets of symbols are used in apocalyptic rhetoric: one describes what ought to be, and the other describes what is. The "ought to be" portrays hope, the other reality. The language is primarily "commissive language," which calls "for commitment to the actions, attitudes, and feelings uttered."[56] This expressive and evocative language is powerful. As expressive language, Revelation creates a virtual experience for the hearers; it expresses a perspectival view of history, suffering, and reality. As evocative language, it elicits a response from the hearers in terms of thoughts, attitudes, and feelings by the use of effective symbols and dramatic plot, inviting imaginative participation.[57]

The rhetorical effect of the imagery of Christ in Revelation is intended to give hope and assurance (confident faith) to Christians under persecution. The self-surrender of Jesus is a sacrifice of self for humanity and serves as an example, albeit a divine and inimitable one, to empower believers through persecution. The community is called to believe that it has access to the celebration of the saving work of God by sharing in the present suffering of Christ and participating in the fullness of Christ's glory in the future. The beast will arise to deceive all who dwell upon the earth, and those who refuse to worship the beast will be slain (13:11–14:5). The challenge for the faithful, says John, is not to compromise but to overcome and conquer (2:7, 11, 17, 26; 3:5, 12, 21).

Since the end of history has now been revealed and made known, the audience is invited to participate in that future by anticipation, for God alone, the purposeful actor in history, has the power to bring history to its unification and dynamic consummation, "incorporating each temporal present as it occurs"[58] to the end of time. It is for this reason that one can anticipate with assurance that God the Almighty reigns. That is the central message and purpose of the Apocalypse.

Conclusion

To summarize the millenarian, apocalyptic, and eschatological views of history in the Bible, I want to point out the biblical understanding of time before listing the significance of millenarian language.

A Biblical Understanding of Time and the Modern Myth of Time

The linear and historical worldview is a critique of the natural, cyclical view of time. A historical and linear notion of time is meaningful because the events of God and the events of humanity interact—God's story intertwining with our stories, God's vision intersecting with ours. Thus the biblical narratives from Abraham to Paul describe the acts of God in history; the incarnation of Christ, his death and resurrection, and his coming are all historical events of God's intrusion in human history. A linear and historical framework allows us to see God's genealogy and eschatology of cosmic salvation in our experiences.

But the linear understanding of time in the modern myth of mechanical and quantitative perspectives can easily distort the biblical worldview because modern time-consciousness is measured by precision of *chronos*—"tick, tock, tick, tock." Our local and communal time is dictated by universal Greenwich Mean Time. Past, present, and future become the tenses in which we use a calendar to plot the timeline. The present is perceived to be all that we possess, so our worth, purpose, and meaningfulness are measured by the present. Past and future are defined by the present. The past is obsolete, because it is the passing of the present. The future is our prolongation of the present, the progression of the space. Bauckham explains how such a "modern historicist, progressivist myth of time" is most clearly "seen at its purest in Hegel and at its most typical in the nineteenth-century liberal and Marxist versions of the idea of inevitable historical progress."[59]

The modern myth of time has three presuppositions: (1) continuity, that is, a single and homogenous movement; (2) causality in the sense that a sequence of events is determined by the first and determined or caused subsequently; and (3) progress, the idea that the movement of history is the cumulative progress towards an ever-nearer utopia.[60] Once the modern myth of time is read with the Christian providential view of history, we witness utopian visions of scientific progressivism, capitalist optimism, and technological omnipotence (perfectibility and hegemony). The problem with the modern myth of time is that there is no assured hope of the future; the future millennium is only wishful thinking of what will be. The future cannot erupt a radical *novum* that the apocalyptic eschatology talks about.[61] The division between past, present, and future offers the images of a disjointed sense of time within a closed system. In other words, what comes to pass will cease to be, and what is in the future will come in the present and cease to be in the past.

This modern myth of time is, of course, not the biblical understanding. With a historical understanding of time, the biblical tradition understands past, present, and future as modes of existence, aspects of actions, or potentialities of events. Basic Hebrew and Greek grammars confirm this reading. This is not to say that Jews and Greeks (and the Chinese as well) did not have the notion of tenses present in English grammar. Moltmann writes, "Future is the sphere of the possible, past the sphere of the real, present the frontier on which the possible is either realized or not realized."[62] As such, the future is the driving force and springhead of time in which events take place. The present is the continuous realm of happenings, the moment when events unfold themselves and when decisions are made, such as the moment of faith (see Rom. 13:11; 2 Cor. 6:2). The present is "a relative eternity, for simultaneity is one of the attributes of eternity."[63] The present is the *kairotic* moment in which "the continuity of the flow of time is ruptured and the believer stands in the dawn of the eschatological future."[64] The past is the realized aspect of acts that confirm what is real and what is not. The death of Jesus as the past aspect of God's action confirms the sacrificial love of God, who surrenders his omnipotence. The resurrection of Jesus as the past aspect of God's actions confirms the realized ability of God to raise the dead to new life. The past shows what is real, not what is obsolete.

The reality of the past regarding the cross-event is that violence and death must come to an end in God's kingdom and future. The world of injustice and annihilation was truly interrupted by God, whose kingdom and future are characterized by resurrection and new life. "The eschaton is neither the future of time nor timeless eternity. It is God's coming and his arrival."[65] The future is the arriving (what is coming) and not what will be. Bauckham explains the New Testament concept of time according to Moltmann's interpretation: "*Adventus*, the future that comes to meet us, enables one to think of God as exercising the power of the transcendent future over time, and as the God whose eschatological coming to the world is also the transcendent *novum*."[66] Moltmann writes:

> The linear notion of time does not fit the experiences of history: for us, history narrows down apocalyptically, and expands messianically. This is a question of God's providence, which leads us into experiences of the end, and into experiences of the beginning. The "nearness" of God's kingdom and the "nearness" of the end cannot be measured in temporal terms. They are *aggregate conditions of history* which we experience when we find ourselves in them. At times when history is open we have to know about history's end, and at times when history is closed we have to know about the new beginnings.[67]

The transcendence of the eschatological future defines God's future as open-ended and wholly new moments. God's eschatological future transcends historical future; in fact, it is in the historical future that God's future "intrudes," transforms, renews. With the eschatological coming of God, the historical future comes to an end (the eschaton), and eternal time—that is, God's future—persists.[68]

The Significance of Millenarian Language

Millenarian language is significant in at least five ways. (1) It views history as one story, not as broken and disjointed. Thus some speak of dispensations, epochs of differences yet of continuity. It has the conviction that significant events of history are for all history and all humanity. It assumes the present crisis or ambiguity as the context in which apocalyptic eschatology works. (2) It views history as a drama, developed in different dispensations, with God as the main actor, who directly works out his will in history despite the suffering of God's people. It sees history as development with an intentional beginning and a climactic goal, not as mere progress (improving periods). (3) It views the consummation of history (eschaton) as either God's event or a product of the human will. While all forms of millenarianism view history as the fulfillment of a specific intention, the details of that intention vary from the consummation of re-creation to human struggle, from the climax of redemption to historical progress, and from the vindication of God to the vindication of a messianic figure. The intention never involves annulment, abandonment, or termination. Jewish and Christian theologies look to the eschaton of history as the climax and fulfillment of God's intention for human history, not as abandonment. This divine intention produces hope, not uncertainty. (4) It views the present history as involving conflicting or opposing forces. Thus history is not melioristic in character, and millenarian movements expect judgment or revolutions of struggle. It looks upon the end time as the period of birth pangs, that is, the most intense period of conflicts and struggles. (5) It looks to a future utopian hope—whether the conviction/hope of the new heaven and new earth or communism—in order to survive the present. It looks to the new events of the end time (transition period) rather than to the past as its hope for historical movement.[69]

Millenarian theology in the Bible is not just the hope of a golden age, whether reminiscent of the past or anticipatory of the restoration and consummation of the paradise yet to come. It looks to the future, the ideal state of a new era; it is "the once and future Paradise . . . primitive Paradise and Promised Land."[70] Millenarian theology believes in the end of this world, the coming of a new world, ushered in by a messianic and charismatic figure of unprecedented magnitude. Millenarian theology also believes in the drastic conflict between good and evil on earth and global tribulations of some sort before the radical interception of deliverance. It confidently believes in the victory of the good, the imminent arrival of the Savior, and a new millennium of peace, prosperity, and purity.

Whereas paradise or utopian thinking might not necessarily have a particular view of history (except for the social reform or political revolutions in that period of history), millenarian thinking presupposes a certain working principle in history, such as an epochal scheme in which history is either cyclical or, more frequently, a linear progression from creation to fall to a present (of wars and tribulations) to a future (of last judgment) and a final consummation of a perfect age (millennium).[71] The cosmos that is the new heaven and the new earth is reminiscent of but more glorious than the original cosmos before the fall (Isa. 30:23; 35:1–7; 65:17; 66:22; Ezek. 34:14, 27; 36:9–35; Rev. 21:1–5). And the earthly paradise will not be destroyed again; it will have no end.

2

utopian views of history from ancient and modern china

Ideal Society and Ideas of History

The universal ideal is happiness and joy, but the expressions of such utopian visions are always culturally conditioned. For the exiled Jews and the Thessalonian Christians, millenarian and apocalyptic eschatology revealed for them a divine destiny of assured hope and salvation despite the harsh social and political situation. Likewise, for Chinese seeking to make sense of dynastic change and cultural deterioration, different groups have postulated what would be best for China. Different groups can coexist with their diverse views of utopia, but competing views of historical unity often result in violence. Even within the Bible, competing views with regard to the salvation of the world remain a problematic issue for biblical scholars.[1]

Paul's eschatological view of history would seem to imply that, among the competing truth claims, divine revelation in universal history ought to be tested by the criteria of the unity of history and the openness to the future that constantly critiques our present reality.[2] Löwith maintains that the teleological and eschatological scheme of the historical process allows history to become universal. He writes:

[F]or its universality does not depend merely on the belief in one universal God but on his giving unity to the history of mankind by directing it toward a final purpose. When II Isaiah describes the future glory of the new Jerusalem, his religious futurism and nationalism are actually teleological universalism. . . . It is an idea and an ideal of the future, the necessary horizon for the eschatological concept of history and its universality.[3]

In a time of global consciousness of political correctness, this interpretation may sound like "theological imperialism," but the truth of the matter is that either we have a grand narrative whose *telos* is written by the coming God or we accept the violence of tribal or imperial narratives.

The more difficult issue is that our belief in one history (diversities that are interrelated) or more than one (diversities that are not interrelated) depends on whether we hold to a cyclical or an eschatological view of history. It appears that in a cyclical view of history, such as that of Chinese dynastic changes, the concept of universal history is simply absent; there is only dynastic history. This will become clear as we review the Chinese utopian visions of ideal history within her complex consciousness of time.

Chinese Views of Ideal History[4]

Semantic Range of Happiness and the Ideal

While the Thessalonian letters use such words as *peace* (wholesomeness, i.e., shalom) and *blessing* (benefactions from God) to describe the utopian human condition amidst suffering and persecution, the Chinese words and concepts are quite different. In Chinese, the common words describing people's ideal hope may be subdivided into three interrelated categories: (1) religious benefaction (*chen*), joy (*zang*), happiness (*xiang*), and honor (*za*); (2) the social offering of joy to one another during an abundant (*kang*) period or celebrative (*ching*) occasion, blessedness (*xing*), happiness (*chi*), good (*xi*) time, favor or take pleasure in (*hao*), joy (*le*), contentment (*xian*), gladness (*huan*), joy (*xin*), and lucky (*ji*); (3) the material well-being of prosperity (*fu*), including having many children and being wealthy (*fu*).[5] The word *utopia* is used to describe an ideal society not yet realized, being translated into Chinese phonetically as "wu tuo pang." Together the three Chinese words mean "the state without foundation." Though an excellent translation, it is not as popular as *Datong*—the age of Great Harmony, Great Togetherness, or Great Unity. *Wutuopang* is generally referred to as the outopia, "the nowhere." Any political regime wanting to affirm its sociopolitical vision as a workable reality would rather use *Datong* because of its rich heritage and thus capture the Chinese conviction that the ideal age would soon be realized.

Datong is akin to the myth of the Garden of Eden without the theological motifs found in the Genesis account. *Datong* is a highly cultural concept, referring to a paradise of an agrarian, communal lifestyle characterized by justice, equality, sufficiency, simplicity, purity, and harmony. It is a period that existed before the introduction and corruption of bureaucracy, social classes, hard labor, and machinery control.

Pre-Confucian Myths of the Ideal Age

During the Predynastic period (before 2205 B.C.E.) and the Xia dynasty (2205–1766 B.C.E., Bronze Age), China was ruled by legendary sages and heroes. The Huang Di ("Yellow Sovereign") of the twenty-seventh century B.C.E.—Yao, Shun, and Yu—were adored by later generations as ideal rulers who restored peace and prosperity. Thus the Chinese understanding of history is similar to Jewish and Christian views of history: it assumes the existence of suffering and ambiguity and hopes for an ideal age that will bring restoration.

During the Shang dynasty (1600–1050 B.C.E.) in the Yellow River area, another means of restoring peace and prosperity became popular, as seen in the scripts discovered on bones and tortoise shells. These are known as *mantics*. The *mantics* are the art of the matriarchal society, traceable probably to the Shang dynasty, during which shamans and oracle priests acted as visionaries and seers reading future events, thus enabling people to find blessings and avoid curses. Their experiences probably became part of the teaching of *Yi Jing* (I Ching; *The Book of Changes*) and Daoist (Taoist) traditions in later Chinese history. However, China is dominated by Confucianism,[6] not Daoism, since Chinese family, political, and social institutions are structured according to the Confucian ethos. The tension between Confucianism and Daoism is visible later in the Zhou dynasty (1050–256 B.C.E.), though at that time Confucianism had not yet existed long enough to be a strong cultural force. The transition from shamanism to intellectualism is evidence of Zhou's view of history.

When Zhou, a patriarchal society, conquered Shang, a matriarchal society, the kings of Zhou claimed the right to perform the rites of heaven by arguing that heaven had mandated that Shang should fall and Zhou should rule. Thus the oracle priests' divinations by means of bones and shells were replaced by a complex, ambiguous system of dried milfoil stalks, which contained the wisdom of the law of changes. In other words, the matriarchal society of shamanism was appropriated gradually into the maturity of a philosophical system of changes and was formulated eventually in *The Book of Changes*.[7] This dynastic change not only brought about the victory of the Zhou's philosophical tradition but also realigned the power of rulers along family lineage and consolidated the power of the rulers as political and religious leaders.

With the demise of Shang, oracle priests perished, and the division between political rulers and religious counselors (or rite performers) began to merge into one person: the king or emperor. This explains why, in Chinese history, the messianic hope of national prosperity has always fallen on the shoulders of the head of state. Chinese people from the earliest written history until the communist regime always thought of their emperors as vested with the divine right and privilege to lead China. Emperors were thought of as men-deities. Emperors had ultimate political and religious power as the son of heaven (*Tian Zi*); this is true of Zhou's kings down to Mao Zedong (1893–1976).

Tian in the Shang period referred to the ancestors of the Shang rulers, as the pictograph portrays "a human figure with a large head and powerfully developed limbs." Bauer analyzes the changes that took place with regard to the understanding of *Tian* from the Shang to the Zhou dynasties:

> It was only natural that the Zhou should not have been interested in obeisance to the Shang ancestors, yet they did not simply want to drop this weighty concept. Because heaven [*Tian*] was worshipped in their religion, they identified this earliest ancestor with Shang-ti, the "God-emperor on high," who was revered by the Zhou. . . . Gradually, he came to be used to merely designate the place where the earliest ancestors of the Zhou sat on their thrones. . . . Thus he lost not only his character as a person but also the personal chosenness that had been his up to this moment. . . . Hesitantly but unmistakably, a split between this world and the beyond, between these two realms which had still been so closely integrated during the Shang period, becomes noticeable. . . . Psychologically, the recognition of heaven meant that a new world was created which might well serve as a place of refuge, of distant vistas and of happiness. But it also established clear boundaries; it made the earth more of a place for men, living men, than ever before and suggested that these boundaries against the spirits be made as impenetrable as possible.[8]

The history of the Zhou dynasty is important in showing the rise of Confucianism in Chinese political history and its continuous influence, even during the eradication campaign of Qinshihuangdi or of Mao Zedong.

The Confucianist View of History and Datong

Confucius, or to be precise Kong Zi (551–479 B.C.E.), regarded the Western (Earlier or Former) Zhou (1050–770 B.C.E.) as the "golden age," only two hundred years or so earlier than "Spring and Autumn" (Chun Qiu 770–476 B.C.E.), when he was born. Later Confucians were also fond of looking to antiquity as a prototype of an ideal age in order to save their own disintegrating society. However, to them antiquity was not a precivilization Garden of Eden but the golden age of Zhou.

THE *DATONG* WORLD ORDERED BY *YUE, LI,* AND *REN*

Confucius's understanding of *Datong* was not mere nostalgia for the good old days. His utopian vision of a past golden age served primarily to stretch backward the imagination of those Chinese currently living in a state of cultural and moral deterioration—the Spring-Autumn period. Confucius wanted them to contemplate the Great Harmony (i.e., *Datong* in Chinese) in the perfect world. In other words, his *Datong* utopian hope was a critique of their chaotic and deteriorating society.

In imagining the existence of goodness and beauty in a perfect society, Confucius's *Datong* vision emphasized music, propriety, character, and harmonious interpersonal relationships (*ren*), because the Zhou dynasty was the prototype of *Datong*. Confucius always looked to the king of Zhou, who employed two principles as the common ground for unifying the people: *yue* (as the harmony of emotion/feeling) and *li* (behavior expressed artistically as propriety, such as bowing). Confucius believed that beauty and goodness were the foundations or the source of music and propriety and that the potential for beauty and goodness resided in every person. It was up to each person to practice, cultivate, and express that beauty and goodness.

THE HEAVENLY MANDATE (*TIANMING*) AND SELF-PERCEPTION OF CONFUCIUS

The *Datong* vision as a transhistorical reality can be seen in Confucius's teaching of *Tian Dao* (the Heavenly Principle or Heavenly Way). Confucius believed that *Tian* not only gave birth to the people but continued to regenerate and sustain them. Confucius also regarded *ren* (love) as the fountainhead of all virtues. He exhorted all to actualize *Tianming* (the Mandate of Heaven) by committing themselves to *ren*, because *ren* is what makes human beings human. The sage-rulers were to be virtuous, providing an example for others to follow, and thus bring about the renovation of society (*Great Learning* [*Da Xue*] 1:1). *The Doctrine of Mean*

(*Zhong Yong*) likewise states that if a sage-ruler knows how to cultivate his own character, he will know how to govern other people (20:11).

Confucius identified himself with the duke of Zhou (Zhou Gong), the brother of the dynasty's founder, Wuwang (Warrior King), who was regent for Chengwang, Wuwang's son and successor. *Lun Yu* (*The Analects*) often mentions the duke of Zhou, and some scholars suspect that perhaps Confucius longed to be such a personality in order to restore the lost golden age.[9] Yet Confucius's vision of the ideal regent was of an ethical but not a religious person, largely because of his preoccupation with society and because of the changes in worldview from the Shang to the Zhou: the new worldview emphasized the here and now. The significant point in Confucius's yearning for the restoration of peace and order in the world was his understanding of the heavenly mandate: the calling from the world beyond for him to fulfill the mission of saving the society in which he lived. Throughout Chinese history, few people had as clear a calling as Confucius, who, according to Bauer, was a self-conscious messiah of his own society.[10] *Shi Ji* (*Historical Records*) contains an account of Confucius as the ideal ruler:

> Three months after Confucius had assumed the government of the state [Lu], even cattle dealers no longer cheated others by demanding excessive prices; men and women walked along different sides of the road, and objects lost on the streets were no longer picked up. Strangers came from the four directions of heaven, but when they arrived in the towns, they never found it necessary to turn to the police, for they were treated as if they were in their own country (*Shi Ji* 47:667b).

A popular Chinese understanding of political messianism holds that in a five-hundred-year cycle there would supposedly be a ruler vested with the heavenly mandate to reign over China. Bauer gives examples of messianic consciousness in Chinese history, and not all these figures were political rulers. The first was the duke of Zhou (who died in 1105 B.C.E., according to traditional chronology); following him were Confucius (551–479 B.C.E.), the historian Sima Qian (Ssu-ma Ch'ien, ca. 145–90 B.C.E.), the illegal emperor Wang Mang (45 B.C.E.–23 C.E.), and the philosopher-emperor Yuandi (508–555) of the Liang dynasty.[11] Bauer notes, "Curiously enough, men who did not live during these periods of renewal also believed that this messianic idea applied to them, particularly Meng Zi (Mencius, 372–289 B.C.E.). He is the first to explicitly discuss this five-hundred-year rule (*Meng Zi* 2B, 13; 7B, 38)."[12] Discerning whether Mao's conviction to be the "savior of New China" arose from a Marxist understanding of historical force, a Chinese egotistical vision for the heavenly mandate, or a mixture of various factors is difficult. It is very likely that, since Mao's thinking was deeply influenced by a mixture of Chinese and Marxist ideas, this Confucian messianic mandate of saving the world lay in the consciousness of his political commitment.

Meng Zi's Social Utopias: Politicizing Confucius's Ethics into Democratic Socialism

Meng Zi (Mencius, 372–289 B.C.E.) was the first to develop fully Confucius's ethical and social philosophy in the political realm. His sense of vocation to save the world is clear, even though the time cycle for him was not ripe. His commitment was based on two beliefs. First, Meng Zi believed in the goodness of human nature, that every human being should have a messianic consciousness. His democratization of an inherently good human nature motivated the conscience of the people toward social responsibility. Second, he believed in the "quasi-mystical notion of a salubrious force pulsating through all beings"[13] (*haoran zhi qi*). In other words, because "heaven does not speak . . . people are the only court of appeal and decide whether or not a dynasty has the 'mandate.' A new ruler must be 'introduced' to both heaven and the people before he can be certain of his office. It is therefore a basic premise of every ideal government that the prince own everything in an 'equal manner' with the people."[14] Thus, Meng Zi's second point was also a democratization, in this case, of the mandate of heaven. Such a view suggests that the validity of a heavenly mandate depended on the people's approval.

Meng Zi's social-utopian understandings combined to form a government that was responsible to the people. He also taught that a royal government (*wangdao*) should seek to benefit all, distribute resources fairly according to the "well field system" (*jing*), and require all to contribute according to his or her abilities.[15] Meng Zi taught King Xuan of Qi the reason of Wenwang of Zhou. He possessed a large piece of land, yet it was considered too small by his people. Why? Wenwang shared it with his people.[16] One cannot help but note the similarity between this vision in Meng Zi's time and that of the establishment of communes in the New China. Again, it is difficult for one to tell if Mao's vision of the communes was influenced by the Paris communes, by Meng Zi's model, or (most likely) by a combination of various traditions.

Mo Zi's Radical Socialism: Inclusive Love

In contrast to the Confucian ideal of society and justice based on traditional social roles, classes, hierarchies, and family structures, Mo Zi (Mo Ti, 479–381 B.C.E.) envisioned a utopian society in a radical social-

63

ist state where inclusive love knew no boundaries. That Mo Zi's utopian vision was not taken seriously and never became a major movement in Chinese socialist history is perhaps a result of its radical nature.

Mo Zi's ideal state was based on "inclusive love" (*jian-ai*) for all, beyond the boundaries and differentiations of family hierarchy. This inclusive love was universally egalitarian and truly undifferentiated in nature. When asked, "What is *jian-ai*?" Mo Zi replied:

> It means that one makes no distinction between the state of others and one's own; none between the houses of others and one's own; none between the other person and oneself. If princes love each other, there will be no more wars. . . . If all the people in the world love each other, the strong will not overpower the weak, the many will not suppress the few, the rich will not mock the poor, the highly placed will not despise the lowly, nor the clever take advantage of the simple (*Mo Zi* 15:64–65).[17]

Mo Zi explained the effect of *jian-ai* as peace and order in a society.[18] His utopian state always worked on the principle of *shangtong*, that is, reciprocity and mutuality. *Shangtong* worked from top to bottom, meaning that those from below assimilated with those from above.[19] Mo Zi's system did not involve complete reciprocity between those above and those below, for those above had the power to enforce their values with punitive sanctions, and those below had to conform. The principle of *shangtong* suggested that punishment enacted by both *Tian* (heaven) or *Tian Zi* (son of heaven) enforced the order of those below.

Mo Zi's socialist vision of inclusive love and assimilation of leadership among the common people may find its parallel in modern communist government, yet there is a subtle, and therefore significant, difference. Mo Zi's political system may sound like totalitarian rule, yet abuse cannot be tolerated in this system, and love remains the basic principle of the Mohist view of government. Maoist communism might also argue that "Mao's love of the people" is evident in songs commonly sung by Chinese adults, children, and students and that all demands, struggles, and hardships under the Maoist regime were meant to inculcate the spirit of patriotism against the evils of imperialism and feudalism. Maoist communism might also defend the dictatorship democracy by claiming that family members who dared criticize one another before the government were practicing just and inclusive love similar to that of Mo Zi but different from that of Confucius.

The crux of the matter is one's definition of love, one's understanding of the scope and working process of love. It is true that in many respects Maoist socialism is similar to Mohist socialism: both are based on inclusive love of the people beyond that which is found in the family. It is not that Confucianism does not have an understanding of love. To Confucius, *ren* means the love of humans that must progress from family members to relatives to friends and then to all. The patriarchal lineage becomes the necessary structure and unit in which one's love for people is expressed. If one does not love one's parents, those who are closest, dearest, and most intimate to one, how could one think of loving others whose relationships are distant? So the Confucian critique of Mo Zi's (and Mao's) socialism focuses on the lack of intimacy among family members or close friends because of their priority of love for the wider scope of people. The main Confucian insight is that any other form of morality will be heteronomous and hence doomed to failure. Mo Zi and Mao command love and threaten punishment if disobeyed, but the Confucian system is grounded rather on spontaneous affect, cultivated and channeled through personal and social delight in obedience for the sake of sagehood.

Both Mo Zi and Mao, on the other hand, would contend that the problem with the Confucian understanding of *ren* (love) is its insistence that the starting point of love comes from family members. This patriarchal logic of love in the political life of Chinese history is most vividly revealed in the divinely ordained right of sons to succeed their fathers as kings. Imperial rule became a family affair, and that was the root of evil in the state and the palace. The palace was the place where sons sabotaged one another, fathers killed sons, and mothers competed with and hated one another. There have been hatred, violence, and bloodshed in the "royal" families throughout Chinese history. Yet this royal practice of patriarchalism was typical of Zhou's politics, which the Confucians considered to be the golden age. Against this, Mo Zi advocated an egalitarian monarchy based not on royal bloodlines but on the qualification of the individual, whose commitment to *shangtong* served as a check-and-balance strategy to develop a more inclusive monarchy.

The Daoist[20] View: Harmony with Primordial Nature and Apolitical Utopianism

Confucius found the golden age in Zhou, when ritual/propriety (*li*) served to create a cultured and regulated society of peace and order, while Mo Zi found it in the legendary Xia, when sage-rulers such as Yao and Shun overcame the destructive force of the primordial condition (e.g., flood) to create a paradise inhabitable for humans by means of *shangtong*. The Daoist utopian vision presented a utopia radically different from either of these. The Daoist utopian vision was subversive to the dominant Confucian vision because it pushed human limits beyond its hard realities to human imagination. The imaginative function of the Daoist utopian quest critiqued the humanism of Confucianism at its core.

A Critique of the Confucianist Utopian Vision

According to the Daoist tradition, human predicaments and problems, far from impeding humans, caused them to flourish and to develop the virtues by which Confucianism wished to realize the ideal social-political world. The Daoist vision of utopia was by no means against "culture," "civilization," or theories of "government." Rather, it perceived them to be the problem that one can transcend to attain utopia. The Daoist answer to a utopian state and political society was to be "apolitical" and natural as much as possible. The rationale was that simplicity could replace sophisticated programs that created inequality; withdrawal or nonaction (*wuwei*) could replace the activism that created chaos; silence could replace vigorous deliberations that created pride; and nothingness could replace power that created domination and abuse. Along these lines, Zhuang Zi (Chuang-tzu, 369–286 B.C.E.) gave an extensive account of the paradisaic human life before sages came to contaminate it.[21]

The Daoist utopia was to be found far removed from the social-political realities because one was in harmony with the primordial nature. Paradise was to be found in nature, in the nonhuman world, both in space and time, that is, in a *realm* such as a mountaintop, a deep jungle, or a wilderness uncontaminated by human existence and activities, and in a *time* prior to the inception of human civilization.

Openness of Truth and Priority of Cosmology

The Daoist utopian vision offered a harsh critique of the social aberrations and political conflicts in the Chinese society of the fourth and fifth centuries B.C.E. It saw two main problems: (1) people at that time were overconfident in their intellectual optimism regarding truth claims; (2) people placed themselves above the cosmos and sought to subjugate it. Overconfidence bred self-boasting, while seeking to dominate nature brought about self-alienation. When Lao Zi (Lao-tzu, 604–521 B.C.E.) and Zhuang Zi attempted to overcome this cultural deterioration and conflict, their utopian hope portrayed truth or Dao as one. Although everyone has his or her own perspective, each person sees only part of the truth. As a result, each person has his or her own reading of reality.

They also saw that cosmology is prior to anthropology. Consequently, peace and order can be achieved only if human beings become less involved in social and political activities and participate more in the harmony of the cosmos. The solution to cultural conflict and claim of superiority is "nothingness," that is, the act of letting go or of putting down one's own presuppositions and biases. Even truth comes from nothingness, and all shall return to it. In *Dao De Jing,* Lao Zi says, "The Dao that can be told of is not the Eternal Dao. . . . The Speaker knows not; The Knower speaks not." Once one speaks of Dao with human language and concepts, one conditions and limits the Dao within one's criteria and conditions, thus distorting the original Dao. The best way to know the Dao is to meditate and to keep silent.[22] For Lao Zi, Dao is the creative reality. Daoist utopianism stresses, therefore, the broadening of one's mind and lifestyle until one is harmonized with the cosmos and achieves a mystical, artistic way of life.

The uniqueness of the Daoist utopian vision is in its ecological cosmology, which, in contrast to Confucian humanism, seeks to subsume anthropology under it. Confucian philosophy would collapse without the intrinsic logic of humanity and the social world. However, the Daoists' utopian realm of "plainness and simplicity" has its intrinsic logic in ecology.[23] The precivilized human existence of simplicity and purity[24] qualifies Daoists to be "true human beings" (*zhenren*). They are without desire and labor, but they are also content and self-sufficient.[25] The ideal age is the one of perfect virtue (*zhide*):

> In an age of Perfect Virtue, the worthy are not honored, the talented are not employed. Rulers are like the high branches of a tree, the people like the deer of the fields. They do what is right but they do not know that it is righteousness. They love one another but they do not know that this is benevolence. They are true-hearted but do not know that this is loyalty. They are trustworthy but do not know that this is good faith. They wriggle around like insects, performing services for one another, but do not know that they are being kind. Therefore they move without leaving any trail behind, act without leaving any memory of their deed (*Zhuang Zi* 12:200).[26]

It is interesting to note that the Daoist vision of paradise is similar to that of Genesis. A city is considered to be a human construct and a place of great temptation (Gen. 11), while a garden is considered a divine blessing and a place of plenitude (Gen. 2–3). It is true that, with the rise of nation and empire, the biblical vision of paradise takes on city imagery (see Rev. 21), but the ideas of perfection and restfulness of the new city of God (new Jerusalem) are said to be heaven-sent and not of human construct.

DEATH IN THE CYCLE OF COSMIC LIFE

The Daoist view of utopia as "nothingness" (*wu*) or "not-doing" (*wuwei*) may be considered pessimistic by others, but many Daoists do regard death as a state of unconsciousness, such as the dreamlike state, providing them with a state of metamorphosis toward happiness.[27] The description of death was common in the Daoist tradition, yet Daoists did not fear it. In fact, they accepted and welcomed disintegration and death as an ongoing, cosmic process of cycle and renewal.[28] The Daoist view of death remains a dominant view in Chinese culture even today, perhaps because the Confucianists are hesitant to discuss issues related to death and the afterlife. Today most Chinese use "an extinguished lamp" as a metaphor for death.

Classical Chinese did not have a linear worldview, but a cyclical one of time and space. They believed in the creative principle (creator) that humanity and the cosmos were in a gigantic cycling process of disintegration and reintegration. Though modern Chinese, including Mao and the Chinese communists, were not able to decisively articulate their view of death, it is clear that the Chinese worldview has a predominantly impersonal and ecological understanding of life and therefore would not take death and suffering personally. Such a cosmic and ecological understanding of death as part of the overall life cycle suggests to the Western world that "human rights" are a secondary category in the Daoist tradition, for anthropology is subsumed under cosmology. Such a philosophy does not suggest that Chinese do not feel pain when tragedy strikes, nor does it suggest that Mao and the Chinese communists were heartless when they saw the hardship and death of the masses during revolutions. This is only to suggest the different perspectives on life and death in the Western and Chinese societies. If death is a part of the natural process, it is not a thing to be saved from, for death itself is a purifying and redeeming process.

Immediately following *Zhuang Zi* 6:116–19, one reads another story about death that portrays Confucius's explanation of life and death, most likely from a Daoist perspective. That is, death is a purification transition from one existence to the next.[29] The story shows the fluidity between the realms of life and death in the Daoist tradition. Because of that fluidity and the obvious differences between the two realms, the yearning for life in the next world is also found in Daoist tradition, as if death is most desirable for the living.[30] The fluidity between the world here and now and the world beyond is akin to the undifferentiated experience of one's dreaming of a butterfly or a butterfly's dream.[31] The parable also offers an explanation of metamorphosis from this state to the next and back; in other words, a dream is the transformation between states and enables one to overcome death. Thus, later popular Daoist tradition sought to eliminate death and to prolong life to immortality. There is a dialogue between Qu Qiao, probably a disciple of Confucius, and Changwu Zi, a legendary sage in the past, that speaks of a dream as the vehicle to overcome death in Daoist tradition.[32]

The utopian vision of the Daoists in the forms of anarchism and *wuwei* (nonaction) are expressed in the doctrine of the "absence of princes" (*wujun lun*). This doctrine does not argue for regression, barbaric domination, misery, or laziness. It simply promotes a governmentless political life that will usher in peace and order and a rulerless society that will bring about the maximum participation of all citizens in their quest for life. The Daoist assumption of *wujun lun* is that the less the government and political leaders intervene, the more peace and order a society will enjoy.

The Legalist (Fajia) View: The Ideal State Ordered by Means of Militarism and Legalism

The Daoist utopian vision was largely a critique of the humanistic perfectibility of Confucian utopianism. Daoism and Confucianism seem opposed to each other in their visions of an ideal state for China. However, the Legalist utopian vision by means of the military and the law was the result of the confluence of the works of Daoism and Confucianism. The Legalist school can be traced back to the seventh century B.C.E., but it took definite form only at the time of Shang Yang, Xun Zi, and Han Fei Zi.

SHANG YANG (DIED 338 B.C.E.)

The Legalist vision of an ideal state maintains that order can be achieved by the administration of the law. During the Qin dynasty (221–206 B.C.E.), the Legalist Shang Yang looked not to the age-old past but to the implementation of the law and militarism in the Qin: "The 'Way' of the sage consists neither in imitating the past nor in following the present, but in acting as the times demand" (*Shang Jun Shu* 8:19).[33] For Shang Yang, the penal law was the absolute guide to the stability of a society and the welfare of its people. Shang believed that the enforcement of corporal punishment, even for minor crimes, and the extension of punishment to family and clan would cause enough fear among people to keep them from doing wrong: "If the punishments are so strict that they even extend to the entire family, people will not dare to try and see how far they can go, and if they do not try, the punishments will no longer be necessary . . . and no one will be punished anymore" (*Shang Jun Shu* 17:29).[34]

Under such conditions, it is no surprise that messianism became pervasive during the flourishing of Qin Daoism. The story is told that an old man by the name of "Master of the Yellow Stone" gave a Daoist priest, Chang Liang, a book entitled *Military Strategy of the Taigong (Taigong Pingfa)*.[35] It resembles the *Taiping Jing (The Classic of the Highest Peace)* in that a divine king is prophesied to rule the land anew in the Han dynasty with the assistance of the warrior Taigong (Wang), who is the teacher of the Zhou dynasty founder.[36]

XUN ZI (298–238 B.C.E.)

Xun Zi was a Confucian who envisioned an ideal and orderly government by means of ritual and music. He explained, "The nature of man is evil; what is good in him, is artificial" (*Xun Zi* 17 [par. 23]).[37] An earlier Legalist, Guanzi (died 645 B.C.E.) had long believed that "the human disposition is to hate; because of the wickedness of the human heart, laws had to be brought into existence."[38] Here Xun Zi assumed that human nature or cosmic nature were artificial or unnatural and thus needed to be tamed and cultivated through ritual. Confucius considered ritual to have its religious function of sacrificing to ancestors and *Tian*, but Xun Zi took ritual to be a basic means of becoming human, against the unnatural forces of life. Xun Zi described the ideal government as follows:

> To make a state content, one must be moderate in one's own consumption, and generous toward the people: that is the best way of garnering the surplus of the country. If one brings about moderation through ritual, and the government is generous toward the people, the people will enjoy abundance. If the people are treated generously, they will grow; if they grow, the fields, being properly cultivated, will yield a rich harvest, and if they yield a rich harvest by being properly cultivated, their fruit will grow a hundredfold. If the superiors follow this rule and gather the wealth of the country, and the inferiors follow the ritual and are moderate in their consumption, the surplus will pile up and form hills and mountains, so that no space will be left to hoard it unless one sets fire to it from time to time. . . . But ritual means that high and low have their place, that there be a difference between old and young, and a relation between important and unimportant. That is the reason that the Son of Heaven, the feudal princes, the high dignitaries, and the officers have the clothing appropriate to their station. . . . Those endowed with physical strength are thus the helpers of the "virtuous" ruler. It is only through the physical strength of the people (*bo xing*) that he achieves success everywhere. Because it forms a society, he attains harmony, because it is capable, he acquires wealth,

because it is steady, he achieves peace, and he lives long because it attains an advanced age. Father and son cannot help loving each other, older and younger brothers cannot help obeying each other, nor men and women making each other happy. Children are raised without misery, and the aged are fed. And it will be as the proverb says: "Heaven and earth have created it, the sages have perfected it."[39]

A wise ruler would create a ritual of fixed social differences for an ideal society:

The old kings saw to it that people did not suffer heat strokes in summer and the cold of winter; that, when speed was called for, their strength was not taxed; and that when there was a chance to let up, this did not mean that they let the right moment pass by. Thus, . . . both the highly placed and the lowly were rich, and the people loved its superiors. The people arrived as in a flowing stream, enjoyed the presence of kings and felt about them as they had about father and mother, and they were happy even when ordered to die on the field of battle. . . . The earlier kings created a clear ritual and a clear law so that all might be of one mind. They induced loyalty and fidelity, so that all loved each other; they honored the sages and assigned tasks to the able so that a hierarchy might arise. They invented gowns for the nobility and ceremonies to instill respect. Work was imposed on the people as the times demanded, and they easily shaped its responsibilities to make all men equal (qi) and to help all of them.[40]

Thus, ritual piety became the central virtue and principle of social order in Xun Zi.

Han Fei Zi (died 233 b.c.e.)

The most famous Legalist is probably Han Fei Zi, a disciple of Xun Zi. Han Fei Zi was a Confucian philosopher whose critique of Confucian and Meng Zi filial piety in the family structure and whose advocacy of militarism of law created a Chinese legalism that influenced later history, even that of communism. Han Fei Zi explained:

Ha, in a strictly run household there are no recalcitrant servants, but a "tender mother" has spoiled children! . . . Ha, when a sage governs the state, he does not count on the people to do what is beneficial to him. Instead, he sees to it that their utilization can do him no harm, he can employ all the people in the entire state in the same manner (*chi*). . . . Therefore he works with the law, and not with "virtue."[41]

Han Fei Zi disagreed with his mentor Xun Zi, who argued that the patriarchal family structure was to be replaced by cultic laws, and agreed

71

with Shang Yang that militarism was the correct means of establishing an ideal society. Many centuries later Mao's harsh critique of Chinese familial emphasis over the welfare of the nation found its philosophical basis in Han Fei Zi.

The emphasis of militarism in Han Fei Zi's philosophy constituted a critique of the intellectualism then present in China. Thus Han Fei Zi wrote:

> Although every family owns copies of the writings of Shang Yang and Kuan Chung about the "law," the state becomes poorer and poorer. The reason is simply that too many talk a lot about tilling the soil, but only a few actually take plow in hand. . . . Although every family owns copies of the writings of Sun Wu and Wu Ch'i, the armies keep getting weaker, simply because too many prattle about the art of war, and too few put on their armor. Therefore the enlightened ruler uses the physical strength of men, but does not listen to what they say. . . . That is also the reason literature does not exist in the state of an enlightened ruler. Only the law is taught. Nor do we find the traditional sayings of the sage kings. . . . Thus it happens that the people inside the borders of the state always follow the law when they talk, always have worthy objectives when they act, and excel nowhere but in the army when they seek recognition. Because of all this, the state is rich in times of peace, and the army is strong in times of war.[42]

In other words, militarism is a knowledge that is practiced, while the pure theory of the intellectual is nothing but empty talk. Mao's ideology, which emphasizes praxis, labor-intensive work for intellectuals, and strong physical health, may be traced philosophically back to Han Fei Zi's thinking. While Mao's praxis political philosophy overcomes the vanity of pure intellectualism, hidden in the militarism of Maoist political theology is the inevitability of violence in his utopianism. Maoist language of praxis always subordinates life to the violence of the state. In its assumption of divinity, Maoist language of praxis claims the sovereign "will to power" and intends to build a "holy empire" by all might in accordance to the heavenly mandate.

LEGALIST AND QIN SHIHUANGDI

The three Legalists mentioned above were instrumental in bringing about the authoritarian rulers of the Qin dynasty (221–206 B.C.E.). Legalism was a response to cope with the chaos of the Warring States (Zhan Guo, 475–222 B.C.E.). The first Chinese emperor, Qin Shihuangdi, whom Mao adored, attempted to create the first united Chinese empire by means of the Legalist visions of law and military. Qin Shihuangdi looked to the future and intended to build a new and everlasting dynasty. His strategy was to burn all Chinese classics except *The Book of Changes,* perhaps because the former were preserving the old ways and the latter was a prophetic book envisioning the future.[43] As the new emperor reigning in the new era, Qin Shihuangdi proclaimed himself to be the first divine emperor, taking the title the First Divine (Shihuangdi). Prior to his reign, the two characters in the title (Huangdi) were used separately: one for sage emperors (Huang); the other for emperors who had died (Di). In other words, before his time, it was popularly believed that emperors were sons of heaven mandated to rule China. After his rule, emperors were regarded as divine even before their death. The divinity of the emperors connoted their claim to absolute power as well as the wish for the emperor's immortality and thus eternal reign.

Mao emulated Shihuangdi, and the similarities between these two personalities is not mere coincidence. Shihuangdi was able to deal with the daily workload of 120 pounds of records written on bamboo sticks. In his twelve-year reign, he set up provinces, unified China, standardized one system of writing, and standardized weights and measures. He built roads as well as the Great Wall and ruled over an age of the greatest peace in Chinese history up to his time. We will assess Mao's leadership of China in the next few chapters; suffice it to say here that Mao's contributions certainly surpassed those of Shihuangdi, given the number of people and the large territory Mao had to rule.

Shihuangdi thought that stability could continue for a long time through the exercise of law and military might, held together by the controlling power at the top. Indeed, he even tried to prohibit his officials from telling anyone the news of his death; it was kept secret for weeks. Yet only a year after his death, his son, the Second Divine, was killed and the Qin empire was destroyed when a rebellion arose (which eventually became the Han dynasty, 206 B.C.E.–220 C.E.). Shihuangdi, a self-proclaimed emperor, pursued happiness until he died, but he failed to find it.[44] He was a paranoid figure, and his greatest enemy was death. The story was told that he had heard of three distant islands—Penglai, Fangzhang, and Yingzhou—where immortals enjoyed everlasting life. He sent his magician, Xu Fu, to discover these islands. Xu Fu came back with nothing but invented a story about a medicine that would prolong life. Shihuangdi again sent out Xu Fu, this time to get the medicine, but the latter never returned.

The Chinese views surveyed above are distinctively different from the Jewish-Christian views outlined in chapter 1. Both motifs of messianic consciousness and national salvation are present in Jewish, Christian, and Chinese utopian history, but dynastic change and the hope of a return to the golden age are distinctive of Chinese history. Jewish and Christian views look to a transcendental reign of God beyond national history. In those views, eschatological and millenarian hope is not limited to national salvation; rather, their visions extend to the salvation of the universe. In critiquing the domination of various empires, Jewish and Christian views of history do contain a periodization process, but the purpose of such is to portray the ultimate God of history whose intended will of salvation "invades" the world and becomes the *telos* of history. In contrast, the majority of Confucianists viewed the Chinese Great Togetherness (*Datong*) as a realization of a past golden age. The Daoists also looked to the past or a time before the existence of time, viewing utopia as the precivilization, primordial cosmic union. The Legalists looked to the future, hoping to achieve and further prolong peace and order through law and military might. Generally speaking, the Chinese view of history is dominated by the Confucianists and the Daoists. For the sake of simplicity, I have delineated the various views in the Chinese traditions; in reality, however, these cultural forces are like crosscurrents clashing with each other and reuniting to form new currents. For example, Mao's thought was influenced not only by these dominant traditions (Confucianism, Daoism) but also by the Legalists as well as the Marxists. Thus, before we look in depth at Maoism as the Sinification of Marxism, it is important to understand the Chinese view of the historical process.

The Chinese View of History: Cyclical Periodization and Permanent Revolution/Recycling

The typical Chinese cyclical worldview works well with the periodization view of history. Since the view of historical time is cyclical, such a periodization cannot be progress but an alternation between order and disorder. Long ago, Meng Zi said: "Since the appearance of the world of men, a long time has indeed elapsed, consisting of alternating order and disorder" (3B, 9). Thus Meng Zi (2B, 13) delineated cycles of history in the following dispensations: (1) from the sage-kings Yao, Shun, and Yu (twenty-fourth to twenty-third centuries B.C.E.) to the founder of Shang; (2) from the founder of Shang to the founders of Zhou (twenty-third to twelfth centuries B.C.E.); and (3) from the founders of Zhou to Confucius (twelfth century to 551 B.C.E.). The alternating sequence of old and new periods was attempted in the Qin dynasty to periodize Chinese history though the old-new-old pattern was evident in the earlier years of the Han dynasty (206 B.C.E.–6 C.E.). The Five Elements school also held to an endless, cyclical view of history: "Starting from the time of the separation of Heaven and Earth and coming down, Zou Yan, the founder of the school, made citations of the revolutions and transmutations of the Five Powers (Five Elements), arranging them until each found its proper place and was confirmed (by history)."[45] Coding the period of history with the color of the element used by the Five Elements school produces the following diagram:

Element	Color	Period
earth	yellow	Yellow Emperor (third millennium B.C.E.)
wood	green	Xia dynasty (2200–1600 B.C.E.)
metal	white	Shang dynasty (1600–1050 B.C.E.)
fire	red	Zhou dynasty (1050–256 B.C.E.)
water	black	Qin (221–206 B.C.E.) or Han dynasty (206 B.C.E.–220 C.E.)

Dong Zhongshu and the Various Cycles of History

Dong Zhongshu (179–104 B.C.E.) understood the significance of color in relation to a dynasty's heavenly mandate. Dong wrote: "Only after one has received the Mandate of Heaven can he become the ruler. The ruler determines the first day of the calendar for his dynasty, changes the colors of court costume, establishes regulations for rituals and music, and unifies the entire empire."[46] In his work, *Chun Qiu Fan Lu* (*Luxuriant Dew of the Spring and Autumn Annals*), he used *Chun Qiu* (*Spring and Autumn Annals*) to interpret the Han dynasty. Based on the assumption that heaven, humanity, and earth are linked, his interlocking system of cycles explained events in the world of nature corresponding to those of the world of humanity. Thus Dong introduced various cycles in his works: the *yin* and *yang* two-phase, the heaven-man-earth three-phase,[47] the four seasons four-phase, the five elements five-phase, and the antiquity sage-kings nine-phase.[48] The five-element speculation was the most common for dynasty changes and was probably earlier than Dong's systematization. But during the Han dynasty, the earth (according to Dong) or fire became a matter of dispute. The two-phase cycle was based on alternating simplicity (*zhi*) and refinement (*wen*). So, for example, one could structure Chinese history as follows: pre-Xia was simplicity and Xia was refinement; Shang, simplicity and Zhou, refinement; Qin, simplicity and Han, refinement; Sui, simplicity and Tang (618–906), refinement; Later Zhou (951–960), simplicity and Sung (960–1280), refinement; and so on. The four cycles is the shang-xia-zhi-wen representing spring-summer-autumn-winter. No example was given for the nine cycles.[49]

Dong believed that events in heaven and earth interlock in such an intricate manner that paradise on earth happened in certain opportune periods:

If the king is of the right kind, the primordial forces (Yin and Yang) are in harmonious relation to each other. . . . The ancients were honored, relatives had feelings of kinship for each other. . . . Since families were given all they needed, the grief born of excessive hopes or furious disappointment did not exist. . . . People did not engage in libel or theft. . . . The desire for riches and positions of honor was unknown. . . . Poisonous insects did not bite, wild animals did not attack other creatures, and evil beasts harmed no one. That was also why sweet nectar dripped from heaven; the reed grass of happiness grew. . . . The prisons were empty, . . . the people did not transgress. . . . The sentiments of the people were plain and unaffected, sacrifices were offered to heaven and earth.[50]

Dong's paradise differed from the earlier Confucian and Legalist views in that the world of humanity and the world of gods were not kept apart. Dong's thought resembles the Daoist view on the union between humanity and cosmology but differs from the drastic Daoist subordination of anthropology to cosmology (much like a Chinese painting of a tiny person in the dominant background of scenery or when the artist's spirit looms larger than even the nature that he or she paints). In Dong's vision,

A balance is created between these two spheres, and it is consistent that the concerted action of heaven, earth and man should bring forth a harmony which creates "supernatural" conditions. As in the ideal world of the Taoists [Daoists], there is the intimate contact with wind and rain, with plants and animals. In contradistinction to them, however, this contact is infused with an elevated human morality. It resembles the ideal world of the Legalists in the strict mechanism of the laws, but these laws do not represent a value above man, as is the case with them. Instead, man occupies a mediating position between heaven and earth, between spirit and matter. Particularly as king or emperor, he thus holds in his hands the key to the happiness of the entire universe.[51]

Kang Youwei: Book of the Great Unity (Datong Shu)

Regardless of their philosophical tradition and historical period, Chinese scholars and political leaders were concerned with finding the key to the happiness of the entire universe. Kang Youwei (1858–1927) was no exception. Kang Youwei was a Confucian humanist and a reformer.[52] His utopian ideal influenced the intellectual Chinese of the nineteenth century. He is older than Mao by about forty years, and Mao read his work with enthusiasm and adored his proposal of reforms.[53]

In his *Datong Shu* (*Book of the Great Unity*) Kang argued that the age of disorder was Confucius's era, that the age of approaching peace was his own time, and that the age of universal peace would be a period in the future in which worldwide harmony and freedom would be real-ized.[54] Since he regarded Confucius as a reformer, Kang was the first Chinese leader to date Chinese chronology from the birth of Confucius. During the One Hundred Days Reform in 1898, he also tried to help the young emperor Guangxu (1871–1908)[55] to reform China by keeping the Confucian tradition (New Text School).

In his study of *Li Ji*, Kang learned the idea of the Three Ages and sought in his *Book of the Great Unity* to write in detail his vision of the ideal age and of the transitional stages leading to it. Kang's vision of a utopian world order began with the elimination of differences and boundaries and thus the "disarmament and the outlawing of war . . . [according] to the teachings of the ancient philosopher Mo Ti [Mo Zi]."[56] The next step was the unification of states through the internalization of the armed forces. A global standardization of monetary and metric measurement followed so that a world state of Great Equality could be created. Kang thought that 1900, the year following the Hague Confer-ence, was the first year of the Great Equality. Bauer explains the ration-ale of Kang's speculation regarding the year 1900:

> This year also seemed particularly appropriate to him because the cycli-cal signs Keng-tzu, which are assigned to it according to the old Chinese cyclical calculation, are phonetically close to the expression "changed beginning" which he thought of as a kind of new reign title. . . . Kang also gave much thought to a uniform world language. . . . [Kang writes,] "If we adopt the Chinese terms for things, but give the sounds by means of an alphabet, and write them with a new simple script, then [the new world language] will be extremely simple and fast." . . . To avoid the possibility of a cult of personality, the office of prime minister is intentionally com-mitted. . . . there will be no world president.[57]

Though a Confucian, Kang was quite critical of the family system, explaining:

> To wish to attain Complete Peace-and-Equality and yet to have the fam-ily is like carrying earth to dredge a stream, or adding wood to put out a fire: the more done, the more the hindrance. Thus, if we wish to attain the beauty of complete equality, independence, and the perfection of [human] nature, it can [be done] only by abolishing the state, only by abolishing the family.[58]

Thus Kang sought to replace family with a world state of socialism: "For enabling the farmers to obtain equality in subsistence, we may perhaps advocate the methods of communism. But if we have the family, if we have the state, selfishness is then extreme."[59]

The idea of communism during the early twentieth century was not merely a European phenomenon. The Chinese history of utopianism had always been interested in socialism and communism, and of course, young Chinese students at this time were studying overseas and were exposed to ideas of anarchy, socialism, and democracy. Kang and his associates Tan Sitong (1865–1898) and Liao Ping (1852–1932) attempted to harmonize evolutionary meliorism with the Chinese belief in devolutionary cyclicism. All three men were Confucianists who knew Western literature; they all somehow embraced both the West's progressive and evolutionary view of history and the East's cyclical regeneration view of the cosmos. But it was the "Western influence, in the form either of scientific writings on the theory of evolution or of theological literature about a coming millennium"[60] that would lead China to a Chinese communist state. Mao once commented that "K'ang Yu-wei wrote the Ta-t'ung Shu but he did not and could not find the way to achieve Great Harmony."[61] Influenced by Kang, Mao was determined to realize the Great Harmony—or at least try to realize it.

The Language, Movement, and Unity of the *Yin-Yang* Worldview

Language That Forms or Reinforces Chinese Historical Consciousness

The Chinese view of history is cyclical; this is true especially in China's political life, where dynastic change is linked with heavenly mandate. Bauer explains:

> In the doctrine of the transmission of the heavenly mandate, there had already existed certain phenomena which were interpreted as the signs of a beginning, a flourishing or a declining dynasty. . . . But during the Han period . . . it no longer tended to express itself in the language of the people and its right to revolution, as had been the case in Mencius [Meng Zi], but in the language of nature. . . . Of course, reports of this sort concerning comets, earthquakes, mountain slides, hail storms and similar events had been provided in earlier chronicles. . . . What was new was their systematization, and especially the opinion that they were not mere reactions of heaven to the way the ruler governed, but were frequently devoid of moral overtones. This was the case when they announced by certain signs the dawn of a new dynasty destined to rule under a different element.[62]

This cyclical view was formed or reinforced by the Chinese language, in which verbs do not differentiate past, present, and future tenses. This is not to say that past generations of Chinese could not tell the present from the past, merely that the linguistic apparatus that informs and constructs the Chinese worldview is such that there is a fluidity between the past, the present, and the future. The past and the future can collapse into the present; realized events possess potential for future ones; every actualized situation points to others in latency.

The Alternating Sequence of Time in the Yin-Yang *Worldview*

The Chinese concept of the cyclical sequence of history is traceable to the *yin-yang* philosophy of Daoism. The notion of cycles in time is the result of cosmological deduction, not speculative argument. The Chinese understand the cyclical movement of time not simply as a bipolar process; according to the *Classic of Changes*, it is change that is the ultimate, noncontingent reality. This is where the *Classic of Changes* understanding of change differs from Western process theology. Reality is conceived ultimately as change (*yi*)[63] rather than as being. Change is the absolute category or frame of reference; it is an *a priori* category of existence. It is not that substance or being changes to create process or becoming but that change itself creates substance and being. It is change that changes all things, but change itself is changeless.[64] Since being is the manifestation of change, an unchanging being cannot exist in reality. Since change is responsible for the changing world, it is the ultimate reality, which is also known as *tai ji* (great ultimate).[65] "The great ultimate is the change."[66] The great ultimate is the changing changeless one.[67]

Yin-yang is simultaneously inclusive of both the changing and the unchanging; *yin* and *yang* are two fundamental components or two cardinal principles of change. In the fact of change, being and nonbeing are synthesized. It is change that produces being, process that produces existence with a purpose in dynamic time. I am not opting for the cyclical view of time (as was the ancient *yin-yang* view) nor for the linear view, but for a three-dimensional view of *kairos*, qualitative time. Chinese seldom talk about absolute time but rather about time associated with events—dynamic time. Fang explains this view of time:

> The essence of time consists in change; the order of time proceeds with concatenation; the efficacy of time abides by durance. The rhythmic process of epochal change is wheeling round into infinitude and perpetually dovetailing the old and the new so as to issue into interpenetration which is continuant duration in creative advance. This is the way in which time generates itself by its systematic entry into a pervasive unity which constitutes the rational order of creative creativity. The dynamic sequence

of time, ridding itself of the perished past and coming by the new into present existence, really gains something over a loss. So, the change in time is but a step to approaching eternity, which is perennial duration, whereby, before the bygone is needed, the forefront of the succeeding has come into presence. And, therefore there is here a linkage of being projecting itself into the prospect of eternity.[68]

In the Confucian process of production and reproduction, time never comes to an end or repeats itself. Every production has an element of novelty, since it requires a new relationship of *yin* and *yang*.

Because *yin* and *yang* constitute the bipolar nature of reality, reality is always perceived as relatedness: "Change always operates in the bipolar relationship known as yin-yang."[69] *Yin* is the opposite but not the antagonist of *yang*, since the two poles are mutually complementary. Because they are bipolar, one cannot exist without the other. *Yin* is *yin* because of *yang*, and *yang* is *yang* because of *yin*. *Yin* needs *yang* to be *yin*; neither can exist without the other. They are mutually inclusive and relative.[70] Since *yin* is relative to *yang*, they form a holistic category of "both/and" and not merely "either/or." Therefore, the yin-yang worldview denies absolutism (absolutism of dualism or monism) yet affirms absolutism (of both dualism or monism) simultaneously.[71] As such, both/and thinking does not negate either/or thinking but includes and deabsolutizes it.

Observing the seasonal change and the night-and-day alternating process, the Chinese suggest that the movement of time is cyclical. Bauer describes the different cyclical notions of time in a typical Chinese worldview:

> Specifically Chinese was the sexagenary cycle which developed from the combination of a decimal and a duodenary cycle where the former was in a manner of speaking based on a human (fingers of the hand), the latter on a cosmic (months) elementary number. . . . The isolation of five elements (earth, wood, metal, fire, water) and their differentiated ring-shaped arrangement (enumerated here in the "order of victory" following their mutual conquest) can be found long before the beginning of the Han period. It is alleged that their inventor was the philosopher Tsou Yen (third century B.C.). This is naturally even more true of other cycles one was always aware of, such as day and night, the course of the year with its four seasons and, in a way, the alternation of life and death as well.[72]

The best summary of Chinese worldview is that given by Bodde, whose brilliant insight I quote at some length:

> The universe, according to prevailing Chinese philosophical thinking, is a harmoniously functioning organism consisting of an orderly hierarchy

of interrelated parts and forces, which, though unequal in their status, are all equally essential for the total process. Change is a marked feature of this process, yet in it there is nothing haphazard or casual, for it follows a fixed pattern of polar oscillation or cyclical return; in either case there is a denial of forward movement, save in proximate terms only.

This cosmic pattern is self-contained and self-operating. It unfolds itself because of its own inner necessity and not because it is ordained by any external volitional power. . . .

Human history belongs to the total cosmic process and, therefore, in the eyes of many Chinese, moves according to a similar cyclical pattern. Another and probably earlier Chinese view, however, sees antiquity as a golden age and all history since that time as a steady process of human degeneration. Some thinkers combine the two theories by saying that history does indeed move in cycles but that we moderns happen to be living during the downswing of one such cycle. . . . all of them reject the idea of historical progress, meaning by this a process of progressive improvement.

Though the universe is self-acting and not guided by any volitional power, it is far from being merely a mechanistic universe. Indeed, the very fact that its movements result in life is enough to show that in them must be a principle of goodness. More than this, however, even what we humans regard as evil—for example, death—is, from a higher point of view, an integral part of the total cosmic process and therefore inseparable from what we choose to call goodness. In short, whatever *is* in the universe must be good, simply because it *is*.

The vital link between the nonhuman and human worlds is man's nature, and it necessarily follows from the foregoing that this nature must be equally good for all. If, nevertheless, some men fail to actualize the potentialities of their nature, this is because of their inadequate understanding of how the universe operates. This deficiency, however, can be removed through education and self-cultivation, . . . for all men without exception to achieve sagehood. It thus becomes clear that evil, in Chinese eyes, is not a positive force in itself. It is . . . simply an inherent factor in the universe . . . the result of man's temporary distortion of the universal harmony.

Human society is, or at least should be, a reflection of this harmony. Hence it too is an ordered hierarchy of unequal components, all of which, however, have their essential function to perform, so that the result is a co-operative human harmony. . . .

Cutting across both the human and the natural worlds there are, in Chinese thinking, many antithetical concepts, among which . . . those of man and nature (Heaven, or Tian), being and nonbeing, quiescence and movement, the yin and the yang, and li (Principle) and ch'i (Ether). In each of these dualisms the Chinese mind commonly shows a preference for one of the two component elements as against the other. At the same time, however, it regards both of them as complementary and necessary partners, interacting to form a higher synthesis, rather than as irreconcilable and eternally warring opposites. Thus here again there is a manifestation of the Chinese tendency to merge unequal components so as to create an organic harmony.[73]

As Bodde has so well articulated the Chinese worldview, Fritjof Capra has diligently elucidated the primitive yet scientific, antique yet holistic worldview in his book *The Tao of Physics: An Exploration of the Parallels between Modern Physics and Eastern Mysticism.*[74]

East and West

The Chinese worldview sees the universe as an integrated whole of matter and space in a dynamic interrelationship with each other, similar to the New Physics.[75] The Chinese worldview in the eighteenth and nineteenth centuries was influenced by modern science, which was introduced to some extent by the efforts of the Christian missionaries. Unfortunately, neither the Christian West nor the Christian missionaries in the early twentieth century knew New Physics nor appreciated the more dynamic worldview of the traditional Chinese as much as their own modern science (which actually was influenced to a great extent by the rationalistic and mechanical worldview of the Enlightenment). Neither Mao nor the Chinese students at that time were sympathetic toward their own Chinese worldview. We will see in the next few chapters how the interactions between East and West brought about Mao's rejection of Christian theology, his acceptance of modern Western science, his critical reaction to the traditional Chinese worldview, and his acceptance of the Marxist worldview—which is critical of Christian eschatology.

Our survey of utopian worldviews in the East and the West points to various plausible systems that are open to seeing the redemptive activities of God. Unfortunately, the secularization process in both the East and the West often distorts the religious worldview in the name of science and humanism. Differentiating the two basic views of historical movement is in order.

Basically, there are two views of history: progress to utopia[76] or the apocalyptic (manifest destiny) eschatology (end of destruction, *telos* of salvation) of God. The former could be labeled the secular utopian view, the latter the millenarian view of the Bible. Both views contain problems of their own. The first is a secular view that history will progress toward utopia and that ideology moves the will of humans to improve the society in which they live. While human participation in reconstructing utopian reality is a good thing, the problem of this view is that the meaning of human history is measured by progression and anything less than that is considered regression or backwardness. Thus, in order to realize the necessity of progress, some have considered violence and revolution legitimate means of the human will in history. The fear that historical forces might not move toward progress wears down the human spirit of hope and possibly brings about a bankruptcy or destruction of the self.

The second view of history anticipates God's eschatology arriving in history, a distinctively Jewish and Christian worldview that can be traced to the millenarian or apocalyptic eschatological movements found in the Bible. It assumes the good and perfect creation of God; the fall of humanity and creation; God's will in bringing about a millenarian peace and order in the historical process of pain and suffering, sin and evil, judgment and transformation; and, finally, God's intervention and consummation at the eschaton. As such, the meaning of history is not measured by progression or regression but by the divine "intervention" of redemption and judgment, through which God's intention for human history is realized when the temporality of history (time) is redeemed toward eternity. Olson summarizes the characteristics of the millenarian view of history: "In millennialism history is conceived of as (1) the locus of divine action and accordingly, the only source of salvation or historical vindication; (2) a strongly periodized drama; and (3) as proceeding to its conclusion in a deeply dialectical fashion."[77]

The differing views of history between West and East influence the ways one looks at Chinese communism (Maoism) and Chinese Christian theology. Western cosmology is based on the laws of nature, while Chinese cosmology is based on the conscientious response of the laws of human nature. Since "law" presupposes heteronomy, "natural law" is almost a contradiction in terms in Chinese. Joseph Needham writes:

Laws of Nature depended upon a totally different line of thought. The harmonious cooperation of all beings arose, not from the orders of a superior authority external to themselves, but from the fact that they were all parts in a hierarchy of wholes forming a cosmic pattern, and what they obeyed were the internal dictates of their own natures.[78]

The traditional Chinese worldview believes in the constant flux of the universe, following a "predictable pattern consisting either of eternal oscillation between two poles or of cyclical movement within a closed circuit. [So] . . . all movement serves in the end only to bring the process back to its starting point."[79] In the Christian world, historical events are dated backward or forward from the birth of Christ, while Jews date events forward from the narrative of the creation; for both, the end of history is the utopian hope of the new Jerusalem. But in Chinese history, events are dated cyclically every sixty years or so from the rise of new emperors. And the dominant view in Chinese history is to look for a golden age in the past—in other words, the circle of degeneration and regeneration characterized in Chinese history—and it is the circle of conscious cultivation of selves in harmony with society or cosmos that will bring back the golden age.

Of all the utopian visions in Chinese cultures, the Daoist utopia is the most "apocalyptic" and millenarian, except that the Daoist utopia does not accept the intrusion of the other world into the present one. Therefore, unlike the Christian eschatology, the Daoist utopia is not imminently realized at the *eschaton* of history. The Daoist utopia mysteriously existed in the past before the beginning of civilization.

3

the meeting of theological and philosophical views of history in marx

Anti-utopian Socialism and Historical Materialism

When Christianity became the religion of the Roman Empire, the countercultural spirit of Christian theology died. Jewish and Christian communities before the Constantinian era lived under the threat of persecution from the empire. But the Christian mission was so successful in the West that Christian eschatology was secularized into the "holy empire." The oppressed became the oppressor, the Lamb of God was reincarnated as the Lion of Judah, millenarian apocalypticism was reinterpreted as historical postmillenarianism, and theology was reduced to mere politics. Apocalyptic and millenarian hope was not needed any longer because eschatology was realized. The Christian millennium conquered the world and set up the new Jerusalem on earth. We have seen how Paul harshly critiqued the *ataktoi* and the men of lawlessness, whose realized eschatology justified their violence of order and power. How would Marx and Mao respond to the Christian theology of the holy empire?

As a trained theologian, Karl Marx (1818–1883) was not ignorant of Jewish-Christian theologies and secular utopian thoughts in the Western world. Was Marx's critique of Jewish-Christian messianism an outright rejection of it? Did he replace the *mythos* of Christian theology with a secular form? Could Marx's secularization of Jewish faith in his political and economic terms sustain a vision of hope? Marx's critique of the Christian theology of the holy empire was valid, but could his own communist utopian thinking overcome the violence of order and power of the already distorted Christian theology of his day?

A Brief History of Utopian Thought in Western Civilization

Utopia in Western civilization blossomed not only in the sacred texts of the Jewish and Christian traditions; it was also pervasive in other philosophical and secular traditions.[1] This chapter will begin with a brief categorization of these utopian thoughts, then move to an examination of the history of the utopian socialists and the views of Marx. Both the utopian socialist and Marxist views critically engage Jewish and Christian utopian thinking.

Categories of Utopia

Doyne Dawson points out several stages or types of utopian tradition. The first was the early stage of folk utopias in myth, fantasy, and messianic expectation, such as those represented by the Greek legend of the golden age, the Elysian fields in Homer, and Hesiod (*Works and Days*).[2] Homer's *Odyssey* depicts the paradise of Elysium, where the Greek heroes were resurrected after their death in the hope of being with the gods. Pindar's *Orphic* portrays a mythic version of the Isles of Blessed for the innocent and the good, in contrast to the nether Hades where the wicked suffered everlastingly.

A second stage was one of political utopianism, including the social and realistic reconstructionist utopias of the philosophers who envisioned an ideal city-state in their critique of the present existing order. This later stage can be subdivided into two types, depending on whether the vision was to be implemented or not: (1) the low utopianism of Plato (*Laws*), Aristotle (*Politics* 2, 7–8), and Cicero (*On the Republic; On the Laws*), and the Pythagorean community of philosophers (mathematicians) and religious moralists, who saw the ideal society not as a theoretical standard but as real, practical, and political programs; and (2) the high utopianism, sometimes called "classical utopianism," which regarded the ideal society as a theoretical construct not to be enacted (e.g., the ideal of Plato in the *Republic*).[3]

As we shall see, the complex Maoist utopianism that spans, changes, and grows over a long period of time will include the three categories listed above. Even in the Western understandings of paradise, a golden age, and utopia, the three categories are not necessarily precise because they overlap each other. The common thread that characterizes all these categories is the hope of a state of rest, ease, freedom, equality, sharing, enjoyment, and abundance. Many believed that the time of such utopia was before or at the inception of civilization, when a primitive society was still in its original condition of purity. It was a time before the fall, when sin, destruction, and evil had not yet contaminated or distorted the rustic environment. It was the state in which nature was blessed with abundance, people's needs were always fulfilled, and humans lived in harmony with one another and animals. Some even thought that humans lived close to nature and the gods.

A Political Vision of an Ideal City

One of the dominant visions of utopian thought was the philosophers' dream of an ideal political city. The three model cities mentioned in Western civilization were: (1) Athens, a city of the ideal democratic government, the boisterous triumph of reason and knowledge over nature; (2) Sparta (in Plato's *Republic*), an authoritarian city of the philosopher-king that was ascetic, communistic, and in harmony with nature; and (3) the new Jerusalem, a city of God ruled by divine law and God's glory.

Reason was the principle that constructed the ideal city, for the ideal city was a reflection or representation of the cosmos in Greek and Roman traditions. But ideal societies do not always have to be in cities, since cities often symbolize a place of work; thus rural areas and villages were also proposed as alternatives.

Both utopian cities and rural areas, however, were critiques of contaminated human habitations. Utopian visions are inevitably social critiques of fallen realities. Thus we see that all categories of utopian visions bear local resemblance or are culturally conditioned because the critical elements of utopia in each category seek to reconstruct its contextual world. Karl Mannheim writes, "[A]ll situationally transcendent ideas . . . have a transforming effect upon the existing historical-social order."[4] Below we will examine social critique and ideology in utopian visions to see how powerfully utopian thinking can dismantle power in history and rewrite the trajectory of history for the sake of the *summum bonum* (highest good).

Utopia, Critique, and Ideology

Mannheim's Category of Utopia and Ideology

In his 1929 book *Ideologie und Utopie* (English *Ideology and Utopia*, 1936), Mannheim uses Weber's sociological theory to differentiate the functions of ideology and utopia. He argues that the notions of utopia and ideology are not incongruent with historical reality but transcend it. However, the two are not identical. Ideology is a conviction or presupposition that one uses to sustain or maintain one's view of reality, while one uses utopia to change or shatter one's view of reality.[5]

Mannheim carefully categorizes four types of utopia based on the utopian community's perception and experience of time: chiliasm (millenarianism); the liberal-humanist idea; the conservative idea; and the socialist-communist utopia. Mannheim argues that chiliasm is concerned not with the future but with the "absolute presentness" and *kairos*. He writes, "For the real Chiliast, the present becomes the breach through which what was previously inward bursts out suddenly, takes hold of the outer world and transforms it."[6] Still, the chiliast conviction of a qualitative leap to a transcendent realm of fulfillment called *kairos* is not just a concern for the now. The now is believed to be impregnated with an intervention from eternity; in New Testament language we call this phenomenon "apocalyptic eschatology."[7] The liberal-humanitarian utopia applies to the middle class, which seeks to transform society through gradual progress (not *kairotic* intervention from the supernatural world) based on education, self-cultivation, reason, and ethics. Conservatism is a movement that opposes the liberal-humanitarian group and is committed to protect the dominant class by conserving the past. Finally, the socialist-communist utopia is a counterrevolutionary group of existing forms of utopia. This group looks at time as a series of strategic events in which socialism will be realized after the collapse of capitalism. While there is a danger of any utopian movement ceasing to be itself when the expectation of change and the reality become one, Mannheim argues that the socialist-communist utopia has a self-correcting matrix whose ideas will continually adjust to what is possible.[8]

Ruth Levitas offers a sharp critique of Mannheim's categories. Levitas points out that the conservative group might better be called ideology rather than utopia but explains that since Mannheim "is examining the shifting constellation of the utopias of different social groups in their conflicts with one another, it becomes necessary to describe this mode of 'incongruous' thought as a utopia as well, in spite of the fact that his description makes it more properly an ideology than a utopia."[9] The dichotomy between ideology and utopia is not formal but functional,

88

and thus artificial and ambiguous. In other words, ideology is linked to the past for the sake of maintaining the status quo, while utopia is linked to the future for social changes; also, ideology is linked to the ruling class, while utopia is linked to the subordinate groups. Levitas further explains:

> Firstly, the categorization of ideas into those which change and those which support the existing state of affairs is extremely crude. . . . The second and third problems, namely the notion of "adequate realisation" and the issue of causality, relate to the criterion of success as a defining characteristic of utopia. The idea of adequate realisation implies that one would not expect a utopia to be implemented in all its details. . . . The issue of causality is a further difficulty: it is not merely a matter of utopia anticipating the future—of wanting something which the future turns out to hold—but of utopia creating the future. . . . A fourth area of difficulty [is] Mannheim's view of reality. . . . [T]he differences between ideology and utopia are in some ways less important than the characteristic which they share, that of being incongruous with or transcending reality, or orientated to objects which do not exist in the actual situation; yet this is to beg the question of what is real.[10]

Along the same lines, Paul Ricoeur, in his *Lectures on Ideology and Utopia*, offers a reinterpretation of Mannheim concerning power and authority. That is, the function of ideology as a means of maintaining the status quo is really about legitimation, positively to integrate a new worldview and negatively to disrupt an existing order. The function of utopia is to challenge, positively by offering a revolutionary new order, negatively by bringing about violent destruction.[11]

The word *ideology* can be a neutral term or a negative term. If used neutrally (with no value judgment), it simply means the basic propositions or ideas that form a person's or a society's values or structures. As a pejorative term, *ideology* is used mostly by Marxists performing class analysis to refer to the biased presuppositions of an insider who projects his or her own conviction as self-evident truth, unaware that the conviction itself is in fact fantasy or distorted truth. If *ideology* is used in that sense (i.e., in a religious sense), then it serves as a superstructure justifying the existing condition or, worse still, dominating and manipulating others.[12]

The Rationalistic Force of the Enlightenment

The rise of *ideology* as a pejorative term is related to the critical, rationalistic spirit of the Enlightenment. After the Enlightenment, the Western world became suspicious, even fearful, of utopian thinking, prophetic eschatology, and messianic millenarianism. It perceived such thinking to be irrational and downright dangerous. Many identify such thinking with religious cults that proclaim a catastrophic end of the world as well as with lunatic actions such as rejecting social norms and causing revolutions. These fanatical cults encourage followers to leave friends and families, withdraw from the sordid world, and bring about various forms of social unrest as well as political upheavals.[13] All these behaviors are religiously and politically disturbing and chaotic, yet they are undertaken in the hope of creating a better world. The issue is not whether we should have utopian thinking or not, even though some of the results of utopian movements might be lunatic, destructive, or simply futile. Utopian thinking and movements appear in every culture, even those with ideologies that seek to reject and deny utopian thinking semantically (such as both Marxist and Maoist ideology). Rather, the issue is how to differentiate utopian movements that are destructive and futile from those that are constructive and meaningful to society.

With the Enlightenment, the tension between *eutopia* (good place) and *outopia* (no place) began to dissolve, because the tenuous relationship between history and myth, science and art, reason and feeling, freedom and determinism began to break down. Most significant for our discussion is the idea that utopia began to be perceived as an ultimate point of the historical process. Thus, the Enlightenment bias was to emphasize the historical optimism of human effort and to distort the utopian model that is actually a critique of the present order in light of its visionary hope for a better reality.[14] The work of Sir Thomas More (1478–1535) is significant precisely because it captures the spirit of utopia as a social and religious critique.

More's Social and Religious Critique

In 1516, Sir Thomas More, the learned Lord Chancellor of Tudor England (Henry VIII) wrote in Latin a sociopolitical satire or fiction titled *Utopia*. In the narrative, which was inspired by the Roman historian Tacitus, More used a traveler-narrator, Raphael Hythloday, to allegorize an imaginary place real enough to be sought after that existed somewhere at the borders of possibility. The connection with historical reality and More's utopia was Columbus's discovery of the New World (twenty-four years prior to the publication of *Utopia*). Thus Hythloday supposedly followed Amerigo Vespucci in his expeditions but made more discoveries on his own. He discovered Utopia some distance beyond what people already knew (America).

More's *Utopia* is a place of freedom, communism, peaceful anarchy, and prosperity. But More's fable of this imaginary world of peace, prosperity, and purity ought to be understood within the context of the Tudor English society that, in its ironies and literary artistry, the book in fact attempts to criticize and indict. Thomas More's description of the Commonwealth of Utopia is the exact opposite, and therefore a critique, of sixteenth-century England. However, More did not issue a social or political agenda to reform England. The transhistorical model of his utopian motif is not first and foremost a belief in historical progress in light of a critique from an ideal model; rather, it is a moral-judgment model that seeks self-critique, contemplation, and transcendence.

The gravest critique in More's *Utopia*, then, is of Christianity. The irony is that, in contrast to the Christian civilization in Tudor England, Utopia is a community of nonbelievers who have maintained a society of near paradise of selfless sharing, abundance, and virtues.[15] More's utopian work is a literary form that seeks to function as social criticism, not for the sake of daydreamers or the bourgeoisie to exercise their mind muscles. More's confession at the end that he "rather wished for than hoped for"[16] the Commonwealth of Utopia may sound like hopelessness with regard to social reform.

More was not anti-God. In fact, his critique of Christianity and Tudor England was based on his uncompromising principle to be "the King's good servant but God's first."[17] More was a committed Christian who could not agree that his master's (Henry VIII) marriage to Catherine of Aragon was invalid because Henry wanted to marry Anne Boleyn. More's protest eventually led to his execution in 1535. His socialist utopianism is thus not a secular one, even though he used a virtuous pagan society to critique a sinful Christian society.

Utopia and Anti-utopia: Secularization and the Historical Materialism of the Marxist

The transition from More's socially and religiously critical utopian vision to Marx's anti-utopian vision is a key issue in our research on Maoism, because Maoist utopian thought was in many respects influenced by the Marxist secularization and de-eschatologization of the Christian vision. The classical utopian vision, traceable from Plato's understandings of the ideal state (in the *Republic*), is a communism[18] that has a hierarchical structure of guardians (philosopher-kings) and citizens. The guardians are to cultivate moral virtues through reason, so they are free from other labors. But as early as Platonic communism, violence is a means to an end: everyone over ten was to be killed. More's

Utopia attempts to break through this hierarchical structure and democratize utopian hope for all. There are two aspects of Marx's view of history that are relevant to our interest: his critique of Christian religion with his critical rereading of Christian eschatology, and his anti-utopian response to utopian socialism.

Hegelian Influence

Louis Dupré has traced the philosophical emergence of Marxist historical materialism from the influence of Hegel, Kant, Fichte, and Feuerbach.[19] Alasdair MacIntyre's work supplements Dupré's by focusing on the relationship between Marxist thought and form as well as the content of Christianity. Löwith's critical assessment of Marxism in terms of its view of history looks at the Marxist distortion of Christian theology.

Karl Marx (1818–1883) was a German Jew, his father a Lutheran. Young Marx did have his own Christian spirituality and theological convictions, and even though he gave up his personal Christian beliefs when he was at Bonn University, his Christian heritage always influenced him. At Berlin University he adopted the dialectical thesis of Hegel, whose idealism is traceable to the Christian tradition.

Hegel was concerned with history in *Judendschriften*[20] and *Phenomenology of Mind* (1807),[21] and it was this that influenced Marx. Hegel defined fallen humanity's "self-estrangement" (*Selbst-Entfremdung*) as a state in which conflicts and alienation characterize human society. To overcome this situation, one creates moral law by means of one's mind and will, setting the law over against oneself and thus "externalizing" (*Vergegenstandlichung*) oneself from society. This "objectification" process creates, however, further subject and object estrangement between humanity and the alienated world. The way back to self-wholeness or redemption is called "coming to one's own" (*Aneignung*), which can be achieved through an individual obeying the inward law of the Jesus religion and the individual pursuit of the other-worldly kingdom over and against the fallen world.[22] Hegel traces his understanding to Jewish history, in which the case of Abraham clearly portrays his estrangement from nature and his own people as he wandered into the unknown, seeking only the promised land of the transcendent God. Later the self-estrangement of the Israelite society led it to objectify the Mosaic law. Finally, Jesus' teaching of the inward law and his separation of religion from politics, the separation of God from humanity, objectified God over and against human existence. The consequence is related to the earlier creation of an outward law that objectified one's self from society.[23]

According to Hegel, history then is a movement from slavery to freedom, a movement that one can make only through the internalization of religion, when one recognizes the Absolute Spirit who is the mind of people.[24] Hegel saw in Jesus the unity of humanity and divinity, but he criticized the Jesus religion for employing myth and symbol, which are nothing but superstition. Hegel argued that philosophy and reason ought to be the tools to replace myth and to overcome human estrangement. Thus, Hegel's philosophy of Spirit had its religious presupposition on the revelational and supernatural foundation of Christianity, though the logic of reason started the secularization process. In Hegelian thought we can see the content of Christianity but not its form. The metaphysical Spirit working in the historical process is a Hegelian rendition of Christ as the Lord and Logos of history. Hegel could be optimistic about history as a movement to freedom for humanity because of his basic belief in the dialectical progress of historical movement. After all, he still assumed that the Spirit is at work in history.

When Marx substituted the material world for the Hegelian idea of reason or Spirit, he replaced and secularized both the form and content of Christianity. Löwith explains how Marx's secularized view of history differs from Hegel's view: "Hegel translated and elaborated the Christian theology of history into a speculative system, thus preserving and, at the same time, destroying the belief in providence as the leading principle. . . . Marx rejected divine providence categorically, replacing it by a belief in progress and perverting religious belief into the antireligious attempt to establish predictable laws of secular history."[25]

Marx's atheistic or secular move began when he followed left-wing Hegelians such as D. F. Strauss, L. Feuerbach, and B. Bauer and critiqued Hegel's *Philosophy of Right*, arguing that "the criticism of religion is the premise of all criticism."[26] Furthermore, he followed Feuerbach's reduction of religion into mere anthropology and believed that human self-alienation is not caused by spiritual sin but by material exploitation. After completing his Ph.D., Marx moved to Cologne and then to Paris, where he met and worked with Friedrich Engels (1820–1895). Marx studied economics and saw economic determinism or scientific socialism as the power behind the progress of society. Thus Marx critically revised the Christian eschatological view of history and human progress in light of economic history.

Promethean Revolution

Marx's historical materialism was based on an atheistic conviction, which was already visible in his doctoral dissertation, "The Difference between the Democritean and Epicurean Philosophy of Nature." He considered Epicurus to be the greatest ancient *Aufklaerer* (rationalist, enlightener) because, as a mortal human, he dared to challenge the gods of heaven and earth. Epicurus dared to rebel against religion and followed Promethcus, "the most noble of all martyrs in the annals of philosophy." Translating the Epicurean story into the context of nineteenth-century Europe, Marx believed that humanity ought to have the same boldness to challenge the authority of the Christian church and the idols of a world market. Marx wrote: "The more the worker labors, the more powerful becomes the estranged, objectified world that he creates over against himself and the poorer becomes his own inner world, and the less he belongs to himself. It is the same in religion. The more man places in God, the less he retains in himself."[27] In other words, the religion of communism is atheism, for atheism is the negation of the religion of estranged humanity.[28]

Regarding the atheistic tenet of Marxist communism, Löwith is correct to argue that

> the final liquidation of the religious consciousness is the prerequisite of man's mastery and control over his world. On the basis of this inherent atheism of earthly self-reliance, Marx undertook his radical criticism of the existing order with the purpose of changing it. His whole enterprise of changing the world by a world revolution has as its negative presupposition the denial of man's dependence on an existing order of creation.[29]

Löwith continues his critique:

> The annihilation of the "illusory bliss" of religion through materialistic criticism is only the negative side of the positive claim to "earthly happiness." Marx is sure that the final withering-away of religion will be caused by this will to earthly happiness, the secular form of the quest for salvation. A strictly materialistic criticism of religion consists neither in pure and simple rejection (Bauer) nor in mere humanization (Feuerbach) but in the positive postulate to create conditions which deprive religion of all its source and motivation. . . . In consequence of this transformation of the traditional criticism of religion into a strictly materialistic one, atheism, too, changes its meaning. To Marx it is no longer a theological problem, i.e., a fight against heathen and Christian *gods*, but a fight against earthly *idols*.[30]

The Promethean revolution in Marxist thought was the development of not only an atheistic philosophy of history but also a philosophy that explicitly challenged Christian theology and wanted to bring about its demise. Christian theology's two most challenging points to the Marxist view of history are: (1) the content of eschatology, which is an understanding that history has a divinely intended goal of consummated salvation; and (2) the belief in God, who is understood to be the main actor bringing about the new heaven and new earth. Marxist critiques of these two points could be seen in its anti-utopian socialism. Utopian socialist beliefs are not the same as Christian theology; the following discussion is aimed at differentiating Marx's and the utopian socialists' views of history.

Against Utopian Socialism

Marx and Engels criticized the utopian socialism of Henri de Saint-Simon (1760–1825) and Charles Fourier (1772–1837) in France and Robert Owen (1771–1858) in England and used the term "utopian communism" to refer to the followers of Cabet in France and Wilhelm Weitling (1808–1871) in Germany.[32] The historical context of utopian socialism was the rise of industrial revolutions. Saint-Simon postulated industrialization as the means to an ideal society, saying that it would eliminate poverty and backwardness. He replaced the moral principle of the gospel, "Do unto others as you would have others do unto you," with "Man must work."[33] Believing in Paul's admonition "If anyone will not work, let such a one not eat," he advocated the universality of work. His projected society consisted of three classes: scientists, artists, and producers. He argued that social harmony would be achieved if people were able to discern their types and gifts. He also argued that a utopian socialism would not need a government per se, only an administration that operated on the principle of persuasion (and not force or violence). Unfortunately, after his death in 1825, the Saint-Simonist movement became an esoteric sect under the high priest Barthölemy-Prosper Enfantin (1796–1864), in keeping with his belief in the New Christianity.[34] The movement became socially quiescent and absent as an active force in social transformation, shifting its attention to moral and religious issues.

Karl Marx harshly condemned utopian socialist ideology; even the word *utopia* took on a pejorative sense in Marxist usage. But what exactly did Marx reject in utopian ideology? Marx and Engels did not adopt an anti-utopian attitude because they regarded utopian socialism as escapist or as speculation about a future utopia. As Maurice Meisner, Vincent Geoghegan, and Levitas point out, the Marxist critique of utopian socialism was not due to the latter's projection of a future ideal society but was concerned with the means of transforming the present to the ideal society. Meisner explains that the Marxist critique of utopian socialism "is essentially a criticism of the failure of the utopians to understand the workings of modern history, neither recognizing the restraints that history imposes nor appreciating the potentialities that history offers."[35] Geoghegan understands that the Marxist critique of utopian socialism does not concern "anticipation as such, but rather the failure to root this anticipation in a theoretical framework cognizant of the essential dynamics of capitalism."[36] Similarly, Levitas explains:

> Since the primary concern of both Marx and Engels was with fostering such [social] changes, the rejection of utopia is a rejection on the basis of its imputed social function—that of distracting the working classes from more suitable political activity. . . . Utopian socialism draws up schemes for the future. Its main fault however is not that it does this . . . but that it entails an idealist model of social change, suggesting that the mere propagation of such schemes will have a transformative effect. . . . Utopia here is . . . seen as a negative, counter-revolutionary, one: "The chief offence does not lie in having inscribed a specific nostrum in programme, but in taking a retrograde step at all from the standpoint of a class movement to that of a sectarian movement."[37]

Thus, Marxism rejects two key aspects of socialist utopianism. First, Marxists deny the belief that the ideas of human genius or the power of truth, rather than *the forces of history*, bring about a better world. Marxists reject the tendency to fantasize in detail about a perfect world; they believe rather in the communist principle to work out an ideal world.[38] Marxist ideology contends that modern utopian socialism, which does not take into account sociohistorical realities, is but the wealthy ruling class's dream of a "no place" (*outopia*), a dream that hampers the transformation of these sociohistorical realities. The will of the working class to have a communist vision of the distribution of wealth and contribution of labor is the movement of history after the capitalist and socialist stages of history. Therefore, Marxists believe that the forces of the sociohistorical process in the capitalist context are the preconditions for socialism and communism.[39]

Second, Marxists reject the hope that socialism will be achieved by imposing an ideal moral model community rather than by understanding *the praxis of the revolutionary working class*. Marx and Engels criticized utopian socialism, but they commended it for its critical spirit of the working class. They wrote in "The Manifesto of the Communist Party":

> Such fantastic pictures of future society, painted at a time when the proletariat is still in a very underdeveloped state and has but a fantastic conception of its own position, correspond with the first instinctive yearn-

ings of that class for a general reconstruction of society. But these Socialist and Communist publications contain also a critical element. They attack
every principle of existing society. Hence they are full of the most valuable materials for the enlightenment of the working class.[40]

Marx's ideology has prior concern for the working class, and it thus con-
demns anything that enhances the power of the capitalists[41] and praises
anything that opposes "the progressive historical development of the
proletariat."[42] In other words, what the Marxist rejects in socialist utopianism is not its ends but its means.

The Marxist vision does not reject the concept of utopianism
altogether. Marxist utopianism believes in a better place in the future,
but Marxist utopianism puts its faith in the potential of history to realize a communist utopia. Here it should be noted that the Marxist usage
of the word *utopian* reflects several meanings. The first meaning
describes what the Marxist rejects: an ideal place that is a "no place"
because, the Marxist believes, it would be futile, naive, and pernicious
to realize such a place by means of ideas and truth without working and
believing in the forces of history. The second meaning, though relatively
rare in Marxist literature, is the concept of an ideal place that will soon
be realized in the communist society (a process rather than a state).
Marx sees the communist society as a process rather than a state,
explaining: "Communism is for us not a state of affairs which is to be
established, an ideal to which reality will have to adjust itself. We call
communism the real movement which abolishes the present state of
things."[43]

Socialist utopianism believes in "pure reason," "individual . . . genius,"
"mere happy accident" as the means for the ideal society to realize itself.[44]
In other words, only the intellectual, powerful, reasonable, truthful, willful, and wealthy could realize the utopian society as they so wished.
Engels pointedly criticized such a mentality:

> Society presented nothing but wrongs; to remove these was the task of
> reason. It was necessary, then, to discover a new and more perfect system
> of social order and impose this upon society from without by propa-
> ganda. . . . These new social systems were foredoomed as Utopian; the
> more completely they were worked out in detail, the more they could not
> avoid drifting off into pure phantasies.[45]

In contrast to socialist utopianism, Marxists believe in the scientific
socialism by which social-historical developments are taken seriously.
In other words, if one takes seriously capitalism as the historical reality
that results in domination of the working class by the ruling class, then

97

one cannot simply impose a utopian order with no thought of the historical context. To do so would only enforce the domination. In fact, taking history seriously means that capitalism is the basis that socialism ought to criticize, and capitalism—along with its social evils—requires the working class to start a revolution against the ruling class.[46] The difference between Marxist communist society and utopian socialism is the process of transition from the present society to an ideal society.

That Engels would consider the millenarian movement of Thomas Münzer to be a revolutionary rather than a utopian movement also indicates that Marxism is supportive of utopian ideas. In his analysis of Thomas Münzer in *The Peasant War in Germany,* Engels argued that Münzer drew his communist idea from New Testament teaching and adapted it to the peasant situation in Germany. So, according to Engels, Münzer anticipated the emancipation of the proletarian peasants and the realization of the kingdom on God on earth, a "society with no class differences, no private property and no state authority independent of and foreign to, the members of society."[47]

The Utopian Communist State of Marx

Marx and Engels did not criticize all of utopian socialism; they appreciated utopian socialism's critique of bourgeois society. In "The Holy Family" they wrote:

> They [the utopian socialists] therefore declared "progress" (see Fourier) to be an inadequate abstract phrase; they assumed (see Owen) a fundamental flaw in the civilised world; that is why they subjected the real foundations of contemporary society to incisive criticism. This communist criticism had practically at once as its counterpart the movement of the great mass. . . . One must know the studiousness, the craving for knowledge, the moral energy and the unceasing urge for development of the French and English workers to be able to form an idea of the human nobility of this movement.[48]

Can Marx's vision of a communist society itself be categorized as a utopian ideal? Steven Lukes believes that "the Marxist utopia is full communism, or human emancipation."[49] Even though Marx critiqued utopianism, his communist theory is not without utopian impulses and visions. For example, he envisioned an ideal future, a state of communist society that would be a "truly human history" marked by a "realm of freedom." Before that ideal state is achieved, however, humans live in "pre-history," which is characterized by the "realm of necessity." Lukes argues that Marxism's self-understanding is scientific and revolutionary and thus anti-utopian, and yet that self-understanding may well seem severely deficient, obscuring the utopian aspects of Marxism from its adherents. . . . Marxism inherited a view that was both anti-utopian and utopian; this was not mere ambivalence but a theoretical position, a kind of anti-utopian utopianism, distinctive of Marxism.[50]

Marx saw private property as the cause of human alienation and poverty. His answer or ideal for overcoming private ownership of property was a communist society. Thus he advocated

Communism as the *positive* transcendence of *private property* as *human self-estrangement,* and therefore as the real *appropriation* of the *human* essence by and for man; communism therefore as the complete return of human to himself as a *social* (i.e. human) being—a return accomplished consciously and embracing the entire wealth of previous development. This communism, as fully developed humanism equal naturalism; it is the *genuine* resolution of the conflict between man and nature, and between man and man—the true resolution of the strife between existence and essence, between objectification and self-confirmation, between freedom and necessity, between the individual and the species.[51]

Marx described the ideal communist society as having four features: abolition of forced divisions of labor, development of individual potential, transformation of work, and increase in prosperity.

In a higher phase of communist society, after the enslaving subordination of the individual to the division of labour, and therewith also the antithesis between mental and physical labour, has vanished; after labour has become not only a means of life but life's prime want; after productive forces have also increased with the all-round development of the individual, and all the springs of cooperative wealth flow more abundantly—only then can the narrow horizon of bourgeois right be crossed in its entirety and society inscribe on its banners: From each according to his abilities, to each according to his needs![52]

The ideal state of the communist society would be "where the free development of each is the condition for the free development of all."[53] The ideal communist society would guarantee freedom in human productive activities:

[I]n communist society, where nobody has one exclusive sphere of activity but each can become accomplished in any branch he wishes, society regulates the general production and thus makes it possible for me to do one thing today and another tomorrow, to hunt in the morning, fish in the afternoon, rear cattle in the evening, criticize after dinner, just as I have a mind, without ever becoming hunter, fisherman, shepherd or critic.[54]

The equality and distributive principles in the communist utopia are positive, being found also in biblical texts. For example, the popularly quoted Pauline formula in 2 Thessalonians 3:10 ("If anyone will not work, let such a one not eat") was used by Saint-Simon, Louis Blanc (1811–1882), and Marx, all emphasizing the universality and necessity of work. Similarly, "From each according to his abilities, to each according to his needs" has its biblical complement in the distributive justice expounded in Matthew 25. In short, Marx's concern for the poor, commitment to justice and equality, and idea of communism were indirectly influenced by biblical socialism.[55] However, MacIntyre argues that Marxist communism has a weak thesis of Christianity; that is, it adopts Christianity's form but not its religious content.[56] The problem of Marxism is its form as a "religion" without the content of the eschatological God, which produces a paradise without eschatological hope and salvation. While MacIntyre offers his critique of Marxism as a Christian theology, Bloch offers his as a Marxist philosopher—that Marxism needs the principle of hope.[57]

Bloch's Principle of Hope and the "Noch Nicht"

Ernst Bloch, a Marxist and Romantic philosopher, has worked laboriously to argue that Marxism should integrate utopia and the principle of hope (thus the name of the 1400 pages of his work). Bloch defines utopia broadly, including daydreams, myths, and fairy tales, and in the second part of the work, designates utopia as "anticipatory consciousness." This understanding is dependent on the central concept of his earlier work: the "not yet" (*noch nicht*). The "not yet" concept has two interrelated aspects: the not-yet-conscious and the not-yet-become. The not-yet-conscious is Bloch's critique of Freud's idea that the unconscious is a closet full of repressed trash. Bloch believes rather that the not-yet-conscious is the creative source of potency for change. But the not-yet-conscious is not simply a psychological category (abstract utopia) once it is correlated by means of cognition to the not-yet-become (concrete utopia), that is, the material reality that is not yet finished. The not-yet-conscious is always in the process of fulfillment, looking to a future full of possibilities in the concrete utopia. Utopia is thus the expression of hope.[58]

Bloch's hermeneutic of hope "is the restoration of lost or hidden meanings, the recovery of the genuine element of aspiration and anticipation which is at the heart of various utopian expressions."[59] Bloch argues that utopia is not a wishful but a willful thinking: "There is never anything soft about conscious-known hope, but a will within it insists: it should be so, it must become so."[60]

The Marxist fears that utopian ideology can easily become the instrument of the ruling class, luxurious fantasy, the mystification of domination are well founded. Yet the utopian model can also be used as an ideological critique, as Bloch's model suggests: the not-yet-conscious and the anticipatory dimension of utopia for a better world. Jürgen Habermas comments:

> In contrast to the unhistorical procedure of Feuerbach's criticism of ideology, which deprived Hegel's "sublation" (*Aufhebung*) of half of its meaning (forgetting *elevare* and being satisfied with *tollere*), Bloch presses the ideologies to yield their ideas to him; he wants to save that which is true in false consciousness: "All great culture that existed hitherto has been the foreshadowing of an achievement, inasmuch as images and thoughts can be projected from the age's summit into the far horizon of the future."[61]

Bloch's works have influenced many Christian theologians, some of whom are Marxists. For example, the work of Lutheran theologian Jürgen Moltmann, *Theology of Hope* (German in 1965; English in 1967), was influenced by Bloch.[62] In addition, Catholic theologian Johannes Metz's "political theology" places hope within the context of political struggle.[63] Finally, Bloch also influenced Gustavo Gutiérrez's *Theology of Liberation* (Spanish 1971; English 1973). Gutiérrez writes:

> Christian hope . . . keeps us from any confusion of the Kingdom with one historical stage, from any idolatry toward unavoidably ambiguous human achievement, from any absolutizing of revolution. In this way, hope makes us radically free to commit ourselves to social praxis, motivated by a liberating utopia and with the means which the scientific analysis of reality provides for us. And our hope not only frees us for this commitment, it simultaneously demands and judges it.[64]

Bloch's principle of hope advocates that people grasp the three dimensions of human temporality. Kellner writes:

> He offers us a dialectical analysis of the past which illuminates the present and can direct us to a better future. The past—what has been—contains both the sufferings, tragedies, and failures of humanity—what to avoid and to redeem—and its unrealized hopes and potentials—which could have been and can yet be. For Bloch, history is a repository of possibilities that are living options for future action; therefore, what could

101

have been can still be. The present moment is thus constituted in part by latency and tendency: the unrealized potentialities that are latent in the present, and the signs and foreshadowings that indicate the tendency of the direction and movement of the present into the future. This three-dimensional temporality must be grasped and activated by an anticipatory consciousness that at once perceives the unrealized emancipatory potential in the past, the latencies and tendencies of the present, and the realizable hopes of the future. Above all, Bloch develops a philosophy of hope and the future, a dreaming forward, a projection of a vision of a future kingdom of freedom. It is his conviction that only when we project our future in the light of what is, what has been, and what could be can we engage in the creative practice that will produce a world in which we are at home and realize humanity's deepest dreams.[65]

The Marxist view of history has rightly pointed out that there are power differentiations between classes in any society and that the dominating groups often use history to enhance their power and rewrite history to erase the workers' memory. The liberation theologies of Latin America and Asia have creatively made use of the Marxist critique of orthodoxy in favor of orthopraxy, of religiosity that embodies the righteousness of God and justice in a society, and of the God of Jews and Christians who identifies with all humanity through the hypostatic union of Christ.[66]

Marxism's materialistic historicism and concrete utopianism is a philosophy of political economy. Marx's materialist interpretation views history as an economic process of moving toward an ideal world of revolution and renovation in which bourgeois-capitalist society will disintegrate and proletarians will rule with equality and freedom:

> But it is just as empirically grounded that through the overthrow of the existing social order, through the communist revolution, i.e., the abolishment of private property, . . . the emancipation of every single individual will be achieved to the same extent that history transforms itself completely into world-history.[67]

And in the "Manifesto of the Communist Party," Marx listed ten measures the proletariats were expected to enact when they had power: to wrest capital from the bourgeoisie, to centralize all properties under the state, to increase production as much as possible, to abolish all private ownership, to centralize communication and transportation under the state, to centralize all credit under state bank monopoly, to equalize all divisions of labor, to abolish distinctions between towns and cities, to provide free education to all, and to combine education and industrial production.[68]

A Critical Assessment of the Marxist View of History

Much more could be said about the Marxist utopian dream of communism from a biblical perspective—and also from a theological perspective. In its rejection of the eschatological God, the Marxist view of history lost sight of the continuous and ultimate intrusion of God in the world he created and redeemed.

Marxism as a political-economical view of history is liberating to the working class, but Marxism's theological deviation and philosophical presuppositions distort its political-economical dimension, thus making it nihilistic and destructive. Marx sought to empower the working class politically and economically; he sought to give them freedom in his revolutionary change of the world. Yet his denial of the divine possibility to work in the hearts of humanity and his rejection of the spiritual vitality of humanity inevitably lead his followers to push for his radical changes even when it violates the people's freedom and runs counter to their will. The Marxist revolution inevitably uses violence to realize its goal.[69]

This is, no doubt, one reason why Marxism has come under sharp criticism, some of it crude, some of it insightful. Arnold Toynbee's analysis of Marxism fits into the former category:

> Marx has taken the goddess "Historical Necessity" in place of Yahweh for his deity, and the internal proletariat of the Western World in place of Jewry for his chosen people, and the Messianic Kingdom is conceived of as a Dictatorship of the Proletariat; but the salient features of the Jewish Apocalypse protrude through his threadbare disguise.[70]

Far more apt is the assessment of D. R. Davies, a former communist: "Marx without knowing or intending it, revealed the ultimate bankruptcy of mere humanistic thinking at its best."[71] In other words, Marxism is a pseudoreligion, a critical Jewish-Christian messianism in its secular form. The falsity of this religion stems from its lack of the fundamental conviction of the Jewish-Christian view of history: the acceptance of the divine providence in history that redemptive suffering is the condition of apocalyptic hope.[72]

Marx's secularization of the Jewish faith in his political and economic terms was studied by Löwith in depth. Here I quote at length his conclusion:

> For the secret history of the Communist Manifesto is not its conscious materialism and Marx's own opinion of it, but the religious spirit of prophetism. The Communist Manifesto is, first of all, a prophetic docu-

ment, a judgment, and a call to action and not at all a purely scientific statement based on the empirical evidence of tangible facts. . . . The final crisis of the bourgeois capitalist world which Marx prophesies in terms of a scientific prediction is a last judgment, though pronounced by the inexorable law of the historical process. Neither the concepts of bourgeoisie and proletariat, nor the general view of history as an ever intensified struggle between two hostile camps, nor, least of all, the anticipation of its dramatic climax, can be verified "in a purely empirical way." It is only in Marx's "ideological" consciousness that all history is a history of class struggles, while the real driving force behind this conception is a transparent messianism which has its unconscious root in Marx's own being, even in his race. He was a Jew of Old Testament stature, though an emancipated Jew of the nineteenth century who felt strongly antireligious and even anti-Semitic. It is the old Jewish messianism and prophetism—unaltered by two thousand years of economic history from handicraft to large-scale industry—and Jewish insistence on absolute righteousness which explain the idealistic basis of Marx's materialism. Though perverted into secular prognostication, the Communist Manifesto still retains the basic features of a messianic faith.[73]

Indeed, the denial of God forces the Marxist utopia to delete the power by which humans can create a proletarian society. The rejection of divine providence makes the Marxist utopia erase historical changes and progress. The refusal of the redemptive suffering of Christ renders the *telos* of history chaotic, aimless, and without eschatology—without redemption and with endless revolutions of violence. That is why the secular form of Christian utopianism is so delusive, destructive, and distorted, because the secularization of Christian eschatology is anti-eschatology. Secularization is not only anti-God but also anti-humankind and anti-history.

Conclusion

The philosophy of history, as first used by Voltaire (1694–1778) in the modern sense, might be a modern invention. Yet Löwith (in *Meaning in History*) has shown that, while the theological view of history in the West originated in the Jewish and Christian traditions, the philosophy of history ends with the secularization of the Judaic-Christian eschatological pattern.[74]

Both the philosophy of history (secular view) and the theology of history (biblical view) have attempted to present unified views of history, so that historical events could be interpreted systematically according to a perennial principle and the ultimate meaning of history could be discerned. Yet these two views offer different understandings of history. The philosophy of history suggests that human will and reason are the organizing principles of history; the theology of history believes that God's will and providence are the hermeneutical principles of history. The philosophy of history looks to progress as the measure of historical meaning, while the theology of history looks for God's salvation in the midst of ambiguities and distortion. The philosophy of history seeks to rebel against historical ambiguities and destroy enemies by imitating the mythic Prometheus, while the theology of history seeks to redeem suffering, transform evil, and recreate heaven and earth by means of faith in Jesus Christ, the God-Human.

While the philosophy of history looks to progressive and triumphal thinking, a Christian theology of history looks to the paradoxes of the cross: death and resurrection, suffering and hope, now and the future. The Christian meaning of history seeks to find life in human suffering and ultimately redemption in eschatology. In other words, the Christian view of history is concerned with salvation. Thus in the historical context of pain and suffering, humanity poses an existential question of the spatial-temporal reality of utopia.

4

the meeting of marxist and chinese views of history in maoism

Sinification of Marxism

Maoism seems able to allow the East wind and the West wind to meet, forming a new current of syncretic utopianism for the New China.[1] That is, Chinese culture and Marxist socialism met in the thought of Mao. Christian traditions and Western secular philosophies have encountered the Chinese worldview in a similar process. I intend to show the unfortunate turn of interpretation in both Marxist and Maoist political theologies whereby the Christian eschatology that was secularized by Marx was further distorted by Mao. The Maoist utopia is an inherently Chinese one (Confucian, Daoist, etc.) attempting to find new expression in Marxist ideology. This accounts for the contradictory personalities of Maoist revolutions. It will be helpful if we can discern in Mao's theologizing of the Marxist, Chinese, and Western utopian resources—his political theological construct for the New China—a narrative of hope and salvation. We will also ask: In his theologizing, has Mao's utopian view of communism moved closer to Paul's vision of "*agapic* communalism," or does the Maoist cyclical view of history inevitably end with contradiction and "permanent revolution"?

I have already shown that the Marxist view of history was critical of the traditional Western worldview that is informed by a Christian view, especially Christian eschatology. I will now show that the Maoist appropriation of the Marxist view constituted his critical adaptation of the Western resources in the Chinese context. Maoism was a unique product of Western scientific and evolutionary Marxist theories incorporating traditional Chinese ideals. These ideals were codified in the power structure and self-strengthening of Maoist hope for the reformation of a nation (Confucianist) by means of the rural transformation of the cities (Daoist), peasantry collectivities (secret societies) in the historical force of eternal changes (*yin-yang*), and the rule of law and militarism (Legalist).[2]

Marxist Maoism

The word *Maoism* does not appear in Chinese. It is used by Western scholars to refer to the common expression used in China, "the thought (*sixiang*) of Mao Zedong." *Sixiang* is thought or, to be more precise, "the thinking." That is, Mao's thought is a dynamic process of development. Yet we can also speak of "the thought" of Mao to refer to the core, consistent, and perennial thesis of Mao's thinking despite its development. During the rectification campaigns of 1942–1944, Mao's writings were canonized as the orthodox ideology of the Chinese Communist Party. Even though Mao's intention was not to devise a doctrine for saving China, the development of his thinking can be said to have formed a doctrine or "ism." During the 1964–1965 campaign prior to the Cultural Revolution, Lin Biao (1908–1971) and others began to fix and canonize Mao's thought as the standard for Chinese people to follow: "study Chairman Mao's writings, follow his teachings, act according to his instructions and be his good fighters."[3]

Since Meisner has compared Marxist and Maoist communism,[4] this chapter will focus on Maoist communism's use of utopian sources and views of history. Since one observes a regressive Marxism and a dominant Chinese ideology in Maoism, my thesis departs from that of Meisner, who did not deal with the Chinese influence and sinification of Marxism in Maoism.

Marxist Influence in China

Even though Mao never studied overseas, one should not assume that he knew little of Marxism. In 1913, at the age of nineteen, Mao spent five years at the Fourth Hunan Normal School at Changsha and there met his philosophical mentor and, later on, father-in-law: Yang Changqi (Yang Ch'ang-chi). Yang Changqi was a faithful reader of Zhu Xi (Chu Hsi), Immanuel Kant, Samuel Smiles, and T. H. Green. Yang was an idealist and an evolutionist. Mao learned from Yang the philosophy of idealism, especially Friedrich Paulsen's *System of Ethics*. Mao was concerned with the dilemma of individuality and found insight from Paulsen and Yang to critique Confucian ethics. Thus Mao wrote:

> Wherever there is repression of the individual, whenever there is a violation of individuality there can be no greater crime. That is why our country's "Three Bonds" (the three traditional Confucian social relationships, between prince and minister, father and son, and husband and wife) must go, and why they constitute, with religion, capitalists and autocracy, the four evil demons of the world.[5]

Yang influenced Mao toward a moral philosophy of self-reliance and duty toward society. At that time Mao believed in an ethics that focused on human will and material spirit.[6] Mao professed: "I was then an idealist."[7]

Another Chinese intellectual who influenced Mao in terms of his socialist and Russian communist ideology was Sun Yat-sen (1866–1925). Sun was a Christian who embraced Christianity and socialism. Sun would argue that only a Christian could be a socialist in its best sense. In 1924 he declared in the *Three People's Principles* his intention to harmonize the Three Principles with Marxism:

> The Three People's Principles consist of the People's Nationalism, the People's Sovereignty, and the People's Livelihood. The first principle means that all people of the world are equal. . . . The Principle of the People's Livelihood means that the poor and the rich are of identical rank. . . . The Principle of the People's Livelihood was realized by someone some decades ago, and that was Hung Hsiu-ch'üan [Hong Xiuquan]. In his Heavenly State of Universal Peace, there was a rule that all those who may be called workers controlled the state and that all goods were public property. This was in every sense the implementation of the Principle of an economic revolution, or of Russian communism today.[8]

Sun Yat-sen had high hopes in the communist world revolution and the Soviet Union.

Mao's contemporaries also influenced him on the idea of Marxism. In 1917, Li Dazhao (1889–1927) became one of the editors of *New Youth* in Shanghai. In 1918 he became the head librarian at Peking University, when Mao came to Peking to be his assistant, and that same year Li announced his conversion to Marxism, based not so much on the theory of Marxism but on the triumphal Russian Revolution against the old Tsarist regime. Mao developed a close friendship with Li, and they soon formed the Marxist Study Society in Beijing. Study groups were established in other cities, among them Shanghai and Changsha, the latter being the capital of Hunan (where Mao was the founding member of the study group). These groups anticipated the formation of the Chinese Communist Party.

Deviation from the Orthodoxy of Marxist-Leninist Ideology

One of the central aims of this chapter is to examine how Chinese communism under Mao departed from the orthodox Marxist-Leninist ideology against utopianism.[9] Maoism's critical spirit grew out of the antitraditionalist strain in Marxism that sought to break with the old socioeconomic and political systems. Marx believed that the power of science and education in freeing the French in their communes was the result of the French critique of the church's power.[10] Chinese Marxism took note of this antitraditionalist impulse and concluded that social and economic changes had to be sustained by the creation of a new humanity freed from old habits and old ideas. This antitraditional spirit erupted during the Cultural Revolution into an iconoclastic assault on all traditional values and beliefs.[11] Ironically, the same antitraditional spirit would backfire on Russian Marxism as Chinese communists critically appropriated Russian Marxism.

Mao and the pro-Soviet internationalist faction of the Chinese Communist Party (CCP) engaged in a long struggle between 1935 and 1945. By the fall of 1960, two ideological currents were entrenched: the Marxist-Leninist party line, and the Maoist line, which was supported by the army, who had studied *The Thought of Mao Tse-tung* and *The Sayings of Chairman Mao*. The struggle between the party and the army reached its climax during the Cultural Revolution. Franz Schurmann's study on this issue explains the power struggle among the Chinese communists:

> One of the key issues in that struggle was who should exercise command over policy and operations: Chairman Mao or the collective body of high-ranking Party leaders. In his rare articles, Lin Biao never failed to point out that all successes of war, revolution, and construction were due to the personal command of Chairman Mao. The Cultural Revolution not only launched a great campaign to study the works of Chairman Mao, but made it clear that it was Mao who exercised direct command over all policy and operations in China. The constant publication of pictures of Chairman Mao, particularly on the covers of *Red Flag* and the first page of the *People's Daily* served to drive that point home. Mao was henceforth always referred to as chairman and not as comrade, as had been done earlier.

Thus the Maoist current can be seen as an expression of a political force seeking to restore Mao [Zedong] to direct and personal command of the country.[12]

The Maoist current dealt mostly with thought (*sixiang*), emphasizing the spiritual significance of *The Thought of Mao Tse-tung* for shaping correct individual attitudes. The Little Red Book became a set of maxims for revolutionaries, but Mao's other works were also published. The Red Guard further publicized his thoughts in news tabloids, though the Marxist-Leninist current published their own works prescribing a proper course for socialist countries to follow at home and abroad.[13] Eventually thought triumphed over praxis. Therefore, Mao and his writings were widely quoted and praised, albeit as thought and theories only, as Lin Biao proclaimed in "Long Live the Victory of the People's War": "The whole series of Comrade Mao [Zedong]'s theories (*lilun*) and policies (*zhengce*) have creatively enriched and developed Marxism-Leninism."[14] Lin Biao's intention was to appeal to Mao's theories as the universal basis for the practice of communism. However, new organizational forms did not emerge to allow the implementation of Mao's ideologies and theories. Although Mao's teachings remained "pure" ideology, they still exercised influence. In fact, most Chinese under Mao studied and recited the Little Red Book, a sort of Communist Bible.

In 1964 Mao "abandoned two of the three basic axioms of Marxist and Hegelian dialectics, including the negation of the negation. . . . [I]t could be argued that he was already leaning in the direction he was to follow in the statement that 'the law of the unity of opposites' is 'the fundamental law of thought', which seems to place this axiom in a higher category than the other two principles (the negation of the negation, and the transformation of quantity into quality) Mao subsequently rejected."[15]

Part of the Chinese move toward socialism took place between 1947 and 1957, when Mao became critical of Marxist ideology. After gaining victory in the Chinese civil war, Mao stressed the need to follow Leninist and Soviet models of reform, focusing on industry and cities. Mao at first maintained gradual and moderate reforms in the countryside with rich peasants, but the economic policies later became so radical that Mao pushed for collectivization in July 1955. Less than a year later, in April 1956, Mao gave a speech entitled "On the Ten Great Relationships" spelling out the road to socialism in a manner different from that of the Soviets.[16] On February 27, 1957, he spoke on the ways to handle contracts among the people. It was within this context that he denounced Stalin's leftist errors and biases against those who disagreed with him.[17]

Thus, in 1954, when the first session of the First National Congress of the People's Republic took place, members stated: "The theoretical basis guiding our thinking is Marxism-Leninism."[18] But in 1969, the Ninth National Congress of the CCP declared that Mao Zedong's thought was the theoretical basis guiding the Party's thinking.[19]

Historical Forces toward a Proletarian Society

The most notable difference between Marxism and Maoism lies in the identification of the historical forces that bring about a society's socioeconomic prosperity. Maoist ideology found its utopian society in the countryside, where peasants and their labors were regarded as the historical forces that inevitably brought about socioeconomic prosperity in China. Mao's commitment to the peasants in the Chinese context bypassed the sociohistorical forces of modern industrialization and capitalism, forces that Marx had presupposed. For communist China, the revolutionary efforts of the peasants were virtues that the urban people should learn so that they would become the proletariat (*wuchan jieji*). To accomplish this, Mao sought to ruralize the urban, proletarize the city-dwellers, and pragmatize the intellectuals.

Mao's deviation from Russian communism is perhaps most clearly seen in his siding with peasants and rural areas. Mao would agree with Marx on the antithesis between town and country:

> The foundation of every division of labor that is well developed, and brought about by the exchange of commodities, is the separation between town and country. It may be said that the whole economical history of society is summed up in the movement of this antithesis.[20]

But Mao did not agree with Marx's views on modernizing society. Marx wrote:

> The bourgeoisie has subjected the country to the rule of the towns. It has created enormous cities, has greatly increased the urban population as compared with the rural, and has thus rescued a considerable part of the population from the idiocy of rural life. Just as it has made the country dependent on the towns, so it has made barbarian and semi-barbarian countries dependent on the civilized ones, nations of peasants on nations of bourgeois, the East on the West.[21]

Cities were not the stage for Chinese revolutions because they were the stronghold of foreign imperialism and not at all ideal places (utopia). Western bourgeoisie dominated China through the power of their wealth in major Chinese ports. Therefore, Maoist revolutions sought "to overthrow world capitalist imperialism."[22] To appreciate the rise and nature of Maoist utopianism, one needs to understand that Mao regarded Western capitalism and industrialism as forms of foreign imperialism.[23] In Mao's analysis of recent Chinese history, foreign invasions and domination had to be overcome by nationalism and patriotism. The unfair port treaties the Chinese government had signed with the foreign perpetrators of domination revealed the fact that cities were contaminated places and that countrysides were ideal places for Chinese society.

Mao regarded imperialism as the principal cause for revolution, and there were two fronts on which Chinese revolutions should attack: foreign imperialistic ideologies in urban areas, and landlord imperialistic ideologies in the countryside. The imperfect realities of China during Mao's era were the problems of foreign and internal imperialism. *Foreign* imperialism refers to capitalistic ideologies from other nations. *Internal* imperialism refers to feudalism, landlords, warlords, and intellectuals who aligned themselves with foreign capitalists ideologically.[24] Mao understood the Chinese feudalism of the last three thousand years as internal capitalism[25] and the nineteenth-century foreign imperialism as a full development of the embryonic form of capitalism in the feudal system.[26]

The link between capitalism and feudalism was that they were both imperialistic, whether externally or internally. Up until the era of Deng Xiaoping (1904–1997), who promoted "rethinking socialism" and the Four Fundamental Principles (adherence to Party leadership, to Marxism-Leninism and Mao Zedong's thought, to the socialist road, to the people's democratic dictatorship), modernization, industrialization, and capitalism were despised because of their divisive nature in Chinese society. There was a division between those who could accumulate wealth and those who were enslaved in labor. In Mao's era, capitalism and feudalism were "contradictions" (Mao's word) of the Chinese masses, with the peasants as the victims. Both foreign and internal imperialism caused the peasants to experience the "internal and external contradictions of imperialism, as well as the essence of the oppression and exploitation of China's broad masses by imperialism in alliance with China's compradors and feudal class."[27] Internal foreigners such as the intelligentsia of the Confucianist tradition and business persons had all been corrupted by imperialistic ideologies.

Mao saw the energy of the masses, the ready spirit of the peasants, and the pristine character of peasants as his true friends in the revolutions, and the people's youthful energy and creativity as true assets to the communist revolutions. Unlike Marxism, Maoism never criticized the cultural backwardness of the countryside; rather, the countryside provided him an opportune space to construct utopian ideologies of the peasants' moral and spiritual integrity. That vision promoted uninterrupted revolutions as the means to achieve the end of communist utopia. In Mao's thinking, "backwardness" was the asset that placed great value on struggle and self-sacrifice. So the aesthetic, moral, and spiritual value of a new communist human was to engage in perpetual struggle and self-sacrifice.

Much praise could be accorded the Maoist visions of liberation, identification with marginal groups, and class analysis of Chinese society. Still, although Maoism is committed to creating a socialist and utopian society in China, there are many aspects of Maoism that one can criticize. First, Mao's political ideology reinvented a utopianism that Marx himself had rejected. Mao's theory and practice often showed unrealistic expectations of an ideal communist society and a divorce from the objective laws of reality and historical development.[28] Second, Maoism looked to Marx's brand of socialism that distorted Christian eschatology and the Christian view of history. Third, the critical adaptation of Marxism in the Chinese contexts presented a challenge for Maoism. We deal with the first two points in other chapters of this book. Here we will focus on Mao's adaptation of and departure from Marxism as he assimilated it into his creative use of his own Chinese traditions.

Chinese Maoism

Mao's Writing and Chinese Influence

That Maoism at its core reflects Chinese influence should surprise no one. Maoism is not merely Marxian. Mao's writings quote Chinese classics from Lao Zi and occasionally from Confucius. Mao's first article cited the Chinese classics to a great extent. Of about twenty citations, a dozen came from the Confucian *Four Books*, one from the Confucian realist Xun Zi (precursor to the Legalists), two from the Sung idealist Zhu Xi (the interpreter of Confucianism), one from the late Ming critic Yan Yuan, and three from Zhuang Zi. A large number of these quotations were left out in the Little Red Book, perhaps because during the Cultural Revolution (1966–1976) the right-wing traditionalists charged the leftists with preserving the old traditions. Before that period, especially during 1949–1965, a group of brilliant Chinese scholars conducted research in humanities and social science in order to maintain traditional Chinese culture in the new socialist China. For example, there were favorable assessments of peasant uprisings, tracing them to the teachings of Mo Zi, Lao Zi, and the anarchists Bao Jingyan and Deng

Mu, as well as the Confucian New Text School with Kang Youwei. Right-wing communists, however, offered a counterattack to such developments as early as 1958.

In the end, traditional Chinese philosophies influenced Maoism in four categories: the five Confucian classics and Daoist philosophical works that Mao studied as a young person; the vernacular novels and historical romances (*wuxia*) that Mao read secretly; historical chronicles such as *Sima Guang's Zizhih Tongjian* (*Comprehensive Mirror for the Aid of Government*); and contemporary political-criticism essays in journals or newspapers.[29] The Chinese classics were learned in school by rote memory (to Mao's dislike), and much of Mao's thought was influenced by the classical material.[30] The chivalric novels, such as *Shui Hu Zhuan* (*The Marsh Heroes*), *Sankuo Yanyi* (*Romance of the Three Kingdoms*), *Xi You Ji* (*Tales of Westward Journey*), *Yue Fei* (*Jin Zhong Zhuan*), and *Hong Lo Meng* (*Dream of the Red Chamber*), were popular readings of all Chinese youth, disseminating ideas of stereotypical heroic and villainic characters, the righteousness of self-sacrifice, boldness to defend good causes in society, dynastic rise and fall, and commitment to *pao*—reciprocity of revenge or reward. These tales informed Mao of the complex operation of Chinese society and interpersonal relationships.[31] Even though he criticized the feudal values inherent in many of these stories, his cognitive language and emotive imagery were informed by this familiar Chinese material.

Traditional Chinese Religious Symbols

The most convincing evidence for the suggestion that Maoism is a Chinese product can be seen in the Chinese symbolism Mao used, much of which was religious. The sociological functions of religious symbols are "legitimation, consolation, orientation . . . [and these] are abundantly fulfilled by Maoism."[32]

The most vivid religious symbols Mao applied to himself involved the sun, brilliant light, the color red, and water. The name Mao Zedong literally means "Mao rules the East." Since the middle character "Ze" is not the given name, Mao Zedong can also mean "the East Mao" or the "Mao of the East," where the sun rises. It is no coincidence that the first verse of Red China's national anthem, entitled "The East Is Red" ("Dongfang Hong"), portrays the destiny of China and Mao as the glorious sun and savior:

> The East is Red.
> The sun rises.
> China has brought forth a Mao [Zedong].

He works for the people's happiness,
he-er-hai-yo! He is the people's great salvation-star.

Chairman Mao loves the people.
He is our guide.
To build the new China,
hu-er-hai-yo! He leads us forward.[33]

One often sees in Red China portraits of Mao with the red rays of the sun shining on his face. The People's Republic of China is Red China not because the cost of revolutions is blood or because red became the color symbolic of communism but because red signified the cosmic blessings and the brilliant future of China. The thought of Mao Zedong is identified with the red sun; Mao is portrayed as the everlasting sun, as this poem also illustrates:

Rely on the helmsman when sailing the seas,
All living things rely on the sun for their growth,
Moistened by rain and dew, young crops grow strong,
When making revolution, rely on the thought of Mao [Zedong].

Fish can't live without water,
Melons can't thrive off their vine,
The revolutionary masses can't live without the Communist Party,
Mao [Zedong]'s thought is the never-setting sun.[34]

The sun symbol is a vivid one in the context of China's turbulent, hostile, fragile, and uncertain history. The sun was seen as a symbol of life and energy that would remind the people of their source of hope.

Swimming is another ideological symbol that Mao used frequently to express the triumph over natural law, and his life was full of the swimming motif. In front of his boyhood home was a pond where he learned how to swim. At the age of thirteen, he almost jumped into the village pond when he had a conflict with his father, trying to run away from home after his father had publicly humiliated him in front of a number of party guests. During his last two years at the Normal School at Changsha (1917–1918), Mao saw physical education and swimming as one of the remedies for a weak and backward China. He once said, "The principal aim of physical education is military heroism."[35] Mao himself practiced cold-water bathing and swimming.[36] He used to swim in the Xiang River with Cai Hesen (Ts'ai Ho-sen) and other friends during his first Normal School days. In June 1956, at the age of sixty-three, Mao swam in the Yangzi (Yangtze) River from Wuzhang to Hankou. Later that summer he swam across the Yangzi two more times—from

Hanyang to Wuzhang. In June 1966 Mao swam in the Yangzi one last time, not simply to show his good health but also to demonstrate his strength and superhuman qualities (the event was filmed and shown around the world). He swam on both the eve of the Hundred Flowers Campaign and the Cultural Revolution. In 1967, fifty thousand proletarian revolutionaries of Wuhan and the People's Liberation Army commemorated Mao's feat by repeating the swimming act. In May 1956 after a swim, Mao wrote a poem entitled "Swimming":

> Just then a drink of water in the south [Changsha water],
> Now a taste of fish in the north [Wuzhang fish].
> A swim cuts across the Long River [ten-thousand-li-long Yangzi];
> A glance gauges the sky's width [Chu sky].
> Let the wind blow and waves strike,
> This surpasses an aimless stroll in the court.
> Today's leisure is well spent.
> Standing at a ford, the Master once said:
> "Thus life flows into the past!"
>
> Breeze shakes the masts
> While Tortoise [Hanyang] and Snake Hills [Wuzhang] are motionless,
> A grand project is being conceived—
> A bridge will fly across
> And turn a barrier into a path.
> To the west, new cliffs will arise;
> Mount Wu's [Wushan] clouds and rains will be kept from the
>   countryside.
> Calm lakes will spring up in the gorges.
> Were the goddess still alive
> She would be amazed by the changes on this earth.[37]

Moreover, in 1966, at the beginning of the Cultural Revolution, Mao explicitly used a "wave" metaphor to describe life: "No need to be afraid of tidal waves; human society has been evolved out of 'tidal waves'. . . . Let it come, I think it is a good thing to have this tidal wave."[38]

Water means change; it is a cosmological metaphor to depict the changing world. The imagery of swimming is a common Chinese metaphor to depict triumph over the forces of nature (water pressure), certitude in the face of the confusion of one's position in the water (space and depth), and endurance through time to reach the other side (transcending this world). Being unable to withstand any of these would mean death. Swimming is a knowledge that is informed by experience. Those who are able to swim experience the freedom, the joy, the victory of a "super" human.

The Daoist Understanding of Death

While the Confucianists did not say a great deal about immortality, the Daoist tradition glorified death. Along those lines, I mentioned in chapter 2 the Daoist vision of realizing utopia by means of dreams and death. The Daoist acceptance of death as a natural process of life is pervasive among Chinese people. The success of Mao's revolutions depended to a great extent on the people's willingness to die for the cause of revolutions. Mao glorified soldiers' boldness in facing death and their readiness to die. For example, the three most widely read articles by Mao speak of sacrifice for the benefit of society as a way to overcome death. The first article is "Serve the People" (September 8, 1944), a speech given at a memorial service for a soldier who had died in his service. In that speech Mao explicitly cited traditional Chinese material:

> All [people] must die, but death can vary in its significance. The ancient Chinese writer Szuma Chien said: "Though death befalls all [people] alike, it may be weightier than Mount Tai or lighter than a feather." ["Reply to Ren Shaojing's Letter"] To die for the people is weightier than Mount Tai, but to work for the fascists and die for the exploiters and oppressors is lighter than a feather. Comrade Chang Szu-teh died for the people, and his death is indeed weightier than Mount Tai. . . . we have the interests of the people . . . at heart, and when we die for the people, it is a worthy death.[39]

The second piece, "In Memory of Norman Bethune," dated December 21, 1939, is an obituary for Bethune, a Canadian physician in China who had died of blood poisoning.[40] The third document, dated June 11, 1945, "The Foolish Old Man Who Removed the Mountains," teaches that human collective effort is akin to a divine overcoming of hindrance and that human death can transcend time. Mao wrote:

> Today, two big mountains lie like a dead weight on the Chinese people. One is imperialism, the other is feudalism. The Chinese Communist Party has long made up its mind to dig them up. We must persevere and work unceasingly, and we, too, will touch God's heart. Our God is none other than the masses of the Chinese people. If they stand up and dig together with us, why can't these two mountains be cleared away?[41]

Mao knew how to appeal to the psychology of the masses to communicate his message that revolutions were a matter of life and death: "Unless it is swept away, no new culture of any kind can be built up. There is no construction without destruction, no flowing without damming and no motion without rest; the two are locked in a life-and-death struggle."[42] Once the masses of people became involved in the rebellions, they committed themselves with frenzy to fight for Mao at all costs, for Mao asked for nothing but total commitment: "The Chinese people are suffering; it is our duty to save them, and we must exert ourselves in struggle. Wherever there is struggle there is sacrifice, and death is a common occurrence."[43]

A typical Chinese understanding of death is that it is a dreamlike state akin to an extinguished lamp. This view is best summarized by the exposition of immortality given by Wang Shouren (Yangming, 1472–1529), an idealist and a Neo-Confucian of the Ming dynasty. Wang replied in a letter to a friend in 1508:

> You ask if "Immortals" really exist. . . . It is said that there were some extraordinary men in antiquity who had pure virtue and realized the perfect way. They harmonized the Yin and the Yang within themselves, adapted to the four seasons, and gathered their physical and psychic energies until they could allegedly walk anywhere. . . . It is true that such things have been reported about Kuang Ch'eng-tzu, who is said to have retained an undiminished vitality to the age of 1500 years, and of Li Po-yang [Lao Zi], who lived throughout the course of the Shang and Chou dynasties, and finally went west through the Han-ku pass in Honan. . . . Perhaps immortality is a gift of heaven rather than the result of some human effort. At a later time, it was said that Taoists had ascended to heaven, taking their houses along with them, and that they could transform or conjure up things. . . . But these are matters which even Taoists such as Yin Wen-tzu call "magic" and the Buddhists "false beliefs." . . . Scholars such as myself also have a doctrine about immortality. The philosopher Yen Hui died when he was a mere 32 years old, yet he is remembered today. . . . If you really want to find out something about immortality, you have to live in the mountain forests for 30 years. If you succeed in perfecting your eyes and ears there, if you harmonized the heart and the will so that your mind becomes clear and pure and free of all that is evil, you will be able to discuss the matter. As things stand, you are still far from the path of immortality.[44]

The Chinese belief in death as a possible gateway to immortality encouraged people to sacrifice their lives. In their view, this life is a temporal and mortal existence that leads to the next life of immortality.[45]

Cosmological Utopia: Death, Journey of Life, Nomadism

Mao and the Chinese communists considered the Long March (1934–1937) to be the most memorable journey of all, since 270,000 out of 300,000 sacrificed their lives trekking across six thousand miles of unbearable terrain.[46] It was also depicted as the initiation of Mao's revolution because of its cosmological utopian appeal to Chinese mentality. Homelessness appeared to be the pattern or structure of Maoist communism. It was certainly anti-Confucian, but it found its traditional appeal from the Daoist source. While Confucian politics preferred to administer the state through the structure of a patriarchal family, Daoist politics emphasized a cosmological base for nonaction (*wuwei*): become one with nature and take a walk away from the cities. Speaking of the Maoist idea of revolution, Bauer also points to its affinity with the Daoist tradition: "The old Daoist idea of a wholly anarchistic society living in small village communities persisted as an ideal [in China]."[47]

Homelessness persisted as a central theme during the Great Leap Forward, when children lived away from parents, husbands and wives separated, and everyone ate at community kitchens. During the Cultural Revolution, the Red Guards roamed around China making homelessness the test of revolutionaries. The youths and the military were like the secret societies of traditional China, making nomadism, revolutionary movement, and guerilla tactics their heroic lifestyle. All these seemed designed to take China back to a utopia before the contamination of home and society; unfortunately, violence and anarchy were often their devastating results.[48]

The homelessness and rootlessness of individuals were glorified, as the favorite readings of Mao depicted. Though fictional, the stories in *The Marsh Heroes* allude to the Sung period, when 108 heroes of brotherhood fought robber bands with a spirit of self-sacrifice. Mao also read *Romance of the Three Kingdoms* and Sun Zi (Sun Tzu) before he began revolutionary wars from 1927 onward.[49] The guerilla tactics of Mao's typical strategy had its Chinese source from Sun Zi's (500 B.C.E.) military strategy. Sun Zi's principle was: "Dissolve the whole into pieces and integrate the aggregates into a unit." He also wrote: "By discovering the enemy's dispositions and remaining invisible ourselves, we can keep our forces concentrated while . . . the enemy must be split up into fractions. Hence there will be a whole pitted against separate parts of the whole, which means that we shall be many in collected mass to the enemy's separate few. . . . And if we are thus able to attack an inferior force with a superior one, our opponents will be in dire straits."[50] Mao adapted Sun Zi's military strategy into a guerrilla warfare of mobilism and quick decision:[51]

> The enemy advances, we retreat;
> The enemy camps, we harass;
> The enemy tires, we attack;
> The enemy retreats, we pursue.

Mao's guerilla strategy secured victory over the KMT (*Kuomingtang*, Nationalist Party) forces even when the Red Army was inferior in number: "Our strategy is 'pit one against ten', and our tactics are 'pit ten against one'; these contrary and yet complementary propositions constitute one of our principles for gaining mastery over the enemy."[52] This strategy depended much on superior intelligence, which in turn depended on effective networking among the people. Mao excelled at mobilizing the peasants against the enemy troops.

Mao's guerrilla warfare made the socialist revolution and national liberation of China a great success. Mao intended to organize and arm the Red Army "not merely for the sake of fighting, but exclusively to agitate among the masses . . . and to help them establish political power."[53] Mao's strategy was that, "With the common people of the whole country mobilized, we shall create a vast sea of humanity in which the enemy will be swallowed up."[54] He wrote, "Our strategy and tactics are based on a people's war; no army opposed to the people can use our strategy and tactics."[55] In the midst of corrupt and unjust power, Mao identified with the outlaws, the knight-errants (*wuxia*), and the peasants of the traditional Chinese stories and chivalric novels.

Peasant Uprisings and Peasant Power

Mao's background and analysis of China's problems enabled him to see the role of peasants in the success of Chinese revolutions. Mao was brought up in the village of Shaoshan (or "Shaoshanchong" in Chinese, meaning "splendid peace silt") in Hunan. His family were middle-class peasants, formerly poor, under the weak leadership of his grandfather. Thus Mao grew up able to identify with the poor and became ambitious to gain power to help the peasants.

Mao adored nature and the rural areas where large numbers of Chinese lived. There is an account that he and his friends used to run in the rain and under the burning sun wearing only pants. When certain peasants laughed at them, he replied: "The sun is the source of all strength. Doesn't it make the rice grow? So why too much clothing?" A friend described Mao this way:

> I think it was at that time that Mao set his face away from the townspeople. . . . He approved of the peasants; he approved of no one else. What he particularly approved of in the peasants was their courtesy and their loyalty to one another. He said that the townspeople . . . simply followed accepted customs. In a sense he was split between his admiration for scholarship and scholars, and his admiration for the peasants. He thought he would be a teacher, and he would spend his time teaching peasants.[56]

121

In his identification with the peasants, Mao was influenced by Li Dazhao, who in February 1919 wrote an article entitled "Youth and the Villages." Reinforcing the idea that the countryside was an ideal place, Li observed: "Our China is a rural nation, and a majority of the laboring class is composed of these peasants. If they are not liberated, then our whole nation will not be liberated."[57] Later Mao declared that the peasants were his "vanguard of the revolution. . . . 'Long live the peasants!' "[58]

In 1926, Mao called the 395 million peasants his true friends in revolution, as opposed to the merely four million middle-class bourgeoisie of the urban areas.[59] Mao's trust in the peasants was so great that, he argued, not even the Communist Party could judge the power of the peasants; rather, the peasants were to judge the success of the revolutions. Without them, there could be no revolution. As early as 1927, Mao attributed the creative energy of revolution not to the Party but to the spontaneous movement of the peasantry:

> For the rise of the present peasant movement is a colossal event. In a very short time, in China's central, southern, and northern provinces several hundred million peasants will rise like a tornado or tempest, a force so extraordinarily swift and violent that no power, however great, will be able to suppress it. They will break through all shackles that now bind them and dash forward along the road to liberation. They will send all imperialists, warlords, corrupt officials, local bullies, and bad gentry to their graves. All revolutionary parties and all revolutionary comrades will stand before them to be tested, and to be accepted or rejected as they decide.[60]

Mao's wisdom was to celebrate the contributions of the peasantry, knowing that the most persuasive interpreter of the masses will be the hero and that the most powerful person is none other than the leader who can gain maximum support from his followers. It was with such conviction that Mao, during his political career, could bypass the Communist Party and go directly to the peasantry for support. The agricultural collectivization campaign in 1955 was a case in point: Mao bypassed the central committee of the Party and went to the provincial Party cadres and to the masses. Mao repeatedly admonished revolutionaries to merge with the peasantry, to "become one with the masses,"[61] to "learn what the peasants demand."[62] In 1915 only 5 percent of the Party membership were peasants; by 1928 the figure had risen to 70 to 80 percent.[63]

Mao's trust in the morality of peasants had its parallel with, or influence from, the traditional Chinese utopian visions, specifically the ideal place of nature in Daoism and morality as the ideal humanity of Confucianism.[64] Mao also knew the power of peasant uprisings in Chinese history. In "The Chinese Revolution and the Chinese Communist Party" he stated:

> The Chinese nation is known throughout the world not only for its industriousness and stamina, but also for its ardent love of freedom and its rich revolutionary traditions. The history of the Han people, for instance, demonstrates that the Chinese never submit to tyrannical rule but invariably use revolutionary means to overthrow or change it. In the thousands of years of Han history, there have been hundreds of peasant uprisings, great and small, against the dark rule of the landlords and the nobility. And most dynastic changes came about as a result of such peasant uprisings.[65]

Mao continued to declare:

> Our Chinese people possess great intrinsic energy. The more profound the oppression, the greater its resistance; that which has accumulated for a long time will surely burst forth quickly. The great union of the Chinese people must be achieved. Gentlemen! We must all exert ourselves—we must all advance with the utmost strength. Our golden age, our age of brilliance and splendor lies ahead![66]

In his speech "On the People's Democratic Dictatorship" after the wars in 1949, Mao twice referred to the communist ideal society as the "Reign of the Great Harmony" (i.e., *Datong* in Chinese).[67]

The imagination and energy of the Chinese revolutionaries and rebellions, including that of Mao, were sparked by Daoism and its subsects, not by Confucianism. While Daoism was popular among common people, Confucianism was popular among the intelligentsia. The Chinese communists may have been critical of Confucianism because Chinese communism's rationality was incompatible with Confucian rationality with regard to their understandings of social structure and class. Moreover, Chinese communism took on a religiosity of renewal, mobility, and revolutions that Confucian propriety, rationality, and preservation of tradition would not allow.

The Anti-Confucianist and Confucianist Mao

Mao had a love-hate relationship with Confucianism. Mao's fondness for youth and the power of the peasant caused him to despise intellectuals and formal education. He once remarked that reading too many books was harmful.[68] Citing historical examples, he despised Liu Xiu, an academician, because Liu Xiu had put down a peasant rebellion, and he praised Liu Bang, a peasant rebel, for becoming an emperor from his peasant background. Mao prided himself on being a "rough fellow, not cultured at all,"[69] perhaps out of humility or because he sought to identify with the commoners. But Mao was still a philosopher, a poet, and one who read constantly even when he was on the run during the guerilla years of revolution.

Mao's anti-intellectual mentality was related to his anti-Confucianist feelings, for Confucius was regarded as the greatest scholar and teacher of all time in China.[70] In Mao's marginal note to an ethics textbook by a German neo-Kantian, Friedrich Paulsen, Mao revealed his anti-Confucian sentiment (see the citation in note 5 in this chapter). In reaction to the evil of *sangang wulun* (three cosmic principles and five ethical norms) in Confucian ethics, Mao proposed the abolition of the master-subject relationship between father and son, prince and subject, husband and wife, officers and soldiers. In reaction to the old society and its obsolete ethics, Mao's vision was to create a new China and a new humanity, with essential renovations in cleanliness (e.g., plain costumes), physical fitness (e.g., mass gymnastics, acrobatics, and circuses), and scientific advancement (e.g., surgical miracles, acupuncture). In reaction to scholars' elitist dissemination of knowledge in printed form, Mao invented large-character posters for all to accumulate and disseminate collective ideas.

Mao thought that the grave evils of Confucianist ethics in ancient and modern China were the three thousand years of Confucian feudalism, ethical ritualism, and chauvinism, all of which led to landlordism, bribery, famine, and disease. Maoism was sympathetic to anarchist socialism and opposed Confucianism because it was a highly hierarchical political system that had kept China backward and rigid for the last two thousand years. In 1918 a famous modern Chinese writer, Lu Xun, wrote in the *Diary of a Madman* that the sickness of his contemporary society was *chiren de lijiao*, that is, the propriety and religion of carnivalism. Using sarcastic language, he attacked Confucianism. Students protested against the decision of the Versailles Treaty and turned against Chinese traditions, especially Confucianism, because Confucianism was unable to empower any action that would prevail over the technological and powerful West. The intellectuals during the May Fourth Movement wished to *fan lijiao*, "to rebel against the old traditions," implying that the old elite had lost its moral charisma.

While Maoism was critical of Confucianism, ironically enough Maoism at times walked under the shadow of Confucianism. The consolidation of political power by those in the highest positions in Communist China was often expressed in a Confucian paternal structure of authority. The problem of Confucianism had long been recognized, for example by Mo Zi, one of the ancient Confucian revisionists. Mo Zi offered a critique of family and a proposal of communism with which Maoism would later agree. Mo Zi's radical utopian system of government (inclusive love and deconstructing the family system) was reminiscent of the government before the Zhou dynasty, probably in the Xia dynasty, when the two sage rulers Yao and Shun were the two best royal figures. "Yao and Shun were careful not to make their own sons their successors because they wished to raise the worthiest person to the throne."[71] Even though they were legendary figures, Mao admired them, along with the historical figures Qin Shihuangdi (reigned 221–210 B.C.E.) and Wudi (Han dynasty, governed 140–86 B.C.E.), both of whom were founding rulers. Chinese emperors had sought to draw their divine authority and closeness to the divine through the use of rituals, but Mao legitimated his authority by means of "entering into the masses" (*shenju qunzhong*).[72]

It is well known that all Chinese rulers are oriented toward patriarchy. Perhaps Mao and the Chinese communists wished to break through that tradition and thus found Mo Zi's vision of leadership based on inclusive love and social equality more appealing. The irony is that since Confucianism, not Mohism, had been such a strong sociopolitical tradition in Chinese life (both private and public), even Mao and the Chinese Communists could not escape the bondage of family ideology. Like any other ruler in Chinese history, Mao ran the country as if China were his big family. After all, "country" (*kuojia*) in Chinese literally means "country-family," and the Chinese people then and now call Mao "grandpa." Since patriarchs, such as father or grandfather, have absolute say regarding family matters, the masses of the people had to listen and obey as if they were his children.

Before we leave this section, we need to discuss Mao's and Confucius's understandings of the transcendent world. Mao was a Marxist, not a Confucianist. Confucius was aware of both the human and the spirit realms, but he made the former an ideal place for humans to actualize themselves fully by means of ethical and social political virtues. *Tian*, the world beyond, does exist, but its life-giving and mandating functions are prior to our human existence; other than that, *Tian* does not intervene in the human world. Confucius was not an atheist, for he prayed to *Tian* (*Analects* 2,3) and advocated honoring "spirits and gods" (*Analects* 6,20). Confucius was not antireligious; he was at most an agnostic, a person who did not know, or sought not to know, the realm beyond human affairs. Therefore, his sole, or prior, focus on this world and human affairs made him a humanist. The prior focus is evident in his dialogue with his disciple Zi Lu. Zi Lu asked him how the spirits should be served. Confucius replied: "If it is impossible to do justice to humans, how can one do justice to the spirits?" (*Analects* 11,11). Mao's views, however, were so different from the Confucian religious view that Mao categorically rejected Chinese traditional religions and Christianity. The Maoist religious view was informed by Marxism, a Marxist influence that unfortunately distorted reality and brought about much pain to Christians and non-Christians in China.

Even though Mao's attitude toward other-worldly matters differed from that of Confucius, both could be categorized as "humanists." First, both maintained a clear division between the world here and the world beyond. This worldview is radically different from more primitive Chinese views, such as that of the Shang period, where fluidity was thought to exist between the worlds beyond and here (i.e., the *yin-yang* worldview discussed in chapter 2). Second, because both Mao and Confucius held to the disjuncture between the world now and the world beyond, both sought to reconstruct the ideal world in the here and now and tended to be skeptical of the world beyond as *outopia* ("no place").

The Sinification of Marxism in Maoism

Having looked at the influence of Marxist and Chinese traditions on the thoughts of Mao, our next task is to observe the sinification of Marxism. In 1945, during the Seventh Congress of the CCP, Liu Shaoqi (1898–1969) hailed Mao's thought as "thoroughly Marxist, and at the same time thoroughly Chinese."[73] In 1946, Liu wrote:

Mao [Zedong]'s great accomplishment has been to change Marxism from a European to an Asiatic form. Marx and Lenin were Europeans; they wrote in European languages about European histories and problems, seldom discussing Asia or China. . . . Mao [Zedong] is Chinese; he analyzes Chinese problems and guides the Chinese people in their struggle to victory. He uses Marxist-Leninist principles to explain Chinese history and the practical problems of China. He is the first that has succeeded in doing so. . . . He has created a Chinese or Asiatic form of Marxism.[74]

The phrase "sinification of Marxism" was actually used by Mao in 1938:

Today's China is an outgrowth of historic China. We are Marxist historicists; we must not mutilate history. From Confucius to Sun Yat-sen we must sum it up critically, and we must constitute ourselves the heirs to this precious legacy. . . . A Communist is a Marxist internationalist, but Marxism must take on a national form before it can be of any practical effect. There is no such thing as abstract Marxism, but only concrete Marxism. What we call concrete Marxism is Marxism that has taken on a national form, that is, Marxism applied to the concrete struggle in the concrete conditions. He who is a part of the great Chinese people, bound to his people by his very flesh and blood, and he who talks of Marxism apart from Chinese peculiarities, this Marxism is merely an empty abstraction. Consequently, the *sinification of Marxism*—that is to say, making certain that in all of its manifestations it is imbued with Chinese characteristics, using it according to Chinese peculiarities—becomes a problem that must be understood and solved by the whole party without delay. We must put an end to writing eight-legged essays on foreign models; there must be less repeating of empty and abstract refrains; we must discard our dogmatism and replace it by a new and vital Chinese style and manner, pleasing to the eye and to the ear of the Chinese common people.[75]

Mao's "sinification of Marxism" encouraged the Chinese people to resolve their own problems their own way. Sinification of Marxism was necessary because Russia and China differed in their cultural forms of language, their customs, and their economic and social realities. Unlike Russia, China was a precapitalist agrarian country.

The Maoist Cyclical View of History, Necessity of Contradiction, and Uninterrupted Revolution

The sinification of Marxism in Maoism is a crucial issue on which our investigation hinges. How does Mao apply a Marxist view of history to solve the problems of China? For Mao, Marxism's materialistic view of history and the anarchist rule of China by means of a people's dictatorship presented a new alternative that might solve China's sociopolitical problems.

Neither a materialistic view of history nor anarchist politics was entirely new to the modern Chinese. The rise of anarchism in modern China found its source in traditional Chinese and modern European ideas. The radical idea of anarchism was imported by Chinese intellectuals who had studied abroad, mostly in France in the early 1900s. Wu Zhihui (Wu Ching-heng, 1864–1954) wrote an article in Paris in 1906, eulogizing "anarchy":

The name anarchy is the most auspicious in the world. . . . [With anarchy] each country can do away with national boundaries. . . . each will give up all the different and numerous languages and adopt a common tongue; the governmentless state uses seventy or eighty percent of its total effort to import the ethics of nongovernment. The result is that anarchy is inevitable. Anarchy will have its "ethics" but no "laws." One will have

127

"From each according to his ability," but cannot call that "duty"; one will have "to each according to his need," but cannot call that "right." When everyone "voluntarily places himself in the realm of truth and equity" and when there is no longer the state of "the ruler and the ruled," then there is true anarchy.[76]

Wu was a thoroughly Westernized Chinese who loved Western (European) cleanliness, morality, technological advancement, and evolutionary theory. He and the Paris cell were anarchists.

Another person influential on Mao was Li Dazhao (1888–1927). Li was a Chinese Marxist, and in 1918 he published an essay entitled "Now" ("*Jin*") to explain his view of history: "All historical phenomena are always revolving and always changing and at the same time they still forever remain indestructible phenomena in the universe. . . . Unlimited 'pasts all find their resting place in the 'present' and unlimited 'futures' all originate in the 'present'."[77] This view of history is similar to the classical *yin-yang* understanding of time, and Li critiqued the Confucian golden-age mentality of dwelling in the past. He saw the *now* as the moment.

Mao was not convinced of the anarchist idea until January 1921, when he replied to his friend Cai (who had been arguing for proletarian dictatorship and anarchism for China): "The materialist view of history is our party's philosophical basis. . . . In the past, I had not studied the problem, but at present I do not believe that the principles of anarchism can be substantiated."[78] By 1940 it was clear that Mao had found a grassroots democracy under the Communist Party to unite and lead China down the road to socialism. In the essay "On New Democracy" he explained that the purpose of revolution was

> for a cultural revolution as well as for a political and economic revolution, and our aim is to build a new society and a new state for the Chinese nation. That new society and new state will have not only a new politics and a new economy but a new culture. In other words, not only do we want to change a China that is politically oppressed and economically exploited into a China that is politically free and economically prosperous, we also want to change the China which is being kept ignorant and backward under the sway of the old culture into an enlightened and progressive China under the sway of a new culture. In short, we want to build a new China.[79]

THE MAOIST VIEW OF HISTORY

The Maoist view of history was meant to solve the unsolvable: mortality and change. That is, how could a ruler guarantee the revolutionary process so that continuous reforms would eventually usher in a communist utopia? This ambitious task was challenged by the fact that historical processes and political leaders rise and fall. Mao was fully aware of dynastic change and personal mortality, despite the increasing praise from the lips of his people: "Mao Zedong Wansui" ("Long Live Mao Zedong"). Mao knew from the first paragraph of the popular novel *Romance of the Three Kingdoms* that "Empires wax and wane; states cleave asunder and coalesce. When the rule of Chou weakened, seven contending principalities sprang up, warring one with another until they settled down as Ch'in, and when its destiny had been fulfilled arose Ch'u and Han to contend for the mastery. And Han was the victor."[80] This knowledge of dynastic change deepened Mao's fear of his regime repeating Chinese history: a vigorous and dedicated beginning giving way to laxity and lack of vision on the part of his successors.

In 1966, Mao's comrade Lin Biao addressed the Politburo and mentioned retrogression and revisionism within a political regime. He mentioned the rise and fall of the dynasties of Qin, Sui, Yuan, and Qing as well as how Yuan Shikai (1859–1916) had gone against Sun-Yat Sen. Lin argued that "these reactionary coups d'etat should have terrified us and hastened our vigilance. Our seizure of political power has already lasted sixteen years. Will this regime of the proletarian class be overthrown and usurped? If we are not careful enough, we shall lose our political power."[81] However, as early as January 1962 Mao was already keenly aware of the problem and suggested that the Central Committee adopt the mass line policy, "developing democracy by encouraging and listening to criticism . . . letting other people speak" so that the sky will not fall on one person or small group of leadership.[82] By May of 1963, Mao advocated continued class struggle for fear of "counterrevolutionary" activity turning China into a fascist nation. For the next year or so, Mao attempted to purify the vision and gain greater momentum for the communist revolution as he accused "rightists" in the party who held authority but took the "capitalist road."[83] He cautioned that these rightists, such as Peng Dehuai and Liu Shaoqi, were the "greatest danger" posed to the party because they sought revisionism of Chinese communism.[84]

The Inevitability of Contradiction

The Maoist view of history trusted in the power structure and self-strengthening of the communist utopian hope to reform China against the historical force of dynastic change. Maoism believed in the rule of law and militarism. This Maoist view of history has its theoretical basis in two essays Mao wrote on July 7, 1937, at Yenan: "On Practice: On the

Relations between Knowledge and Practice, between Knowing and Doing" and "On Contradiction."

The first essay deals with the age-old problem of the Chinese psyche: inner and outer. Unlike the Christian problem of sorting out the relationship between transcendent grace and human will (or similarly the question of providence and freedom), the Maoist view of history was concerned with inner or outer personhood. Mao's position, as suggested by the title, placed the emphasis on practice and doing. Mao wrote: "If you want to know a certain thing or a certain class of things directly, you must personally participate in the practical struggle to change reality, to change that thing or class of things. . . . If you want knowledge, you must take part in the practice of changing reality."[85] Mao also quoted a Chinese proverb: "How can you catch tiger cubs without entering the tiger's lair?"[86] He explained, "If you want to know the taste of a pear, you must change the pear by eating it yourself. If you want to know the structure and properties of the atom, you must make physical and chemical experiments to change the state of the atom."[87] Since the historical process is changing and since there is no objective meaning discernible from history, the role of human beings to change reality became crucial for Mao. Bauer explains:

Mao derived it [the theory] . . . from the conceptual framework of the Book of Changes which is also merely half-determinist, as it were. . . . Mao's conviction that knowledge was not only practice but also a practice that changed objective reality, also led to his doctrine that the process of cognition was necessarily infinite simply because it transforms reality and constantly gives it a new appearance. Reality and cognition, object and subject, which are fundamentally inseparable, are thus in a constant process of change which does not approach a distant, fixed pole, but forms part of the nature of being and cognition. Consequently, Mao only acknowledges an "absolute truth" which consists of "innumerable" relative truths, and which thus loses its quality of absoluteness.[88]

Mao wrote:

Marxists recognize that in the absolute and general process of development of the universe the development of each particular process is relative, and that hence, in the endless flow of absolute truth, man's knowledge of a particular process at any given stage of development is only relative truth. The sum total of innumerable relative truths constitutes absolute truth. The development of an objective process is full of contradictions and struggles, and so is the development of the movement of human knowledge. . . . The movement of change in the world of objective reality is never-ending, and so is man's cognition of truth through practice. . . . Practice, knowledge, again practice, and again knowledge. This form repeats itself in endless cycles, and with each cycle the content of practice and knowledge rises to a higher level. Such is the dialectical-materialist theory of the unity of knowing and doing.[89]

The second essay, "On Contradiction" (written in 1937, published in 1952), begins with this sentence: "The law of contradiction in things, that is, the law of the unity of opposites, is the basic law of materialist dialectics."[90] Mao differentiated materialist dialectics and metaphysical dialectics. The latter worldview sees that things are capable of only quantitative change and thus only bring about vulgar evolution. The former worldview sees that "the fundamental cause of the development of a thing is not external but internal; it lies in the contradictoriness within the thing."[91] Mao writes:

Contradictoriness within a thing is the fundamental cause, while its interrelations and interactions with other things are secondary causes. . . . There is nothing that does not contain contradiction; without contradiction, nothing would exist. Contradiction is universal and absolute, it is present in the process of development of all things and permeates every process from beginning to end.[92]

Since it is universal, contradiction forms the fundamental law of reality for communism, and so oppositions, struggles, and revolutions become continuous in the historical process. This view is reminiscent of *Dao De Jing,* and at one point Mao quoted Chinese proverbs in support of his view: "Things that oppose each other also complement each other."[93] Mao's understanding of dialectical relationship was strongly influenced by Daoism in traditional Chinese thought. He adapted Chinese thought as revolutionary tactics in the context of Chinese society.[94]

The philosophical understanding of "contradiction" first appeared in Hegel's philosophy, then again in the materialist dialectics of Marx, Engels, and Lenin in their view of historical process and class struggles. Mao's view was informed by Marx, Engels, and Lenin. Various scholars have seen that the notion of contradiction was emphasized by Mao more than by Marx, Engels, or Lenin.[95] Contradiction as used by the Marxists often referred to logical contradiction in philosophy or argumentation. But contradiction to Mao was a technical term, which did not mean philosophical contradiction; rather, it meant the conflicting interaction of two opposing entities common enough to be in that relationship.

Mao found Marxism convincing because he used the Chinese philosophical *yin-yang* worldview to read the Marxist meaning of contradiction. In the *yin-yang* system, contradiction means the opposing and unifying forces of interaction between two conflicting things or groups, such as contradictions in nature: life and death, dark and light, cold and heat. Indeed, the *yin-yang* philosophy conceptualized the necessity and the complementary relationship of opposites as well as the harmony of conflicting forces. Maoism's problem in using the *yin-yang* philosophy was its "secularized" assumption that the cosmos contains only a historical and materialistic process. The ancient *yin-yang* worldview was fluid, comprehensive, interactive, and holistic precisely because it was cosmological and attempted to describe both divine and human activities. Applying the *yin-yang* philosophy to the historical materialism of Marxism reduced the *yin-yang* worldview into a humanistic and mechanical class analysis. Thus we see that in 1956 Mao listed the ten most important contradictions of relationships in Chinese society: (1) between industry and agriculture; (2) between coastal and interior industry; (3) between economic and defense construction; (4) between units of production and government; (5) between central and regional authorities; (6) between various ethnic groups; (7) between revolutionary and counterrevolutionary parties; (8) between the Party and those outside the Party; (9) between right and wrong; and (10) between China and other nations.[96]

Applying this theory of contradiction to his view of the sociopolitical history of China, Mao wrote:

> In human history, antagonism between classes exists as a particular manifestation of the struggle of opposites. Consider the contradiction between the exploiting and the exploited class. Such contradictory classes coexist for a long time in the same society, be it slave society, feudal society or capitalist society, and they struggle with each other; but it is not until the contradiction between the two classes develops to a certain stage that it assumes the form of open antagonism and develops into revolution. . . . Contradiction and struggle are universal and absolute, but the methods of resolving contradictions, that is, the forms of struggle, differ according to the differences in the nature of the contradictions. . . . Lenin said, "Antagonism and contradiction are not at all one and the same. Under socialism the first will disappear, the second will remain."[97]

According to Mao's writing on contradiction, the ideal society is now and not now, similar to the "already and not yet" concept of Christian eschatology. The major difference is Mao's naturalistic and secular view of history, thus his emphasis on contradiction rather than wholeness, and the means of struggle/revolutions. Fundamentally, Maoism differs from the Christian view of history because Mao rejects the eschaton/end/goal of history. Mao believes in the progress of history from primitive communism to slave society, feudal society, bourgeoisie society, capitalism, socialism, and finally communism. Thus while the socialist and Marxist view of history believe in the command of the historical forces as the necessary conditions for socialism and communism, the Chinese communist view of history constituted by Mao (and also Li Dazhao) trusts only human will. Li said: "There are some people who misinterpret the materialist view of history by saying that social progress depends only on natural material changes. They therefore disregard human activity and sit around waiting for the arrival of the new situation."[98]

THE NECESSITY OF UNINTERRUPTED REVOLUTION

Mao believed that struggles and contradictions were not merely the law of a class society but were the eternal laws of nature, the laws found also in a communist classless society. With the cyclical worldview of eternal changes and the necessity of complementary opposites, Mao understood that the social transformation of China would need uninterrupted or continuous revolutions.[99] Mao even stated: "I stand for the theory of continuous revolutions."[100] He also said: "The transition from socialism to communism is a struggle, a revolution. With the advent of the communist era, there will also be many, many stages of development. . . . All kinds of mutation and leap are a kind of revolution and must go through struggle."[101] Mao's deep concern was how to prolong his reign after the "empire" had been founded. Lu Chia, founder of the Han dynasty, once said, "The empire could be conquered from the saddle, but could not be governed from it" (*Shi Ji* 97:989a).

Mao's deep conviction of the uninterrupted revolutions in the 1950s set his communist vision in a greater program of the Great Leap Forward. In February 1958, before the Great Leap Forward, he made a statement that became a slogan: "Let a hundred flowers bloom, let a hundred schools of thought contend." Then the People's Commune was established, and revolutions one after another rolled over Chinese history. In "On the Correct Handling of Contradictions among the People" Mao wrote:

> Many dare not openly admit that contradictions still exist among the people of our country, although it is these very contradictions that are pushing our society forward. . . . they do not understand that socialist society will grow more united and consolidated through the ceaseless process of the correct handling and resolving of contradictions.[102]

The doctrine of uninterrupted, continuous, or permanent revolution taught by Mao is the means by which the communist revolutions can achieve the communist state. The ideal of communism is not a future utopian peace; it is an everlasting struggle or revolution in the prolongation of the now, and such achievement depends not on objective historical forces but on the continuous revolutions of the masses. Thus, history does not have an end.

The idea of uninterrupted revolution works well in a Chinese worldview. According to a Daoist understanding of life, the forces of history are in constant transition and renewal and society is in constant flux, just as the cosmos is in eternal change.

A New Humanity: Red and Expert

Mao believed that the realization of his utopian vision of a Chinese socialist society and universal communist state did not depend on an objective working out of the historical forces. Indeed, Mao believed in the moral virtues of the new humanity, who must work hard at their socialist consciousness. This is another trait of Maoism that distinguishes it from Marxism. To achieve *Datong* (Great Harmony) Mao used traditional Chinese terminology and proposed uniting the hearts of both the little people (*xiaoren*) and the superior people (*junzi*) on the basis of thought and morality.[103]

Maoism envisioned creating a spiritual transformation of the ideal humanity, the new Maoist humanity. In August 1967, Mao wrote:

> We must train a large number of revolutionary vanguards who have political vision, militant spirit, and readiness to make sacrifices. They are frank, honest, active, and upright. They seek no self-interest; they are completely dedicated to national and social emancipation. They fear no hardships; they are always firm and brave in the face of hardships. They are never boastful; they covet no limelight. They are unpretentious, realistic people. With a large number of people like this, the tasks of the Chinese revolution can be easily fulfilled.[104]

The "Three Constantly Read Articles" of Mao also emphasized the moral values of persistent hard work, diligence, self-discipline, honesty, courage, and sacrifice for people.[105] Mao's idea of concrete human nature was conditioned by class consciousness. He wrote:

> Is there such a thing as human nature? Of course there is. But there is only human nature in the concrete, no human nature in the abstract. In a class society there is only human nature that bears the stamp of a class; human nature that transcends classes does not exist.[106]

134

The new humanity in Maoist ideology was the "red and expert." The "red and expert" were virtues honoring two new groups of people in the late 1950s. The color red referred to the political cadre and the elite, the word *expert* to technological professionalism. During the Great Leap Forward the formula "red and expert" was used to call upon the masses to be well-rounded revolutionaries, able to integrate both the professional elitism of experts and the political fervency of red. Meisner explains:

> The "red and expert" was the model for a new "generation of all-rounded men who combine a capacity for mental labor with a capacity for manual labor"; he was a politically conscious "jack of all trades" (*duomi-anshou*, literally, "many-sides hand") capable of engaging in "scientific and cultural undertakings" as well as in physical labor. He was an exemplar of "communist" social and moral values. He was typically antitraditionalist, for he knew (or was told) that those who make creative accomplishments are those who have freed themselves from "the fetters of tradition." He was "a fully developed red and expert laborer who can handle both civilian and military work," combining theory with practice, "brain work with brawn work," and thus capable of switching from one job to another as the needs of society dictated. He was, in short, the "new Communist man, red and expert," who would realize Mao [Zedong]'s dream of a whole nation of "socialist-conscious, cultured laborers."[107]

The "new Communist man, red and expert" was to be a revolutionary engaging in practice, such as engaging in physical labor. Even the last Manchu emperor, Pu Yi (1905–1967), was forced to work as a gardener until his death. In the New China, everyone was to be a proletarian and revolutionary figure. Mao explained in "On New Democracy" (1940) that the bourgeoisie and intelligentsia could be reeducated to be poor and blank so that China could always retain its newness.[108]

Mao's attempt to "renovate the people" was inspired by *The New People Magazine,* edited by Liang Qichao (1873–1929), a reformer whom Mao admired. Mao founded the New People Study Society in Changsha in 1917. This vision was not borrowed from Marxism; it was mentioned in the Confucian tradition. The first sentence of the *Great Learning* says: "The Dao (teaching) of Great Learning is to illustrate illustrious virtue; to renovate the people, and to rest in the highest excellence."[109] Confucius's vision of an ideal person sought to renovate the people by being a moral example for others to follow. Such was the vision of Mao as well. He wanted every Chinese person to be "expert and red."

The Divinization of the Masses and the Atheist View of Maoism

The "success" of the Cultural Revolution was attributed to the energy of the socialist masses, who were "red and expert." The agents of the Maoist revolution were the masses, and the masses produced euphoria for themselves in the frenzy of revolution. The egalitarian impulse of the Maoist vision worked on the formidable force of crowd psychology that everyone was equal, that everyone was useful, and that the total effectiveness of their work together was greater than the sum of their individual actions. This demonstrates again Mao's faith in the masses, who, in his eyes, were equivalent to God.

Instead of theology, Maoism seemed to lift up anthropology, even to the position of the divine. This move was intentional, for in the Seventh National Congress to the Chinese Community Party in June of 1945, Mao reinterpreted a classical Chinese fable (Lie Zi) to portray a utopian possibility:

> [A]n ancient Chinese fable . . . tells of an old man who . . . was known as the Foolish Old Man. . . . [He] called his sons, and hoe in hand they began to dig up these mountains with great determination. Another greybeard, known as the Wise Old Man, saw them and said derisively, "How silly of you to do this! It is quite impossible for you few to dig up these two huge mountains." The Foolish Old Man replied, "When I die, my sons will carry on; when they die, there will be my grandsons, and then their sons and grandsons, and so on to infinity." . . . Having refuted the Wise Old Man's wrong view, he went on digging every day, unshaken in his conviction. God was moved by this, and he sent down two angels, who carried the mountains away on their backs.[110]

Why would Mao, an atheist, want to invoke the mercy of God? In fact, Mao's interpretation of the fable was utterly humanistic, spelling out the lesson of the fable as follows:

> We must persevere and work unceasingly [the traditional teaching of the parable], and we, too, will touch God's heart [Mao's "religious" or mythological interpretation]. Our God (Shangdi) is none other than the masses of the Chinese people [Mao's divinization of humanity].[111]

Mao might not have believed in his own divinity, but he did believe in the power of the collective masses of people. Their self-reliance constituted strength, and he felt responsible to lead these people correctly. In September of 1949, Mao harshly criticized the American idealist conception of history and proclaimed, "Under the leadership of the Communist Party, as long as there are people, every kind of miracle can be performed."[112] The "mass line" is the policy of the Chinese communist.

The Antithetical Chinese Personality of Maoism

The intention of this chapter is not to provide a clear-cut analysis of Mao as a Marxist or as an adherent to Chinese ideology. The thought of Mao, or of anyone, for that matter, cannot be teased apart so precisely. Yet it would be inaccurate simply to list the different traditions that influenced Mao and assume that the combination reflects his thought. The thought of Mao was not the sum of all its aggregates. The impact of different traditions formed Mao's thought into a new one. This analytical reading seeks to show how diverse traditions influence one's thought.

The implication of this chapter is that while the thought of Mao was complex, it was also at times confusing. Maoism is assumed to be Marxist, yet as we have seen, many old Chinese ideas reappeared in Mao's thought even when Mao deliberately wanted to reject them. These thoughts (such as Mao as the emperor, peasant rebellions, Chinese commune) came back through Marxist ideology. I conclude that Mao sinified Marxism with Chinese thoughts, thus making them more prominent than Marxism.

Maoism, in its sinification of Marxism, retained the Chinese personality, which is difficult to change and nearly impossible to abolish. The Chinese personality can be defined as a commitment to be loyal (*zhong*) and to stay in balance or in the middle course (*zhong*), not wavering about or becoming extreme in anything one does. The Chinese words meaning "be loyal" and "middle" are the same phonetically. Playing on this, one might argue that the Chinese personality is to walk on the way defined by the mean, the middle, and not to depart from it. But *zhong* can also mean mediocre and so-so.

Mao's "heavenly mandate" was to rule China and to ensure that China became self-strengthened and renovated against the tyranny of imperialism and feudalism. Mao's vision was to rebuild a *Xin Zhongguo*—New China. *Xin Zhongguo* means New Middle Kingdom. The Middle Kingdom was first unified during the Qin dynasty (255–206 B.C.E.) by Qin Shihuangdi, whose name literally means "Qin the first emperor-lord." Mao's vision was inspired by Qin Shihuangdi. The word *Zhongguo*, which appears in *Lie Zi* 3:35,[113] defines China geographically, nationally, and morally.

The Chinese personality, however, in its struggle with the tension between the antithesis of the inner and the outer and its attempt to stay on the middle of the way, often becomes mediocre and confused. The Doctrine of Mean states: "If equilibrium and harmony are secured, Heaven and Earth will dwell in it and all things will be nourished by it." The contradictions Mao so uniquely expounded reveal the age-old problem of "antithesis between the inner and outer" of the Chinese personality.[114] The most significant problem of Maoism "was the contradiction between objective history and subjective will."[115] The Chinese dialectic is constantly aiming to live a life of inner and outer balance, of individual and social being, of private and public, of loyalty to family and country.

The inner and outer antitheses are not dualistic opposites between matter and spirit; they are, rather, bipolar necessities to maintain the equilibrium of inner and outer spheres of life. The inner and outer antitheses are not necessarily sets of dichotomies; they are not diametrically opposed to one another. If they are, then China and the West are an irreconcilable pair, always in conflict. Another example will suffice: a human being is an individual *and* a member of a society, not simply one or the other, though the Chinese personality often struggles with the tension between individuality and social interaction.

This is the inescapable destiny of a mandarin person, *Zhongguo Ren*, whose personality at times seems to be wisely holding all the ambiguities of life in a healthy tension, at times split in confusion and contradictions. Is this the Chinese personality of Maoism? This discussion will unfold in the next few chapters. The next focus of our inquiry will be the rise of the Maoist cult and religious policy regarding Chinese Christianity. After sketching those issues in the next chapter, we will then move to the final task of allowing Maoism and Paulism to meet face to face.

5

the meeting of maoism and christianity in red china

The Maoist Cult and Chinese Christianity

Western science and Christianity's encounter with Chinese political messianism was most rigorous in the late nineteenth (Manchu dynasty) and early twentieth centuries (founding of the Republic). This period of national messianism was set during a time when a sense of Western superiority in China was at its height. Chinese intellectuals went overseas to study and looked to the West for utopian hopes. Most looked to science and democracy for the hope of modernization and salvation for feudalistic China.

Understood in the context of the two great enemies then faced by China in the twentieth century—imperialism and feudalism—Maoist utopian ideology dismissed both traditional Chinese culture and Christianity in the name of nationalism and proletarianism. However distorted a view Mao might have had of traditional Chinese cultures (especially Confucianism) and Christianity (whose identification with Western culture he justifiably categorized as imperialistic during the nineteenth and early twentieth centuries), I am convinced that the Chinese utopian tradition has encountered Christian eschatology in Maoism. Unfortunately, Maoism also adored Marxism's evolutionary and materialistic views.

139

My intention in this chapter is, first, to investigate why Maoism criticized both the old Chinese culture and Christianity; second, to show that Maoism is a secular millenarian cult even though it saw itself as strictly a sociopolitical movement; third, to investigate whether the Maoist cult could have functioned as a sacred canopy for Chinese society during Mao's era; and fourth, to examine how Chinese Christianity, caught between the "holy empire" of Western Christianity and Maoism, responded to the emerging antireligious policy of Maoism.

Background of the Maoist Critique of Religion and Chinese Traditions

We must first reflect on the cause of Maoism's critical spirit toward Chinese tradition and Christianity—and its origins in the Versailles Conference and the May Fourth generation. To begin with the latter, during World War I (1914–1918) China aligned with the Allies and helped fight the war in Europe. After the war, China wished to take back its sovereignty over Shandong, which had been ceded to Germany under the "unequal treaty" in 1897. As early as 1915, however, Japan had claimed the right to Shandong in the "Twenty-One Demands" document. To the dismay and outrage of China, the Western powers transferred the rights to Shandong to Japan at the Versailles Conference (1919). Among the Chinese representatives sent to the conference was a Catholic, Lou Tseng-Tsiang (1871–1949), who was the foreign minister for a short period of time but later joined a Benedictine abbey in Belgium.[1] About 30 percent of the Chinese delegates to Versailles were Protestants.[2] Sun Yat-sen was enraged at the decision of the Versailles Conference, and he determined to form a revolutionary government in China. Students throughout China's universities protested, and the famous May Fourth Movement was formed with the student riots and demonstrations held in Tiananmen Square in Beijing on May 4, 1919. Antiforeign and anti-Christian sentiments were intense.

The May Fourth Movement was a literary and cultural revolution in the name of modernization (against rigid traditionalism), science (against superstitions and religions), and democracy (against monarchy). Its mission was to build a new and modern China that would be strong enough to overcome any aggressors. Two initiators of the May Fourth Movement were influential in forming the antitradition and anti-Christianity sentiments of the modern Chinese. Hu Shi (1891–1962), a student of John Dewey, was not a Marxist but a humanist who saw poverty, disease, ignorance, corruption, and destitution as the five great evils in China. He was the key proponent of a literary revolution in the

May Fourth Movement that would replace the archaic classical Chinese language, called "eight-legged letter," with modern popular Chinese, called *paihuawen*—literally, "plain language." He hoped to popularize colloquial dialect in order to spread modern ideas and to highlight science and democracy. Chinese writers began the new era of experimenting and writing various genres of literature in modern Chinese.[3] This modernization process for China meant that old traditions would have to change or be rejected.

The literary revolution was coupled with a cultural revolution. A second figure, Chen Duxiu (1879–1942), was instrumental in encouraging the younger generation to use their pens to bring about social and political reforms in China. These writers condemned the old China and praised the new. In 1915, Chen Duxiu founded the journal *New Youth*, which intricately linked the modernization of China with the rejection of the West, old traditions, and foreign religions. Chen was a Marxist nationalist who rejected the aggression of the West and refused to join Sun Yat-sen's national revolution because he disliked the anti-Manchu society called Dongminghui. Chen saw capitalism and imperialism as China's two great enemies. He became a Marxist in 1920 and was responsible for founding the Chinese Communist Party (CCP) in 1921.

As the editor of *New Youth*, Chen emphasized from the second issue of the journal "the superiority of the dynamic, militant, individualistic and utilitarian attitude of the West over the weak world view of China" and advocated the industrialization of China.[4] The *New Youth* had an editorial board and articles that were politically aggressive and ideologically communist, and it was instrumental in molding the ideology of Chinese communism. In 1918 Chen Duxiu wrote a scientific critique characterizing religions as "the useless things . . . rubbish and idols." "If such idols are not destroyed," he said, "mankind will never be delivered from deluding superstitions and irrational beliefs."[5] Chen argued that China had to walk either on the "enlightened path to republicanism, science and atheism" or "the obscurantist path of despotism, superstition, and theocracy."[6]

Meanwhile, the antireligious and anti-Christian sentiment of Chinese students, both in China and overseas during the 1920s, was significant, as Whyte observes:

Chinese students in Paris had already tried to impose a ban on religious believers joining the Beijing-based Young China Society. Then in early 1922 it was announced . . . that the forthcoming WSCF [World Student Christian Federation] conference was to be held in Beijing. In response a small group of Shanghai students formed the "Anti-Christian Student Federation" and issued a manifesto on 9 March. . . . The Anti-Christian Federation attacked Christianity and the missionaries, saying that Christianity was dead in the West and the missionaries make up the loss by "implanting in foreign areas the remnants of their superstitions in order to prolong their parasitic existence."[7]

Mao belonged to the generation of the May Fourth Movement, and the momentum of the antireligious movement was evident in his ideology. The deification of the masses as God in Maoism was consistent with the Marxist critique of religion. One might try to explain Maoism's atheistic and antireligious views within the contours of the humanistic traditions of Chinese culture. This would not be accurate, however, because the Chinese humanistic traditions, such as Confucianism, are not antireligious; they are at most areligious. The worldviews of Daoism and *yin-yang* philosophy embrace religions.

Mao appealed to the masses, not the intellectuals, for the success of revolutions. But as an intellectual and leader himself, he adopted the antireligious view of the Chinese intelligentsia. In other words, Mao identified with the peasants for power, but he criticized religions by means of intellectual persuasion. While Daoism was popular among the common people, Confucianism was popular among the intellectuals. It was Daoism and its subcults, not Confucianism, that sparked the imagination and energy of most Chinese revolutionaries, and it was this religiosity that China's homemade humanist tradition—Confucianism—protested against. Confucian rationality and structure, in both its ethical and social patriarchy, could not contain the anarchist religiosity of Daoism.

Looking at the religious and humanist interaction in China's long history of utopianism, we see that Maoism was critical of Confucianism. Chinese communism took on a religiosity of renewal, mobility, and revolution (revolutionary fervor, subsuming to authority, etc.) that Confucian propriety, rationality, and preservation of tradition refused. One might say that Mao was Daoist in his revolutionary spirit but Confucianist in his critique of religion—and empowered by the Marxist rationality.

Maoism's antireligious sentiment reflected the popular antireligious and secularization sentiments of the Chinese intellectuals of his generation. We have seen how the intellectuals during the May Fourth Movement wished to *fan lijiao*, that is, rebel against the elitism and moral rigidity of the old traditions. It was also the antisuperstition scientism of the May Fourth Movement that taught people not to tolerate religions, which mesmerized people and led them away from the down-to-earth activities of reconstructing China.

Moreover, Christianity and the Western powers were held responsible for the domination of China during the previous hundred years or so. Christianity was categorically regarded by students and intellectuals as an opiate poisoning China and obstructing her on the road to modernization. Some of the students' argumentation came from the Western sociological sources that challenged and critiqued traditional Christian belief. They read, for example, Chinese translations of Thomas Huxley's *Evolution and Ethics*, the works of Charles Darwin, Adam Smith, John Stuart Mill, Rousseau, and Spencer—which Mao also read.

To claim that Maoism has an antireligious ideology of Mao is not the same as saying that Maoist thought does not have its own understanding of religion. It would be ironic, though, if we were to find that Maoism functions as a religion in its own right, perhaps taking the place of the superstitions and religions Mao sought to annihilate.

Communism As a Religion? A Maoist Cult?[8]

How does one begin to speak of Chinese communism as a "religion" or of Maoism as a "cult"? The works of C. P. Fitzgerald and Arthur Wallis on the "religiosity" of Maoism and Chinese communism might be too direct, but their interpretations are perceptive. Fitzgerald writes:

> It is obvious to any observer that in China the Communist doctrine has established itself as a religion and that a great part of its success is the appeal which it makes to men of religious temperament. . . . From Christianity Marxism has undoubtedly borrowed much, sometimes with no acknowledgment; sometimes with a nod of recognition such as Zhou Enlai [1899–1976] bestowed upon the Protestants.[9]

Similarly, Wallis argues:

> During the Cultural Revolution every household had a white plaster cast of Mao, and each day all the family members had to bow before it twice. The saying was "In the morning ask for instructions; in the evening report back what you have done." For those of us who survived, the Cultural Revolution was a good thing. We learned a lot. I could never put another god in my heart like Mao.[10]

Since Mao was an atheist, what was his view of God? There is a well-known story that relates how Edgar Snow interviewed Mao in January 1965 and how Mao told him that he "was getting to see Shangdi (God) very soon."[11] *Shangdi* is a classical word for the high God or God in heaven; it is also the word that the Chinese Christian Bible used for Yahweh. Snow was not entirely clear what Mao meant, so he inquired further: "I wonder if you mean you are going to find out whether there is a God. Do you believe that?" Mao denied believing in God but added that "some people who claimed to be well-informed said there was a God." The context here reveals that it was Mao's intention to show that people use the name of God to justify their political views.

A similar incident took place on October 25, 1966, when Mao gave a talk to the Central Work Conference. In his address he stated, "When I go to see God. . . ,"[12] meaning when he died. But in 1971, Mao delivered a talk to the people in the provinces, and it was clear that he did not believe in God: "[Lenin tells us] that slaves should arise and struggle for truth. There never has been a supreme savior, nor can we rely on gods or emperors. We rely entirely on ourselves for our salvation. Who has created the world of men? We the laboring masses."[13]

Mao might not have believed in the existence of God, but his worldview accounted for aspects of life that have affinities with ideals, the highest good, immortality, transcendence, achieving the impossible, *Tian*, the purpose and goal of history, and so forth. All these are not simply political, social, or philosophical concerns but also religious categories. Mao was an atheist, yet he created a religious worldview that sought to replace God or gods with his personality cult and the power of the peasants! In other words, Mao was a secularist and humanist who secularized religions. The cult of Mao secularized all realms of life.

The Religious Phenomena and Function of the Maoist Cult

When one speaks of the Maoist cult, one speaks of Mao and his thoughts being adored as divine. The cult of Mao is more than a normal adoration of examples (*bangyang*) or heroes (*yingxiong*), such as Norman Bethune, a Canadian surgeon who died of blood poisoning; Chang Zede, a soldier who died in a civil war; Yu Kung, the foolish old man whose determination removed the mountain; Lei Feng; or Jin Xunhua, who drowned in the Xun River saving flood victims.[14]

Since Maoism rejects the need for religion in a socialist society, it is difficult to use religious language to analyze the Maoist cult. However, Peter Berger speaks of the social reconstruction of the world as the main function of a religion.[15] Wakeman argues that "to say 'the cult of Mao' is to risk melding usages, so that the term sounds deprecatory, implying superstitious idolatry. Yet, like a purely religious cult, the veneration of Mao does help secure a theodicy in the form of a person. But Mao . . . his cult, though liturgical, distinctly lacks ritual specificity."[16]

I will therefore employ sociological and functional categories to read Maoism. Maoism may not be a religion proper, but it is a religious phenomenon in the sense that the Chinese revolutions under Mao dealt with the issues of national survival and reconstruction, the significance of life and death in a society, the peace and prosperity of different classes, and social and personal ethics. The Maoist conviction of human mastery over nature was religious, touching on the question of transcendence and human finitude, divine providence and human freedom, God's purpose in history and human responsibility. The selfless sacrifice in Maoist teaching was honored as heroic martyrdom and seen as human power equated with divine power. The "regeneration" process of *pi-dou-gai*, criticism, combat, and revolution, does show its religious function of the inner and spiritual transformation of humanity.

In 1927, Mao appealed to the peasants on the basis of class solidarity to create a cult based on human power. Mao proclaimed:

> For the present upsurge of the peasant movement is a colossal event. . . . They will smash all the trammels that bind them and rush forward along the road to liberation. They will sweep all the imperialists, warlords, corrupt officials, local tyrants and evil gentry into their graves. Every revolutionary party and every revolutionary comrade will be put to the test, to be accepted or rejected as they decide.[17]

The cult of Mao emerged in this context and filled the vacuum of many years of incessant wars and privations. The incipient form of the Maoist ethos[18] could be detected again in October 1934, when only thirty thousand of the original 300,000 survived the six thousand miles of the Long March, trekking through unbearable terrain under the leadership of Zhu De (1886–1976) and Mao.[19] Though many died from starvation, drowning, exposure, and enemy attacks, the miraculous story of those who traversed vertiginous obstacles, slippery mountains, cliffs, and foaming rivers inspired many peasants to look on Mao as the invincible liberator who would lead impoverished, exploited, illiterate China to the promised land of rice, iron, and will.[20]

In 1938 Mao declared an unprecedented glorious moment for China in world history:

> This process, the practice of changing the world . . . has already reached a historic moment in the world and in China, a great moment unprecedented in human history, that is, the moment for completely banishing darkness from the world and from China and for changing the world into a world of light such as never previously existed.[21]

Mao began to distribute land to the peasants and to restore Chinese sovereignty and independence. On October 1, 1949, he declared to the masses at Tiananmen Square (Gate of the Heavenly Peace), "We have stood up."[22] Early in 1940, Mao already envisioned communism as "the most perfect, the most progressive, the most revolutionary, and the most rational system ever since human history began."[23]

The charisma and logos of this messianic figure was unprecedented in the millenarian history of China. Meisner mentions a secret speech Mao delivered in March 1958 regarding people's reverence of him and the relationship between personality cult and truth:

> There are two kinds of cult of the individual. One is correct, such as that of Marx, Engels, Lenin, and the correct side of Stalin. These we ought to revere and continue to revere forever. . . . Then there is the incorrect kind of cult of the individual in which there is no analysis, simply blind obedience. . . . The question at issue is not whether or not there should be a cult of the individual, but rather whether or not the individual concerned represents the truth. If he does, then he should be revered.[24]

There is no doubt that Mao considered himself to represent the truth.

Even with the unexpected failure of the Great Leap Forward, the Maoist cult was growing in the army. Because of production shortages, organizational disintegration, and economic crisis,[25] Mao retreated from the public in 1958–1959. At this time, the relationship between Moscow and Beijing was tense, culminating in the eighth plenary session of the Eighth Central Committee at Lushan in July 1951. Marshal Peng Dehuai (1898–1974) criticized Mao's leadership and vanity, at one point comparing him to Stalin and Tito. Mao also spoke at the Lushan conference, denying that his power was slipping away: "The rightists said: why did [Qin Shihuangdi] collapse? Because he built the Great Wall. Now that we have constructed the T'ienanmen, we would also collapse; that's what the rightists alleged."[26] Mao threatened that, if the Chinese state collapsed, he "would go to the countryside to lead the peasants to overthrow the government." He continued: "If the Liberation Army won't follow me, I will then find the Red Army. I think the Liberation Army will follow me."[27] The subsequent voting indicated strong support for Chairman Mao against that of Peng Dehuai.

With the unrealized promises of good times and a prosperous society during the bitter years of 1960–1962, Mao's popularity dropped to the lowest point of his career. Since his power over the Party was eroding, he turned to the People's Liberation Army, made up mostly of peasants, to regain power. This was a political move, as Meisner writes:

The People's Liberation Army [was], the most bureaucratic and hierarchical agency of the state apparatus, but the one which provided Mao with his main political base at the time and the only institution he regarded as still uncorrupted by "revisionist" ideology. It was the Political Department of the Army that published the first edition of *Quotations from Chairman Mao* in May of 1964, and then proceeded to print almost a billion copies of "the little red book" over the following three years, along with 150 million copies of *The Selected Works of Mao [Zedong]*. It was the head of the Army, the then eminently Maoist Lin Paio, who orchestrated the 1964–65 campaign to study Mao's works, to the virtual exclusion of all other writings, and who made the most extravagant claims for the power of Mao's thought. "Comrade Mao [Zedong] is the greatest Marxist-Leninist of our era," Lin proclaimed, and his genius had raised the doctrine to "a higher and completely new stage." Masses and cadres alike were enjoined to "study Chairman Mao's writings, follow his teachings, act according to his instructions and be his good fighters," for once grasped by the people Mao's thought was "an inexhaustible source of strength" and nothing less than "a spiritual atomic bomb of infinite power."[28]

By 1965, Edgar Snow, an American reporter, had confirmed the complete glorification of Mao in China, and Mao himself acknowledged it.[29] Snow heard from Mao that Nikita Khrushchev had lost his power three months before because he had had no personality cult at all—which was not true of Mao himself. Snow writes:

Giant portraits of him now hung in the streets, busts were in every chamber, his books and photographs were everywhere on display to the exclusion of others. In the four-hour revolutionary pageant of dance and song, *The East is Red,* Mao was the only hero. . . . I saw a portrait copied from a photograph taken by myself in 1936, blown up to about thirty feet high. It gave me a mixed feeling of pride of craftsmanship and uneasy recollection of similar extravaganzas of worship of Joseph Stalin seen during the wartime years in Russia. . . . The one-man cult was not yet universal, but the trend was unmistakable.[30]

There were sociopolitical motivations and consequences for this glorification, but irrationality and zealotism were also crucial components. For example, in the three-year Great Leap Forward, pure ideology was used to incite the masses. That ideology tended to take the form of utopianism.[31] During this period, professionals, intellectuals, middle administration in national bureaucracy, and middle management in industry were ruthlessly attacked, and many were discharged from their positions. Young cadres were told to lead the masses and the production teams. Furthermore, intense ideological propaganda was widespread.

"Utopian preaching of the imminent advent of pure communism"[32] was heard in the summer and fall of 1958, as Schurmann describes it:

> Party cadres often go into the industrial and agricultural production teams preaching *Weltanschauung* to the workers and masses. Most characteristic of this preaching was its utopianism, the promise of a bright future just in the offing, in the literature of the Cultural Revolution. In 1958, the cadres told the peasants that three years of suffering would lead to a thousand years of happiness. . . . The morality tales, such as those about the soldier-hero Lei Feng or about the self-sacrifice of Dr. Norman Bethune, have become a prominent part of the preachings of The Thought of Mao [Zedong].[33]

In 1965, two years before the Cultural Revolution, a story was conveyed to Edgar Snow that peasants came to the October anniversary and bowed before Mao. The Chinese official "had to keep guards posted there to prevent them from prostrating themselves. It takes time to make people understand that Chairman Mao is not an emperor or a god."[34]

That the Maoist movement and revolution led to a personality cult does not come as a total surprise. The period between 1966 and 1976 was characterized by cultural deterioration and disaster, yet the cult of Mao became full blown. The Cultural Revolution not only celebrated heaven on earth but also carried out the "great judgment." The rhetoric of Maoism was evidenced in such images as bulls, ghosts, serpents, monsters, and demons, all of which were used to describe the uncooperative lost ones. The Cultural Revolution intended to assault and eradicate Chinese traditions and Western bourgeoisism; it ended up turning Mao into a religious symbol, such as the son of heaven. Mao-sun was hailed as "a locomotive, a compass, a lighthouse, a bright lantern lighting up the road,"[35] "the reddest of all suns," whose radiance dwelt in the hearts of all true revolutionaries, the commander-in-chief of the Chinese people and army, and the leader of all revolutionaries—especially the communists—in the world. The glorification of Chairman Mao reached such proportions that he seemed to be revered as a divine being: he was addressed as "Great Teacher, Great Leader, Great Supreme Commander and Great Helmsman" during the Cultural Revolution. Paul Rule's thesis that "It is not a cult of Mao, but of Maoism, the thoughts of Mao [Zedong], and Mao is honored as the thinker of the thoughts"[36] is only partially correct, because the religious experience of Mao in the lives of many Chinese people touched on transcendent power and divine adoration. Schurmann writes, "Chairman Mao had indeed become a charismatic leader, in the full sense of that much-abused term."[37]

He was greeted by every Chinese with "Long live Chairman Mao!" Drawing on the imagery of Daoist mysticism, "the 'thoughts of Mao' were said to be a 'magic weapon' that would vanquish his foes. . . . Exhibition halls commemorating Mao's revolutionary deeds . . . [were] referred to . . . as 'sacred shrines'."[38] Traditional Buddhist terms such as "monsters," "demons," "cow-ghosts," and "snake-gods" were used to describe Mao's opponents. In contrast, Mao was called "star of salvation," "savior," "genius" by the Chinese people. Meisner writes:

> Exhibition halls commemorating Mao's revolutionary deeds were built across the land, their halls facing east to the source of light, their floors laid in traditional-style mosaics decorated with sunflowers. The official press referred to these halls as "sacred shrines." . . . Increasingly massive numbers of people came on organized pilgrimages to pay homage at the "sacred shrines" built to commemorate the life of Mao [Zedong]. The test of loyalty to Mao came to be measured less by revolutionary acts inspired by his "thought" than by the ability to memorize his maxims and sayings, and by the size of his portraits carried in the streets and hung in homes. At the beginning of the Cultural Revolution, the Mao cult had stimulated the masses to take revolutionary and iconoclastic actions; at the end of the upheaval it simply produced icons for the masses to worship.[39]

Villagers had "tablets of loyalty" in their homes where Mao's portraits hung, and city-dwellers had little portraits of Mao hanging in their vehicles, both symbols of an object of reverence and of good luck. The daily ritual of paying allegiance to Mao included receiving instruction in the morning (from Mao), reporting at noon (to Mao), and repenting in the evening (to Mao). People also devoted about ten hours a week to *xuexi*, small-group studies of political literature (government directives, select Marxist writings) and exegetical examinations of Mao's works. Such gatherings also involved criticism sessions, including self-criticism as self-cultivation, and frequent "reports" in which people expressed political consciousness and loyalty by confessing or informing to Party leadership about themselves and others.[40]

The Cultural Revolution, if viewed from the perspective of Mao's consolidation of power from the reverence of the masses, was intentionally a cult-building process to address the descending position of Mao after the Great Leap Forward. By now, Mao was struggling with his own mortality as well, but the main motive was his securing of power and the ongoing movement of the communist utopian vision. Politically, the Cultural Revolution was set off to curb those "capitalist restorations" and "counter revolutionaries."[41] However, the thesis that the Cultural Revolution was only a sociological and cultural phenomenon does not hold water. The Cultural Revolution ought to be understood from a religious perspective because its ideologies, characters, language, and related objects were nothing less than religious.

Mao's message of good news and his rhetoric were so widespread that by 1976, during the waning of the Cultural Revolution, school children across the land still chanted, "May Chairman Mao live ten thousand years ten thousand times!"[42] However, the energy, jubilation, revolutions, and hopeful spirit soon faced the reality of hardship, turmoil, and dissatisfaction. By the end of 1976, the Chinese woke up and were disappointed that communism had not realized the promised utopia.

Even before his death, Mao knew that his personality cult was widespread in China, especially among the peasants. In an interview with Edgar Snow he confessed that the cult-worshiping might have been overdone, but the cult itself was of political necessity. He continued to say that the Chinese people were accustomed to three thousand years of emperor worship, so the practice of a personality cult was not very difficult for them.[43]

An Assessment of the Maoist Cult

So, then, is Maoism a substitute religion, a pseudoreligion, an antireligion, a humanistic religion, or a form of atheism? I agree with the position of Paul Rule:

> Perhaps Maoism is a substitute-religion, deliberately usurping the traditional religious ground. The attempt to apply an ultimate criterion, that of transcendence, has revealed an aspect of transcendence but one that is ambivalent and inconclusive. The New China is certainly overtly anti-religious in its policy toward traditional Chinese and foreign religions. Yet again, paradoxically, this very inability to tolerate rivals may be evidence of Maoism's ambitions to be the one, true faith of China. It leaves no room for rivals precisely because it ambitions to occupy fully all spheres of human activity including that we call religion. If it is not a religion, it looks remarkably like one.[44]

Mao's success in creating a personality cult lay in his wisdom to gain the faith of the masses and to secure power through the use of Chinese imperial means (emperors were sage-rulers in China). Li Jie writes that "the victorious Mao combined the elements of sage-ruler (based on a belief system) with that of the political hero (realized through his autocracy)."[45] Indeed, the cult of Mao was able to blossom because Chairman Mao assumed the role of patriarch (sage) and emperor (ruler) of China, even though the nomenclatures differed. Mao was able to sinify Marxist historical materialism by means of Legalist, Daoist, and (anti-)Confucianist wisdoms (see chapter 2 for background).

The Maoist cult did not need a religious institution, structure, and doctrine, because the Chinese worldviews did not differentiate clearly between the secular and the sacred. Sacredness is found in the ideal society of virtues in Confucianism, in the harmonious relationship with nature in Daoism, and in the law and order of the Legalist tradition. The cosmological worldview of the *yin-yang* philosophy was able to accommodate both human and divine activities. Consequently, the Maoist cult found its indigenous structure in the traditional religions, without necessarily creating a religious nomenclature or structure for itself.

To be more precise, the Maoist cult thrived on the structure of the Legalist militarism (ruler) and the Confucianist patriarchalism (sage). The consolidation of power in the sage-ruler personality of Mao made the Maoist cult active without imperatives, persuasive without dogma, pervasive without institutions. All Mao needed were rules of law and to be head of the big family called "country."

Readers may recall the conflict between the Legalists and the Confucianists (see chapter 2) with regard to the rule of an ideal society. While the Legalist tradition of law and militarism sought to critique the Confucianist ethics and patriarchal structure, Legalist traditions turned out to be another form of family structure, that is, "state-family" (*guojia*). The concept of state-family was not alien to Confucius's teaching found in the *Great Learning*, whose vision of a peaceful state began with self-cultivation and extended to universal peace within the world. The Confucian ideal state was based on morality and ritual. But when the law and the military were in the hands of an assumed family elder, such as Mao, the family became as big as a country, and the elder became the lawgiver and commander in chief of the military. As such, we see in Chinese history that the Legalist tradition was nothing more than a chief's arbitrary rule of the country, a personality cult of patriarchy. This only shows the pervasive influence of Confucianism in China's political life, so much so that the Legalist tradition in China, from its beginning to Mao's era, is not without the Confucian impact as well. The inevitable problem of Chinese rulers, then, was to be caught in between the Legalist and the Confucianist, with the result that emperors were always autocratic and not subject to reproof. The Chinese Legalist tradition was not based on a democratic idea of public discourse, on political rule by means of rhetorical persuasion, and on majority rule and representation of good and right. The Chinese Legalist tradition was always based on a personality cult of the emperor.

The dangers of regarding a ruler as lawgiver and father of the people were many. First, being the "father" of the Chinese people meant that critiquing or disagreeing with him would constitute an insult to the father. After all, filial piety is the Confucian virtue and propriety that holds the family structure together. Second, the "father" of the people, especially a typically stern Chinese father, would often rule the people with absolute authority as the head of a family or state-family. The more power one has, the more power one wants; the benevolence of the emperor required the total submission of the people. Third, the conflict of roles as lawgiver and a rewarding judge, between a justice enforcer and a forgiving parent, often turned an emperor into a dictator. Fourth, the logic that the emperor was the "father" of the country provided a legitimate justification for the notion that the emperor could do no wrong. Even if an emperor admitted that he did something wrong, he could not bear any punishment; only his royal garment would be beaten. The problem of the emperor and the personality cult was that he thought of himself as divine, not human. Mao's principle of securing power and relating to comrades was: "Those who go against me will perish, and those who side with me will serve!"

Emperor Cult

Mao was not the first political leader whose status was elevated to divinity. The theological politics of an emperor cult inevitably maximizes its power and allows the emperors to consider themselves gods. We find a parallel case in Thessalonica, in 42 B.C.E., which had become a free city rather than a Roman colony. It was during this time that the cult of the goddess Roma and the benefactor Romans emerged.[46] The temple of Caesar was built during the reign of Augustus, and numismatic evidence as early as 29 B.C.E. indicates that the image of Caesar's head was designated as a god on one side of a coin and as Augustus on the other side.[47] Consequently, Augustus, Julius Caesar's adopted son, who had been acknowledged to be a god, enjoyed the status of *divi filius* (son of the deified). This numismatic evidence reveals that the head of Augustus had replaced the head of Zeus, and Octavian/Augustus was seen as "son of god." The priesthood and royal theology of the divinity of the emperors is indicative of the legitimation of Roman emperors and their successors. Not only is an imperial cult worshiping Roma and Augustus evident from inscriptions and coins, but other evidence indicates that the priest of Roma was the Benefactor of Rome and Agonothete of Augustus.[48] It is clear that the *pax Romana* claimed to be ushering in a millenarian reign and that the emperors were divine figures.

Chinese Christianity in Communist China

Chinese Christian responses to the Maoist cult and millenarian Maoist thinking were conditioned by the sociopolitical situations of Red China.

Chinese Christian responses were different (though quite consistent with Paul's theology in 1 and 2 Thessalonians), and its concerns were multiple. Here I will simply focus on one response from the Three-Self Patriotic Movement.

The Chinese communists viewed religion (especially Christianity) as a foreign imperialist's ideological tool to exploit common people.[49] Christian missionary work in China was considered to be a form of foreign cultural aggression. Seen through the eyes of the Chinese, the treaties in the nineteenth century were both totally unjust and acts of blatant imperialism in exploiting China's resources and forcing its people to accept opium. The Boxer Uprising of 1900 was the culmination of sixty years of antagonism toward all foreigners.[50] That some missionaries had condemned the opium traffic and that they had never been part of imperialist or colonialist activity against China, as Leslie Lyall contends, may be correct.[51] But, in fact, imperialists had often used the name of Christianity to conquer, the preaching of Christianity had often been dominated by Western culture, and the native churches had always been tied to the leadership and control of overseas mission boards. Thus the "three-self" and "patriotic" movement was a political move by the Chinese churches to overcome imperialism. The three-self idea was a theological and ecclesiastical response to Western domination in Chinese churches and society.

The Three-Self Patriotic Movement[52]

The three-self concept was first proposed by two administrators of missionary societies: Henry Venn (1796–1873) of the Church Missionary Society and Rufus Anderson of the American Board of Commissioners for Foreign Missions. Venn explicitly advocated that "the elementary principles of self-support and self-government and self-extension be sown with the seed of the Gospel . . . in the Native Church" in China.[53] Anderson recommended that missionaries "ordain presbyters . . . and to throw upon the churches . . . the responsibilities of self-government, self-support and self-propagation."[54] The idea of "three-selfs" was also proposed by two American missionaries, S. L. Baldwin and V. Talmage, in the 1800s.[55]

There were already indigenous Chinese churches even before the official Three-Self Movement. In 1873, for example, Chen Mengnan founded at Guangzhou (Canton) the East Guangdong Zhaoqing China Evangelization Society, an independent organization that set up churches. In 1906 Yu Guozhen founded the Chinese Jesus Independent Church in Shanghai. In the 1950s this church was led by Xie Yongqin, who later played an active role in the Three-Self Movement. More and more independent Chinese churches were founded in Jinan, Qingdao, Yantai, Enxian, and Wiexian, which also set up schools, hospitals, and service centers. Then in the 1920s the larger independent churches such as the Little Flock and the True Jesus Church were founded.

The Three-Self Movement, however, was unique because it had government involvement. When the communist government came to power in 1949, it seriously adopted the policy of religious freedom and tolerance but added a political twist. C. M. Chen, an official of the Religious Affairs Bureau, once said that the purpose of the government was not outright extermination of the church but restriction, reformation, and control. Chen pointed out that the Three-Self Patriotic Movement (TSPM) had been created to make religion serve politics and to make the church politically harmless.[56]

The Separation Strategy and United Front

The Religious Affairs Department was set up in Beijing in 1950 and was commissioned to cut off all Christian bodies in China from their overseas ties, to expel foreign missionaries, and to promote an autonomous church movement.[57] This separation strategy also required the Chinese churches to work more closely with the communist leadership. The Communist Party required that Chinese churches had to be loyal to the Chinese government and not to any foreign body. Then, in the mid-1950s, Zhou Enlai met separately with Protestant and Catholic leaders. He assured them of the government's intention to protect freedom of religious belief but requested that they separate themselves from overseas imperialist control and express their patriotic sentiments by adapting to the new political situation in the New China.[58]

The separation (from foreign bodies) strategy was reinforced by the formation of a united front (with the government). Mao Zedong, in his 1940 essay "On Coalition Government," had proposed the willingness of the communists to form a *united front* with any political, religious, and idealistic group to fight against feudalism and imperialism, despite his clarification that "we can never approve of their idealism or religious doctrines."[59] Therefore, the Chinese Communist policy toward religion was officially "seeking common ground while retaining differences."[60]

But earlier, in 1949, the Vatican decreed that Chinese Catholics should not support the CCP or the People's Government, warning that Catholics who showed support would be suspended from the sacraments and excommunicated. The Catholic Church had explicitly viewed communism as "atheism," "deception," and "barbarism." "Communism is by its nature anti-religious. It considers religion as the 'opiate of the people' because the principles of religion which speak of a life beyond the grave dissuade the proletariat from the dream of a soviet paradise which is of this world."[61] The Vatican also stated: "The communism of today . . . conceals in itself a false messianic idea. A pseudo-ideal of justice, of equality and fraternity in labor impregnates all its doctrine and activity with a deceptive mysticism, which communicates a zealous and contagious enthusiasm to the multitudes entrapped by delusive promises."[62]

On the Protestant side, Y. T. Wu (Wu Yaozong) advocated the Three-Self Movement in 1950. Wu, a visionary and first president of TSPM, was influenced by the worldwide Christian socialist movement of the 1930s and became more and more sympathetic to the ideas of Chinese communists.[63] He saw that a crucial task neglected by Christians and the churches was being fulfilled by the communists. He explained that the Chinese Christian church was in a tragic situation because

> China is today face to face with the greatest change in its history, and in this period of great change the Christian church, besides the negative reactions of feeling sorry for itself, and trying to escape reality, has nothing to say or to do.[64]

The Christian Manifesto

During that year (1950), nineteen Protestant leaders, led by Y. T. Wu, met with Chinese Premier Zhou Enlai to prepare a statement, called the "Christian Manifesto," concerning the difficulties the churches faced in New China. By that time war had broken out in Korea, anti-American sentiment was high, and patriotic fervor was rampant. A massive campaign was launched to get Christians all over China to sign the manifesto.[65] The manifesto called on Chinese Christians to heighten their "vigilance against imperialism, to make known the clear political stand of Christians in New China, to hasten the building of a Chinese Church whose affairs are managed by the Chinese themselves." It stated further that Christians should support the "common political platform under the leadership of the government."[66] It called upon churches relying on foreign personnel and financial aid to discontinue those relations and to work toward self-reliance.[67] The controversial document stated specifically the political viewpoints of the Christian church, not its theological ones.[68] It is understandable that the Christian Manifesto would agree with the Communist Party's view, stating that since "missionaries who brought Christianity to China all came themselves from these imperialistic countries, Christianity consciously or unconsciously, directly or indirectly, became related with imperialism."[69]

In October 1950 the biennial meeting of the Chinese National Christian Council was held for the purpose of adopting the Christian Manifesto and implementing means to bring about the "three self reform."[70] In April 1951, the Religious Affairs Bureau of the government invited 151 Protestant leaders to a conference in Beijing, where they voted "to thoroughly, permanently and completely sever all relations with American missions and all other missions, thus realizing self-government, self-support and self-propagation in the Chinese church."[71] Thus they officially established the Protestant TSRM (Three-Self Reform Movement)[72] in order to carry out this policy.[73]

The Christian Who Loved China and the Communist Party

What made the TSPM unique was its willingness and courage to cooperate with the Communist Party at least on the common ground of sociopolitical issues. It is little wonder that the Christian Manifesto was prepared by Y. T. Wu and Premier Zhou Enlai.[74] In 1958 Wu wrote in *Tien Fung* (*Heavenly Wind*) that "without the Communist Party there would not have been the TSPM or the Christian Church. . . . I love the Communist Party."[75] At that time, the TSPM drafted a "message of respect" to Chairman Mao that articulated four main goals: (1) to promote the greater unity of all Christian churches by carrying out the three-self policy in response to their love for both the country and the Christian religion; (2) to support the Draft Constitution of the People's Republic of China and to strive with the people of the whole nation to construct a socialist society; (3) to oppose imperialist aggression and thus safeguard the peace of the world; and (4) to encourage all Christians of the nation to seriously learn patriotism.[76]

In Wu's provocative essay "How the Communist Party Has Educated Me" we see a perfect example of how a Chinese Christian was able to praise communism and be critical of his own religion. He focused on the social and political contributions of the Communist Party: not to be a pacifist in condoning wrong or accepting "imperialist opiate to keep oppressed peoples quiet." Wu wrote:

> Now I know that capitalism is an oppressive system that must necessarily produce many domestic and international contradictions and threaten world peace; it is communism, and the socialism and new democracy that form the foundation of communism, that constitute the world's only road to safety. . . . Christianity is inseparable from culture. . . . the larger part

of Christendom today is already completely controlled by the capitalist class and by imperialist elements, and has become a tool for their aggression and an enemy of the proletariat.[77]

Y. T. Wu was not alone; other Christian leaders likewise accepted the communist regime to be a political entity they could work with: YMCA leaders (Y. C. Tu, Kiang Wen-han, Liu Liang-mo, Cora Deng), T. C. Chao (president of Yenching University), Bishop Z. T. Kaung (senior bishop of the Methodist Church), Robin Chen (Chen Chien-chen, bishop of the Anglican Church), H. H. Tsui (general secretary of Church of Christ in China), and Marcus Cheng.[78]

By supporting the TSPM, the Chinese Christians were choosing common ground between Christianity and communism rather than magnifying their differences. This did not necessarily compromise the Christian truth. No doubt these two competing "ideologies," each supremely assured of its own understanding of reality, had "compatible and partly convergent positions regarding the dignity and destiny of man and his call to transform the world."[79] Julia Ching calls this alternative way "that of collaboration in the humanist cause . . . a faith in man which can be acceptable to Christians, in so far as it is open to God."[80] The TSPM regarded the policy of religious freedom "a reasonable one" but had no illusions about communism's atheistic views.[81] The TSPM therefore worked with the state on the "common ground" explained above for the sake of Christ and the benefit of the people.

Most of the resistance to the TSPM came from conservative preachers such as Wang Ming-dao and Watchman Nee, some underground house churches, and the Roman Catholic Church,[82] who reacted against the more "liberal" theology of the TSPM and its cooperation with the Communist Party.[83] Obviously, the Roman Catholic Church in China could not break its ties to Rome.[84]

Maoism and Antireligious Ideology

Maoism's attitude toward religion departed radically from the traditional Chinese attitude, which tended to enculturate (such as Buddhism, Nestorian Christianity) and be open to transcendence in the human world (such as Daoism, *yin-yang* philosophy). I suggested at the beginning of this chapter that the Maoist religious attitude may be similar to that of the Confucianist whose worldview is preoccupied with political affairs. But I also differentiate the areligious worldview of Confucius and the secular or antireligious worldview of Maoism, for a Maoist view of religions is influenced by Marx.

157

The Feuerbachian and Marxist Influences on Maoist Views of Religion

Religious freedom in Communist China is guaranteed only in article 88 of the 1954 constitution: "Citizens of the People's Republic of China enjoy freedom of religious belief."[85] The Chinese constitutional idea that religion must not become an exploiter of the people agrees with Marx's famous dictum that "religion is the opiate of the people."[86] According to the Marxist dogma, religion originated in primitive society as a way of dealing with the unexplainable forces of nature. But as society developed, religion became a tool of the upper class to exploit and control the lower class by taking "the minds of the exploited off their present condition of misery."[87]

Marx and Engels's communist understanding of religion was influenced by Ludwig Feuerbach's *Essence of Christianity:* "The idea of the species becomes the idea of God, who again is himself an individual being, but is distinguished from human individuals in this, that he possess their qualities according to the measure of the species."[88] Feuerbach viewed "religion in general, and Christianity in particular as a conceptual manifestation of man's projection of his own understanding, will and especially feelings."[89] Religion, according to Feuerbach, is a human projection of a pseudo self-realization because a human being projects and calls God whatever he or she cannot attain. Feuerbach explains: "The personality of God is thus the means by which man converts the qualities of his own nature into the qualities of another being— of a being external to himself."[90] In the socioeconomical realm, this religion is used by the oppressor on oppressed people to give them a false hope of a future world.[91] Thus Marx, following Feuerbach, viewed religion as a human protest against social alienation by offering imaginary, otherworldly consolation that would doom one's destiny.

The Chinese communist view of religion adapted Marx's and Feuerbach's ideas and concluded:

> Religion is a social ideology, "the fantastic reflection in men's minds of those external forces which control their daily life." . . . The fantastic interpretations by religion of natural phenomena, social phenomena, and especially of oppression and class exploitation, play the role of paralyzing the minds of the working people, and disintegrating their combat will.[92]

From 1959 to 1964 some Chinese communist theorists discussed the difference between organized religions (Daoism, Buddhism, Christianity) and feudal superstitions (ancestral cult, physiognomy, geomancy). Ya Han-chang distinguished the two groups, but Yu Hsian and

Liu Chun-wang argued that they are the same because they are not scientific. The government, for its part, explained that all these religions are oppressive:

> Before the liberation of the whole country, China's Catholicism and Protestantism were principally controlled by imperialism, and were tools of imperialism in the aggression against China. Buddhism, Islam and Daoism were principally controlled by domestic reactionary classes, used as tools for preservation of their reactionary rule.[93]

In theory, Chinese communism did not consider organized religions dangerous; only superstitious cults and socially destructive sects were to be eliminated. The government policy was to guarantee the freedom of organized religions such as Christianity—but only *if* that policy was practiced accordingly by factions of the government concerned, and *if* religious institutions or movements were not deemed a threat to the government. The "if" clauses were significant but were often subjected to different interpretations, and the choices were many in a land ruled by the law of personalities. There are examples of ultraleftists and, of course, the Gang of Four, who willfully disregarded the religious policy and persecuted Christians.

There was religious tolerance *if* the constitutional policy was observed. But the problem was that Christianity in rural China could also surface as a superstitious cult, similar to local gods and ghosts, preoccupied with miracles and healings. The eradication of these superstitious cults had been carried out by the government, not for religious (atheist or theistic) but for economic and social reasons. In other words, cults and religions did not contribute toward the reconstruction of Chinese society. Worse still, superstitions and cults caused social unrest, and believers spent too much time in religious activities that were not productive at all. Many gave their properties to these cults and wasted their resources in superstitious practices. Not all Christian churches in China functioned according to the dogma expounded in the biblical and theological orthodoxy of the Christian traditions.

Scientific and Materialistic Views of Religion

Even though both Christianity and science came from the West, communist China identified only Christianity as coming from the imperialist West; it saw science as the universal truth for the modernization of all nations. The anti-Christianity argument from the Chinese communists was thus adopted in the name of science. Science was used to discount all religions as the opiate of the masses, a hindrance to progress, and the tool of the oppressors. After 1949, under the regime of Mao, pastors and other Christians were harassed and placed under constant surveillance and suspicion. Many were persecuted, imprisoned, and even killed.[94] Many had to go through "accusation meetings," being suspected of "counterrevolutionary" activities. They were accused of subscribing to, and being brainwashed by, the unscientific foreign religion.[95]

The Christian life became even more oppressed during the Cultural Revolution, when all of China was in turmoil. In 1966, Mao approved the organization of the Red Guards; under this banner millions of teenagers indoctrinated with fanaticism ravaged the country and wrecked structures of orderly society, including religious institutions.[96] A correspondent describes what happened in Shanghai on August 24, 1966:

> On that day all the churches, active and inactive, whether conducted by their meager congregations or preserved by the Shanghai Municipal Bureau of Religious Cults, were stripped of the crosses, statues, icons, decorations and all church paraphernalia by the revolutionary students, wearing Red Guard armbands and determined to eradicate all traces of imperialist, colonial and feudal regimes.[97]

Again:

> Throughout the Guangxi region, the ranks of open believers were decimated by these early persecutions. In 1949 in the provincial capital of Guilin were four Protestant churches. . . . But as this wave of persecutions took its toll, attendance dwindled. Finally all churches were combined into one. . . . In 1966 that church was closed by the Red Guards of the Cultural Revolution. . . .[98]

Many churches installed a large white statue of Mao at the center. Posters such as the following, in front of the YMCA at Shanghai, became common:

> There is no God; there is no Spirit; there is no Jesus. . . . How can adults believe in these things. . . ? Protestantism is a reactionary feudal ideology, the opium of the people. . . . We are atheists; we believe only in Mao Tsutung. We call on all people to burn Bibles, destroy images, and disperse religious associations.[99]

On yet another poster in Shanghai, the Red Guards wrote: "Hang God!"

Between 1949 and 1954 the communist indoctrination was intense in all walks of life. It was used as a scientific means to heal the contamination of foreign religion in the mind of the Chinese people. "Self-examination" was meant to be introspection into one's emotions, thoughts, and actions for the purpose of remaking the inner person. Self-examination was thought to be the reform or remolding of thoughts.[100] Many people were required to write long papers, sometimes forced to write over and over again to satisfy the communist leaders.

Maoism believed that as the Chinese people's ideological consciousness increased, religions such as Christianity would gradually dwindle and their role in human society would decrease to zero. Along the same line, Mao's wife, Jiang Qing (1914–1991), declared during the Cultural Revolution that "Christianity in China has already been put into a museum. There are no more believers."[101] Jiang Qing's announcement of the death of religion and the total destruction of everything old, including religions, forced churches to close, with the exception of two in Beijing—for the diplomatic community. There was sporadic persecution, and in places such as Pingyang in Zhejiang province, the "model atheist district," all religious activities were eliminated.[102]

Utopianism and Eschatology

In the darkest moment of Chinese church history, Christians turned to utopianism, whether that of Maoism or Christianity. Here lies the central and ultimate agenda of this project: to research the eschatological worldview of Chinese communism and Chinese Christianity. Chinese Christians during Mao's regime should have clarified for the church and the society the possible fruitful interaction between Christian eschatology and Chinese utopian messianism. Unfortunately, little attention has been paid to the eschatological viewpoints of Maoism and Christianity. Why?

First, Christian scholars and biblical interpreters have often distorted the understanding of and have biases against biblical eschatology, especially apocalyptic eschatology. Few would consider early forms of Christianity as millenarian and apocalyptic movements. Even if scholars think they are, they think these movements should be critiqued rather than followed as models. Why? Some independent churches and fundamentalist groups in the Western world or in China maintained eschatology as God's schedule of judgment on and destruction of the world, thus making the entire doctrine a taboo in Christian proclamation and scholarship. Some Christians took the opposite extreme position of denying eschatology altogether.

Second, Chinese Christianity during Mao's era struggled with self-survival. They could not focus their energy on theologizing, since they were going through shock and suffering and did not have the luxury of sitting down and reflecting on Maoist utopianism as a distortion of Christian eschatology via Marxism. But their reflection on suffering had by itself a healing effect. Wallis writes:

> Hence the history of the church in China since 1949 has been a history of suffering. Yet by going through different stages of suffering, the church in China has been transformed from a timid, foreign-coloured institutional church into a bold, indigenous institutionless church, and it has been changed from a dependent mission church to an independent missionary church. It is a church that has gone through the steps of the cross, following the footsteps of her Lord: betrayal, trial, humiliation, abandonment, suffering, death, burial, resurrection, and the gift of Pentecost.[103]

Third, the notion of "evangelism" as defined by Chinese Christianity was limited to the saving of the souls of unbelievers for the kingdom of God. However, evangelism should include repentance in the sense of "turning around" one's worldview regarding history, God, and humanity. Thus Chinese Christians should have examined the "theology" of Mao's secular ideology and sought to help people to turn around to the theocentric, Christo-redemptive, and Spirit-permeating worldview.

Fourth, perhaps there was the intention to compare and contrast Mao's worldview to that of Christianity, but *the doctrine* the Chinese communists prohibited Christians from preaching and teaching was the doctrine of *eschatology:* "We must oppose sermons on supernatural things, especially subjects like 'the Last Judgment' in Catholicism and 'Jesus will come again' and 'Doomsday' in Protestantism. We must promote propaganda of world peace, patriotism, love of the people, and support for the realistic world."[104] Political pressure and government prohibitions ordered people to have nothing to do with eschatology.

Christians living in China are not to be blamed or accused for this. Indeed, Christians outside of China did not see the need to compare Maoist utopianism and biblical eschatology. Their appraisal of communist China did not assess the utopianism of Mao at all.[105] Moreover, too many Christian analyses of Chinese church history in Mao's era ignore the topic of eschatology.[106] Consequently, our next task is set.

6

mao meets paul I

Faith, Hope, and Love in the Chinese Church and the "Holy Empire" of the Christian West and Mao

Both Maoism and Christianity have utopian beliefs, but Maoism was repulsed by Christian theologies—especially its eschatology and Christology—because Maoism saw the Christian gospel as an otherworldly fantasy that was oppressive and exploitative. Mao saw Christianity as paralyzing "the minds of the working people, disintegrating their combative will."[1] I wonder whether Mao meant that Christianity did not make believers sufficiently violent. Indeed, the Maoist view of religion, informed by the Marxist and Feuerbachian dogma of religion, witnessed again and again the ungodliness and sins of the Christian West. Many missionaries were compatriots with their conquering nation's interests, and much imperialistic activity was carried out in the name of Christ.

Having examined the distortions of Maoism in the previous chapter, I will extend in this chapter the critical dialogue between Mao and Paul to include the Christian missionary movement and the Chinese Christians. After various encounters between Christian theology and Chinese culture, the Maoist sinification of Marxism further distorted Christian eschatology. Though sought after by Chinese patriots, Western science and democracy offered false hope in their aggression. Most Christian missionaries coming to China did not critique Western science and democracy by means of biblical apocalyptic eschatology. Worse still, many missionaries felt called to realize the Christian occupation of China. Amid all this, how could Chinese Christians begin to respond? If there is any sign of hope, they are the last remnants of God's witness in China.

The Maoist Critique of Missionary Ungodliness and the Sins of the Christian West

Missionary Guilt and Christian Sin: Where Is Hope and Who Is God?

Pauline theology in 1 and 2 Thessalonians was intended to critique the social-political realities of the dominant culture. Paul's eschatology was a harsh critique of the complacency and overconfidence of the Thessalonian *ataktoi*. His eschatological gospel was an ideological critique of the emperor cult as Christians proclaimed the new Lord and opposed the decree of Caesar. Paul's message of the imminent *parousia* and the lordship of Christ, as well as his reinterpretation of the grace and benefaction of Jesus, threatened the *pax Romana* and the benefactor Rome. However, the Christian West and the nineteenth- and twentieth-century missionaries to China behaved as the dominant and superior Roman Empire had.

Certainly the most missionary-minded apostle of Christianity was Paul, whose ambition to evangelize the world for the sake of Christ became the paradigm and blueprint for Christians to be passionate about bringing all to Christ at any cost. Unfortunately, the tragic scenarios of the Christian movement in modern Chinese history were not simply religious, because the Christian movement was also a political movement with various cultural and national interests and denominational obligations. The most tragic flaw of the Christian missionary movement was its arrogance and its identification with the dominant Western culture, which preyed on and intoxicated China. The West not only failed to help eliminate or alleviate China's problems; it took on the posture of imperialists in stigmatizing China as the "sick man of the Far East."

While many missionaries were apolitical, wrongly accused, and ill treated by the Chinese, their divisiveness and their unwillingness to help made them look exactly like their compatriots. Mao was right in considering Christian missionary work in China to be a form of cultural aggression from the West. Christian missionaries were guilty in a series of events during the nineteenth century when they stood with the imperialist Western powers to rob and rape China in its weakness. The religious views of Mao were both directly and indirectly shaped by four historical forces and events: (1) missionaries and the unjust Opium Wars; (2) the psychotic gospel of the Taiping Rebellion; (3) the Boxer Rebellion; and (4) Chiang Kai-shek's Christian bias.

Missionaries and the Unjust Opium Wars

While opium has been commonly used in every culture throughout the centuries as both a legal medicine and an illegal euphoric substance, during the Opium Wars the Western powers were guilty of poisoning the soul of China for the sake of silver and gold.[2] A Protestant missionary, Hudson Taylor (1832–1905), wrote from Shantou (Swatow) in 1856:

> Not less than 32,000 pounds of opium enter China every month at this port alone, the cost of which is about a quarter of a million sterling. After this you will not be surprised to learn that the people are wretchedly poor, ignorant and vicious. . . . The people have no love for foreigners.[3]

It was difficult for the Chinese to love the "foreign devils" because foreign traders and missionaries were seen by Chinese as having one pact: both the trading and missionary activities were done under the same powerful East India Trading Company.

China resisted the opium trade for a number of years, but it was too weak to stand against the military power of the West during the series of wars that followed.[4] The result of the First Opium War (1838–1842) was that England annexed Hong Kong in the Nanjing Treaty (August 29, 1842). The German missionary K. E. A. Gutzlaff, appointed as a Chinese Secretary in the British Department of Trade, took part in the drafting of the treaty, thus signaling to the Chinese that Western power and Christianity were one and the same.[5] The Nanjing Treaty demanded that China pay for the confiscated opium and the cost of the war—a total of $21 million. The treaty gave the British extraterritorial rights to reside in the treaty ports; that is, they were not subject to Chinese law and trial. In 1844, China was forced to sign a supplementary treaty at Wangxia, which demanded that China provide immunity from the death sentence to British missionaries. American missionaries Elijah C. Bridgeman[6] and Peter Parker participated in drafting the Wangxia Treaty (1844). In the same year, the French signed a treaty at Whampao demanding the right of the French to establish churches, hospitals, hospices, schools, and cemeteries in China.

The Second Opium War (1856–1860), sometimes called the "Lorcha War," with England and France was ignited in 1856 when Father Auguste Chapdelaine of France was murdered in Guangxi. France protested according to the 1844 Treaty of Whampao, and Britain was informed

165

of the incident, though no serious fighting began at that point. That same year, Chinese sailors on the *Arrow*, a British ship owned by a Chinese settler in Hong Kong, were arrested by Chinese officers. The British immediately intervened and bombed the city wall of Guangzhou. In retaliation for the Chapdelaine incident, France also joined in the attack, but China refused to capitulate or sign a peace treaty. Eventually England captured Guangzhou in 1858, and six months later China was forced to sign the Tianjin Treaty (1858) with Britain and France. China was partitioned by the following countries: Sakhalin was annexed by Russia, Vietnam by France, the Ryuku Islands by Japan, Burma by England, and Kiaochow by Germany. American missionary S. W. Williams participated in the drafting of the Tianjin Treaty. Up to that time, China had refused to legalize the opium trade, but in 1858 England succeeded in forcing China to make opium trade legal.

The treaties signed by China contained some insulting clauses. For example, the thirteenth article of the Treaty of Tianjin (1858) states:

> The Christian religion having as its essential purpose the leading of men to virtue, the members of all the Christian communions shall enjoy entire security in regard to their persons, their property and the free exercise of their religious practices. . . . No hindrance shall be put in the way, by the authorities of the Chinese empire, of the acknowledged right of any person in China to embrace Christianity if he wishes and to practise its tenets, without being liable to any penalty imposed for so doing. Everything which has been previously written, proclaimed or published in China by order of the government against the Christian religion is completely abrogated and is a dead letter in all the provinces of China.[7]

The Chinese emperor was humiliated and furious; he ordered the plenipotentiaries to fire the representatives of the treaty. Still the situation grew worse and worse. The following year the British were determined to capture Beijing. They did so in October 1860 and burnt the old Summer Palace to ashes. The French also vandalized the city. China was forced to sign a series of unequal treaties (1858–1900) with Britain and France that imposed various unfair terms: additional ports in China were given for trade; foreigners were given privileges to travel throughout China and the right to reside in certain cities without being subject to local laws; and China was to pay an indemnity to cover British and French losses in the war. The treaties also granted religious toleration and the protection of foreign missionaries to enter the interior of China. The so-called Convention of Beijing signed in 1860 demanded that the Chinese government restore all religious and charitable institutions confiscated from the Christians since the decree of Emperor Daoguang (1782–1850) on March 20, 1846.[8]

For the twenty years of the Opium Wars, Western traders, politicians, and missionaries found a secure place in China to exercise their interests and callings. But the God of the missionaries was neither the crucified Messiah nor the Coming One. The living witness of the Christian West in the Opium Wars showed that God was the Colonizer, the Imperialist, the Drug-Seller! And the Christian hope was to be found in the spiritual Christ, expressed in the concreteness of opium. Christian hope was to be found in total submission to the Christian aggressors.

While it is unfair to blame the missionaries for everything, one can indict them for not being engaged in critical theology as they interacted with Chinese cultural problems. Perhaps the backwardness of China at the time did not warrant such a need. But as preachers of truth and love and justice, their lack of interest in the relationship between theology and culture resulted in the hegemonic and unreflective dogmatism of the missionary gospel. Missionaries were concerned with their privileges and their safety in treaty ports and in remote places in China, and they were unconcerned with the injustice of the unequal treaties. Missionaries were concerned with getting on board opium-trading ships and were unconcerned with the social redemption of China from such toxicity. Missionaries were concerned with saving souls and unconcerned with saving bodies. Missionaries were concerned with being Christian to the point of prohibiting Christians from being Chinese. In short, missionaries were concerned with "pure" truth only and unconcerned with incarnate truth. Most missionaries of the nineteenth century therefore created a virtual reality akin to that created by opium consumption.

The Psychotic Gospel of the Taiping Rebellion

The Taiping Rebellion (1850–1864) was an anti-Manchu nationalistic movement combined with Christian fanatical apocalypticism; its leader was Hong Xiuquan (1813–1864). Having failed the state examination for a government job several times and eventually suffering from mental depression, Hong obtained a copy of Liang Fa's gospel tract, *Good Words to Admonish the Age*[9] and was converted to Christianity in 1837. In his experience of mental collapse, he began to see apocalyptic visions of himself as the messiah of China and the world. He believed himself chosen to be "God's Chinese Son,"[10] called to exorcise the Manchu demon from China and to lead the elect Chinese to God's kingdom on earth.

Hong's apocalyptic theology derived its insight from the Bible. For example, commenting on Genesis, Hong proclaimed himself to be the Light: "The Father is Light, the Brother (Christ) is Light; the Lord (Hong Xiuquan) is Light."[11] Likewise, Hong's commentary on Matthew 4:16 explains:

> God is fire; the Sun is also fire. Thus God and the Sun (i.e., Hong) have both come to us. God is the Holy Ghost and has come together with the Holy Spirit (i.e., the Eastern King) to us. Thus the Holy Ghost descended on the Pentecost and the fire and wind appeared. Fire and wind both come from God, the source of all things. God is fire, so there was the Divine Light. The Great Elder Brother is fire, so he is the Great Light. I Myself am the sun, so I am also the Light.[12]

Thus, in Hong's view, Christ was the heavenly Elder Brother and Hong the heavenly Younger Brother. Hong "was not satisfied with a brotherhood of grace, he would claim a brotherhood of nature with Christ."[13]

After his conversion, Hong and his friend Feng Yunshan began not only to preach in the Guangxi province in 1847 but also to organize a rebellion. Hong returned to Guangzhou and received biblical training from an American Baptist missionary, Issachar J. Roberts (1802–1871). Hong believed that Chinese Christians were militant agents of God commissioned to usher in God's kingdom on earth and a millenarian peace in China but that before the arrival of peace and victory, the world would be caught in tribulation and crisis. The famine of 1849–1850 seemed to confirm Hong's prophecy. Probably Liang Fa's gospel tract also influenced Hong to envision the wickedness of this world and the apocalyptic redemption that was imminent after the last age of tribulation. But Hong's teaching anticipating universal peace, the practice of equality in land ownership, and training in purity attracted thousands and thousands of followers.

By 1850 this religious-political movement successfully rebelled in the Hunan, Hebei, Jiangxi, and Anhui provinces. On September 25, 1851, Hong named his indigenous Chinese utopian group Taiping Tianguo. Hong led his group and defeated the Ching government forces. The revolt then spread to the central regions of China. By February 1853, Nanjing was taken and designated the Heavenly Capital (tianjing; Hong identified Nanjing with the new Jerusalem in Rev. 3:12), where Hong resided as the Heavenly King (tianwang).

Both imperial China and the Western nations were stunned by the rebellion. The Italian bishop Aloysius Mocagatta, in collaboration with the Ching government, organized armed troops in Shandong to attack the Taiping Heavenly Army in 1861. Finally, on June 1, 1864, Hong committed suicide by taking poison while Nanjing was being besieged by Western allies and Chinese troops under Zeng Guofan and Major Charles Gordon.[14] It is estimated that twenty million people were killed during the rebellion in Nanjing, Yangzhou, and Xinjiang—twice the number killed in World War I.[15] Among the twenty million were thousands upon thousands of Taiping followers.

Even if one acknowledges that biblical eschatology is an explosive doctrine re-expressed in various forms of religious violence, there is no reasonable explanation for the mindset of the Taiping movement except that China's soul was weak and intoxicated with opium, be it a euphoric drug or religious excitement. The later Chinese communist and Maoist equation of religion with opium was a result of their painful analysis of Chinese history. In the midst of the rebellion, Karl Marx wrote to the *New York Daily Tribune* (June 14, 1853) giving a sharp social analysis of the China situation:

> Just as the Emperor was wont to be considered the father of all China, so his officers were looked upon as sustaining the paternal relation to their respective districts. But this patriarchal authority, the only moral link embracing the vast machinery of the State, has gradually been corroded by the corruption of those officers, who have made great gains by conniving at opium smuggling. This has occurred principally in the same Southern provinces where the [Taiping] rebellion commenced. . . . It would seem as though history had first to make this whole people drunk before it could rouse them out of their hereditary stupidity.[16]

The missionaries' silence and neutral position with regard to the opium trade rendered their preaching insensitive to China's problems; the gospel of Christ could only save the "souls" of Chinese but not address the political and national problems. This uncritical cultural spirit may have sent confused and psychotic Chinese Christians into a bizarre apocalyptic vision for China. Here we see how biblical apocalyptic eschatology was distorted into an extreme form. The Taiping Rebellion shows that Christian apocalyptic theology led not to a hermeneutics of meaningful history, a purposeful goal of life, or a hopeful awareness of divine grace. Instead, it resulted in a pseudo-divine justification of utopia by means of violence, a *parousia* of chaos and destruction supported by the citation of biblical proof texts, a deception of self as messiah, and a collapse of time into the space of a personality cult (Hong). It was an example of how Pauline eschatology could be misused and misinterpreted.

169

The Boxer Rebellion

The year Mao was born (1895), China was defeated in the Sino-Japanese War (1894–1895). As a result of the war, China was forced to accept the independence of Korea and was forced to cede Taiwan (Formosa) to Japan. Kang Youwei (1858–1927), a Confucian humanist, staged the One Hundred Days Reform (June to September 1898) to help the young emperor Guangxu reform China, but the Dowager Empress executed six reformers in September 1898, ending Kang's effort. Foreign powers (British, German, French, American) stood ready to annex pieces of China as the empire was dying.

When two Catholic German missionaries were murdered by robbers in Kiachwang in southwest Shandong in 1897, Germany immediately annexed Kiaochow Bay and demanded sole railway, mining, and trading rights in Shandong. In the following year, Russia snatched Port Arthur, France took the Bay of Guangzhou, and England acquired Weihaiwei and Kowloon.[17] Outraged by the international banditry and the dying Manchu dynasty, the Chinese thought seriously of national salvation from the "foreign devils" who preached Christianity and from the Manchus who had dominated China for hundreds of years.

Although the Empress Dowager had resisted the reform efforts of Kang Youwei, she supported the aims of some of the reform societies springing up everywhere in the empire, among them the Boxer Rebellion (Yi He Tuan Revolution or Fists of Righteous Harmony, 1898–1900) and the Da Dao Hui (Great Sword Society). Both forged campaigns against foreign powers. Whyte traced the Boxers' influence to the anti-Christian White Lotus (Buddhist) traditions:

> Without doubt White Lotus traditions lay behind the movement and it was not in the first instance pro-Ching [Qing], for the White Lotus were loyal to the previous Ming dynasty. It was in fact made up of several unco-ordinated groupings united by a common hatred of foreigners and foreign teachings. The primary targets were Christian missionaries ("Primary Hairy Men"), Chinese Christians ("Secondary Hairy Men") and those who used foreign goods ("Tertiary Hairy Men"). "Hairy Men" were all to be killed.[18]

The governor of Shandong, Yu Xian, called for the Chinese to "support the Ching and exterminate the foreigners." The Empress pledged her support to the Boxers.

Western powers intervened after the December 1899 murder of Mr. Books, an Anglican missionary, in Shantung, where the nationalist movements had started. In retaliation, the Germans burned down two villages, and in January 1900 the American, British, French, German, and Italian governments asked Beijing to suppress the Boxers and the Great Sword members. By February 1900, the Boxers had an army of eight thousand. In the midst of turmoil and chaos, 186 missionaries and innumerable Chinese Christians were killed and their churches burned, especially those in Beijing, but also in Tianjin.[19] In June 1900, thousands of Chinese Christians were massacred throughout northern China, Inner Mongolia, and Manchuria. A few days later the empress issued a decree to kill all foreigners.

Finally, Frederick Brown, an American Methodist missionary, led eight allied forces from Tianjin to Beijing to suppress the Boxer Rebellion. British missionary Timothy Richard and American missionary W. A. P. Martin took part in drafting the Peace Protocol of September 7, 1901, in which an indemnity was paid to victims in the revolution: the total payment equaled almost half of the Qing government's annual budget. The China Inland Mission and her missionaries refused to receive the indemnity because of their good faith in Christ. Timothy Richard suggested to the United States government that indemnity payments from the Qing government be spent in developing culture and education in China under the control of American missionaries (1908).

Many Westerners used the name of Christianity to conquer, and many Christian missionaries preached Western culture as the Christian gospel. The most vivid sociopolitical group to revolt against Christianity was the Boxers, who blamed the decline of Ching on the Christian West. Here we touch on the most difficult query in this book: Can the metanarrative of Christianity be the universal redemptive history for all nations? And how can it be so without being imperialistic? I must admit that I do not have a ready answer; consequently, I offer only suggestive answers, turning to resources outside the Thessalonian correspondence.

There was no doubt in Paul's mind that the grand narrative of Christ is the only end of history, yet this grand narrative is not imperialistic for at least three reasons. First, Paul recognized the crucified Christ (Gal. 2:20; 3:1; 5:24; 6:14; 1 Thess. 2:15) as the inclusive symbol without hegemonic connotations because the paradigm of Christ deconstructed his own (sacred) Jewish culture and portrayed the shortcomings of any culture, no matter how sacred it might be. This paradigm also confirms the hope that cultures can be transformed and renewed only through their self-surrender, self-critique, and crucifixion. Christ's crucifixion presents to humans their fear and insecurity even as they boost their egos and hold tight to their cultures as absolutes. They put their trust in culture rather than in God. Paul's Damascus experience (cf. Gal. 1:13–17) enlightened him that the Messiah had been crucified to include Gentiles among the people of God.

171

Second, Paul was also convinced that the coming God had included all—Jews and Gentiles, civilized and barbaric—peoples into his eschatological salvation. This is the eschatological age that is marked by the divine economy of Christ's faithfulness as believers are adopted into the family of God. In fulfillment of the "works of the law," valid for the Jewish elect of God, Gentiles were included in the people of God when they received the blessings of Abraham in the crucified Messiah and thus received God's Spirit in the eschatological age. Since the Abrahamic covenant is derivative of Christ's faith, Abraham's sons are those who are related to Christ's faith.

Third, Paul's exhortations in 1 Thessalonians 5:19–22 have a common denominator of community living in the eschatological Spirit, thus affirming the transcendental critique of human actions and calling for openness to divine truth. The pneumatic activities are signs of the eschatological times. Paul wished the community neither to be ignorant of the power of the Holy Spirit nor to be overzealous in pneumatic excessiveness. Applied to Christian missions, the first injunction of "not quenching the Spirit" (5:19) suggests trusting in "the role of the Spirit as a guarantor of God's final salvation."[20] Hegemony is not produced by adhering to one grand narrative; it is a result of overconfidence without discerning the ways of God's Spirit. The next injunction, "do not despise prophecy" (5:20), is an admonition to let the word of God continue to speak forth, shaping, directing, and strengthening the community. Prophecy is a sign of the inauguration of the new age of Christ, the millennium of bliss. Just like the Thessalonian case, in which prophecy was trashed, those who reject the grand narrative of Christ will turn either to anarchism or tribalism, chaos or despotism. Without the prophecy of the Spirit, people will live in alienation and darkness. Suppression of the Spirit-inspired activities will result in great loneliness and loss. The Spirit of God re-presents the divine transcendence, and the role of the Spirit unveils the intention of the divine mystery. Paul's third injunction of "testing of all things" (5:21) is a necessary counterpart to the reception of the Spirit, in order that good might be upheld. Thus, missionaries' spiritual gifts can be abused, but Paul is unhelpful here because he does not spell out the testing criteria.

Chiang Kai-shek's Christian Bias

By the early twentieth century, Chinese intellectuals were experiencing an increasing awakening of national salvation. Though influenced by Western ideas and concerned with the national salvation of China, the revolutionary ideas eventually split into two groups: the Sun

Yat-sen group, which was informed by Western Christian modernism; and the Mao Zedong group, informed by European socialism and Russian Marxism. Unfortunately, in the immediate aftermath of Sun's death in 1925, China was again immersed in civil war between the Kuomingtan (KMT, Nationalist Party) under Chiang Kai-shek and the communists under Mao (CCP). Between 1925 and 1949, China observed both Christian (Chiang) and anti-Christian (Mao) sentiments as the two parties struggled for dominance.

Because of the government's antagonistic attitudes toward missionaries, the number of Christian missionaries in China dropped drastically in the 1920s: from six thousand missionaries in 1920 to five hundred in 1926. Chinese Christians were called "running dogs of the imperialists,"[21] but missionaries called communist units "bandits."[22] The year 1927 marked the end of the first united front, in which the CCP and KMT were able to work hand in hand to bring about political and economic changes in China.[23] But by 1927 Chiang Kai-shek successfully led the Northern Expedition and controlled major cities and urban areas. In April 1927, the KMT killed a fairly large number of communists and their supporters in Shanghai.

Between 1927 and 1937, Chiang Kai-shek was able to rule China with the KMT based in Nanjing. Chiang's political philosophy drew on the Confucian socialism of order and discipline, European fascism, and liberal Methodism. Chiang Kai-shek was baptized on October 22, 1930, as a Methodist, based on his Christian confession (his funeral in 1976 in Taiwan was held in a church). From 1927 to 1934 there was relative peace, revival, and economic growth in Chinese society. But history soon witnessed a reversal of fate for Christian Chiang and atheist Mao in their control of China.

While Chiang triumphed over the CCP in 1927 and focused his energy on urban rebuilding and elitist investment, the defeated communists retreated to the countryside and focused on the agrarian revolution (e.g., Mao's peasantry uprising in Hunan in 1927). Chiang's vision of the urban rebuilding was typical of his contemporaries' Christian vision, for 66 percent of the missionaries and 34 percent of the Christians lived in 176 cities all over China; 71 percent of Christians lived on the east coast alone.[24] Yet more than 90 percent of China's population lived in the rural areas.

In 1929 growing communist groups moved to the Jianxi-Fujian border. Because of the CCP's antireligious policy, Christians were killed and churches in those areas were sacked and destroyed. While Chiang's forces did not counterattack the CCP on religious grounds, Chiang's determination to exterminate the communists in a series of encirclement campaigns did attract the attention of Protestant missionaries. The three campaigns of annihilation against the communists (November 1930–July 1931) could not penetrate the communist base in Jiangxi. The fourth (June 1932) and the fifth (October 1933) encirclement campaigns forced Mao to take the Long March (October 1934–1935) westward. Then Chiang's government turned to Protestant Christians for help.

As early as the summer of 1932, a group of American Protestant missionaries met in Jiangxi to curb the problems posed by the "communist bandits" in China. The group met again the following year. Because of his connections with Madame Chiang, William Johnson of the Protestant missionaries was invited to set up the National Christian Conference for the purpose of social reforms.[25] Protestant missionaries helped the government in various educational and famine relief programs. But the rural programs were ineffective under these "urban tribes" (Nationalists), partly because of the Protestant priority on evangelism rather than social service. Another reason was the popularity and success of the communists with peasants.

In 1934, Chiang founded the New Life Movement to restore traditional Confucian and Boy Scout values and to promote Christian regeneration in China. The movement gained the attention of Christian groups, who also used the name "new life" to promote new life in Christ. But the mix and match of these ideological concepts proved only superficially helpful to China; the New Life Movement was rejected by serious scholars, Christian and non-Christian alike. Mr. and Mrs. Chiang did meet with Christian groups at times.[26] Other than that, Christian theology did not play a key role in Chiang's political life, though Chiang's identity with Christianity was often perceived by the common people as antisocialism. Meanwhile, more and more of the intelligentsia turned to Marxism as a source of hope for China.

Raymond de Jaeghei, a Belgian missionary, directed the Catholic Youth Patriotic Association (Gongjiao Qingnian Baoguo Tuan) to work with the KMT army and helped them bomb Pingshan in the Hebei province in 1948, an incident in which 130 people died. That same year, reactionary clergymen Li Zhiren and Cao Lishan in Beijing and Tianjing enlisted 1,200 people for the KMT. But by then a majority of the peasants and scholars supported the CCP. Soon the communists occupied Beijing (by January 1949) and Nanjing (April 1949). By then it was clear that the KMT did not have the support of the Chinese people. The civil war (1945–1949) ended with the establishment of the People's Republic of China in October 1949, and Chiang and the KMT fled to Taiwan in November.

Bishop K. H. Ting recounts the history of Christians robbing the glory of God during Chiang's regime:

Why do Chinese revolutionaries reject the God of the Christians? Because many Christians all over the world stood on the side of Chiang Kai-shek, the enemy of the Chinese people; and because in 1949, when the People's Liberation Army was about to cross the Changjiang (Yangzi) River in pursuit of Chiang Kai-shek forces, some missionaries and their Chinese colleagues led Christians in praying that the soldiers of the People's Liberation Army would drown in the river. That was certainly a very political, reactionary and brutal prayer. There was a leader of a certain Christian sect who, several weeks after the liberation of Shanghai in 1949, gave signals to bombers sent by Chiang Kai-shek to bomb the city.[27]

The relationship between Christianity and anticommunist biases found its twists and turns in both politics and the missionary movement in China. Many missionaries intentionally wanted to preach the gospel of Jesus Christ in China, but this did not mean that they were not without their political commitments. They held to democracy against communism. Christians aligned with Mr. and Mrs. Chiang sought to use Christian values to reform and save China, but they were walking a tightrope of being understood as fulfilling the political agenda of the imperialists—the Westernization and Christianization of China. Missionary works and Christian activities could easily be misunderstood as "the Christian occupation of China," which was exactly the title of a book the China Continuation Committee published in 1922.[28] The subtitle also portrays a political consciousness of the missionary ambitions: "A general survey of the numerical strength and geographical distribution of the Christian forces in China." While Chiang's government had a Christian identity, its political bias undoubtedly would have been to allow Christian forces to occupy China.

The biases of Chiang's government and the Christian missionaries may have found their Christian precedence in the militarism and triumphalism of the Judeo-Christian traditions, such as the "Lord of hosts" tradition in the Old Testament, the zealotry of the Maccabees in the intertestamental period, Jesus' Jewish friends hailing him as the "King of the Jews" in early Christianity, the triumphalism of the bishop-emperor Constantine, and the conquest of the Crusaders. In the Thessalonian correspondence, however, even though political critique was part of Paul's theological motif, there is no indication at all that the Thessalonian Christians were called to topple the Roman government or to put up any military resistance. Instead, they were taught to live in imitation of Christ and Paul, accepting the inevitability of suffering (1 Thess. 3:3), bearing witness to their oppressors, and loving fellow believers and non-Christians neighbors alike (5:13).

The tragic consequence of Christian leaders siding with the Chiang faction was spelled out by K. H. Ting:

> He was defended on the ground that being a regenerated man, he could not sin, even when committing acts that in themselves were evil, since he was no longer under law. Justification by faith becomes lawlessness. If you profess faith in Christ, everything is permitted. This is antinomianism. It describes a God who permits Christians and the "Christian Nations" to do anything they please.[29]

Might not the fear of "justification by faith [becoming] lawlessness" be the reason for Paul's silence on Christian military resistance against Rome? In the book of Romans, Paul taught that any governmental authority is delegated by God; thus government is under God and submission to governmental authority is an act of faith in God. But by no means have all governments acted according to God's will. That was why one government might be replaced by another and, more important, why all governments are eventually accountable to God. Without the view of eschatology, the actions of governments are unaccounted for. Eschatology is judgment (2 Thess. 1:5–10) and redemption (1 Thess. 1:10; 5:9; 2 Thess. 1:5); it calls all actions into accountability, including those of God, whose intention for history is redemption.

In the Thessalonian correspondence, Paul did not teach the Thessalonians to be "Christian forces" and to have a "Christian occupation" of Thessalonica. Rather, in 1 Thessalonians 5:8 Paul admonishes Christians to "put on faith and love as a breastplate, and the hope of salvation as a helmet." The military imagery, however, does not suggest a military revolt; in fact, the military terms used here are defensive. Christians were encouraged to live their witness of faith, hope, and love despite the political oppression. They were "to live lives worthy of God, who calls them into his kingdom and glory" (2:12). The "kingdom" language does not refer to national or political occupation of a government. Rather, it speaks of God's rule of faith, hope, and love among those who trust him.

Pauline theology does not prohibit Christian involvement in politics; otherwise, to be a Christian would be to assume a politically passive role. Paul's theology cautions Christians not to use the name of God to justify one's political stance, such as in thinking that democracy is the divine economy and that communism is satanic. Paul's benefaction theology calls the Thessalonian Christians to critique the ideological deception of the Roman cult, but as Christians and Roman citizens they are responsible to be benefactors to the faithful community and the larger society. Thus 1 Thessalonians 5:15 says: "Always seek to do good to one another *and to all*."

The Pauline Theology of Faith, Hope, and Love Relived by Chinese Christians in Red China

In this section about the critical interaction between Paulinism and Maoism, it is proper to observe how the Chinese Christians living under Mao's regime lived out the Pauline theology of faith, hope, and love. The enduring question is: Is it possible to be a Christian and yet be submissive to Maoist ideology? The question might be rephrased as: How can one be a Christian in a communist state?

Christian Fear of Communism and the "Socialist Religion"

The first question reveals the fear of many Westerners and overseas Chinese, who often dualistically contrast Christianity and communism to the extreme.[30] C. K. Yang in the early 1960s, for example, perceived communism and Christianity not to be mutually tolerant but conflicting faith bodies "because of the nature of Communist faith and its interpretation of religion." He wrote: "The absolute certitude of its own historical destiny and the centralist nature of its organization ('democratic centralism,' 'democratic dictatorship') prevents any genuine tolerance of theistic religions."[31] Fred Schwartz likewise believes that Christianity and communism are incompatible:

> Communism without atheism is cancer without malignancy, a contradiction in terms. Either the one or the other is true. They can't both be true. The Christian can find no place in his thinking for the militant atheism of Marx and Mao, and Communism can find no place in its materialism for idealism—the supremacy of ideas—or the conception of a Supreme Mind, the truth of God the Creator. Even to contemplate the possibility of becoming a practising Communist while remaining a convinced Christian requires either the most utter self-deception or the most abysmal ignorance both of Christianity and of Communism.[32]

Because of the critical posture I have taken, the present work may give the impression that it is hostile to Maoism. Indeed, I have shown the wide range of differences that exist between Paulinism and Maoism on an intellectual level. Yet the narrative section concerning the TSPM (chapter 5) and the critique of the missionary movements (chapter 6) have indicated possible fruitful consequences of a critical dialogue between Paul and Mao, between Chinese Christians and a communist government, especially under the conditions of hoping to make the best of the limited choice the Chinese Christians had. Chinese Christians believed that Christian socialism was an attainable reality and in fact had been one of the visions of the Christian tradition.[33] Unlike Westerners or overseas Chinese, who have greater freedom of expression and whose views of communism are inconsequential, Chinese Christians must overcome their phobia of communism and work with the Chinese government as a "dialogue partner" in the matter of the reconstruction of Chinese society.

Many have misunderstood the way Chinese Christians dealt with communism in New China. For example, Lyall calls the Christian manifestos "Christian betrayal" without understanding the complex sociopolitical context of New China.[34] Gao Wangzhi argues that Y. T. Wu's proposal of Chinese Christianity as a "socialist religion" was naive and that Wu failed to safeguard the Chinese church when he stated he felt no "anxiety about the future of Christianity [in China]. The Communist Party does not believe in religion, but it protects religion and respects religious faith."[35] Wu's overreliance on the communist government to motivate the mission of the Christian church was indeed naive. But his proposal of a socialist religion motivated the TSPM to think critically of the identity and mission of Chinese Christianity and to call Chinese Christians to be patriotic benefactors in Chinese society.

Any discussion concerning "socialist religion" ought to be held on the same ground as our discussion of whether a "capitalist Christianity" is a better option and provides a more biblical understanding of Christianity. Might not the position of "capitalist Christianity" be a secular view and therefore culturally biased? Lyall tends to criticize China from an American perspective (individual freedom, human rights, religion, etc.) when he identifies communism as the ancient serpent who is the reincarnation of the devil and Satan.[36] Such a view seeks to erase all the contributions made by communism in China, which include decreasing the education illiteracy rate from 90 percent in 1949 to under 30 percent in 1978; improving health care, transportation, communication, and the status of women; and abolishing and condemning sexual immorality, drug traffic, banditry, prostitution, gambling, pornography, child marriage, polygamy, and concubinage.[37]

My appraisal of Chinese Christians and the TSPM is positive and commendatory. Given the communist framework, the complexity of the sociopolitical context, and the revolutions and deprivations that surrounded the church, their task was difficult, to say the least. Chinese Christians were living out their faith and seeking to bring about transformations in themselves and in the society. Those of us outside a totalitarian state where freedom abounds tend to contrast democracy and communism and see things only in black and white terms, but in a communist state Christians have a wider range of perspectives about atheism. For example, K. H. Ting, in his essay "A Chinese Christian's View of the Atheist" (delivered in Vancouver, November 1979),[38] divides atheists into three categories: (1) unscrupulous atheists, who are morally bankrupt, such as King Herod; (2) honest atheists, who find it impossible to believe in God seriously because of the injustice, alienation, and evil around them; and (3) revolutionary humanist atheists, who protest and reject God because they were told that God is the defender of the oppressor.[39] While this categorization may sound like a sympathetic defense of the communists, the Chinese church and political history reveal again and again how Christians demonstrated the "evils" of this Christian God who empowered the imperialists, sided with the Nationalists against the communists, and forced China to become opium addicts, the "sick man of the Far East." Missionaries and Western powers have caused horrendous aggression against China and have confused and distorted the identity of Christianity.[40]

In the end, neither demonizing nor Christianizing communism is helpful. The Christianizing approach is evident in the words of Joseph Needham, a Christian Marxist:

> [T]he China which broke the hearts of the missionaries has accepted the Spirit of Christ from another source, namely Marxism. . . . If the Chinese have indeed created a society with more faith, more hope and more love than the "Christian" West, they deserve not only attention but allegiance. As apostles of Christ we must follow where the spirit flows.[41]

An alternative approach is to think theologically about how God acts through history. The response of K. H. Ting in "New Initiatives" (1957) is apt: "Many Chinese Christians see the liberation of their country by the People's Liberation Army, and the new socialist order itself, not as God's punishment or judgment, but as an act of God, showing God's love for China."[42] Ting proposed an innovative view of evangelism to a revolutionary atheist:

> Should we not try to get inside the mind of the revolutionary humanists; recognize the honesty of their search; appreciate the depth of their reservations and fear about the social consequences of much of our preaching about God; tell them that we are almost as atheistic as they are when it comes to the kind of God that they reject; and join with them in the quest for a social system in which love would be made available to the masses of people? In so doing, we shall not be giving up our faith in God, but pre-

179

senting ourselves as evangelists to the revolutionaries, thereby making progress in our own spiritual pilgrimage.[43]

The challenge of the Chinese Christians was to be the bearers of the holy and to offer a redemptive interpretation of Chinese history.[44] After all, the Pauline eschatological view of history believes that we are living in the "already and the not-yet"; thus no interpretation of history is absolute. Listening to other voices, no matter how conflicting they may be, is a redemptive and reinterpretive process that will work toward the greater unity (harmony, *datong*) of God's *telos* in history, namely, the consummated salvation of humanity and the world.

Chinese Christians As Bearers of the Holy to the "Revolutionary Atheists"

As Chinese Christians in New China began to reflect seriously on the relationship between God's creative work and God's redemptive work,[45] they understood that the gospel of Christ not only is concerned with the reconciliation of people to God but also has a mission for the state and society. After years of breaking off all relations with imperialism and gradually learning to rule, to support, and to propagate, the Chinese Christian church has come to recognize that China's government leadership is sincere in its policy of freedom of religious belief and its willingness to help the church in difficulties it may meet. It has also come to recognize that to participate in the government is one way to bear witness for the Lord.[46] Bishop K. H. Ting, for example, has observed that Christians must learn to live with atheists in New China, not being seduced by them but learning how to present the gospel to them.[47] In his article "A Call for Clarity: Fourteen Points from Christians in the People's Republic of China to Christians Abroad," K. H. Ting affirms the positive attitude the TSPM has toward the New China. His point is that the Chinese Christians' patriotism is "not without a prophetic and critical character."

The Christian Manifesto was correct in condemning the missionaries as "imperialistic" and in noting that Christianity "consciously or unconsciously, directly or indirectly, became related with imperialism."[48] Because the cult of Mao viewed religion, especially Christianity, as a deceptive, foreign imperialistic and ideological tool for the exploitation of the common people, all Christian missionary work and Christian activity were associated directly or indirectly with foreign cultural aggression.

180

In a situation that was less than ideal, for example, in the political struggles of the communists during the Cultural Revolution, Chinese Christians and Chinese people were caught in between the rightist and the ultraleftist campaigns. Chinese Christians suffered greatly with the people. It is a living testimony that during the ten catastrophic years of the Cultural Revolution, when all the churches were closed, many congregations attempted to meet in house settings or underground. These "underground" churches, most of which lacked pastors or elders, found resources and met regularly to nurture one another. They kept meeting, praying, witnessing, and studying in families and close-knit groups. There were seven hundred thousand Protestant Christians in a population of about 500 million in 1949, when Mao envisioned his new society and humanity for China. By September 1976, at the end of the Cultural Revolution and at the death of its cultic savior, there were an estimated ten million Christians.

Chinese Christians had accepted the more coherent vision of reality that Paul discusses in 1 and 2 Thessalonians. That vision included the understanding that God called them with a purpose, even the purpose of enduring affliction and persecution (1 Thess. 1:4–10). Like the Thessalonians, they understood that they had to endure many afflictions (1:6; 2:14; 3:3–4); they would trust God even if God destined them to suffer. But suffering never concerned these Christians; their concern was to find the assurance of God's love, a meaning in suffering, and a purpose in life as they read the Scriptures.

Chinese Christians were able to see the final destiny of this despairing world in the divine purpose. Their faith abounded and their love increased (cf. 2 Thess. 1:3). The belief that the righteous of God ruled over his world encouraged Chinese Christians to counter the communist worldview. Certainly the righteous seemed to suffer while the wicked flourished; the world seemed to be ruled by evil, not by God; the communists seemed to be correct. But that was only part of the picture. Though there are a series of events that will take place before Christ's coming (2 Thess. 2:1–11), his coming is nevertheless sure (2 Thess. 1:7; 1 Thess. 5:1–11). The eschatological worldview assured Chinese Christians that God's kingdom will surely reign and that they should maintain their faith in the one, all-powerful and righteous God in the face of the harsh realities of evil in the world, especially the political evil of the oppression of God's faithful people by a pagan regime. It is the hope portrayed in the Thessalonian correspondence that sustained Chinese Christians to endure to the end, to do good works, and to be morally effective and joyfully alive.

Hope has produced miracles among Chinese Christians for the past forty years. The blood of the martyrs is the seed of faith, and Christian hope nurtures that faith. Most of these groups loved to study the eschatological theology of the New Testament, from which they derived strength, faith, and hope. Similar to the believers of Mao, the Christians "remembered" (1 Thess. 2:9) and "knew" (1:5; 2:1, 2, 5, 11; 3:3, 4; 4:2, 4, 5) what they had been "told" (3:4; 4:6) and instructed (4:2, 11), what they had "received" (2:13; 4:1). But in contrast to Mao's followers, Chinese Christians have seen the whole picture of God's revelation working itself out in history. They have seen the end of history, and that grants them assurance of victory, comfort in suffering, and hope in the midst of dismay. They have learned to be open to God and to the future in an attitude of obedience and surrender.

Chinese Christians have learned that the crucified God in his death does not accept the "will to power" (Nietzsche), the violence of the *pax Romana*,[49] the murderous jealousy of Cain (Gen. 4), or the oppression of the Lion of Judah (Revelation). The crucified God becomes incarnate as the Lamb of God who accepts not tragic meaning but redemptive meaning. The blood of Abel, the son of man (Adam), cried out to heaven (Gen. 4:10). The blood of Jesus, the Son of Man, also cried out to heaven. Both are victims of violence, and both of them do not retaliate. Both are vindicated by God. Retaliation against the Red Guards was not the revenge of the Chinese Christians, for Christ's death is the only death God wills to offer and accept. Because Christ dies, no one needs to die, and violence must stop.

Christ's violent death on the cross demonstrates publicly God's wound of love rather than the human power to kill. But the participation of Christians in the cross-event is not simply that of purity, forgiveness, and passivism. The church, as the body of Christ, is to live out the faithful life of the incarnated and crucified Logos (Christ). Toole writes of the atrocities in Sarajevo surrounding the struggle of the church, and this applies to the Chinese setting as well:

> Because the incarnation reaches a crescendo with the crucifixion, Christians learn how to name, but not escape, violence. The crucifixion is the definitive example of both love and sin, nonviolence and violence, and Christians are forever nailed to the center of the cross where love and sin intersect. . . . Jesus interrupts history. But history is vengeful. The Church as history's wound in itself born of a wound that history inflicts. The Church is born where spear and heart meet to form the flow of a wounded Word.[50]

The church is a unique group among Thessalonian or Chinese guilds and associations because it believes in the interconnectedness of classes and backgrounds under the love of one God, equality of the gracious

Benefactor, and the mysterious *koinonia* of the Holy Spirit. The Pauline vision of the church is a constructive critique of the secular world of guilds and associations as well as the religious ideology of the imperial cult through the wound of the cross and the coming God.[51]

Relevance of Pauline Eschatology in Response to the Cultural Millenarian Worldview

Paul writes to the church of Thessalonica that God calls the Christians "into his own kingdom" (1 Thess. 2:12). The Pauline eschatological theology provides relevant resources for Chinese Christians to respond to a secular millenarian worldview, whether that of an emperor cult or of a Maoist cult. Can Paul's language of "into his own kingdom" be understood as an attack on the *pax et securitas* program of the early principate (5:3)? Pauline eschatology has an assured expectation of the complete transformation of the social world by means of a cataclysmic event. However, such a millennial expectation of a replacement of this world by a new, blissful, perfect world of the Edenic time or place was already present in the Thessalonians' thinking. This was a belief in personal invulnerability, ranging from radical change to passive belief in an assured present and future.[52] If the old age meant wrath, the new age meant salvation.

If Paul was merely using indigenous theology by employing the language of the people, he was being too politically naive regarding the implications of his language. It would be more natural to assume that the Pauline theology and gospel in 1 Thessalonians was intentionally expressed as a critique of the ideology of the imperial cult. In Luke's account, Paul's preaching in Thessalonica concerning another king could have been charged by Roman law as defying "the decrees (*dogmata*) of Caesar" (Acts 17:7). Now in 1 Thessalonians, he critiques the Roman emperor by saying that the Lord will descend from heaven (4:16). In critiquing the *securitas et pax Romana* (5:3), he asserts that the day of the Lord will come suddenly. Disguising the Roman emperor as the man of lawlessness, Paul points out the false lordship, false *parousia*, and false power of the emperor; he argues that "the Lord Jesus will slay him with the wrath of his mouth and destroy him by his appearing and his coming" (2 Thess. 2:8). E. A. Judge even suggests that 2 Thessalonians 2:5 ("Do you not remember that when I was still with you I told you this?" RSV) might be referring to Paul's prediction of a change of ruler; such a prediction was of course prohibited by Caesarian edict.[53]

Paul uses three distinctive words to describe the second coming of Jesus, and all have political connotations: epiphany, *parousia*,[54] and apocalypse. Epiphany and *parousia* are used to mean the manifestation of a divine figure, either in personal form or through an act of power demonstrating his or her presence.[55] The unexpected return of Christ means not only a public and powerful manifestation of power and presence but also the overcoming and overthrowing of the lawless one who claims to be God. In 1 Thessalonians, the term *parousia* (4:15) may suggest either the epiphany of a god or the royal language of arrival (of Caesar); the political connotation is clear.[56] A *parousia* was a festive occasion in which all rejoiced in the presence of the royal and authoritative one.[57] Robert Evans is correct in claiming, "*Parousia* puts stress upon the presence of Christ with his people; *epiphaneia* draws attention to his manifestation as already having taken place; apocalypsis points toward a future consumation [*sic*]."[58] These three terms are highly charged with connotations of political treason. As such, when employed in a Chinese context, Pauline eschatological language continues to present a vision of theological politics that is abrasive to an existing political system.

Other politically explosive—and thus countercultural—terms and concepts that Paul uses include *apantesis* (presence), *kyrios* (lord), and *euangelion* (good news). *Kyrios* appears in 5:2, where it has royal nuances. The term *apantesis* (4:17) denotes citizens' expectation of a ruler's arrival;[59] it is a political term. A *kyrios* (4:15, 16, 17) was a political lord, a Roman emperor.[60] Edgar Krentz writes: "Deissmann has shown that the title is applied to the Roman emperors beginning with Augustus by people in the eastern Mediterranean. . . . *euanggelion* was also used in the eastern ruler cult and the political tone triumphs over the apocalyptic."[61] *Euangelion* means the good news of the royal person and all the benefactions of that person. There is no indication that Paul intended to destroy a political system. Perhaps his use of contextual language indicates the inevitable nature of the gospel, that is, to be ideologically incompatible with any other political system.

Even though the politarch system of government in Thessalonica left the people to rule for themselves, the security and peace of Rome still entailed the patronage and benefaction obligations of paying homage as well as loyalty to Rome. In one sense, to hope for the arrival (*parousia*) of the royal was the hope that freedom and prosperity would be granted by Rome. In another sense, the true freedom that the Thessalonians waited for could never be fully realized and found in the human realm. However, at the end of history transcendent freedom would be bestowed beyond Rome's yoke and propaganda.

The political and cultural environment of Thessalonica (and China) provided a fertile soil for an eschatology in which dissatisfaction with an existing social order was interpreted to mean desiring a better world order. Among the Christians, their deprived and insecure positions in relation to the social guilds and workplace meant that they were doubly alienated. "The fullness of time was 'full' because it was pregnant with the 'end' of time. . . . Paul's prophetic presentation of Jesus Christ fell upon ready-prepared soil."[62] Eschatology and the hope of a better future was a message that was music to their ears. The message of eschatology would make better sense to the poor than to the rich, since in times of constraint and deprivation, the promise of peace, prosperity, and abundance would meet their need. With the presence of a diverse class spectrum, the eschatological message of Paul received mixed responses: some believed, others rejected. Those responses are indicative of the conflicting worldview of different classes. "These contradictions illustrate the different points of view rooted in different social classes—the millennial dreams of the poor and hungry, and the mystical escapism of the more comfortable. . . ."[63] Despite this confusion and conflicting reaction to the gospel, the new Christian community of the church presents a new world order in which all are included, if they can overcome their sociological differences.

The ideological clash between Christianity and the emperor cult is visible in the charges the mob placed upon Jason and other Christians whom they dragged before the city magistrates of Thessalonica (Acts 17). They charged that these Thessalonian Christians opposed Caesar's decrees by proclaiming another king named Jesus. Paul's message of the imminent *parousia* (arriving or presence), the lordship of Christ, and the grace and benefaction of Jesus posed an obvious challenge and threat to the *pax Romana* and the benefactor Rome.[64]

Relevance of the Calling Language of Honor, Service, and Hope to New China

While Chinese Christians under Mao's regime have a clear view differentiating Christians from communist atheists, they have not stopped short of proclaiming the redemptive grand narrative in Christ by means of their words and, especially, their lives. Chinese Christians have not stopped evangelizing because of persecution. They have not predestined, as it were, the eternal damnation of unbelievers and sought for their own salvation. They have found comfort in the gospel and, despite their many limitations, have sought to transform Chinese society.

Indeed, Paul's election/calling language in 1 and 2 Thessalonians is not so much concerned with the predestination of believers and unbelievers as it is with the believers' acceptance into the family of God. The Pauline rhetoric of hope, assurance, and purpose in the benefactor Christ speaks against the predestination millenarian cult of the Thessalonian

185

ataktoi. In 1 Thessalonians 1:4 ("We know, brethren beloved by God, the choice of you"), Paul affirms the congregation through the most intimate form of rhetoric, the thanksgiving prayer, that as brothers (and sisters) beloved by God (repeated in 2 Thess. 2:13), they are accepted by God's unconditional love.[65] The problem the community faces is persecution, which tends to alienate the individual from the faithful community. Thus the idea of "election" to salvation expressed in terms of being part of a family enables the congregation to cope with suffering in the context of a community bonding in a hostile world. The Pauline "language of belonging"[66] to God's family reinforces the Thessalonian Christians' hope for a new social reality, or utopia.

In Paul's day, the Greek word *ekloge* (call) was a military-political term, meaning to be chosen for a purpose or to perform a task.[67] Paul's rhetoric here encourages the audience so that they will continue to encourage others, even those Christians in Macedonia. Paul's encouragement aims not merely at group sufficiency or maturity but at the goal of being benefactors to each other. This community building in turn helps them deal with the problem of persecution. Paul's reassurance can thus be categorized as a rhetorical oxymoron, a "literary mysticism,"[68] or a rhetorical "figure" to reestablish "a coherent vision of reality . . . by dissociation."[69] Granting help to others does not exhaust one's energy; rather, it builds one's stamina to deal with persecution.

Another dissociation is between the appearance of paradoxical life and the reality of the gospel: calling with a purpose, and how that purpose can be one of affliction. This is, of course, the primary sense of the purpose clause. Paul has to affirm a more coherent vision of the reality of "commitment of faith."[70] More than spelling out the divine purpose in the congregation's life, Paul also confers special honor on the congregation (the classical Greek use of the words *kaleo* and *klesis* ["call"] conveys that meaning).[71] In other words, Paul proclaims that the gospel is not without affliction, a sharp contrast to the radical millenarian belief.

Paul's consolation is a correction of the audience's radical millenarian idea of realized elect status and elitism. Paul writes in 1 Thessalonians 2:12: "Exhorting, encouraging, and charging you to lead a life worthy of God who calls you into his own kingdom and glory." Here Paul illustrates how his own Thessalonian ministry has encountered opposition and hardship.[72] In a sense, both the congregation's and Paul's faith are assured (1:5) despite tribulation, because God is the God who calls (2:12). The kingdom and glory language[73] is best understood in the context of the political messianism of the time: the Augustan expectation of the new age with a divine ruler.[74] This form of messianism must have appealed to some in the audience when they compared it to Paul's message of a Christ whose kingdom is *yet to come*. The realized eschatology of the *ataktoi* was a case in point. But Paul uses the present tense of *kalountos* ("calling") in 1 Thessalonians 2:12, suggesting the dynamic progressive and yet-to-be-consummated reality of the kingdom and glory of God.[75]

A calling to kingdom and glory does not mean the elimination of affliction. Best highlights this point with a radical phrase, "normality of persecution."[76] Among the Thessalonian Christians was a lower-class population of handworkers;[77] the calling language to kingdom and glory appeals to their needs. This message offers hope and prosperity to the deprived and marginalized laborers who yearn for utopia and messianic triumph. In 2 Thessalonians 1:11, Paul prays for the suffering congregation, that God will make them worthy of his call and fulfill every good resolve and work of faith by his power. Paul uses the phrase "deem worthy" (*axiose*) in 2 Thessalonians 1:5 to connote the suffering that the congregation has experienced in the expectation that the members will be made worthy of the kingdom. This verse identifies the suffering they endure as part of the purpose of the calling.

The calling language of 1 Thessalonians 2:12 not only brings hope and comfort but also points to the fact that God calls the audience into his *own* kingdom, in contrast to the kingdom of Caesar. After all, the ministry of Paul and his coworkers was considered politically inflammatory to those who sought to enforce the decrees of Caesar. Against such imperial forces, Paul proclaims another Lord, another good news, another kingdom. Despite the political critique in 1 Thessalonians 5:3, the reference to wrath in 5:9 ("For God did not place/appoint us into wrath but to obtain salvation through our Lord Jesus Christ") is not a reminder to the audience of the ultimate fate of the evil ones, because God does not "appoint" wrath.[78] What is "ordained" or "appointed" is the salvation, rather than the determined destinies of the sheep and goats. Thus, 1 Thessalonians 5:3 is "a frontal attack on the *Pax et Securitas programme* of the early Principate."[79] First Thessalonians 5:2 is a politically loaded sentence, with the word *parousia* ("coming") signifying the arrival or presence of a person, emperor, king, or other official in the city.[80] The helmet as the hope of salvation (5:8) may be linked to the helmeted head of Roma.[81] The word *Lord* clearly denotes a royal figure, politically the emperor[82] and religiously the epiphany of a god.[83] During Paul's day, emperors were revered as gods (parallel to the Chinese cult of personality). Paul uses the vivid and popular imagery of his day to convey his rhetoric of hope, though in a contrasting way. Paul believed that Christ will bring the benefactions to completion. Therefore, "be sober, and put on the breastplate of faith and love, and for a helmet the hope of salvation" (5:8 RSV). The end is not yet here, but it will surely come; there is hope for the salvation that their Benefactor will bring. Thus, 1 Thessalonians 5:9 provides motivation both for vigilant behavior by the community and for the hope that they are living with the Lord whether they wake or sleep (5:10).

In contrast to the behavior of the *ataktoi* in 2 Thessalonians 3:1–15, therefore, Paul prays for the audience that they will "fulfill every good resolve and work of faith" (2 Thess. 1:11 RSV). The call to salvation is a form of benefaction to public service (good work, faith, and service). Frederick W. Danker and Robert Jewett elaborate: "In the manner of public servants who bring prestige to their cities at terrible personal hazard, these converts through their faithful endurance of trials and tribulations bring luster to the name of God, the Supreme Benefactor, and the Lord Jesus Christ, the Great Benefactor."[84]

The intercessory prayer of Pauline rhetoric intends to sustain the Thessalonian Christians in the apocalyptic trial.[85] Paul continues to pray that God "mightily fill them with all choice desire for goodness and faithful performance," a reference to the exceptional nature of the audience.[86] After clarifying the confusion over the return of the Benefactor (2 Thess. 2:1–12), Paul praises the Supreme Benefactor and the benefaction of the people (2 Thess. 2:13–17). The calling and election language of Paul has its goal in urging the audience to live lives honorable to God.

Calling or electing is therefore God's work of creating, sustaining, saving, and sanctifying his creation out of love and grace. It is the divine purpose to call his creations into relationship with him. The divine yearning is expressed in the benediction of 1 Thessalonians 5, whose calling language affirms the possibility of experiencing the *shalom* (wholeness and harmony) of God in the destructive perils of life. Germane to the apocalyptic theology of Paul is the rhetoric of hope, a rhetoric of recapitulating the End (who is Jesus Christ).[87] That rhetoric of hope encourages the Thessalonians by declaring the working presence of God, Christ, and the Holy Spirit in their midst, confirming God's own "nursely" and fatherly example and concern and nurturing the community by an exhortation of faith, love, and hope in the midst of a hostile environment. Paul at times also recasts the elitist election language of the audience and the intertestamental traditions christologically so that his rhetoric sustains the audience in the tension of God's faithfulness and the apocalyptic hope and joy. In short, the Pauline language of calling and election has a rhetoric of hope that produces trusting perseverance in the context of afflictions and a rhetoric of purpose that creates meaningful obedience in the midst of an apparent dissonance between the promise and the reality of the gospel. Finally, Paul's language has a rhetoric of assurance that comforts the audience in their beloved status in God against the background of the "already-but-not-yet" *parousia*.[88]

The words of Paul in the Thessalonian correspondence remain relevant to the Chinese who seek peace, justice, food, equality, and hope in the face of afflictions. Paul's eschatological theology speaks to both the first-century Christian and twentieth-century Chinese audiences despite the time gap of almost two millennia. As a contrast to the radical millenarian usage, Paul's calling language is not a language of predestination but a rhetoric of reconfirming their beloved status. This language assures some but does not prejudge the destiny of others; it operates in the already-and-not-yet eschatological matrix rather than in a fulfilled eschatological grid; it grants a dynamic and realistic hope rather than promising a false expectation of escapism or triumphalism; it acknowledges rather than denies suffering; it imitates not the superheroic leader but the *exemplum* of the suffering benefactor; it urges the audiences not to misplace their faith in a problem-free, crisis-proof system but to accept the vulnerability of life.

Conclusion

This section has revealed two tenets of Christian eschatology in China. The first tenet is the role of the *ekklesia* in God's apocalyptic involvement in history. Christianity is not a doctrine; it is the new community that is born, called, and sanctified by God to be the agent of God's benefaction and salvation in the world. The church is a politically theological reality in that, though it does not seek to form a government for a nation-state, it is the radical realization of God's grace and justice upon the world to create God's community of trust, faithfulness, equality, and accountability. *Ekklesia* is a common term referring to the assembly of the free in civil or political guilds; it was then taken over by early Christianity as a sacralization of the secular *polis* into a heavenly *politeuma:* the church as the body of Christ that practices the love feast, proclaiming the divine future of hope, wholeness, and salvation in the harsh reality. It seeks to understand the Logos of God incarnated in the Emmanuel Son, the grace of God tabernacled in the world, and the Spirit of God sanctifying his creatures to intended wholeness. The church is not created and called for its own sake but for the sake of God's kingdom in the world. The church's task is to proclaim the radical future of God that offers hope and possibilities in a world where violence and possible destruction are the old scripts of life. Its task is to call upon people to make a decision of faith in God and to give new courage to live against the odds in life. As bearers of the holy in China, the Chinese churches are new community of God in New China.

Second, the church is a theological movement whose *religio* bonds the new community of God and sacralizes all social bodies. *Religio* is defined as the *virtue* that binds the community together and envisions the salvation of the world. The problem of both a conflated Christian state and the separation of church and state is the same: the elimination of the *religio* of the church. The separation of church and state was the reaction to a Constantinian form of Christianity that reduces itself to an earth-bound *mythos,* which is a distortion of the Christian eschatology called "de-eschatology" or the "secular" view of history. Once the sacred bonding among people and the salvific vision were stolen and replaced, societies began to collapse. In the Constantinian form of a Christian nation, it is not that God became the emperor (theocracy) but that the emperor became divine; such is the typology of the "divine nation" to which many Chinese emperors, as well as Mao Zedong, belonged. *Religio* in the Christian or "divine nation" is eliminated because the political leader has claimed his divine status and power; thus the *religio* of the church is subsumed under the assumed divinity of the political leader, and the result is an authoritarian state. The Pauline interpretation of the "antichrist" who claims to be God remains the most illustrative example of how a political or religious leader claims to be God and assumes hegemonic power, thus bringing about lawlessness and chaos in the elimination of *religio* virtue among people. The problem here is not that we should avoid the notion of a Christian state altogether; rather, the problem (as revealed in 2 Thessalonians) is caused by the kind of eschatology a Christian or "divine nation" has. In the cases of the "antichrist" in 2 Thessalonians and Mao Zedong, realized eschatology and de-eschatology were their political theology—or political *religio.* When the *mythos* of a politics and a theology become one and the same and de-eschatology is the view of history, the Christian church loses its *religio.* However, in the separation of the church and the state, the *religio* of the church is replaced by the new *religio* of politics; that is, the secular state now dictates that the people believe in a schizophrenic vision of religion/church pertaining to the sacred realm and of state pertaining to all that is not religious. This secular *mythos* first reduces theology and church to a fragment of our social life that is termed "sacred" (theology is no more the comprehensive view of God's redemptive activities in the world), and then it replaces the *religio* of the church with its own secular vision of salvation, hope, and progress.[89] As I have shown, the "secular" *mythos* does not mean that the interpretation itself is ignorant of transcendence. In fact, as in the cases of Marx and Mao, their secular *mythos* was a direct critique of the Christian *mythos.*

190

7

mao meets paul II

Canonization, Power, Rebellion and the Similarities/Differences of Chinese and Thessalonian Society

Maoism and Paulism are both millenarian according to Y. Talmon's and John G. Gager's definition of the word. Talmon, a social scientist, defines millenarianism as an ideology that brings about "total, imminent, ultimate, this-worldly, collective salvation."[1] Similarly, Gager, a biblical theologian, defines the "millenarian movement" as a group believing in the utopian dream of imminent salvation, in the immediate transformation of the social order, in the outburst of energy for social activism, in the prophetic figure of charismatic persona, and in sets of belief as well as practices for its followers.[2] We will investigate the ways in which the millenarian thinking of Mao was helpful or destructive to China. Does the theology of Paul and the thought of Mao clash ideologically? Is the "united front" proposed by Mao and accepted by the TSPM theologically coherent? The crosscultural interaction between Paul and Mao is based on a historical reading of the texts of both writers. Since this is a hermeneutical reading, rather than purely exegetical and literary, critical dialogue will take place in the interpreter's juxtaposition of the Pauline vision in 1 and 2 Thessalonians over against Maoist utopianism (based on the works of Mao).

The critical dialogue between Mao and Paul on the utopian or eschatological views of history will illuminate how Chinese Christians survived and thrived in a difficult time of persecution and oppression, as well as how they responded to two utopian texts of radically different natures, namely, the secular text of Maoist utopianism and the theological texts of biblical eschatology. The dialogical analysis will help us to understand whether different political systems, especially communism or democracy, are motivated by differing ideas of utopianism.

The dialogue might be unfair, since there is a wide range of differences between Mao and Paul in their cultural backgrounds, their societal roles, the number of people under their leadership, and so forth. Yet the contrast will reveal the ethos, strategies, and ideologies that might otherwise be sublimated without the critical dialogue. The dialogue will intentionally center on the differences between Paul and Mao in their deliberations on hope in history while paying attention to the millenarian nature of both Mao's and Paul's ideologies.

Canonized Thoughts of Mao and Paul

As charismatic leaders of social and religious movements, Paul and Mao were not ordinary persons. Both had extraordinary ideas that had worldwide impact. If they had not been great persons, their ideals would not have been canonized. But neither Paul nor Mao thought of writing "scriptures." Both were practical theorists writing out of the necessity of situations and addressing problems in their communities. The canonization process of both Mao's and Paul's thought reached a point of becoming divine (the divine word itself or an agent of divine word) when devotees began to memorize and imitate the rhetoric. Any canonized text contains codes that believers assume to be the lenses through which reality should be viewed. Christians believe that sacred Scripture views reality as God sees it; Maoist followers believe that the Little Red Book views reality as Mao sees it.

Canonization, Authority, and Reading Practices

Pauline writings were probably the earliest New Testament documents to be read publicly, circulated among Pauline churches, collected by the Pauline school, and copied for the sake of circulation and preservation.

The ideology of Mao was also enshrined and preserved while he was alive. It was the Pauline school, probably in Ephesus, that first collected, redacted, and began the canonization process of Pauline writings. The canonization process was undertaken in part to circulate Paul's teaching among the churches. Paul's prestige and power soared as the canonization process gained momentum. This was true especially after Paul's death, when his legacy gained its mystified and divinized qualities. For example, Acts 27 describes the divine and miraculous preservation of Paul in the face of a shipwreck and poisonous snakebites. Later, Christian Gnostics called Paul "the apostle," without the need to mention his name.

However, Mao's fame and prestige superseded even that of Paul, for while Mao was still alive, at the 1945 Seventh Party Congress, the *Thought of Mao Tse-tung* was singled out as the guide for the Party's policies. "The Chairman's already enormous personal prestige and power" was further solidified in the victory of the 1949 Communist revolution to the extent that "he was indeed a 'savior' and 'the star of salvation.'"[3] Mao's popularity and revered status were boosted not only by the charisma of his personality but also because the Red Guard newspaper was the key medium to advertise and disperse Mao's thought. In this glorification process, it was not so much that Mao's lifestyle was emulated as that his thoughts and writings were widely read.

The canonization process established and legitimated Mao's and Paul's authority. Paul's authority was enhanced as his writings became canonized in the Christian Scriptures. The Bible, especially the New Testament, is the most widely circulated and read book in the history of the world. But the works of Chairman Mao also enjoyed exceedingly widespread circulation. The political department of the army published one billion copies of the first edition of *Quotations from Chairman Mao* in May 1964, along with 150 million copies of the *Selected Works of Mao Tse-tung. The Quotations from Chairman Mao Tse-tung* originally was printed for the People's Liberation Army, but copies were soon given to all young citizens so that they would show diligent and exemplary behaviors. By August 18, 1966, *The Quotations from Chairman Mao Tse-tung* was circulated to the public at Tiananmen Square and was known popularly as the "Little Red Book" because of its size and color. Since the Little Red Book was given to cadres and citizens, their political participation was expected; there was to be no difference between leaders and masses. From 1967 onward, study groups were formed nationwide to study the Little Red Book.

Seeking to appeal to the masses, the Little Red Book intended to structure and guide the mind of the masses, especially the youth, because they were seen as the hope of future revolutions.[4] For example, Lin Biao orchestrated and revived the 1964–1965 campaign to "study Chairman Mao's writings, follow his teachings, act according to his instructions and be his good fighters."[5] Lin Biao proclaimed in the foreword to the Little Red Book that Mao's thought was "an inexhaustible source of strength and a spiritual atomic bomb of infinite power."[6] The Little Red Book was considered to be magical and sacred, able to accomplish anything. The famous little book was believed to be the supernatural guide of the national as well as personal life of the Chinese; thus it was not only a practical operational guide but a magic wand of success and prosperity.

The Quotations from Chairman Mao Tse-tung is called *Mao Yu-lu* in Chinese, meaning proverbs or practical wisdom that contain eternal truth, similar to the words "Holy Scriptures" that Christians use to refer to Paul's writings. In Chinese, "holy scripture" means sacred classics or sacred edicts from the gods or the imperial courts. Wakeman compares the similarities between *Mao Yu-lu* with the sacred edicts of the Qing imperial courts, noting especially the authority invested in both documents.[7] *Mao Yu-lu* represents a traditional prototype of catechetical or scriptural function. The term *yu-lu* was first used during the Tang dynasty by Buddhist monks who took notes of their masters' teaching so that they could preach to greater masses. Mao's teaching contained in *Mao Yu-lu* served the same purpose and was of a similar genre as the Buddhist *yu-lu*.[8]

Being *yu-lu* and a sacred edict, *Mao Yu-lu* had a sacred—and thus unchallenged and absolute—authority. Here the first difference between *Mao Yu-lu* and Paul's writings begins to surface: their differing claims of authority on their readers. The Pauline corpus consists of highly contextual epistles addressing specific problems of various local congregations in the first-century Greco-Roman world. Their claim of authority on readers outside the original contexts was not achieved by means of selective quotations from Paul's texts. Rather, their claim of authority on the lives of believers in later periods was effected by the hermeneutical and theological processes of biblical exegesis and criticism. That is, the Pauline texts are by themselves not sacred, but the sacredness of the texts is found in hermeneutical relevance as they are interpreted. The volumes of commentaries on Pauline corpus are a clear indication that a sacred and authoritative text does not fear criticisms; in fact, the scrutiny clarified puzzling issues for later readers.

Many Chinese scholars studying in the United States have told me that the Chinese way of studying *Mao Yu-lu* was similar to Christians' study of the Bible. Serious study would involve historical-contextual and literary methodologies. Many others would engage in devotional readings. Serious communist scholars studied and interpreted *Mao Yu-lu*, but none dared to scrutinize and criticize it, for the very words of *Mao Yu-lu* were considered sacred. For instance, it was common practice to keep a copy of this good-luck charm and magical power as close to the heart as possible during the Cultural Revolution. In addition, selective quotations of Mao in the *Yu-lu* were interpreted out of context or were assumed to be true for all situations. When two opposing factions were uncertain about the interpretation, it was up to Mao to offer the correct one. But Mao would not spell out the procedure and process of the interpretive methodology. Thus it was not uncommon to see two groups of Mao loyalists fighting over their different interpretations of the same text. The great masses of people continued to imitate Mao's accent and speaking style, even while different factions quoted *Mao Yu-lu* in debates and attacks on each other. They all cried, "We swear to protect Chairman Mao with our lives." These chaotic and conflicting situations often generated more factions seeking to gain personal power in the midst of the struggle, as was the case during the Cultural Revolution.[9]

A similar division existed in the Pauline circle. The immense redaction that went with canonization indicated that different factions of Paulinism used Paul's texts to fight each other in defense of truth. When the canonization process was complete in the New Testament, there were hints of both the Pauline and deutero-Pauline schools.[10]

Absolute and Collective Power in the Canonization Process

Comparing the power of Mao and Paul is neither fair nor accurate because the canonical authorship of the Christian Scriptures is collective and communal. Even in his many letters, Paul credited his colleagues who contributed or helped draft the letters with him. Collective authorship, such as we see with the letters, decentralizes the absolute authority of any one person. The canonical process of the Christian Scriptures throughout church history confirms that divine revelation and divine activities work through communities. Thus we hear polyphonic voices within the New Testament while the centers of their unity shift from Christ and Christian ethics to Christian communities.[11] While equality is a foreign concept in the canonical process of the Scriptures (and thus "canon within a canon" is a default mode of scriptural reading),[12] the authority of the Pauline corpus is shared with other apostles within the larger groups of divine agents.

It is difficult to see "shared leadership" and "shared power" in Mao's regime. Interestingly, the Commission on Publication of the Selected Works of Mao Zedong of the Central Committee of the CCP published "The Chinese Revolution and the Chinese Communist Party" in December 1939, saying, "This is part of the textbook written jointly by Comrade Mao [Zedong] and several other comrades in Yenan."[13] However, later publication attributed sole authorship to Mao.

In another example of Mao's centralized power, at the Eighth Congress of the Chinese Communist Party in September 1956, Liu Shaoqi (1898–1969) and Deng Xiaoping (1904–1998) advocated "collective leadership" of the Communist Party, adding that the phrase "guided by the Thought of Mao Zedong" be deleted from the Party's constitution. Deng offered a "Report on the Revision of the Constitution of the Communist Party of China," in which he said: "Love for the leader is essentially an expression of love for the interests of the Party, the class, and the people, and not the deification of an individual."[14] Liu and Deng may have been aware of the danger of the personality cult and thus intended to save China and the Communist Party from the devastation caused by the Maoist cult. But the tension between Mao and the Party and other key leaders would get worse from then onward. Soon Liu and Deng were criticized and rejected from the leadership circle.

The Leadership and Power Structures of Mao and Paul

Paul and Mao were both powerful figures, but their styles of leadership and their practice of power differed greatly. As spiritual leaders and visionary messengers, they played a significant role in creating and disseminating visions of an ideal world. They were charismatic leaders, intellectual geniuses, persuasive communicators, and skillful organizers. Both counted on the collective responses of the masses and the power differentiation between leaders and followers to become the catalyst that moved their utopian movements forward.

In an article, "Toward a Critique of Power in the New China," Philip Shen names the polarity of the power issue in Red China:

> The experience of the Chinese people since liberation is preeminently an experience of power, of its awesome liberating and transforming effects, and at the same time of its awful dominating and threatening character. . . . The will of the leadership, that speaks and acts in the name of the people, is pervasive and exacting, and often arbitrary and capricious.[15]

Shen continues by suggesting the need to analyze the "coercive and persuasive" nature of the state's power on the Chinese people, especially "the series of mass campaigns as well as the regular political education and remolding processes, including the study groups, the struggle meetings, the criticism and self-criticism sessions, and the like."[16] While this study cannot do all that is suggested, I do want to analyze the power structure of Mao in contrast to that of Paul, which will help us understand the nature, means, and devastation of the Maoist revolutions.

"Mass-Line" Superman and "Agapaic Communalism"

The "mass-line" vision of Mao and the "agapaic communalism" of Paul were both communist in structure. In his 1943 essay "Some Questions Concerning Methods of Leadership," Mao explained the organizational communication of his mass-line policy:

> In all the practical work of our Party, all correct leadership is necessarily "From the masses, to the masses." This means: take the ideas of the masses (scattered and unsystematic ideas) and concentrate them (into concentrated and systematic ideas), then go to the masses and propagate and explain these ideas until the masses embrace them as their own, hold fast to them and translate them into action, and test the correctness of these ideas in such action. Then once again concentrate ideas from the masses and once again go to the masses so that the ideas are persevered in and carried through. And so on, over and over again in an endless spiral, with the ideas becoming more correct, more vital, and richer each time. Such is the Marxist theory of knowledge.[17]

Mao's emphasis on the masses revealed his belief that masses should control the state and not vice versa.

In order to bring about ideal self-sufficiency and egalitarianism for the peasants and the cadres in Red China, Mao suggested that the commune be the basic unit of agricultural and industrial productions. He wrote:

> In 1958, a new social organization appeared. . . . This was the large-scale people's commune in the rural areas of our country which combines industry, agriculture, trade, education and military affairs and in which government administration and commune management are integrated. . . . Within a few months starting in the summer of 1958, all of the more than 740,000 agricultural producers' cooperatives in the country, in response to the enthusiastic demand of the mass of peasants, reorganized themselves into over 26,000 people's communes. Over 120 million households, or more than 99 percent of all China's peasant households of various nationalities, have joined the people's communes.[18]

Whether in villages or in urban areas, the peasantry and the proletarian young cadres were in control. They were the masses with the power. They were the ones who broke with traditions and old institutions and formed the new institutional structures called communes, which were to accelerate production and create new social and revolutionary order.

Even though the congregation size at Thessalonica was incomparable to that of the Chinese masses, the Thessalonian Christians living in apartment houses called *insulae* were also practicing a communal lifestyle—sharing resources and supporting one another.[19] A large percentage of the free and slave population resided in these *insulae*. These households "represented a considerable cross section of a major portion of society, made up of manual laborers and trades people. Such households were part of an intricate social network, being linked to other households by ties of kinship, friendship, professional advantage, and so on."[20] Besides the house church under the patronage of Jason (if such an assumption is correct), the possibility of tenement churches and love-feast communities in Thessalonica (proposed by Robert Jewett)[21] influenced Paul in proposing "agapaic communalism" for the Thessalonian community. They probably ate from a common kitchen in the building because basic facilities such as heat, running water, toilets, and a kitchen were not available for each small apartment of about ten square feet.[22] Jewett's study of the tenement churches in Thessalonica indicates that

> In contrast to house churches that have an upper or middle class patron along with his or her slaves, family, friends and others, the tenement churches consisted entirely of the urban underclass, primarily slaves and poor freedmen/women. Lacking a patron who would function as a leader, the pattern of leadership appears to be egalitarian in tenement churches.[23]

Both the Maoist and the Pauline community structure have a passion for the poor, the laborers, the ordinary people; and the Pauline community's practice of shared power is also similar to Mao's. But unlike the new order for the people of God—the church, whose bonding principle was agapaic communalism—the people's commune was the base unit for socioeconomic and political activities: "It is the basic organization of the socialist state power."[24] Thus the power structure between the leaders and the followers in the communes was not of an egalitarian, mutual, and sharing type.

Mao's mass-line policy sounded as though he had a willingness to share power with all. Yet in the midst of an actual power struggle, his strategy was to consolidate his own power. He did so by intensifying the struggle between the masses and the Party leadership rather than by allowing there to be a struggle between the Party leadership and himself. The Party leadership in a power struggle with him were people such as Liu Shaoqi, Lin Biao, and Deng Xiaoping.[25] Mao would ask or approve the masses to criticize the Party leadership, thus siding with the people and putting himself at odds with the Party's leadership. In February 1957, Mao delivered a speech deliberating on the many contradictions in Chinese society, specifically the contradiction between the people and the Party leadership.[26] If the division was between the people and the Party leadership (though, of course, the masses were not in any position to criticize the Party leadership), Mao stood above both the Party leadership and the people. The fact that the people were powerless unless they were approved by Mao indicated that the real contradiction existed between Mao and the Party leadership. It follows that anyone who was not backed by Mao, whether from the masses or from Party leadership, was in fact contradicting Mao. This strategy might not have been deceptive, but it was clearly manipulative. Charismatic leaders can demand support from followers and gain more power by means of wisdom and persuasion, or they can do it by means of manipulation and deception.

Paul's leadership style with the tenement churches and the laborers in Thessalonica was drastically different from Mao's. The egalitarian lifestyle and mutuality of the "God-taught" community at Thessalonica might, on the surface, bear a certain similarity to the Maoist vision of communism and the mass-line structure, but the agapaic communalism of the Thessalonian community presents a radical alternative to the Maoist myth and personality cult. The eschatological meal celebrated by the Thessalonian community signified that leaders and followers alike were *all* vulnerable humans in need of grace, love, and hope. That is, all people need the grace of God, the love of the beloved community, and the sustaining power of sacredness and utopia amid the mundane and evil realities of life. Since the Pauline group at Thessalonica lacked patrons to sponsor the resources for the Lord's Supper, they used the common renter space or workshop areas for activities such as common meals.[27] The celebration of the Lord's Supper within the context of the love feast was "marked by eschatological joy at the presence of a new age and of a Master who had triumphed over the principalities and powers. At times an overly realized eschatology in some of the agape meals led to Christian forms of the Saturnalia in Thessalonica."[28]

The truly mass-line principle of agapaic communalism is evident in the biblical texts. First, the casuistic law of 2 Thessalonians 3:10 reflects the sharing lifestyle and power of the Thessalonian community and Paul.[29] In order to enforce the absolute prohibition of "eating" (without any qualification), one has to assume that the community had control on the matter of eating for individuals.[30] The casuistic law of 2 Thessalonians 3:10 makes sense only if the community was sharing the common table in their daily meals. Second, the references to "brotherly love" (1 Thess. 4:9) and "well doing" (2 Thess. 3:13), which means to labor and to share bread, depict members of the faith community sharing in the common kitchen within the tenement setting. The notion of "brotherly love" is primarily a familial understanding that connotes Christians living together as a new family in Christ instead of staying with their earthly families. Third, the phrase "work with your own hands" in 1 Thessalonians 4:11–12 implies brotherly love expressed by "members of the new Christian family contributing their fair share to the love feast, signifying the transformation brought by Christ."[31] This eschatological community of the Thessalonian Christians was an egalitarian and mutually supportive community, for all depended on the Patron of Grace, the Benefactor Jesus Christ.

In contrast to other leadership styles in the ancient world,[32] Paul's style was closer to that of the benevolent patriarchal leader than that of the populist, demagogic leader.[33] The former is "modeled on the well-intentioned, kind, superior father" who will continue to rule the subject by gaining trust. The populist leader "accommodates the people, he lowers himself socially, and his motivation is gain." Paul's use of the nurse (1 Thess. 2:7) and father (2:11) imagery reflects his benevolent patriarchal model of leadership. Paul stressed the importance of sticking to the tradition received (1 Thess. 1:5, 6; 2:13; 2 Thess. 1:8; 2:15), but his rhetoric of noncoerciveness and his model of apostleship in care and the "love of nurse" were indications that he took time to let the truth be persuasive in the lives of the congregation. Paul contrasted himself to the deceptive sophists, whose words often manipulated the truth (see 1 Thess. 2:4–6).

The Maoist practice of power was manipulative of crowd psychology, without which the personality cult would not have existed; the result was detrimental, because when power is not shared, it is invested in one person. Either that person is God, who has absolute power, or that person is someone who merely claims the absolute power that does not belong to him or her. And in political settings where power struggles are inevitable, human leaders such as Mao have the temptation to claim to be God. In other words, if a communal unit was a political one (rather than a religious one), ushering in a utopian society by means of political struggle, military might (rather than divine grace) would become the guiding principle of the exercise of power. In a political regime that rejected God, Mao and the masses became gods—in no need of divine grace.

Neither Caesar nor Mao was the mover of history; the resurrected slain Lamb is. The power of *pax Romana* and Mao was built upon "the will to power"; the christological eschatology of Paul was built on the "wound of love." The myth of Romulus, the founder of Rome, was that he was the murderer of his brother Remus. John Milbank notes that, according to Augustine's interpretation, "the Romans continued to 'live out' this mythos: within the city gates, the goddess most celebrated was *Bellona* [meaning 'War'], the virtues most celebrated were the military ones. The statue of the goddess *Quies* [meaning 'Peace'], by contrast, stood outside the gates, as if to indicate that peace was a benefit brought through war by Rome to others."[34] The Roman Empire and the Maoist Empire were established by human blood and weaponry. In contrast, "the crucified Jesus is a more adequate key to understanding what God is about in the real world of empires and armies and markets than is the ruler in Rome, with all his supporting military, commercial, and sacerdotal networks."[35] Following the thesis of John Howard Yoder, David Toole writes that "The cross is a political alternative to insurrection because it stands at the end of a path of resistance that refused violence."[36] Yoder highlights the arrest scene at the Garden of Gethsemane, where Jesus commanded his disciple to put his sword back into its place and assured the group that if he wanted to use force, his Father would at once send him more than twelve legions of angels (Matt. 26:52–53).[37]

Ironically, Maoism intended to liberate people from sociopolitical bondage but ended up with a totalitarian and oppressive state. Besides the problem of a political utopian state that rejected divine grace and love, there was also the Maoist monolithic ideology that emphasized its firmness and purity. Therefore, in Maoist political utopia there is no margin for error, and various antirevolutionary campaigns were used to purge any deviant or alternative views.

The Managerial, Political Ideology and Redemptive Use of the Benefaction System

Power sharing in Paul and Mao was similar in the sense that both wanted the masses to assume the responsibility of collective edification. But the difference between Paul and Mao in their power sharing was the manner in which political ideology got in the way of the communist revolution, while Paul's power structure followed the benefaction system of honor and shame redeemed in Christ.

The Chinese Communists' ideology had a managerial structure of organization,[38] at least in the theory that was explicitly laid down in the Party rules and the volumes of *The Selected Works of Mao Tse-tung.*[39] Mao was aware that any organization should facilitate managerial delegation of work, but such organization would inherently result in bureaucratic red tape and the wasting of resources. Thus, to overcome the problem and keep the organization alive, the Communist Party sought to eliminate routinization by bringing in ideological critique and to prevent bureaucratization using managerial leadership. Communism was working toward a liberated peasantry, a new class of young technocratic administrators and entrepreneurial managers. For example, Mao Zedong called specifically for the recruitment of young workers and peasantry to be the core of his party, and those youths were then assigned the special mission of implementing his programs of rural reconstruction.[40] Positively, the CCP did provide organization that would sustain the young, the poor, and the peasants to create the destiny of China. Collective communization allowed all to participate in the public pattern of the work organization. But on the negative side, many of the masses were young intellectuals and students whose utopian dreams were less realistic than those of the older leadership of the Party. Furthermore, the young were asked to rebel, and Mao could not provide them with realistic and practical ways of rebellion. Attacking social order without being able to produce a new order was destructive to the society. In that regard, Schurmann's analysis of the problem of replacing organization with ideology in Communist China is perceptive. He believed that "The Communists saw the trends of history and fought to complete the revolution. . . . [T]hey looked to the future, and began to prepare for it with ideology and organization. When they triumphed, they replaced system by organization, and ethos by ideology."[41] Thus, since the 1960s the Maoist revolutions have taken on a purely ideological character, while the practical managerial organization has subsided into the background; ideology has taken precedence over all. The Chinese Communist Party was on the verge of collapse if a revolution were not unleashed to transform the purely ideological structure.

Mao's power structure lies in ideology, whereas Paul's depends on values and norms in the society that feed on the reciprocity of benefactions. Maoist ideologies were sets of ideas whose unity lay not in the ideas themselves but in the unconsciousness of the collective or individual groups,[42] namely, the masses. In contrast, in the enculturation (socialization) process, Paul made use of values and norms of contemporary culture to express his authority. In other words, whereas Maoism secularized religion and power (power is always beyond the control of anyone) and then took the power that was to make him divine (e.g., Mao as savior and Maoism as a supernatural power), the apostle Paul attempted to transform the secular into a sacredness in which people could experience the holy. The genius of Paul was his use of secular language and the fact that he redeemed it for religious functions, thus empowering believers through the meeting of the secular and the sacred. The redemptive use of benefaction language is an example: in Paul's hermeneutic the language called the community to share power and to benefit all people.

Because of radical differences of theological politics between the emperor cult and Christian believers, their respective understandings of benefactor and beneficiaries' response differed. This is clear in the Thessalonian case, but it requires careful articulation in the Chinese case. In the Thessalonian case, Frederick W. Danker has shown that the dominant feature of the Greco-Roman culture was its association with the benefaction motif, both in the display, claim, and acknowledgment of the benefactor's merit or excellence and in the beneficiaries' response to the merit.[43] The pervasive nature of this cultural pattern is evident in the variety of the benefaction media (city council documents, publishing edicts, civic decrees, biographies or autobiographies, oaths), the benefaction subjects (esteemed members, community, military personnel, emperors, deities, statesmen, physicians, freedom fighters, philanthropists, judges' clerks), and the benefaction merit (exceptional character, investment in sport, *pronoia* = foresight) or honor (*proxenos*, savior, divine).[44]

With regard to the Thessalonian material, the ideological clash between who was the benefactor and who received benefaction became a key issue. But Paul creatively readapted the cultural benefaction tradition and critiqued it by means of the new Christian benefaction system. It can be shown that the exemplary character motif in the benefaction tradition (e.g., awards to Opramoas, or decree from Priene in honor of Herakleitos, cf. Danker, *Benefactor*, 348–49) is reflected in 1 Thessalonians 1:6–7, where Paul says that the congregation should become a *typos* (model or example) for all Christians in Macedonia and Achaia.[45] In 1 Thessalonians 2:2 Paul describes the hostility he encountered at Philippi as a "great contest/struggle" (*pollo agoni*). Nevertheless, he was determined to proclaim the gospel fearlessly.[46] Paul is using benefaction language to show his commitment to be an apostolic benefactor of the Great Benefactor God in proclaiming the benefaction of the gospel, Jesus Christ.

The benefaction the community receives now is not that from the Roman emperor, who claims to give "peace and security" to those who pay their *philia* loyalty. Paul understands peace and grace as coming from God the Father and Jesus the Son (1 Thess. 1:1). The benefaction now comes from God's grace and salvation, especially in the assured, consummated form in the *parousia* of Christ. God the Father is their new patron who is capable of protecting and saving the clients from all afflictions and keeping them whole (1 Thess. 5:23). The new family network (3:11–13; 5:23) is formed through Christ. It is significant that Paul begins to explain the identity of the audience right from the beginning in the exordium of 1 Thessalonians 1:1–2.

Benefactors are essentially those whose task "is to ensure the safety and the well-being of those who rely on their services."[47] The self-offering benefaction ("give oneself") that Paul "shared his very life" (1 Thess. 2:8) finds its cultural parallels in Akornion, a priest who gave himself to serve the city, and Menas, who "dedicated himself unstintingly" for the welfare of his city.[48] The "respectfully and uprightly and blamelessly"

(2:10) public activity of Paul parallels the blameless service and character of Moschion II (a priest of Herakles) and Nikasippos, who were praised for their blamelessness and righteousness in the benefaction tradition.[49] In 1 Thessalonians 2:19, Paul uses the semantic field of the benefaction language to describe the Thessalonian Christians as his "crown of boasting." The crown of boasting was the award granted for an achievement in which one took pride as a head of state or as a generous citizen. The Thessalonian Christians were the crown for which Paul wished (2:19). They were his glory; that is, they made his reputation as a benefactor (2:20). Like Demosthenes, Paul did not hesitate to boast of the virtue that he manifested among his converts in Thessalonica (2:1–12). At the same time, he classified his detractors as antibenefactors (2:14–16).

Danker's reconstruction of the Pauline ministry as that of an apostolic benefactor of the gospel provides a corrective lens with which to view Paul not as an egocentric, pompous, autocratic theologian but as a committed and thankful agent of the Great Benefactor because of his realization that he is not the supreme benefactor. All are called to be benefactors to one another, not to gain power but to empower one another and share divine benefactions to all. Three key words in the Thessalonian correspondence —"appoint," "choose," and "call"—have a common denominator in God's purpose and not in human manipulation or predetermination. The subject of these words is always God, who initiates an event with a purpose. The purpose may be holiness, enduring affliction, obtaining glory, sharing salvation, or rendering good resolve and good work. The benefaction tradition illuminates our understanding of the goal or purpose of God's calling as receiving benefactions from the Benefactor. The calling and election language of Paul in 1 and 2 Thessalonians has its goal in motivating the audience to live a life honorable to God: Paul is encouraging, comforting, and urging the Thessalonians to lead lives worthy of God (1 Thess. 2:12). They are to be benefactors to each other for the purpose of catalyzing the benefactions of God throughout Macedonia.[50]

Salvation in the Thessalonian correspondence bears the meaning of receiving benefaction.[51] In the Thessalonian correspondence Paul portrays Jesus as the apocalyptic Great Benefactor who will reward the persecuted Christians in his *parousia* but who will also bring down vengeance on the persecutors.[52]

Rebellions of the *Ataktoi* and the Red Guards

Maoism came to power through revolutionary struggles against Chinese traditional and Western normative values. In order to rebuild the country and to improve the condition of life, Maoism strategized to create a systematic structure that had similar ideology of the *ataktoi* (rebels) in the Thessalonian correspondence. Peasants and urban working-class people "proclaimed total loyalty to Mao, professed faith in his teachings, and performed the rituals of his cult."[53] Youthful Red Guards replicated the Long March across the streets of the nations to testify to their faith in the deified Mao. They believed Mao had freed them from imperialism, feudalism, and oppression. The development of economic and social prosperity required a continuous process of ideological transformation, political revolution, and social struggle: this is what Mao meant by *buduan geming*, an "unceasing" or "continuous revolution."[54] Mao believed that after a victory they must at once put forward a new task so that all cadres and masses would forever be filled with revolutionary fervor. This fervor was most vividly seen in the Red Guards, who behaved just as the *ataktoi* (rebels) of the Pauline congregations in Thessalonians did. The word *ataktoi* does not denote laziness but a rebelling against order.[55] The Thessalonian *ataktoi* were not merely lazy or without jobs; they refused to work (2 Thess. 3:10), rejecting church order (3:6) and thus creating dissonance within the church.

The Red Guards were instrumental in carrying out the ideology of Mao, whose "directives" and "instructions" were set forth in the "Sixteen Articles," approved by the Party Central Committee (the Eleventh Plenum) in August 1966. In that same year, Mao approved the organization of the Red Guards. Many Party leaders were absent when Mao made his decision; instead, their places were taken by the Red Guard representatives. Millions of teenagers indoctrinated with fanaticism ravaged the country and wrecked structures of orderly society, including religious institutions. This was intentional in light of the twofold purpose spelled out in the "Sixteen Articles on Working Methods": to overthrow those in the Party who had authority and were treading the path of capitalism, and to destroy the "four olds" (old ideas, old customs, old cultures, and old habits).

On August 5, 1966, Mao posted his big-character message on the door where the Central Committee was supposed to meet. Feeling that his opponents had been exercising bourgeois dictatorship, he urged his followers to "bombard the headquarters" of his Party. The Red Guards were commissioned to be the vanguards of mass rebellion against the Party's high-ranking leaders and state authorities. The traditional word for "treason" now became the word "rebel," used by the Red Guards and masses to indicate that they were rebelling against the despotic Party leaders. Among the latter, they accused Liu Shaoqi as "the leading person" and Deng Xiaoping the "second leading person in authority taking the capitalist road."[56]

On August 18, 1966, a significant event marked the "blast-off" of the Cultural Revolution. Hundreds of thousands of people, wearing red armbands to signify their allegiance, assembled in the square of the Gate of Heavenly Place to hail their Supreme Commander, Great Teacher, Great Leader, and Great Helmsman.[57] Mao launched the Great Proletarian Cultural Revolution in 1965, calling on the masses to "dare to rebel" against established authority with "life and death."[58] They carried with them the "supernatural powers . . . great invincible thought" of Mao and perceived themselves as the incarnation of Mao's persona.[59] Red Guard groups were organized in almost every university and high school; they rallied under the slogans "it is justified to rebel" and "destruction before construction."

The Red Guards marched through streets, cities, towns, and countryside carrying out the Maoist command to destroy all ghosts and monsters. They rampaged throughout the nation in an iconoclastic crusade against the "four olds," using violence and vandalism against traditional architecture, old buildings, and historical and cultural treasures in Canton, Hangchow, Xian, and Hofei. Since one of the four olds that needed to go was religion, including the Jesus religion, the Buddha religion, the Dao religion, the Confucius religion, and the Hui (Islam) religion, the rebels desecrated many religious buildings. They physically assaulted and psychologically abused many people, Christian and non-Christian alike. Zhou Enlai had to step in often to minimize or stop the rebels' frenzied wrecking and destructive activities.

By August 1966, the revolutions were getting out of control, as the August 18, 1966, demonstration precipitated a highly charged and emotional rebellion. China was on the verge of civil war; physical violence was breaking out sporadically in various cities as Red Guard groups fought each other for control of power. The Red Guard movement became an orgy of bloody fighting. Fortunately, the army, which was entrusted with legal power, held on to the fragile unity of the country.[60] Mao then ordered Lin Biao and the People's Liberation Army to intervene. Schram writes:

> His last years are marked by increasing bafflement and frustration, as he becomes more and more desperate to resolve China's problems while he is still in command, and less and less capable of doing so. At the end, he is scarcely able to think, let alone to speak, and has become indeed, as he complained of being in 1966, a dead ancestor at his own funeral, or at the burial of his hopes.[61]

The conflicts and bloodshed during that period were horrendous. During the summer of 1968, the People's Liberation Army attempted to repress the radical rebellions of the Red Guard and workers' organization. Forty thousand were killed in the province of Kwangtung alone during that resistance measure.

The Cultural Revolution failed to establish the political successors of the Chinese government, at least during the time when the original aim of the Cultural Revolution was to "train revolutionary successors." In the summer of 1968, Mao summoned the leaders of the Red Guard to end their rebellions.[62] At that time, the Red Guards were hailed as "new people" (*xinren*) and "revolutionary successors" of earlier Chinese communists (*koming jiebanren*).[63]

The Red Guards were akin to the "people of lawlessness" described in 2 Thessalonians 2:1–12. Information on the description, activity, character, and destiny of the man of lawlessness in 2 Thessalonians 2:1–12 is not detailed enough for readers to pinpoint the identity of the Antichrist. Perhaps it is rendered in that way deliberately to provide for a paradigmatic identification rather than an individual witch hunt. Our interest here is to look at the character, activities, and destiny of "lawlessness" as a social and religious movement and to observe how the phenomenon surfaced not only in Thessalonica but also in Red China.

Interpreters have identified the Thessalonian man of lawlessness with Caligula, Nero, and other persons of past centuries—and with the Antichrist elsewhere in the New Testament. No matter how antireligious or anti-Christian one's destructive activities were, no political individual could be pinpointed as the Antichrist. Paul described the character of the man of lawlessness in a strict sense as a man without the law (*anomia*), but the word "lawlessness" rapidly acquired the meaning of "against the law." Since the law was the law of God, lawlessness meant the impulse to work against the mandates of God. The Red Guards were said to be "lawless" because they placed themselves above the law, similar to the man of lawlessness in 2 Thessalonians 2:4, who arrogated himself to divine status.[64] The prototype of the man of lawlessness was Antiochus Epiphanes, who exalted himself over every god (see Dan. 11:36).[65] That human claim to be divine had a long history in Jewish thought (Ezek. 28:1–10 on the king of Tyre; Isa. 14:4–20 on the king of Babylon).[66] It is also not uncommon in other cultures, where we find the antichrist phenomenon in people assuming themselves to be divine messiahs and rebelling against law and order.

The lawless one often appears with a splendor and power that is associated with Satan, probably because he is Satan's agent. Paul suggests in 2 Thessalonians 2:9 that the man of lawlessness is not simply a human with bad ideas but that his evil ideas are empowered by Satan. Thus it is said that he comes "with all power and pretends signs and wonders."[67] He imitates divine miracles in order to lead people away from the true

God. If the expression "with all power and deceptive miracles and wonders" describes the character of the deeds accompanying the lawless one's coming, then the phrase "with all wicked deception" describes the effect of his activity in seducing people into destruction.

The frenzied destruction of the Red Guards could not be explained simply as abnormal or deviant human activities. In the beginning of the Cultural Revolution, the Red Guards "took seriously the talk of old habits, and defaced historical monuments, beat old people, attacked bourgeois and Overseas Chinese."[68] Later they attacked the "capitalists" (that is, not just those with the love of profit and private ownership but also the love of power and authority), school officials, and the Party committee as well as government officials. Party officials "were paraded with dunce caps on their heads through the streets. Students broke into Party offices. More and more of their fire was leveled at high officials. Mayors, governors, and Party first secretaries were forced to attend meeting after meeting in which they were subjected to humiliating criticism."[69]

If the following destruction does not describe satanic work, what would? In all the catastrophe of the Cultural Revolution and the damage done by the Red Guards, there was a estimate of 400,000 people killed nationwide.[70] Statistics indicate that more than 729,000 people were framed and persecuted in "witch-hunt" campaigns, one after another, and nearly 35,000 died related to these campaigns. Millions limped away from the repression; thousands upon thousands were beaten and tortured. Families were broken and destroyed as parents and children became enemies denouncing one another. Children were persecuted for the alleged political "sins" of their parents. Life and career were robbed as millions were exiled to remote areas such as Manchuria and Sinkiang for hard labor. This period of ten years was sometimes called "Cultural Destruction," "Ten Years of Calamity," or "Ten Years of Madness."[71] The aim of the Maoist movement was to fight off imperialism and foreign domination, yet the actions of the Red Guards pitted the Chinese against their own people. Alas!

I find Paul's description of the man of lawlessness in 2 Thessalonians coming to do satanic activity a helpful lens with which to sift through the chaotic events during the Cultural Revolution. The Red Guards took the slogan "to rebel" seriously, and the violent means of justifying their cause meant that they would perform powerful and counterfeit miracles. Is not a regime that discounted religion as opium and Satan as superstition still under the influence of religious and satanic forces? Only the view of history that evil is antitruth, anti-God, and antihumanity can explain the rebellions of the Red Guards.

Radical Eschatological Excitement and Violence of the Ataktoi and the Red Guards

If history does not have an end in which accountability (judgment and reward) is required by God and humanity, then religious faith or ethics do not matter; everyone can do what is pleasing in his or her own eyes. But 2 Thessalonians 2:8 emphasizes the destiny of the lawless one who defies God. The second part of the phrase "and destroy him by the appearing of his coming" is intended to emphasize the destruction of the lawless one and, in particular, the breaking of his power by the coming God, the Lord Jesus Christ who is the end of history. The appearance of the Lord will overcome and destroy the lawless one. Religious faith and ethics matter, for in the eschatological view of history, there is judgment and hope.

The theological problem of the *ataktoi* in Thessalonica and the Red Guards was their disruptive behavior informed by their distorted eschatology. The word *ataktoi* came from the verb *tassein*, "to order." Traditionally, *ataktoi* is understood as "loafers" or "idlers."[72] Jewett, following the studies of Ceslas Spicq, argues "that the basic meaning of the term is standing against the order of nature or of God."[73] More significantly, the word *tassein* was "used in Jewish and early Christian literature to indicate the order which is ordered in the Law by God and by Moses. . . . The order instituted by God at the creation is indicated in the same way."[74] The most obvious order is in Genesis 3:17–19, where Adam (human being) was made to work for his living.[75] The words "work" and "eat" are found in Genesis 2:15–16; 3:17–19; and 2 Thessalonians 3:6–10. "Cursed is the earth because of you" in the Masoretic Text of Genesis 3:17 becomes "cursed is the earth in your works" in the Septuagint (3:18).[76] Palestinian Targumim have: "So let us rise and work with the work of our hands and we shall eat food from the food of the earth."[77] All these show that in Jewish and early Christian apocalypticism, the absence of hunger, thirst, and labor were often seen as signs of new age when the bliss and abundance would provide for human needs.[78] The "paradise lost" of Genesis brings with it toil and hardship, whereas the paradise to be regained in the new age (Isa. 51:3) is often looked forward to as abundance without toil.[79] Menken rightly says, "It is quite probable that the conviction combated in 2 Thessalonians 2:2, that 'the Day of the Lord' had come, implied a conception of this day in terms of . . . the restoration of Paradise or of paradisiac conditions."[80] If the day of the Lord was assumed to have arrived (as was the case with the *ataktoi* and the Red Guards), then the *ataktoi* would naturally assume also that the curse of toil was lifted and annulled and that the eschatological bliss had come to provide for the abundance of human needs.

Yet Paul considered their behavior to be disruptive to others because the end of history had not arrived. Paul presented them with the eschatological realism of 2 Thessalonians 2:1–10, then with the validity and necessity of a work ethic, because paradise had not been regained: Christ had not yet returned.

The behavior of the *ataktoi* and their eschatological expectation were related because the discussion of the *ataktoi* (3:6–12) immediately follows the steadfast expectation of Jesus in 3:5 and the eschatological error refuted in 2:1–12.

The Red Guards' overconfidence in themselves as the bearers of truth was a logic derived from their assumption of a realized utopia. In assaulting and eradicating Chinese traditions and Western bourgeois capitalism, the Red Guards were overconfident in ushering in millenarian communism. The social behavior of the *ataktoi* and the Red Guards was caused by the radicalization of the millennial hope into irrational eschatological excitement. Their ideology was therefore one of eschatological excitement.[81]

The Prophetic Realism of Pauline Apocalyptic Eschatology

Paul corrected their mistaken eschatological and ethical assumptions. In 1 Thessalonians 5:13, Paul exhorted his readers to be at peace among themselves, in response to the disruptive behavior of the *ataktoi*.[82] Paul's work ethic is characterized by peace so that the poor majority would not be burdened by the *ataktoi*, who refused to work.[83] The problem may have been the social strife of the *ataktoi* with regard to the patron in the city. Paul would not want such a problem to hinder the mission of the church in Thessalonica. More probably, the political problem of causing "bad witness" for the church and "false realized eschatology" to the outsiders was too great a risk to take. So Paul admonished them to live a quiet life. *Quiet* does not mean passive or inactive but rather not causing social and political problems in such a way that the mission of the church would be in jeopardy. Given his commitment to a social ethic, Paul wanted Christians in Thessalonica not to burden other Christians but to continue to do good for the welfare system of the city.[84]

More important, Paul gave his response to the *ataktoi* in the eschatology deliberation in 2 Thessalonians: at the end of history the invisible world that controls the present order will be revealed. Either God himself or God's appointed representatives will appear to direct the consummation of God's plan for the universe and the realization of history's appointed goals. This will be accomplished through a series of cataclysmic events, such as a final cosmic struggle, which will radically alter the existing natural, physical, and spiritual order. As a result, the physical and spiritual world will yield to the absolute rule of God. Resurrected individuals will be judged and assigned to their several destinies.[85]

Pauline eschatology has a prophetic realism built into it as its core of existence—eschatological ethics. Without prophetic realism as its foundation, Pauline eschatology is wishful thinking, akin to that of the Red Guards, inspired only by empty ideology. However, Paul's eschatological ethics in 1 Thessalonians 5:10 exhorts the Thessalonians: "Whether we are awake or sleeping, with him we will live." Living and eschatological hope are inseparable; without eschatological hope, living is mere existence.[86] Eschatology and ethics are also inseparable in Pauline thinking.[87] The Pauline community was born through a faithful response to the preached word and the imitation of Jesus, as well as by enduring suffering with hope through the eschatological gift of joy given by the Holy Spirit. Living is a matter of ethical living in Jesus Christ.

Pauline ethics in the Thessalonian correspondence finds its base in eschatology. Paul responded to the question of "times and seasons" with the ethical advice of "not sleeping" (negatively expressed) and being watchful (positively expressed)[88]—being ever ready for the *parousia*. Paul does not give a timetable, an eschatological answer; rather, he asks believers to be sober, which is an ethical answer.

The prophetic realism of Paul's eschatological ethics critiques the disruptive behavior and unwillingness of the *ataktoi* to work. Paul exhorts them to work and not to burden anyone (3:11–13), just as he toiled and worked as an apostle (3:7–10). The rhetoric of prophetic realism enables persecuted believers to hang on in the tension between the pain of suffering and the promise of rest, the ambiguity of life and the sureness of victory, the coming of Christ and the consummation of *parousia*, the waiting for *parousia* in sobriety (eagerness to earn one's bread) and hope. Prophetic realism nurtures hope for believers, which constantly challenges them to view their present situation in light of the future.

Conclusion

Paul's prophetic realism of eschatological ethics is relevant for the Red Guards and the *ataktoi* alike. This Christian hermeneutic of hope constantly qualifies the present existence and brings about salvation. This hope will not result in overconfidence or legalistic endurance. Evans explains this point well:

Paul is endeavoring to make the Thessalonians mature men rather than teaching them a morality. The Church must live with a future which is open; she should not claim to have ready-made answers for all ethical problems. Her ethical program is a direction. Her future is governed by the coming Lord, so that the Church lives proleptically for *God's* sake and not for *good's* sake.[89]

The eschatological ethics of prophetic realism is not only a critique of cultural hopelessness but also a sustaining force for the faithful community to live meaningfully in the world of conflict and dead ends.

In his critique of the *pax Romana* of his day, where the *telos* of history comes before the terminus, Paul warns of the unexpected and imminent *parousia* of Christ for the purpose of gathering believers (1 Thess. 5:3). The Pauline apocalyptic ethos is to sustain the constant critique of the social and political injustices on behalf of the powerless, a critique of complacency and comfort for the discovery of greater truth. Ultimately, apocalyptic thought seeks to actualize human existence both through its constant critique by the divine word and by drawing it into openness of future possibilities.

8

mao meets paul III

Eschatology, Utopia, and Hope

We have seen how the demise of the Maoist revolution came because of its shift from the socioeconomic level to the ideological and political levels of the Great Leap Forward and the Cultural Revolution. This shift from the socioeconomic to the ideological and political is the inevitable but necessary failing of most political movements, and Maoism is no exception. The socioeconomic revolutions of the 1950s brought changes to management and institutional levels of the Party and society, but during the 1960s the changes were purely ideological and political and did not meet the concrete needs of the people. Perhaps one exception was the education revolution of the Cultural Revolution; but even there, the higher school's cadre training functioned more to teach empty slogans than to expand knowledge or enculturate virtues. The Ninth Plenum of January 1961 released ideological and political controls on the social and economic needs of the country. State and society were separated; thus, the means and ends of the Maoist revolutions were separated. "Ideology and politics, being in the realm of the state, took on an auto-cephalous character."[1] As a result, the Maoist revolution, having alien-ated itself from the real needs of the people, began to feed on itself. It finally rolled on like an overwhelming tidal wave that swept on fren-ziedly and turned into the hurricane of the Great Proletarian Cultural Revolution.

This chapter continues the critical dialogue between Paulinism and Maoism, paying particular attention to their different understandings of the historical process ([de]-eschatology) and the means and ends of utopia. The knotty issue is the contradiction between the utopian impulse (the hope for a better world) and the anti-utopian ideology (the Marxist historical-materialistic assumption that rejects a future, otherworldly utopia) of Maoism, which reveals its problematic: "the contradiction between objective history and subjective will."[2]

Utopian and Anti-utopian Ideologies

Both the Thessalonian millennialists and the Maoist revolutionaries can be said to have held to a "utopian ideology," a term defined by Karl Mannheim as "a state of mind . . . when it is incongruous with the state of reality within which it occurs. . . . Only those orientations transcending reality will be referred to by us as utopian which, when they pass over into conduct, tend to shatter . . . the order of things prevailing at the time."[3] Pauline Christians in Thessalonica and the Chinese in Mao's era faced similar problems of deprivation and crisis—suffering, dissonance, hardship, hopelessness—that inevitably caused them to look to utopian ideology for survival. However, the Pauline and Maoist utopian movements were radically different in their means and ends of utopia as well as in their view of historical process.

The Means and Ends of Realizing a Utopian Society

Whereas the Marxist critique of socialist utopianism (of Saint-Simons, etc.) focuses on the means rather than the ends of a utopian society, the Pauline critique of the Maoist form of utopianism is largely on its ends rather than its means. Paul was a Jewish Christian who saw the end of history in Christ, which provided the ultimate reference point for the hope and meaning of history; Mao, on the other hand, was a Chinese Marxist who sought to offer the socialist hope of utopia by means of mass struggles and uninterrupted revolutions. In other words, Maoism has a utopian impulse that is anti-eschatological: it hopes for a better world than the existing reality and at the same time rejects a transcendent, otherworldly utopia.

The problem in Mao's utopian and anti-utopian ideology is caused partly by its sinification of Marxism. Marxism is a distorted interpretation and heretical adaptation of Christian theology expressed in a social-political context of class struggle. In the process of adopting certain aspects of the Christian tradition, it corrupts the apocalyptic eschatology of that tradition. On the one hand, Marxist ideology co-opts the dramatic transformation of social realities from the apocalyptic tradition. On the other hand, the ideology rejects the in-breaking power from the transcendental world. Further, Maoism uses Marxism's violent struggle and revolutionary transformation and adapts them into the Chinese cyclical worldview. This means that Maoism believes in uninterrupted revolutions without an eschaton; instead, its revolutions will spin on in an eternal cycle. The "uninterrupted revolution" is the means *and* the end of achieving the communist utopia. The ideal society of the communist state is made up of eternal struggles in the prolongation of the historical now.

Hopelessness in a Vicious Cycle and the Prolongation of the Now

Marxism and Maoism's elimination of the end of history produces a lack of hope and future in their political revolutions. Maoism is anti-utopian in the sense that the belief in a better future is simply absent; utopia, if there is one, is found in the constant struggles of the present. According to Maoism, "paradise now" is simply pain and violence. It is because of these contradictions and struggles as both the means and the ends of communist utopia that one cannot call it "utopia" or "paradise." Since Mao believed in the inevitability of continuous class struggle and the permanence of revolutions, even in a communist society, the Maoist utopian society will never have harmony, coherence, and peace.[4] According to Maoism, the historical process does not move in a straight line; rather, it moves in a wavelike spiral.

The problem of Maoist utopian and anti-utopian ideology is the disintegration of time and space that results from the sinification of Marxism, in which the *yin-yang* cyclical worldview is employed to accommodate the de-eschatological, linear, and dialectical worldview of Marxism. When Maoism read "contradictions" into the dialectics of Marxism, the Maoist understanding of time and space began to collapse. As I explained at the conclusion of chapter 4, the inescapable destiny of the Chinese personality is that at times it seems to be wisely holding all the ambiguities of life in healthy tension but at times in confusion and contradiction. There I explained the constant struggle of living in the tension between the antithesis of the inner and the outer person. Here the problem is the collapse of space and time in the experience of the people, because the *yin-yang* worldview of change is intensified in the prolonged now of everlasting revolution. Bauer writes on the "now" intensification of Maoism:

> [P]recisely because it cannot find a fixed place anywhere in a perpetually changing medium, the ideal society acquires a curious presence. Just as absolute truth is only revealed "in the process of cognition itself," the ideal society becomes tangible reality only in the revolution, during change, which is the "only absolute." But this change is constantly at work in the incessant movement of contradictions in all phenomena and therefore can be realized at any time in the consciousness of it. . . . Happiness thus turns out to be elusive, and that in two respects. It can only be caught in flight, as it were, only in revolutionary movement. It can also always escape again unless one is ready to catch it ever anew. The blissful eternity of heaven and paradise which springs from an infinitely great, quiescent time, is replaced by the intoxicating eternity of earth which is composed of an infinite chain of infinitely small, ecstatic moments where the sudden reversal of contradictions is time and again experienced as the breathtaking rebirth of pulsating life. This "Now" is the dimension of happiness and of the ideal, not the "once" whether this refers to a distant past or a distant future.[5]

Mao's anti-utopian ideology emphasizes the masses and the uninterrupted revolution of the now. The uninterrupted revolutions, one after another, are meant to overcome a socially distorted and conflicted history. To disrupt the temporal and spatial ambiguities as well as evil, Maoist revolutions attempt to overcome and change history (time and space). Thus, political ideology and the euphoric trance of the masses help Red China to overcome pain and suffering. Yet in the success of these revolutions, Maoism keeps reminding the people that there is no transcending utopia, that revolutions must keep on going, or they will be condemned as "counterrevolutionary." To purge the "counterrevolutionary elements," Mao launched in 1950 and 1951 the "Three Antis" (antiwaste, anticorruption, antibureaucracy) and the "Five Antis" (antibribery, antifraud, antitax evasion, antilying, antirevealing state secrets) to "reeducate" millions. This led, in fact, to the lynching, repression, and killing of many.

Realized Eschatology of the Ataktoi

Mao's anti-utopian ideology contained the same weakness as did the conviction of the Thessalonian *ataktoi,* who believed that the day of the Lord had come, that is, that past and future had collapsed into the now. Mao's anti-utopian ideology assumed that the Chinese masses were blank tablets on which traditions and history were bracketed out. Mao

attempted to create a new humanity in the masses, where Chinese traditions (especially feudalism, Confucianism, and superstitions) and
Western capitalism would be rejected and erased. Mao emphasized in
1964 that "the thought, culture, and customs which brought China to
where we found her [in 1949] must disappear, and the thought, customs, and culture of proletarian China, which do not yet exist, must
appear."[6] The consequence of this anti-utopianism was twofold: radical
hostility toward an existing order, and living in an extreme make-believe
world, that is, the reverse of the existing order that would not be realized. Utopianism attempted to counteract and transform the existing
social order. However, in Maoism, not only could the social order not
be transformed but neither could the utopian dream be realized.

This was the case also with some of the Thessalonian millennialists
who thought that Christ had come and who grieved over death in the
new age (1 Thess. 4:13). The "utopia" or "millennia of peace and prosperity" that the Thessalonian *ataktoi* and the Maoist Chinese sought was
no place at all. It simply did not exist. Sir Thomas Moore once noted
that the word *utopia* can mean either a good place or no place;[7] Lewis
Mumford observed that the term *utopia* can mean either the ultimate
in human hope or the ultimate in human folly.[8] The collapse of time into
the now has the utopian definition of "no place" only.

(Anti-)Utopia and Hope(lessness)

Maoist anti-utopian ideology gives rise to a distorted mental structure and worldview because the intensification of time and the revolution of the "now" are ideas that can never be realized in the existing
social order. This utopian ideology as a form of knowledge is no longer
adequate to comprehend reality. Once utopian wish and reality are separated, ideology and utopianism would be sustained only as far as the
dream allowed. The Thessalonians and the Chinese confirm the futility
of anchoring one's faith in a secular utopia of human folly or in having
an idol of a no-place utopia. The hope that Paul theologized comes neither from humans nor from idols but from the true, living God, to whom
Paul enjoined the Thessalonians to turn (1 Thess. 1:9–10). God is faithful and able to realize his kingdom in his time (5:24). The inherent contradiction in Maoism is the Chinese people's simultaneous desire and
inability to find ultimate meaning and hope in mortal persons, whether
in Mao or in themselves. To fill that emotional and cultural void, Mao
injected the idea of eternal revolution and utopian communism among
the masses. These impulses were able to sustain the Cultural Revolution for ten years in a paradigm of "destruction before construction."

In denying the inheritance of history and opting rather for its destruction, Mao made the main thrust of the Cultural Revolution the proletarianization of the masses. He said, "It is always people with a low level of culture who triumph over people with a high level of culture."[9]

The Maoist "utopian and anti-utopian" problematic depicts the universal human problem of overcoming time and space. Time and space are dimensions of human experience that are difficult to conquer, yet the very act of being human is to accommodate ourselves in and to transcend the limitations of time and space. Without the consciousness of a perfect place that transcends history (time and space), humanity is merely existing in the bondage of historical embeddedness, that is, merely living in distortion, ambiguity, and imperfection. As such, human history is constituted of pain and suffering, aimlessness, meaninglessness, and hopelessness. The problem with Maoism is its view that it can project a utopian vision and yet reject the transcendent world.

Undoubtedly, the "better place" is never a fully realized place, so that the never-realized "better place" becomes the engendering force of hope and the driving force of our existence.[10] In fact, if there ever were to be a moment in our existence in which we thought we had arrived at the perfect place, then the *eutopia* (good place) would cease to be a *outopia* (no place); worse still, the assumed *eutopia* of our history would become stagnant self-complacency and even boring, lifeless deterioration. The historical process is always in the state of change and always in need of improvement, redemption, and new interpretation. Once the ambiguity and distortion of historical reality is assumed to be the ideal and perfect state, humans would lose their "will to shape history and therewith [their] ability to understand it."[11] Mannheim puts it well: "With the relinquishment of utopias, man would lose his will to shape history."[12] If *eutopia* ceases to be *outopia*, but fully present in history, we will witness the termination of history and meaning.

The message of 2 Thessalonians 2:1–11 is relevant here: it speaks to the confusion regarding the teaching that "the day of the Lord has come." A utopia such as that which Mao promised did not come. To see Mao as the savior of the Middle Kingdom who ushered in a new era of equality and bliss, as the deliverer of the masses who redeemed the oppressed, as the bearer of social justice for China, was to live in a deceptive world. The Thessalonian correspondence pointed out that there was only one utopia, the otherworldly, eschatological kingdom of God (1:7–12). Mao's promise of security and peace entailed patronage and benefaction obligations of paying homage as well as loyalty to the Maoist ideology. Paul believed, however, that the true freedom the Thessalonians waited for could never be fully realized in the human realm; it could only appear at the end of history, when divine freedom is to be bestowed beyond that of any governmental yoke.

Paul understands "salvation" as future, not present, reality in 1 Thessalonians 1:10 ("Jesus . . . saves us from the *coming* wrath"). The words "hope of salvation" in 5:8 also confirm this reading. The creation motif signified by the word "appointed" in 5:9 is common in Old Testament literature,[13] and this creation of God is viewed in a continuum of past, present, and future. Therefore, this motif implies that God's creation is still in process. The "appointment" of Christians is declared clearly in both positive and negative qualifications: "not . . . in the wrath but to obtain salvation." This appointment is the goal, couched in the connotation of purpose. Paul assures the Thessalonians that their appointment means that their lives are pregnant with divine purpose. Such eschatological hope allows them to live in the difficult present situation with strength and a hope for the future. Thus Paul's rhetoric depicts the movement of hope, evoking the believers' hope to be made aware of God's purpose in their lives in a unifying reality of past, present, and future.[14] That sense of salvation from past to present to future constitutes holistic salvation.

In the Maoist revolutionary experience, the utopian thought of messianic promises without the utopian and eschatological bases drew the masses to embrace uninterrupted revolution. The irony was that such a messianic commitment in the Maoist vision of communism reinforced the totalitarian tyranny of the revolution. Communism, whether that of Marx or Mao, is a utopian vision that is linked with totalitarianism. Meisner explains:

> [T]he most repressive features of contemporary Communist states can be explained, in large measure, in terms of the apocalyptic acceptance of the utopian Marxist promise of the universal advent of a totally egalitarian society; totalitarian domination in the present is not only justified, but also essentially determined, by a belief in necessary laws of historical development inevitably leading to worldwide salvation. Thus Communist totalitarianism . . . is essentially a "secularized sociopolitical religion" [Waldemar Gurian's words] based on the "utopian eschatology" of Karl Marx.[15]

In short, the inevitable problem of a secularized form of eschatology is a never-ending dialectical process of cyclical recourse to humans' own resources, which eventually is self-feeding. Pauline eschatology provides faith in a transcendent being who requires humans to repent, change, and critique themselves. It gives humans the resources beyond themselves as well as the freedom of salvation and new life. The Maoist utopia's denial of God deletes the power of humankind to create a socialist society, for when there is no God, there is no humanity.

Human Will and Transcending Forces in Historical Progress or Personal Sanctification

Actualizing the full human potential for the sake of a harmonious world order is the old Confucian doctrine of becoming a sage. This doctrine of sanctification is humanistic in the Confucian tradition because of its belief in *Tian's* (heaven's) endowment of human nature to live a holy life in the secular and public realm. The Maoist vision of human nature is influenced by this Confucian tradition but distorted by the historical materialism of the Marxist view on human nature. Mao believed in the moral virtues of the new Maoist person, who must work hard at socialist consciousness (for there is no such thing as abstract human nature); he believed that human nature is conditioned by class consciousness.[16] Thus Maoism envisions the realization of Chinese revolutions by large numbers of "vanguards who have political vision, militant spirit, and readiness to make sacrifices. They are frank, honest, active, and upright."[17] The Maoist humanity was the "red and expert," that is, fully sanctified revolutionaries who were the professional elites (expert) and political die-hards (red).

Maoism perceives sanctification as the process of human moral perfection by the fulfillment of political imperatives and the overcoming of class consciousness. In other words, only ideological sanctification exists; there is no such thing as human nature that is pure and divine. Sanctification becomes the ideological process of struggles and revolutions. In the *Yu-lu*, Mao asks: "Where does man's correct thought come from? Does it fall down from Heaven? No. Is it imbedded in his own mind? No." He concludes: "Man's correct thought only can come from social reality, only can come from three realities: production struggles in society, class struggles, and scientific investigation."[18] Struggles and revolutions are essentials of human history.

In contrast to Mao's view are those of the apostle Paul and of Liu Shaoqi. Paul believed that sanctification is an appropriation through faith of one's union with God and a practical realization of God's purpose through the simultaneous working of the Holy Spirit. Following the Old Testament prophets, who used the term *holiness* (Hebrew *qodesh*, translated in the LXX by the Greek *hagiasmos*) not to denote a pure being or a pious essence but rather one belonging to the Holy One (Yahweh),[19] Pauline sanctification is the belief that because one belongs to Yahweh, then one is expected to be ethical, just, and morally good.[20] The one who is related to God must practically realize God's provision of power over impurity or unholiness. The indicative (seen in the phrase *en hagiasmos* in 1 Thess. 4:4, 7) and imperative (seen in the infinitives *apexesthai, eidenai, ktasthai, hyperbainein, pleonektein,* and, most forcefully, *dei*) of holiness are enveloped in the notion that God, who gives the Holy Spirit, prompts believers toward sanctification. The indicatives and imperatives of sanctification are fluid and not artificial; they are two sides of the same coin. This rhetoric of sanctification as the will of God not only defines for the Thessalonians the purpose of their lifestyle but also evokes awareness that the Holy Spirit is constantly guiding, enabling, and empowering them to be conscious of God's presence and to live in a way pleasing to God.

The wording of "spirit and soul and body" in 1 Thessalonians 5:23 reflects the Thessalonian audience's tripartite view of human nature, which is similar to Mao's atomic anthropology. Since trichotomy language is atypical for Paul, and since we have observed already the dualistic understanding of the sexual ethics of the "rebels" (*ataktoi* in 1 Thess. 4:7), Paul's emphasis on "wholeness" is a correction of the audience's misconception. Paul's theology affirms body, spirit, and soul as making up the whole human being, whereas his audience may have viewed the body as degenerative and the spirit as divine.[21] Thus Paul emphasized the wholeness of God's sanctifying action. God will sanctify them to be complete and will keep them blameless in spirit, soul, and body until the end-time.

In contrast to Mao, Liu Shaoqi believed that correct thought could only come from social struggle *within* the Party; in other words, the Party was the key instrument for the transformation of humans to revolutionaries.[22] Liu's ideology was criticized during the Cultural Revolution, at a time when the Maoist current swept to victory.[23] The Cultural Revolution was initially named "socialist" but changed to "proletarian" after the defeat of Liu: "socialist" signified the importance of class struggle for the transformation of human beings; "proletarian" connoted the triumph and continuous struggle against all capitalists (such as Liu and the authoritarian clique that dominated the Party).

So the revolutionaries were the *ataktoi,* to use Paul's words. If there was no class struggle, then there was no spiritual transformation of the inner person. Mao's approach of ideological conversion was aimed at changing "the content of motivation, to provide through continuous and painstaking socialist education, through rectification campaigns and movements, a change in behavior 'within the soul of man'. . . . This conversion has been attempted before, in religious systems, but not with the thoroughness of a science, which is Mao [Zedong]'s treatment of this psychological remarking."[24] In other words, the organizational form of Mao's ideology was the inside-out approach. Schurmann notes that, "given the mystery and intractability of human nature . . . a scientific campaign to change the soul of man seems to be a task which normally only God would set himself to accomplish."[25]

Along the line of placing one's trust in humans, Meisner comments correctly that "The whole vision of a continuous process of revolutionary change that would rapidly transform China into a country both economically modern and socially communist was based on a profound faith in the powers of the human consciousness and the human will to bring about that transformation."[26] Mao put much faith in "the boundless creative powers" of the masses and their "inexhaustible enthusiasm for socialism" for achieving the utopian social, economic, and ideological goals of communism. In launching the Great Leap Forward, for example, Mao was fully aware of the vicious cycle acting on the Chinese masses, causing them to be psychologically restricted and economically backward. To break that vicious cycle, Mao would raise their consciousness to a revolutionary spirit that would unleash their energy for economic development.

Mao did not believe in an objective law of historical progression. He believed that the end of a utopian society was to overcome ever-present contradictions and struggles. This anti-utopian ideology makes Maoist utopian thinking immune to a critique on the grounds of a standard definition of utopia (eternal peace, permanence, security, prosperity), for in Maoist utopian thinking, utopia is not defined as an ideal, good place; it is defined as change, struggle, and a lack of expectancy. The end is not defined, only the means—and the means define the end. Maoist utopia is defined as de-eschatologized revolution.

Eschatology and De-eschatology

The De-eschatology of Maoism and Violence

Mao's revolutionary ideology is a secular eschatology, influenced by Marx, because it proclaims an imminent paradise of human will on earth. During the Cultural Revolution, Mao boldly gave new names to the Chinese and to China, such as "new humanity," "new society," and "New China." By that he implied that the unprecedented new reality of uninterrupted revolution was the communist utopia. Because of his assumption that history does not have a goal of divine redemption, Mao blessed the Red Guards to usher in the communist utopia. Since the anti-utopian, de-eschatological worldview rejected faith in the God of history, Maoism believed in the philosophy of history and human will.

In 1967 Mao declared: "The next 50 to 100 years, beginning from now, will be a great era of radical change in the social system throughout the world, an earthshaking era without equal in any previous historical period. Living in such an era, we must be prepared to engage in great struggles which will have many features different in form from those of the past."[27] This de-eschatological (or eschatologyless) worldview of Mao found its popular expression in the cyclical ideology of uninterrupted revolutions. In other words, violence was the justified means of achieving the ideal, which explains Mao's famous political slogan: "Political power grows out of the barrel of a gun."[28] Mao believed that

> A revolution is not a dinner party, or writing an essay, or painting a picture, or doing embroidery; it cannot be so refined, so leisurely and gentle, so temperate, kind, courteous, restrained and magnanimous. A revolution is an insurrection, an act of violence by which one class overthrows another. A rural revolution is a revolution by which the peasantry overthrows the power of the feudal landlord class. Without using the greatest force, the peasants cannot possibly overthrow the deep-rooted authority of the landlords which has lasted for thousands of years. The rural areas need a mighty revolutionary upsurge. . . . it is necessary to create terror for a while in every rural area, or otherwise it would be impossible to suppress the activities of the counter-revolutionaries.[29]

Maoism as a heretical expression of de-eschatological "apocalyptic" thinking inevitably makes violence and struggle the means of preparing for the new era. Mao's ideology of struggle and revolution was a correction of liberalism, as he wrote in 1937 in an essay called "Combat Liberalism." The liberal heresy was that it "let things slide for the sake of peace and friendship. . . . [it] let things drift if they do not affect one personally."[30]

The liberation motive was inherent in Maoism, and the emphasis on struggle to bring about this liberation from the oppression of imperialism and feudalism was also the emphasis of Maoism, so much so that the revolutions were mandated to be continuous. While Mao's critique was apt, he radicalized revolutionary struggle by making violence and hatred necessary means. Raymond Whitehead writes: "Hatred of the enemy is a positive concept in Mao's thought. Animosity arouses the oppressed to action. Love only leads them to slavishness. The opposite of hatred is not love, but servility, the apathetic acceptance of an inferior position. Hatred of the enemy does not mean random venting of feelings. Hatred is justifiable and creative only when it is 'class hatred,' that is, hatred of oppression and the perpetrators of oppression."[31]

Vindication, Judgment, and Violence in Paul's Theology?

In Paul's teaching, judgment on oppressors and love for all people were held in tension. For example, the *vituperatio* (blame) language of the disobedient Jews in 1 Thessalonians 2:13–16 (which is a digression but neither a scribal commentary nor an interpolation[32]) and of the Roman oppressors in 2 Thessalonians 1:8 serves mainly as vindication language for creating social identity, purpose, and hope for the oppressed group rather than as a vitriolic attack on disobedient Jews and Roman oppressors.[33] The purpose of the vindication language is to legitimate the persecuted group in accordance with the will of God and the persecuting group as incurring wrath in the immediate future.[34] Thus 2 Thessalonians 1:8 speaks of the eschatological judgment of God that calls the actions of oppressors and oppressed into accountability. The language in 1 Thessalonians 2:13–16 is also eschatological or even apocalyptic, and thus the symbolic exaggeration is intended to heighten the readers' sense of God's just judgment and to strengthen the readers' resilience in overcoming suffering.

Paul's theology of the just judgment of God is balanced by his theology of love for all. Thus we read in 1 Thessalonians 5:15: "See that none of you repays evil for evil, but always seek to do good to one another and to all" (NRSV). Note also the peaceful and reconciliation theology of Paul in 1 Thessalonians 3:12—"May the Lord make you increase and abound in love to one another and to all, as we do to you"—and in 4:11–12: "Command the respect of outsiders." Quoting an aphorism in 5:15, the proscription does not concur with the *lex talionis* of Judaism (e.g., Exod. 21:23–25; Lev. 24:19–20), which is implicitly rejected. Even though Paul does not explicitly quote Jesus' Golden Rule (Matt. 7:12), the quotation appears to be common catechetical material (see Rom. 12:17–21; 1 Peter 2:19–21; 3:9) that Paul would simply use freely. Thus he encourages his readers' mutual respect and benefaction toward one another: "Pursue what is good toward one another *and everyone*." In other words, the basic interpersonal relationship of Pauline theology is that of tolerance, not evil for evil. The hallmark of the Christian community is unconditional selflessness and dynamic love toward others. Christians are to pursue the good at all times.

Manifest Destiny of Humanity: Death or Salvation?

In contrast to the secular faith of Mao's view of history, Paul's eschatology is Christ-centered: it has an openness to the future. It acknowledges the limitation of the human and urges one to place one's trust in the Divine, who determines the future. For Mao, death for the people was the highest virtue as well as the ultimate end of the utopian hope. In other words, Mao's utopian vision was a "fully realized eschatology" in the now because of his rejection of the eternal future. Robert Faricy points out:

> The ultimate future of humanity as foreseen by Mao is its extinction, either by the death of the human race or by its transformation into something else. The death of the species: this prospect is surely due to provoke a collective anxiety as the new China builds itself toward the future. If beyond progress there is only the dead end of the mass grave, then the sickness of the dead end is going to set in and grow, unless there is found a basis for hope in an ultimate future.[35]

Faricy continues to offer a suggestive answer to the Maoist internal contradiction from a Christian perspective:

> Jesus risen is precisely that person whose hands hold the ultimate future of each person and of all humanity. . . . He is the answer not only to the death of the individual but, as the personal Center of the world to come, to the death of human society in this world. . . . Mao's conception of permanent [i.e., uninterrupted] revolution is one that, by its very nature and structure, asks for an ultimate justification, for an ultimate meaning. This meaning can be found in the Christian doctrine that the struggle of people on earth is or can be a participation in the struggle, in the passion, of Jesus. Just as Jesus' struggle and death ended in resurrection, so can the struggle and death of each person and of humanity collectively. . . . There is then, an internal contradiction in Mao [Zedong] thought between its stress on the struggle for the development of people and of society . . . and . . . its absence of an ultimate goal to give ultimate meaning to the struggle and to be a solid basis for human hope.[36]

The tension between "the already and the not yet" of Pauline eschatology may be translated into the tension between the "ideal place and the no place" (e/outopia) of utopianism. The "todayness" of God's future is present in our midst. Without the tension, people can easily become complacent or have the feeling of resignation. The utopian tension serves to identify the social, economic, political, ethical, spiritual, and psychological dissonance of their present reality.[37] It also serves to project the hope of possibilities, to offer an alternative order to the present one, and to transcend the present dissonance with a salvific and comprehensive worldview.

Christological Eschatology As Redemptive Telos *of History*

When we speak of the Pauline theology of history and Christ, we are talking about a particular worldview that schematizes the world and provides meaning for our existence. The function of apocalyptic under-standings such as those of Paul is that "it offers a temporal or teleolog-ical framework for understanding evil by claiming that evil must grow in power until the appointed time of the imminent end."[38] Pauline escha-tology helped the Thessalonian Christians cope with pain and suffer-ing, social deprivation, cognitive dissonance, and absence of meaning through the apocalyptic reworking of time. The theological intention of Paul in the Thessalonian correspondence was not to provide a detailed schedule of the world's end; it was, rather, to provide the presence and meaning of history as it is located in Jesus Christ. As such, evil and chaos and meaninglessness will be transformed, the limitations of time and space transcended, and the fear of mortality cast out.

Paul's narration in 1 and 2 Thessalonians must not be taken as a com-prehensive, universal summation of history from its beginning to its eschatological end. Rather, the Thessalonian correspondence consists of pieces or mosaic stones arranged in a certain design, which climaxes in the power of the eschatological Judge and Benefactor, Jesus Christ. Pauline eschatology attempts to stretch human finitude beyond the pres-ent to the historical past (Jesus' death and resurrection) and to the futur-istic end of time (eschatological hope). The Pauline view of history there-fore grants the Thessalonians a vision of the past, present, and future.

Pauline eschatology provides meaning to suffering in history and grants freedom beyond the limitation of time and hope to the sting of mortality. This eschatology challenges the Maoist fear of mortality, as seen in the Cultural Revolution, which was Mao's "quest for revolu-tionary immortality—By revolutionary immortality I mean a shared sense of participating in permanent revolutionary fermentation, and of transcending individual death by 'living on' indefinitely within this con-tinuing revolution."[39] Lifton continues: "The revolutionary denies theol-ogy as such, but embraces a secular utopia through images closely related to the spiritual conquest of death and even to an afterlife."[40]

Apocalyptic Eschatology As Theology of History

Paul's eschatological thought seeks to actualize the fullness of human existence in two ways: by bringing human existence under the constant critique of the divine word and by drawing human existence forward toward future possibilities. Pauline eschatology challenges humanity to face the reality of the finality of ourselves and of the world; its purpose is to prevent us from falling into sterile optimism or downright pessimism. Evans puts it well: "True Christian eschatology calls our present order into question by the final order of God, while making us aware of our social solidarity and responsibility."[41]

The search for the meaning of history begins with our present ambiguities. This search extends to the beginning, which projects backward our human utopian condition before the fall, back to the meaning that was created and intended by God at the very beginning. The search also projects forward our human utopian condition to the end of history, pointing us to what is possible. Thus the search for meaning extends to the whole of history and gives us a holistic sense rather than a disjointed or constructed one. Such enveloping of the past, present, and future meaning of history enables us to transcend any present suffering to embrace the belief of the past and the hope of the future. Löwith argues: "In the Hebrew and Christian view of history the past is a promise to the future; consequently, the interpretation of the past becomes a prophecy in reverse, demonstrating the past as a meaningful 'preparation' for the future."[42] Likewise, the same prophecy in reverse can be said of the future in relation to the now: the eschatological future on one hand exists in our expectation and hope; on the other hand, it is realized proleptically in the present as assuring and consummating the future (cf. "Give us this day our bread of the morrow!"). Thus the search for meaning focuses our attention on the ultimate goal as the ultimate purpose and ultimate meaning of history.

Paul's eschatological thought is therefore a theology and hermeneutic of history in which the future and the present take precedence over his concern for the past. That is, the reality of God's future can extend backward in time, reinterpreting the historical past and present and saving history from being alienated or ambiguous, so that believers can claim that they belong to the absolute future of history, which is the one, living, and faithful God. Jesus as the coming Lord (*ho erchomenos*, the coming one) provides the present struggle of human beings with a goal and purpose whereby all history is proclaimed and believed by Christians to be within the redemptive act of God. It is a dynamic faith lived out in love, anchored in the hope of an assured *parousia*.

9

millenarian hope in the post-paul and post-mao eras

Modern Utopian and A-utopian Visions and Pauline Eschatology

The one-sided view of a secular utopian worldview can either perceive the historical *eschaton* as a goal without ending (continuous progress) or an ending without fulfillment (abrupt catastrophe without salvation). The former is a de-eschatological worldview of secular "messianic presumption of utopian progressivism," as represented not only by Maoism and present-day capitalism but also by technological optimism. The second view is "the apocalyptic resignation of fatalistic acceptance of inevitable catastrophe."[1] Even now we see that globalization of the economy produces ever-greater inequalities, reducing the dignity of people to mere digital identity and market value, converting humans in God's image to machine-cloned slaves. We also see that technological advancement brings the worldview of destruction and violence closer to a reality if people do not understand the christological eschatology of the *finis* of violence and the *telos* of salvation. We do not need the self-fulfilling prophecy that the world will end in violence.

This chapter will investigate the implications of Pauline eschatology and Maoist utopianism for post-Mao China and the modern world. I want to comment on the significance of contemporary society's understanding or ignoring of eschatology and utopianism.

Anti-utopia in the Post-Mao China

The growth of Christianity in China during the post-Mao era was dramatic. By 1990 it was estimated that there were six thousand open churches and fifteen thousand registered "meeting points" (*juhuidian*) for five million believers.[2] Moreover, "Christianity fever" in the post–Cultural Revolution era, especially after 1989, indicated another prosperous growth of Chinese Christianity, and the phrase was used regularly by research institutes in China. Yet religious phobia remains a strong sentiment among government leaders in the post-Mao China, as Alan Hunter and Chan Kim-Kwong describe:

> Religion gained a higher political profile after 1989. The top leadership of the CCP, dismayed by the challenge to its power in spring of that year, attempted to intensify its ideological control over society. It was aware that religious organizations, especially Christian ones, had been influential in opposition to the communist governments of eastern Europe. Stricter regulations were promulgated, and rumours spread that a crackdown on religious activities was imminent. In 1990, Chinese government officials reportedly feared that 70 per cent of the nation's religious activities were out of control, while Premier Li Peng called for attacks on the underground churches. Other senior leaders warned of a transfer of allegiance, especially in the countryside, from the CCP to religious organizations.[3]

Not only in religious life but also in cultural and economic life, there seemed to be a "Second Liberation" in 1978 (the "First Liberation" was in 1949). After ten years of Cultural Revolution, the Bamboo Curtain was lifting, and exchanges in commerce, knowledge, studies, sports, and arts were common.

However, there are dangers in the post-Mao reaction to Mao's utopianism and the total reception of the pragmatism of capitalism.[4] Most Chinese respected the pragmatism and Four Modernizations under the leadership of Deng Xiaoping. But the problem of this one-sided total rejection of utopianism, together with the calamity of its consequences, and the total embrace of industrialized and technologized capitalism is, to say the least, quite serious. The problems of market economy and capitalism have not been recognized by China.

In various lecture engagements and visits to China's main cities in the last ten years, I have witnessed increasing material prosperity, rigorous commercial activities, and the luxurious spending of the rich. University students, Christian and non-Christian alike, have repeatedly told me their fears that the pragmatism of capitalism, technological advancement, and economic modernization will lead to the neglect and robbing of China's ethical, spiritual, and relational wholeness. They lament the disappearance of hope for the future, community building, character integrity, and the spiritual quest.

The danger China now faces is the dissolution of the tension between the "already and the not yet" of eschatology. During Mao's era the emphasis was on the "not yet," as people looked forward to realizing the communist utopia in the New China. In the post-Mao era the emphasis is now on the "already," as people assume that with capitalism (*tzu pen zhu yi*) good times have already arrived.

Even though my critique of Mao's utopianism is harsh with regard to its political and ideological misguidedness, I would not want to dismiss the teleological necessity of Mao's vision for the future. No doubt that vision itself can be taken too far (e.g., by the leftists), and Mao's strategy of realizing that vision by means of violence is demonic; yet the vision for the future does provide drive and hope for the people. With New China's lack of vision for the future, individualism and materialism become the means of satisfaction and the goals of existence.

More important, the lack of a utopian vision in the post-Mao era and the commercial utopia itself might be self-consuming. In the post-Mao era, indeed, the Four Modernizations have gone very well. Yet people are well aware of social impasses, leadership corruption, economic ineptitude, and political nepotism throughout China. In the popular imagination Mao remains a moral and political leader who gave masses of people a ray of hope, "the symbol of an age of economic stability, egalitarianism, and national pride."[5] Geremie R. Barmé believes that since the mid 1980s there has been nostalgia for the old days, including the Cultural Revolution, even though the Cultural Revolution was a painful experience for all. He writes about the reason for the nostalgia:

Nostalgia is a central feature in how people form, maintain, and reconstruct a sense of self and the place of the individual in the world. Nostalgia develops usually in the face of present fears, disquiet about the state of affairs, and uncertainty about the future. Confronted with social anomie and disjuncture, nostalgia provides a sense of continuity. Nostalgia has politically often been used for extremist, particularly totalitarian and nationalist, ends. In mainland China, nostalgia was institutionalized by the Communist Party and its claims to legitimacy that emphasized its role as the inheritor and protector of a codified body of national traditions and that were summed up in terms of China's unique "spiritual civilization."[6]

Without a utopian dream, young people in China today can easily sink into self-doubt, individual struggle, and a sense of helplessness. But for them the nostalgia of Mao reinvents a period of national pride, a collective power to change society, and a purpose in life to revolutionize all cultural evils of the day.

The lack of a utopian vision clearly indicates the lack of a utopian leader in China today. Chang Zhengzhi, a contemporary Chinese author, writes:

> With Mao's death, China's age of great men came to an end. The masses feel a sense of loss. They have not yet found an alternative. That is to say that despite the passage of time, when the masses feel themselves discriminated against and oppressed, they can think of no other leader than Mao Zedong. . . .
>
> The name Mao Zedong will remain eternally a symbol of rebellion against this new order of democracy and capitalism. His prestige may well gradually rise among the masses once more. Of course, Mao Zedong must be criticized in human terms, but ironically, for Chinese like me who continue to oppose neocolonialism, the international balance of power makes it necessary for us to look to him as a bastion of human dignity.
>
> Seen in this light, for the people of China and of the poor nations throughout the world who are confronted with the new international scene, it is possible that Mao Zedong will gain a new lease on life.[7]

The lack of utopian vision in China today presents another problem in de-eschatologizing history, a common problem of secular utopia: "the discrepancy between the piling up of technological and scientific instrumentalities for making all things possible, and the pitiable poverty of goals."[8] But since no person can survive without a utopian vision, we do see in China today, as in the global culture, a contemporary utopian vision prevalent in mass media, popular entertainment, and various religious cults in this New Age. History is viewed as the instantaneous and eternal now, which does not have a purpose or goal, and thus has no meaning as well!

Today the utopian vision of the global culture seems to uphold democratic and capitalistic society as the ideal. People find the golden age in the instantification of the now. Present China seems to be in a state of identity crisis. And if Chinese Christianity is not aware of the problem, it will not be able to contribute to the society or even to love the country (patriotism). Worse still, it will be swept along with the cultural wave of present contentment, mechanical labor, and blind existence. The problem posed for Christianity is usually the secularization of its doctrine, such as the secularization of eschatology by Marxist and Chinese communism. Secularization can easily become a weak thesis or a weak religion that can hardly be called religion, yet it possesses the functions and dangers of a religion. Since it does not fall into the category of religion, people do not have any cognitive apparatus to understand it. Therefore, it becomes a "religion" that has the absolute concentration of power to exert its influence on the people without being questioned. If modernization and secularization in contemporary China constitute a "religion" with absolute power, many are searching for a democracy that, while it might not grant freedom and might actually cause societal evils, would offer prosperity. Many are searching also for a capitalism that, while it might engender greed and decrease societal virtues, would accumulate wealth. The anti-utopian ideology of secularization seeks to challenge the utopian hope of religion. While focusing on the eternal now, an anti-utopian "religion" of democracy and capitalism eradicates hope and dissolves the future.

Pauline eschatology challenges the modern myth that the global economy and global technology will ensure global peace and end wars—as well as history. Faith is not required; technological perfectibility is the logic of modern realized eschatology. Can technology standardize and necessitate one universal way of existence? Can transcendence grounded in a secular state be the logic that legitimates human bonding and freedom? Can autonomy replace theonomy? Moltmann is right in asserting:

> It is no longer a militant anti-theism as it was in the nineteenth century. It is merely a theism that has got lost and become superfluous. . . . Today many people are losing even the ancient over-valuation of the self, and both theism and atheism are being replaced by a cheerful nihilism or a trite complacency about things as they simply happen to be, and by the self's hollow emptiness.[9]

Similarly, Pauline eschatology prohibits us from believing that "the day of the Lord has come" and that the "peace of the empire is here forever." Christ's kingdom is the grand narrative for all empires, and God's glory will save us from nihilism and emptiness. Only in the sacrament of the love feast can modern humanity participate in the new life of God's kingdom by allowing God's future to define our present mode of being. Replacing God with secular narratives of technology and economy will not help. Secular states need God.

Modern people need faith in God. They need to allow God's future to "intrude" into their secular worldview so that God's presence (i.e., *parousia*) will be real in their lives. They need to suspend their technologically controlled schedule so that they can experience God's presence in their Sabbath. The Sabbath is the moment in which people allow God to interrupt their lives as the orders of the world are suspended. "The sabbath rest links the experience of God in history with the messianic hope in God for history."[10] The Sabbath rest is the foretaste of the redeemed world.

Progress in China does not guarantee happiness; that, perhaps, is the irony of a secular utopian vision. Bauckham offers a theological explanation for the destructiveness of secular utopianisms: "By postulating endless time the modern myth of progress has propagated an illusory sense of eternity, but in reality endless historical time, endless transient time, cannot lead to true eternity, the transcendence of transience, but only to universal death."[11] Christian apocalyptic eschatology offers an assured hope to believers in the living God, who raised the crucified Jesus and will usher in a new future of consummated redemption. According to apocalyptic eschatology, God's future of possibility and redemption has already intruded into the present chaotic and afflicted world. God's future counteracts secular historical forces and the human will, overpowering them, for they are nihilistic forces leading human society only to emptiness, paganism, or even destruction. Pauline apocalyptic eschatology of ethical realism rejects the deterministic acceptance of fatalism for the same reason that God's future is intruding into the seemingly dead-ends: to offer seeds of hope. The nature of hope forces us to offer "a radical reinterpretation (reimagining or reimaging) of the real, seeking a meaning for the present which is historical in the sense that it is teleologically determined. The present . . . does not contain its full meaning within itself, but only in its relatedness to what is yet to come."[12] In light of God's promises for the future, our task is to offer new images of the present. Thus God's future opens up the present and shapes it according to God's intention for history, vis-à-vis renewal, transformation, salvation, and wholeness. The power of God's future is thus made present in the now, especially in the incarnated Son and the baptism of the Holy Spirit.

Suicide Cults and Pauline Eschatology

China today needs a biblical eschatology, but Bible reading and interpretation are dangerous religious activities, as history shows. Almost all of the so-called "suicide cults" in China and in the West have used biblical texts to achieve their disastrous ends. Assuming the role of the two witnesses prophesied in Revelation 11:3, Bo and Peep (Southern Californian Applewhite and Nettles, the so-called "Do" and "Ti") traveled around the United States preaching a holy life of purity from sex and drugs and isolation from family. They also preached the good news of a salvation voyage, purportedly on a spaceship at the tail of the Comet

Hale-Bopp and destined for the kingdom of heaven. Twenty-one women and eighteen men died by their own hands at Rancho Santa Fe, California, at end of March 1997. The Order of Solar Temple was also looking for the millennial kingdom of peace and glory, which they located on the star Sirius. Over seventy disciples of this group have taken their lives in Canada, France, and Switzerland since 1974.[13] More than nine hundred members of Jim Jones's People's Temple took Jones's interpretation seriously concerning the end-time message of the Bible. They all died in a mass suicide in Jonestown, Guyana, on November 18, 1978. More and more "end-time cults" appear in China, many under the banner of Christianity, and some import their understanding of eschatology from the West. The Chinese government is fearful of these cults because they are not constructive to society.

We call them cults because they end up in tragedies. But how can one tell in advance that their interpretations of biblical eschatology are so mistaken? We also call them cults because their interpretations do not fit the reading of traditional, mainline churches. But they take biblical eschatology seriously (perhaps excessively so), while mainline churches are silent on the subject. It is ironic that people outside the church are interested in eschatology while those in the church show little or no interest.

A concern for eschatology is found in a world of uncertainty, insecurity, and change. Horoscopes and predictions of the future are popular columns in daily newspapers in China. The fear of nuclear holocaust, ecological catastrophe, social collapse, Satanism, terrorism, sexual perversion, and crime stimulate the hope for the end of the world and for heaven to come on earth.

There is an alleged prophecy of the day of the Lord that encourages people today to assume they are the "terminal generation." The prophecy of Armageddon is still preached today. We know how tricky it is to pin down the date of the end of the world. For instance, the year 1842 was originally thought to be the "Year of Rapture," but it turned out to be the "Great Disappointment." By arbitrarily following the Western calendar, we saw the end of the twentieth century and the second millennium of the common era—the year 2000—as something to trigger fears and hopes concerning our destiny. (If we were to use the Chinese calendar that operates in the lunar cycle of twelve and that has long passed 2000—actually, 2000 c.e. is 4698 on the Chinese calendar—we would not have any "millennial anxiety" concerning the end of our present history.)

The calendrical ending of the century or the millennium for most people using the Julian calendar was enticingly alarming even in the age of Melanchthon (sixteenth century) and Newton (seventeenth century).

Melanchthon predicted the year 2000 to be the final epoch of humankind, and Newton predicted 2000 to be the end of papal rule. The so-called New Age is also based on the Western astrological configuration of the Zodiac system, which asserts that the age of Taurus (the Bull) began around 4000 B.C.E., when Adam and Eve were expelled from Paradise. The age of Aries (the Ram) followed in 2000 B.C.E., when Abraham would have sacrificed his son had it not been for the ram. The age of Pisces (the Fish) characterized the salvation brought by "Jesus Christ, God's Son, Savior" (Greek acronym for "fish"). The age of Aquarius (Water), which dawned in 2000, is thought to supersede the patriarchal and institutionalized religions of Yahweh, Abraham, and Jesus Christ. The New Age religion teaches its new freedom and power, or so it claims, in the unleashing of spiritual power without boundaries, structure, and hierarchy.

Humans have long been caught in the web of sorting out the meaning of the end times. History gives us many examples of how people responded to perceived end times. When the Western calendar reached its first millennium, Europe faced threats and phobias similar to those around the year 2000. Various prophets emerged and proclaimed that the end of the world would come on the last day of 999. Some thought that Armageddon would happen on Christmas Eve of 999.[14] Mass panic, suicide, lawlessness, and indolence occurred as the final eve of 999 approached. George Duby has noted that "[a]t the centre of medieval darkness, the Year One Thousand, antithesis of the Renaissance, presented the spectacle of death and abject submission."[15] Augustine had postulated that the end of the world would occur at the year 1000, one thousand years after the birth of Christ. The year 1033, one thousand years after the *death* of Christ and marked by a great famine, was yet another year of fervent end-time expectation.[16]

A twelfth-century Irish saint predicted that the pope after John Paul II would be the last. In the sixteenth century, the French visionary Nostradamus predicted global conflagration before the end of the millennium. The Jehovah's Witnesses foresaw 1914 as the end, and, consequently, many suffered and were disappointed. Inscribed on the American-made Jehovah's Witness watch were the words "One Hour nearer The Lord's Return." In 1925, Robert Reidt shouted to the skies: "Gabriel, we're ready. Oh Gabriel." He then shouted to reporters: "Every one of my little flock will be transported by a supernatural power to California, possibly on a cloud." Another preacher, Charles Taylor, predicted that the end would be in 1976, 1980, 1988, 1989, and 1992. On the last date, he traveled with his disciples to Israel but could not decide whether to buy a one-way or round-trip ticket. In 1978, the Reverend Jim Jones, hoping to usher in the end, led his followers into the Guyana jungle and persuaded them to drink poison and commit suicide—913 people died.[17] In 1994, the doomsday prophet Luc Jouret led fifty-three followers to a fiery death at the Swiss headquarters of the Renewed Order of the Solar Temple.[18] All these are historical examples of how people responded to anxiety about the end of the world.

The apocalyptic expectation of the end of the world is usually related to the doctrine of the rapture, which "introduces a highly appealing element of escapism into the modern form of apocalyptic theology because true believers are promised they will not have to experience the world-wide destruction of an atomic holocaust."[19] The assumption, prediction, and fear of the rapture, as well as Armageddon, are too often corrosive in the personal, social, and political lives of Christians. Jewett writes:

> The doom boom theology teaches that the apocalyptic end of world history is predetermined by God in our time. Consequently there is nothing we can do to avert it. In this view, peacemaking is both futile and sinful and all efforts to promote international cooperation are inspired by Satan. Every compromise with our adversaries is viewed as a betrayal of divine trust; every effort to achieve arms control and to reduce the danger of accidental atomic wars is a sellout to the demonic powers.[20]

The effects of such rapture and Armageddon thinking are that some believe the world is about to end and thus consider social ethics a secondary responsibility. Some would even deliberately distance themselves from society, since they believe that the world is about to be condemned by the coming Judge. By internalizing the gospel for their own spiritual edification and holiness, they make the gospel simply a personal choice that has no significance for the world. But we see from the Pauline eschatology in the Thessalonian correspondence that Paul combined eschatological preparedness with an ethical responsibility of wholeness (holiness) and orderly living. Paul's eschatology can never be detached from one's holistic, ethical lifestyle. The calling of God is not to separate Christians into a cocoonlike, cloistered existence but to call them to a life of purpose and service.

Worse still, the hermeneutical presupposition of the rapture and Armageddon reading does not do justice to the Bible. It often plays the game of a jigsaw puzzle as interpreters piece together clues from Daniel, Revelation, Ezekiel, the Gospels, and a few verses from the Thessalonian correspondence. They ignore the historical context of each book of the Bible: the preoccupation with the modern generation transports biblical texts to the modern era. At best, the result is an arbitrary interpretation coupled with a constant rescheduling of contemporary events in the time line of apocalypticism. At worst, the result is a self-fulfilling prophecy of destruction as enmity and violence between individuals, cultures, and nations are enforced.

Should hope for the end of the world justify one's living and believing whatever one feels is right? Should the end justify the means? And if, in fact, such means should bring repetitive events of a disastrous end, should anyone in his or her right mind call this mentally healthy, theologically correct, and intellectually plausible? The original message of hope in Thessalonians has become the message of gloom and fear in the modern era, illustrated by an Adventist bumper sticker: "If you hear a trumpet, grab the wheel."

In the Thessalonian correspondence, Paul resisted date setting for any of the end time, least of all for the battle of Armageddon. Armageddon is not a part of Pauline eschatology at all. Fatalistic doctrines and escapist ethics are not at the core of Paul's teaching; rather, realistic hope and responsible ethics are! Paul writes: "See that no one returns evil for evil, but always pursue what is good toward one another and toward everyone" (1 Thess. 5:15). This verse seems to address how the congregation should treat not only the in-group but also the outsiders of the community—"toward one another and toward *everyone*." The imperative "see that" and the shift from the second to the indefinite pronoun (someone) indicate the wider audience Paul has in mind. Paul does not accept the traditional wisdom of *lex talionis*. Instead, he ignores retaliation and encourages respectful coexistence and mutual transformation through love and hope.[21]

The rapture in 1 Thessalonians has to do with the meeting of believers with the Lord, not a unilateral destruction of the innocent or of Christians who somehow do not belong to the right church or have an improper understanding of the rapture. Without the contextual understanding of Paul's message in the Thessalonian correspondence, the rapture's message of hope becomes the message of fear and anxiety. Many young Christians cannot be sure if they are going to make it. Paul is cautious in his deliberation on the rapture not to preach the damnation of the ungodly, whereas certain modern apocalyptic movements stress precisely this. It is true that he mentions the judgment of the persecutors (1 Thess. 2:13–16; 2 Thess. 1:6–10), but understanding the vindictive rhetoric would help to make sense of why a selected group was posed as victims.[22] Such rhetoric does not annul and condemn all without discretion. Specific groups are named (1 Thess. 2:13–16) because they are responsible for their actions.

The peaceful ethic of living with oneself and others is a key teaching of Paul in 1 and 2 Thessalonians. Love and reconciliation are essential components of faith and hope. Paul repeats and praises the love of the Thessalonian Christians (1 Thess. 1; 2 Thess. 1). Even with the separation from the *ataktoi,* who refused to come back, the community's attitude toward them is that of brotherly love rather than hatred (2 Thess. 3:15). Paul does take demonic domination and destruction of the world seriously, but he does not despair. Rather, he constantly works toward love and transformation in light of hope. Paul speaks to the Thessalonians about the possibility of joy, hope, and the ethic of work. The Pauline narrative ends, but there is more to be said and hoped for as Christians are gathered before the returning Benefactor and Judge.

The rhetoric of hope adequately focused on the sureness of the past and of the future, but the Thessalonian Christians had not been able to place that sureness in tension. Thus, those who found hope by recounting their past experience also embraced strict legalism; those who found hope by projecting themselves into the future embraced radical apocalypticism. The former may have been represented by obedient followers of Paul; the latter may have been represented by enthusiastic *ataktoi*, who assumed the imminent coming of Christ.[23] It is difficult for people to strike the right chord with a rhetoric of hope, since all too often they swing to the right or to the left. The sureness of the present is not the middle point of the sureness of the past and the future.

Prophetic realism is the answer to the difficult tension between the "already" and the "not yet" of Paul's eschatology. It is such openness and potential that give millenarian thought its creativity, power, and hope. The belief in *terminus* and *telos* do not necessarily spell fatalism and determinism. Rather, such a belief ushers in a mythic tension of terror and hope, fear and confidence, judgment and reward, ending and beginning. This Pauline eschatology remains valid for our age because of its realistic and hopeful view of history through the Christ event. Modern millenarian movements have often been too eager to eliminate apocalyptic tension with its "already and not yet," its human limitation and divine possibility, its judgment and reward, and its disorder and law (see 2 Thess. 1:12). The results are rebellion, chaos, rejection of God, and delusions of all sorts. The Thessalonian correspondence has an "apocalyptic interpretation of the Christ event," in which Pauline theology points to the imminent cosmic triumph of God over suffering, opposition, lawlessness, and Satan.[24]

The hope of finality can be a creative force in bringing human history to a new beginning, and it is a necessary element in biblical thinking. The problem with present-day utopian dreams is that they do not contain the element of hope. In other words, utopian thinking needs millennial hope. Utopia only sees the end—without seeing the new beginning that comes after the end. Utopia urges us to desire the future and its possibilities; eschatology supplies us with the element of hope.[25] Kumar states it well: "Millennialism supplied the dynamism, the heightened sense of expectation of a coming crisis out of which would rise a new world. Utopia provided the picture of the new world, painted in such colours as to make us want to live in it."[26] If a utopian end "is about making us think about possible worlds, [it] is about inventing and imagining worlds for our contemplation and delight. It opens up our minds to the possibilities of the human condition."[27] Kumar explains:

> We need both millennium and utopia. We need, first, something that lends urgency and the sense of a forward movement. The idea of the millennium sees the whole of human history from the viewpoint of the future. Unlike the cyclical conceptions of antiquity, which saw only eternal return to the starting point, the Christian millennium sees the breakthrough to something radically new. Even if we do not know when we will get there, even if we never get there, the millennium beckons, like a beacon, and draws us on. It is the Faustian spirit in history, preventing us from spending too long in one way of life, or lapsing into a complacent admiration of the present. The millennium is a constant check to a tendency of self-satisfaction. It represents what the Marxist philosopher Ernst Bloch called the principle of noch nicht: which means not only "not yet" but also "still not". It thus carries the sense both of what is expected, what will be in the future, and what is lacking in the present, what should impel us to change our condition. Together they add up to a dynamic progress of becoming whose motivating force is an ever-present future.[28]

Christopher Rowland likewise believes that "[t]he foundational documents of Christianity suggest . . . [that] history is illuminated by apocalypse; vision opens ultimate possibilities, and responsibilities which others could only dream of."[29] Christian apocalypse is preoccupied not exclusively with the future but with "the present as a decisive opportunity for the transformation of the world."[30] Paul's concern in the Thessalonian correspondence is the present survival, meaningfulness, and holiness of the congregation in the midst of suffering, ambiguity, and impurity.

Pauline eschatology constantly nurtures imaginative hope. The imaginative hope, confidence, reward, and beginning, if held in tension with terror, fear, judgment, and ending, will nurture a prophetic realism. Krishan Kumar writes of a Christian millenarianism that "kept alive the hope that the end of the world, which was foreordained and certain, would also be the beginning of a new life. . . . The apocalyptic ending will also signal the millennial beginning. However frightful the contemplation of the end, there is no need to despair: a new world will be born."[31] The cosmic history of the human race finds the meaning of its present and past in light of the finality in which a dramatic and cataclysmic divine intervention will usher in a complete transformation of evil into justice, chaos into peace, deterioration into prosperity. The era of conflict and violence will be superseded by a millennial reign of righteousness, goodness, and bliss!

notes

Acknowledgments

1. Bauckham, "Time and Eternity" in *God Will Be All in All*, 173.

A Note on Style

1. Choosing between the Wade-Giles or the pinyin romanization systems is a matter of political correctness, depending on whether one wants to align with the People's Republic of China (mainland China) or the Republic of China (Taiwan). The pinyin system was developed in Soviet East Asia in the 1930s, and the mainland Chinese revised it and adopted it as the official system in the 1950s. Mainland Chinese also simplified the traditional Chinese characters. Chinese in Taiwan, on the other hand, keep the complex characters and use the traditional phonetic symbols instead of the romanized pinyin. (The pinyin is an attempt to use alphabets to render the traditional phonetic symbols.) Unfortunately, because of the political differences between mainland China and Taiwan, the use of different language systems takes on political significance. While foreigners use the pinyin romanized system out of convenience, the use of pinyin and simplified character or the traditional phonetic symbols and complex character by mainland Chinese or Taiwan Chinese reflects their political identity. My personal preference is to use the pinyin (and sometimes Wade-Giles) and the complex (seldom the simplified) character. I seek first to maintain the richness of the aesthetic and meaning of the Chinese character and use the simplified character only for the sake of convenience.

2. Sun Yat-sen is the popular English name. Actually it is a Cantonese transliteration of another name of Sun rather than the more popular Chinese name Sun Zhongshan.

Introduction

1. One can also argue that "Christian Chinese" is a better term than "Chinese Christian" because race is a matter of givenness and not a choice (i.e., *a priori*), while a Christian worldview or faith, though a divine gift, involves decisive subscription to and practice of one's faith. Here the question of religious faith, such as that of Christian identity, is *not* how and when one is saved or whether one will "go to heaven." The issue is about how those who are ethnically Chinese profess to be believers of Christ.

2. See my *Rhetorical Interaction in 1 Corinthians 8 and 10* and *What Has Jerusalem to Do with Beijing?* Unfortunately, many resources on biblical interpretation and theology and on Chinese Christianity and churches today exist independently in their own fields. For biblical studies, see the works cited in the bibliography. On Chinese Christianity or Chinese politics, see B. I. Schwartz, *Communism and China*; Wickeri, *Seeking the Common Ground*; and D. Wilson, ed., *Mao Tse-tung in the Scales of History*.

3. The fourfold sense of Scripture has been used by the Christian church since John Cassian, Augustine, and Gregory. It was the dominant interpretive method before the historical-critical methodologies were introduced.

4. See Jameson, *Political Unconscious*, 30–32; and Thiselton, *New Horizons in Hermeneutics*, 144–45. For example, the literal sense of the exodus narrative is the Israelites' departure from historical Egypt; the allegorical sense is the church's salvation in Christ; the moral (tropological) sense is the individual soul's departure from sin, while the anagogical sense is the coming of Christ that consummates the meaning of history.

5. See Thiselton, *New Horizons in Hermeneutics*, 183. Steinmetz ("The Superiority of Pre-critical Exegesis," 29) gives the example of Jerusalem in the fourfold sense: historical Jerusalem in Israel, the church, the faithful soul, and the center of God's new creation. Steinmetz also gives the often-quoted rhyme of Nicholas of Lyra (fourteenth century): "Littera gesta docet, Quid credas allegoria, Moralis quid agas, Quo tendas anagogia."

6. The literary exegetical level will include a historical reading of the biblical texts and Mao's writings. Biblical and theological studies on millenarianism as well as political writings of Mao are available in different languages for interested scholars. The research will make use of literary and historical collections as well as their interpretation of data. The crosscultural and dialogical methodology intends to bring together a confluence of traditions, whether the views of utopianism in the West and in China or Paul's and Mao's different views of history. Using the dialogical method, Maoist ideology will be compared and contrasted with Pauline theology. The critically constructive methodology of the project is theological in intention. It asks how the Chinese concern for eschatology reflects the larger issues of revolutionary immortality, the fear of ending (personal death, cosmic catastrophe), the purpose of history (goal and meaning), the hope of a new world, and meaning in life. These larger issues are found inherently in the life and thought of Mao and of Chinese Christians as well as Western Christians today.

7. For the best treatment of the intertwined relationship between theology and politics, see Milbank, *Theology and Social Theory*, 9–26 and 380–438. Arne Rasmusson is probably the first theologian to contrast "political theology" (Jürgen Moltmann) and "theological politics" (Stanley Hauerwas), thus highlighting the sharp differences between subjecting the church to worldly violence and extending the peace and salvation of the assembled community of God to the world. See Rasmusson, *The Church As Polis*, esp. 23–24. To read about the rise of the liberalism in Christian theology that accepts the division of church and state, of theology and politics, see Manent, *Intellectual History of Liberalism*. See also Jameson, *Political Unconscious*, 17 and 20, where he speaks of the political reading of all interpretation as prior and the political horizon of all texts as absolute.

8. For example, I draw Paul's theology mostly from his Thessalonian correspondence; his eschatological thoughts from other works are not dealt with in this volume. In my survey of Chinese utopian traditions, I do not begin to deal with the complex utopian thinking of Buddhism. The Old Testament material is also selective. The same can be said of the New Testament material and the utopian thoughts in the Western world. These are some of the limitations of the work. Since, however, the work deals with the "theological politics" of Paul and Mao, I believe that the essential material is dealt with here.

9. Pauline theology in the Thessalonian correspondence *is* political, especially so in the encounter between Paul's theological conviction and the *pax Romana* of the dominant politics. Paul uses four distinctive words to describe the coming of the Lord Jesus: *epiphaneia* (2 Thess. 2:8), *apantesis* (1 Thess. 4:17), *parousia* (1 Thess. 2:19; 3:13; 4:15; 5:23; 2 Thess. 2:1, 8), and *apokalypsis* (2 Thess. 1:7; 2:3, 6, 8). Their nuances are of theological and political significance. *Epiphaneia* (epiphany) and *parousia* are used commonly to refer to the manifestation of a god or the arrival of Caesar. Similarly, *kyrios* ("Lord," 1 Thess. 4:15–17; 5:2) can refer to a political lord, namely, the Roman emperors, and *euan-*

gelion ("good news," 1 Thess. 1:5; 2:2, 4, 8, 9; 3:2; 2 Thess. 1:8; 2:14) is used to refer to the royal person with all the accompanying benefactions. Paul writes that God calls the Thessalonian Christians "into his own kingdom" (1 Thess. 2:12). Can this language be properly restricted to either theological or political significance?

While one can say Paul had no intention of setting up a "Christian Political Party" in Thessalonica, one cannot assume that the Pauline theology and gospel did not critique the imperial cult. Indeed, Acts 17 contains an account of Paul's preaching in Thessalonica, where he was charged by Roman law as defying "the decrees (*dogmata*) of Caesar." The explicit critique of the *securitas et pax Romana* in 1 Thess. 4:2 shows again that Pauline eschatology was politically subversive.

10. Jameson's term, thus the title of his work: *The Political Unconscious: Narrative As a Socially Symbolic Act.* The "political unconscious" is the assumption in one's discourse/narrative of social reality. In structuralism, it corresponds to the deep structure. It is similar to one's worldview or frame of reference, the master symbol that one uses to image the reality.

11. On my usage of the word *ideology,* see chapter 3, where its usage by Marx merits an in-depth discussion.

12. The definition given here is of Christian theology, since Islamic, Hindu, and Jewish theologies have different parameters.

13. In *Rhetorical Interaction in 1 Corinthians 8 and 10* (34–37), I deal with the metaphorical nature of language and the creative aspect of metaphorization in interpretation. Imagination could be explained as metaphorization. There I use the works of I. A. Richards, Max Black, Paul Ricoeur, and J. M. Soskice to explain the interanimation and reimaging function of metaphors.

14. For excellent discussions of "imagining" and "*mythos*" in theology, see Bauerschmidt, *Julian of Norwich,* 5–12; and Ricoeur, *Figuring the Sacred,* 144–66. On political theology, Bauerschmidt explains: "What I mean is that the metaphysical image, the *mythos,* proffered by Christian theology is one that finds its political correlate in the church as the exemplary form of human community" (9).

15. Moltmann, *Way of Jesus Christ,* x.

16. Moltmann, *Coming of God,* 22.

17. Bauerschmidt, *Julian of Norwich,* 4.

18. Lohfink, *Does God Need the Church,* 154.

19. On the differentiation of future and advent as well as *novum,* see Moltmann, *Way of Jesus Christ,* 22–28.

20. Sauter, *What Dare We Hope,* 11–20, quote from 19–20 (italics his).

21. This is clear in the work of Moltmann, *Coming of God.*

22. J. J. Collins, "Introduction," 9. See also the similar definition in A. Y. Collins, *Cosmology and Eschatology in Jewish and Christian Apocalypticism,* 1.

23. See the standard definition of these terms by Aune, "Apocalypse of John and the Problem of Genre," 67.

24. See Cook, *Prophecy and Apocalypticism,* 1–54; J. J. Collins, "Introduction," 1–20; Duling, *New Testament,* 75–88, idem, "Millennialism," 183–205; Hanson et al., "Apocalypses and Apocalypticism," 1:279–92; and A. Y. Collins, ed., *Early Christian Apocalypticism.*

25. For examples of millennial expectation, see Lanternari, *Religions of the Oppressed;* B. R. Wilson, *Magic and the Millennium;* La Barre, *Ghost Dance;* Olson, *Millennialism, Utopianism, and Progress;* Burridge, *New Heaven, New Earth;* Overholt, *Prophecy in Cross-Cultural Perspective;* Worsley, *The Trumpet Shall Sound.*

26. Milbank, *Theology and Social Theory.*

27. The expression "euthopia" is used by Erasmus, *In Search of the Common Good.*

28. Bloch, *Principle of Hope*, 1:144.

29. Ibid., 3:1320. See also Erasmus, *In Search of the Common Good*.

30. On the human commitment to religious mystery and the utopia of the kingdom of God on earth, see Bloch, *Principle of Hope*, 3:1183–1311. The tension between the imaginary and the real, the wished-for and the possible, has had a dynamic function in utopian literature, such as H. G. Wells, *Modern Utopia*, 6.

31. See Kumar, *Utopianism*, 3; Oscar Wilde, "The Soul of Man Under Socialism," 246.

32. Harrison, "Millennium and Utopia," 61.

33. Kumar, *Utopianism*, 18–19.

Chapter 1: Utopian Views of History from the Bible

1. Lohfink, *Does God Need the Church*, 8.

2. Ibid., 10.

3. See my exegetical work in Yeo, *What Has Jerusalem to Do with Beijing*, 51–105.

4. Lohfink, *Does God Need the Church*, 82.

5. Ibid., 14.

6. Both Cain and Abel offered a sacrifice to God, but Cain did not trust that God would accept his sacrifice. Cain killed Abel and protested to God that he had no responsibility for taking care of his brother. Faithlessness led to alienation, then to violence against his own. See Gen. 4:6–7.

7. Many Christian thinkers throughout the centuries have believed in the literal existence of the Garden of Eden on earth, with medieval maps showing its location. The Christian emperor of Ethiopia, Prester John, searched for it. Columbus thought he had found the Garden of Eden at the mouth of the Orinoco River. See Kumar, *Utopia and Anti-utopia*, 11–12.

8. Lohfink, *Does God Need the Church*, 2.

9. On the cyclical worldview of Babylonian and Greco-Roman cultures, see Eliade, *Myth of the Eternal Return*, 112–30.

10. Eliade contends that in the Jewish theology of history "for the first time, we find affirmed, and increasingly accepted, the idea that historical events have a value in themselves, insofar as they are determined by the will of God. This God of the Jewish people is no longer an Oriental divinity, creator of archetypal gestures, but a personality who ceaselessly intervenes in history, who reveals his will through events (invasions, sieges, battles, and so on). Historical facts thus become 'situations' of man in respect to God, and as such they acquire a religious value that nothing had previously been able to confer on them. . . . The Hebrews were the first to discover the meaning of history as the epiphany of God" (*Myth of the Eternal Return*, 104).

11. I am indebted to Olson, *Millennialism, Utopianism, and Progress*, for the following material on the Jewish view of millenarianism.

12. Ibid., 22.

13. For self-references at the end of a book, see, e.g., Sir. 50:27; John 20:30–31. Malachi 3:13–31 reports that those who remained loyal to the Lord God of Israel were deeply troubled by the assertion ("it is vain to serve God") of those who were ready to forsake their inherited faith. In response to the despondency of the loyal, "a book of remembrance was written before him for those who are faithful to the Lord and think on his name." It would enable them "to distinguish between those who are loyal to God and those who are not, between one who serves God and one who does not."

14. On Israel's exilic experience, see Ackroyd, *Israel under Babylon and Persia*.

15. Von Rad, *Das Formgeschichtliche Problem des Hexateuchs*, 3.

16. Olson, *Millennialism, Utopianism, and Progress*, 16–17.

17. See Jer. 31:3: "Yahweh appeared to us in the past, saying: 'I have loved you with an everlasting love; I have drawn you with lovingkindness.' "

18. See Jer. 33:15, 17: "In those days and at that time, I will cause a righteous branch to spring forth for David, and he shall execute justice and righteousness in the land. . . . David shall never lack a man to sit on the throne of the house of Israel."

19. Olson, *Millennialism, Utopianism, and Progress,* 34.

20. Roth, *Isaiah.*

21. The Babylonian king was depicted in line with the son of Marduk, and the Greek king was in line with Zeus, as the coinages show.

22. We see the self-critical spirit of the biblical canon in which Revelation would use the Lamb of God (wound of love) to critique the Lion of Judah (wound of violence). It is clear from the Jewish prophet Jesus that though his genealogy came from David, his kingdom was not a historical millenarianism, an earthly kingdom, but a New Jerusalem that transcended all empires.

23. Unlike Daoism, there is no discussion about love of death in Jewish literature. Jewish theology postulates that the transcendent utopia will descend to God's people, while the Taoist paradise is a world beyond this filthy one, and only by means of death or sleep can one transport oneself above this world to a world beyond.

24. Käsemann, "Beginnings of Christian Theology," 102.

25. Weiss, *Jesus' Proclamation of the Kingdom of God;* Kähler, *The So-Called Historical Jesus and the Historic, Biblical Christ;* Schweitzer, *Quest of the Historical Jesus.*

26. Representative of these scholars are nineteenth-century theologians such as Richard Rothe, Albrecht Ritschl, and Albert Schweitzer.

27. See, for example, Hays, *Moral Vision of the New Testament;* Lohfink, *Jesus and Community;* idem, *Does God Need the Church;* Yoder, *Original Revolution;* idem, *Politics of Jesus.*

28. L. T. Johnson, "Humanity of Jesus," 53–54. See his footnotes for the primary works of scholars mentioned. For a quick survey of the Third Quest of the historical Jesus, see Witherington, *Jesus Quest.* Anyone doubtful of what one can know about the historical Jesus should read the detailed work of R. E. Brown, *Death of the Messiah.*

29. See E. P. Sanders, *Jesus and Judaism;* idem, *Historical Figure of Jesus;* Casey, *Son of Man;* idem, *From Jewish Prophet to Gentile God.* Sanders interprets Jesus to be God's eschatological viceroy (the last envoy of God), not to bring about military action against the Romans but as "King of the Jews" to restore the imminent eschatological reign of God among the Jewish people. Jesus' words and actions in the temple pose a threat to the temple authorities (for blasphemy, i.e., initiating the eschatological reign of God) and the Romans (for treason). Casey also regards Jesus as an eschatological prophet whose mission was to usher in the coming kingdom in the near future (thus fulfilling John the Baptist's prophecy) and views Jesus' death as an atoning sacrifice.

30. See especially Theissen, *Shadow of the Galilean;* idem, *Gospels in Context;* Horsley, *Jesus and the Spiral of Violence;* Horsley and Hanson, *Bandits, Prophets and Messiahs;* and Kaylor, *Jesus the Prophet.* Theissen believes that the Jesus movement had two essential subgroups: the local Jewish groups and the disciples who traveled around Palestine. Theissen also believes that as a charismatic itinerant figure, Jesus began a "renewal movement" that mediated among different factions in the socially volatile situation. Building on Theissen's reconstruction of Jesus' nonviolent mission, Horsley argues that Jesus sought to transform the existing power structures of family and society socially and politically from the grass roots to the top leadership. Kaylor understands Jesus' social and political movement in the context of covenant theology and God's intervention in history.

31. Horsley, *Jesus and the Spiral of Violence,* 287.

32. Kaylor, *Jesus the Prophet,* 4.

33. Horsley, *Jesus and the Spiral of Violence,* 144.

34. Ibid.

35. These events include his calling of twelve disciples and the church to be God's agents of salvation. Jesus' teaching, healing, and exorcism are indicative of the "intrusion" of God's power in history.

36. Eliade, *Myth of the Eternal Return,* 105–6.

37. Cullmann, *Christ and Time,* 50. Italics added.

38. Van der Watt, "Use of ZAW," 359.

39. R. F. Collins, *Studies on the First Letter to the Thessalonians,* 249.

40. Ibid., 247.

41. Moltmann, *Coming of God,* 279–80.

42. Jewett, "Matrix of Grace," 65.

43. See Danker and Jewett, "Jesus As the Apocalyptic Benefactor," 491.

44. See Krentz, "Traditions Held Fast," 510–12.

45. Ibid., 514.

46. First Thessalonians implies that "children of light and children of the day" (5:5) and those "taught by God" do not need further instruction. They have already received all that they need to determine their future destiny. Building on this, 2 Thessalonians argues that Paul's readers should not form any conclusions about their future destiny on the basis of their present sufferings. The present does not prove anything; only the end will reveal their destiny. Indeed, the suffering of Christians will now be vindicated in the future, and their oppressors will be judged.

47. Jewett, *Thessalonian Correspondence,* 81.

48. See Krentz, "Traditions Held Fast," 515: the "lens through which all of the language of 2 Thessalonians is refracted is the expectation of apocalyptic vindication through the agent of a just God."

49. Cf. Schüssler Fiorenza, *Book of Revelation,* 37.

50. Hellholm, "Problem of Apocalyptic Genre," 27.

51. Schüssler Fiorenza, *Book of Revelation,* 50.

52. Cf. Fannon, "Apocalypse," 33–43.

53. Schüssler Fiorenza, *Book of Revelation,* 47.

54. The idea of a scroll in which the gods' decisions about the future were written was adopted by Jewish apocalyptic from Babylonian religion.

55. *1 Enoch* 81:1–2; cf. also 47:3; 106:19; 107:1.

56. A. Y. Collins, *Crisis and Catharsis,* 144.

57. Cf. ibid., 144–45.

58. Ford, "God As the Subjectivity of the Future," 292.

59. Bauckham, *God Will Be All in All,* 161.

60. Ibid.

61. See Moltmann, *Coming of God,* 27–29.

62. Ibid., 286.

63. Ibid., 287.

64. Bauckham, "Time and Eternity" in *God Will Be All in All,* 188.

65. Moltmann, *Coming of God,* 22. Again on page 25: "The future is God's mode of being in history. The power of the future is his power in time. His eternity is not timeless simultaneity; it is the power of his future over every historical time."

66. Bauckham, "Time and Eternity" in *God Will Be All in All,* 164.

67. Moltmann, "Hope and Reality," 85.

68. Moltmann, *Coming of God,* 26: "The future as God's power in time must be understood as the source of time. It then defines the past as past-future and the present as present-future and future time as future-future. Historical time is irreversible: the future

becomes the past, but the past never again becomes future. That is because reality emerges from potentiality. . . . If transcendental future is the source of time, then it does not abolish time as does timeless-simultaneous eternity, nor does it lose itself in the maelstrom of the general transience of all temporal being. It rather throws open the time of history, qualifying historical time as time determined by the future. . . . With the coming of God's glory, future time ends and eternal time begins."

69. Olson, *Millennialism, Utopianism, and Progress,* 14–15.

70. Kumar, *Utopianism,* 6.

71. Ibid., 7: "Of all ideal society conceptions, it is the millennium which most forcibly introduces the elements of time, process and history. The millennial Good Time restores something of the glory of the Golden Age, but is also at the End of Time. It is a prelude to something radically new, something not experienced even in the original Paradise. It represents and at the same time reveals the completion of God's purpose in relation to man. The peculiar power of the millennial idea comes from the fact that in it eschatology complements futurology."

Chapter 2: Utopian Views of History from Ancient and Modern China

1. A biblical example would be the Galatian debate between Paul and the Judaizers regarding the identity of God's people and whether or not Gentile believers ought to observe the Jewish Law. Likewise, the Matthean tradition focuses on the salvation of the Jewish audience, while Luke-Acts has a more universal and inclusive view of salvation. The Old Testament has diverse views that focus on covenants: Adamic (universal and communal), Abrahamic (racial but universal), Mosaic (legalist and racial), Davidic (national and royal). An intertextual and intracanonical reading of these diverse traditions helps us to form a more comprehensive view of God's salvation for the whole world.

2. See Pannenberg, *Theology and the Kingdom of God,* 62; idem, *Jesus: God and Man,* 82–88. Pannenberg's view of history does not contradict views of liberationists and feminists who see divine revelation in group histories of particular contexts (see Cone, *Black Theology of Liberation,* 62; Ruether, *Sexism and God-Talk,* 12–46). For the role of diversity in viewing history, see Appleby, Hunt, and Jacob, *Telling the Truth about History,* 241–309.

3. Löwith, *Meaning in History,* 18. See also Finger, *Christian Theology,* 1:99–116, 177–212.

4. Much of the following material is indebted to Wolfgang Bauer, who wrote an exhaustive volume tracing the search for happiness in Chinese history (*China and the Search for Happiness*). I will selectively focus on the few main traditions, with an emphasis on Chinese views of ideal history.

5. The categories are taken from ibid., 8–9, but I have changed some of the Chinese translations.

6. On the nuances and development of the term *Confucianism,* see L. Jensen, *Manufacturing Confucianism.*

7. Bauer, *China and the Search for Happiness,* 13–14.

8. Ibid., 18.

9. Ibid., 22.

10. Ibid., 22–23: "Confucius was firmly convinced of his world-shaking, 'heaven-sent' mission. He may already have known of a tradition whose existence during the century following his death is verifiable beyond a doubt and according to which the realm would be saved and restored every five hundred years by a truly spiritual ruler. Along with his . . . theories concerning the messianism of the oracle priests, Hu shih has [shown] . . . the existence of such a tradition for the period following Confucius. . . . Similar to the belief

in a heavenly 'mandate' to rule the world being passed from one dynasty to the next, the conviction that a great restorer would appear every five hundred years thus more probably arose from the precedent created by Confucius's repeated emphasis on the close tie between himself and the duke of Zhou."

11. Ibid., 429–30 n. 44.

12. Ibid. See Legge, trans., *Chinese Classics*, 2:232, 501–2.

13. Bauer, *China and the Search for Happiness*, 49.

14. Ibid., 23. See *Meng Zi* 5A, 5. Legge, trans., *Chinese Classics*, 2:354–57.

15. Bauer, *China and the Search for Happiness*, 24–25.

16. *Meng Zi* 1B, 2. See Legge, trans., *Chinese Classics*, 1:153–54.

17. See Michael Shaw's translation in Bauer, *China and the Search for Happiness*, 26.

18. "If one tries in this way to benefit the world through inclusive love [*chien-ai*], attentive ears and keen eyes will assist each other, bodies will be strengthened through exercise, and those who know the True Way (Tao) will indefatigably instruct the rest. The aged, having neither wife nor child, will be supported and spend their last days peacefully. The young, the weak and the orphans will be cared for and taught so that they may grow up and thrive. Such are the benefits that spring from inclusive love [*jian-ai*]" (*Mo Zi* 16:72–73). See Shaw's translation in ibid., 27.

19. For the two passages where the principle of *shangtong* is discussed with the vision of developing an ideal society and government, see *Mo Zi* 11:44–46; 13:60.

20. We are not sure about the rise and development of the Daoist tradition(s), since their ahistorical philosophy was not preoccupied with the dogmatic preservation of ideas. But since this study attempts to be historical and scientific, my reconstruction of the Daoist tradition is based on Lao Zi's (Old Master) *Dao De Jing* (*Tao-te-ching*) and Zhuang Zi's (Master Zhuang) *Zhuang Zi* (*Chuang-tzu*), allegedly written or redacted by Zhuang Zhou.

21. See *Zhuang Zi* 9:151–52.

22. Nevertheless, Lao Zi used five thousand words to write about the Dao. In a sense, this is because of the self-revealing Dao that invites speaking and interpretation. In chapter 25 of *Dao De Jing*, Lao Zi says: "There is Something undifferentiated, and yet complete in Itself. Soundless and Formless; Independent and Unchanging; Pervasive and Inclusive. It can be regarded as the Mother of the Universe. I do not know Its name. I named It 'Dao.' Only I was forced to give It a name. I regard It simply the 'Great.' For in greatness, It produces. In producing, It expands. In expanding, It regenerates" (Wang, *Commentary on the* Lao Tzu, 74).

23. *Dao De Jing* [*Tao-te-ching*] 19:10:
"Banish wisdom, throw away knowledge,
    and the people will benefit a hundredfold!
Banish 'humanity,' throw away righteousness,
    and the people will become conscientious and full of love!
Banish skill, throw away profit
    and thieves and robbers will disappear!
Yet even if one should let these three principles redound to one's honor, that will not suffice.
One should therefore let the people have something it can hold on to.
It should be given simplicity to look at, and the unhewn to grasp.
It should be given selfless desires!" (Waley, trans., *The Way and Its Power*, 166.)

24. On Lao Zi's idea of the rustic, village-like, precivilization ideal place of simplicity and innocence, see *Dao De Jing* 80:47.

25. See *Zhuang Zi* 6:102–3.

26. Legge, trans., *Tao Te Ching and the Writings of Chuang Tzu*, 373.

27. See *Zhuang Zi* 6:116.
28. See *Zhuang Zi* 6:116–19.
29. See *Zhuang Zi* 6:120–21.
30. See *Zhuang Zi* 18:272–73.
31. See *Zhuang Zi* 2:53–54.
32. See *Zhuang Zi* 2:47–48.
33. Bauer, *China and the Search for Happiness*, 57.
34. Ibid., 58. Likewise, Kuan Zi argued that "Law is that which is observed by the government in orders and regulations, and observed by the people as standards of reward and punishment. Reward lies in obeying the law; punishment is meted out to those who disobey" (Wakeman, *History and Will*, 50).
35. Two Daoist philosophers, Shen Dao and Shen Buhai, also influenced the Legalist tradition. See Fung, *History of Chinese Philosophy*, 1:132–33, 158–59, 319.
36. Bauer, *China and the Search for Happiness*, 124.
37. Cf. Dubs, trans., *Works of Hsüntze*, 301.
38. Wakeman, *History and Will*, 49. The source of Guanzi writing is Guan Zi, "Emperor versus His Officers," 123–24.
39. *Xun Zi* (Hsün-tzu), Dubs, trans., *Works of Hsüntze* 6 (par. 10):114–15.
40. Ibid, 123–24.
41. *Han Fei Zi* (Han Fei-tzu) 19 (par. 50):356; quotation from Liao, trans., *Complete Works of Han Fei Tzu*, 2:306–7.
42. *Han Fei Zi* 19 (par. 49):347; quotation from ibid., 2:290–91.
43. He buried alive 460 officials, killed or deported at least two thousand nobles, and forced the sacrifice of several hundred thousand people in the building of the Great Wall and countless others in the building of his tomb. His tomb is so big and complicated that, two thousand years after his death, it is still intact in Xian.
44. Bauer, *China and the Search for Happiness*, 64–65.
45. Fung, *Short History of Chinese Philosophy*, 160. Cf. *Shi Ji*, ch. 74.
46. Wakeman, *History and Will*, 54.
47. According to Dong Zhongshu, the three-sequence (black, white, and red) periodization of Chinese history is:

Sequence	Dynasty
black	Xia
white	Shang
red	Zhou

On the view of history and the reference of color in modern Chinese thought, Fung Yu-lan notes: "It is interesting that in modern times, colors have also been used to denote varying systems of social organization, and that they are the same three as those of Dong Zhongshu. Thus, following his theory, we might say that Fascism represents the Black reign, Capitalism the White Reign, and Communism the Red Reign" (Fung, *Short History of Chinese Philosophy*, 199).
48. See *Chun Qiu Fan Lu* 21:162; Fung, *History of Chinese Philosophy*, 2:61.
49. Bauer, *China and the Search for Happiness*, 78; see also *Chun Qiu Fan Lu* 1:7; Fung, *History of Chinese Philosophy*, 2:81; and Wakeman, *History and Will*, 53.
50. *Chun Qiu Fan Lu* 6:75–79, taken from Bauer, *China and the Search for Happiness*, 81.
51. Bauer analyzes the role of Confucius in the cyclical history of ancient China: "For Tung Chung-shu [Dong Zhongshu] points out that the periods described by Confucius in the Spring and Autumn Annals could be divided into 'Three Epochs,' each of them consisting of three, four and five reigns of the rulers of Lu.... While this idea does not appear in Tung Chung-shu, there is a barely veiled reference that Confucius had been a 'ruler

without a throne.' The world having rejected him, he ruled in the place of the intellect by writing the Spring and Autumn Annals which, as Mencius [Meng Zi] reported, 'frightened' all the princes of the realm. The accession of prince Yin of Lu, with which the annals begin, happened to coincide with the time of year the Hsia dynasty had chosen as the beginning of its reign. According to the cyclical theory of the 'Three Beginnings,' this could only mean that with this year, 722 B.C., and after the completion of the Hsia-Shang-Chou (black-white-red) cycle, a new 'black' dynasty had started in Lu which signaled its inception with the appearance of Confucius in the realm of the intellect. Tung Chung-shu probably conceived of the Han dynasty with its Confucian orientation as perfecting a 'Confucian' era which had begun with the Spring and Autumn Annals" (Bauer, *China and the Search for Happiness*, 78–79).

52. See the illuminating essay on Kang Youwei by Wakeman, *History and Will*, 115–36.

53. In 1909 Mao's cousin gave him a book describing Kang's reform activities and Liang Qichao's (Liang Ch'i-ch'ao, 1873–1929) *Xin Min Cong Bao* (*Hsin-min ts'ung-pao*). Mao later reflected upon the experience: "I read and reread these until I knew them by heart. I worshipped K'ang Yu-wei [Kang Youwei] and Liang Ch'i-ch'ao and was very grateful to my cousin" (quoted in Snow, *Red Star over China*, 133–34). Two years later, Mao was excited about the reform movement of Sun Yat-sen and posted a bulletin calling for Sun to be president, Liang to be foreign minister, and Kang to be premier (Ch'en, *Mao and the Chinese Revolution*, 130).

54. *Datong Shu* was written during Kang's exile in Darjeeling in 1902 after he failed to bring about reform and overthrow the Dowager Empress Cixi (1835–1908). The complete book was published posthumously. Kang might have begun to write the book as early as 1880. Cixi was a concubine to Emperor Xianfeng (1831–1861) but gave birth to a son, Tongzhi, who became the emperor after Xianfeng's death. As an able mother of the emperor, she became regent to the young emperors Tongzhi and Guangxu, whom she named to the throne.

55. Guangxu was the nephew of Emperor Xianfeng. Guangxu was chosen at the age of four by his aunt Cixi to be the ninth emperor of the Qing dynasty after the death of his cousin, Emperor Tongzhi (1856–1875).

56. Bauer, *China and the Search for Happiness*, 306.

57. Ibid., 307–9.

58. Khang [Kang], *Ta Thung Shu* [*Datong Shu*], 288–89. See also L. Thompson, trans., *Ta T'ung Shu*, 138.

59. Ibid. 354. See also L. Thompson, trans., *Ta T'ung Shu*, 212.

60. Bodde, *Essays on Chinese Civilization*, 253–54.

61. Mao, "On the People's Democratic Dictatorship," 4:414.

62. Bauer, *China and the Search for Happiness*, 72.

63. The word *yi*, meaning change, has pictograms of sun and moon. Technically, *yin* means the shaded area, and *yang* means the sunlit slope of a mountain; cf. Lee, *Theology of Change*, 3–14, for his critique and comparison. Lee writes, "Whitehead then seems to separate God's primordial nature from his consequent nature; Whitehead fails to describe God in the most inclusive terms, the continuum of 'both-and' and 'this as well as that.' Whitehead also separates the world from the world. . . . If God is the ultimate reality, he must be ultimate both in actuality and in potentiality. . . . The *I Ching* concept of change as the ultimate reality must be understood in light of this inclusive way of thinking. In other words, change as the ultimate reality is always conceived in terms of simultaneous change and changelessness" (17–18). This critique is a little unfair to Whitehead, because "creativity" is the ultimate category, though admittedly Whitehead is committed to a kind of atomism of the actual that even *yi* avoids.

64. Cf. Lee, "Search for a Theological Paradigm," 29.

65. Lee, *Theology of Change*, 3.

66. *Da Zhuan*, sec. 1, ch. 11.

67. *Dao De Jing* [*Tao-te-ching*] states, "Essential nature is everchanging-changeless" (ch. 16). The *I Ching* says, "When it [change] is silent, it is immovable; when it moves, it penetrates to all things in the universe."

68. Fang, "The World and the Individual in Chinese Metaphysics," 240.

69. Lee, "Search for a Theological Paradigm," 28.

70. "When the sun goes, the moon comes. When the moon goes, the sun comes. The alternation of sun and moon produces light. When cold goes, heat comes. When heat goes, cold comes. The alternation of cold and hot completes the year. What is going contracts. What is to come expands. The alternation of contraction and expansion produces progression" (*Da Zhuan*, sec. 2, ch. 5).

71. Lee, "Search for a Theological Paradigm," 30–31: "It is both one and two, for one is expressed in two and two is known in one."

72. Bauer, *China and the Search for Happiness*, 71–72.

73. Bodde, *Essays on Chinese Civilization*, 285–87.

74. Capra, *Tao of Physics*, 130–302.

75. See A. N. Whitehead's *Process and Reality*, in which he notes that he learned a similar notion from William James.

76. See Nisbet, *History of the Idea of Progress*, which surveys the Western idea of progress and social development (entelechy) in history from ancient to modern times.

77. Olson, *Millennialism, Utopianism, and Progress*, 7.

78. Needham, "Human Laws and Laws of Nature," 230.

79. Bodde, *Essays on Chinese Civilization*, 239.

Chapter 3: The Meeting of Theological and Philosophical Views of History in Marx

1. See Manuel, ed., *Utopias and Utopian Thought;* Manuel and Manuel, *Utopian Thought in the Western World*.

2. Hesiod looked back to the Kronos's reign when people lived as if they were gods, their hearts free of sorrow, without hard work and pain, living in peace and ease, and the earth yielding its abundance.

3. Dawson, *Cities of the Gods*, 5, 7. On the history of political utopianism, especially in its Greek traditions, see Dawson's work as well as Morgan, *Nowhere Was Somewhere*, 91–151.

4. Mannheim, *Ideology and Utopia*, 185.

5. Ibid., 173. Popularly the word *ideology* may refer neutrally to one's worldview, one's symbolic universe, or one's presuppositions of social realities and conflicts. It may also be used pejoratively to describe one's "false consciousness," a redefinition given by Marx based on his view of historical materialism that life determines consciousness rather than consciousness determines life. In class struggles, the dominant group always exerts assumed ideas on the working class to force the working class to submit, and this is the "false consciousness" or "ideology" of the bourgeois. See Kellner, "Ideology, Marxism, and Advanced Capitalism," 37–41; Berger and Luckmann, *Social Construction of Reality;* Geertz, *Interpretation of Culture*.

6. Mannheim, *Ideology and Utopia*, 193.

7. Ibid., 198.

8. Ibid., 220–21.

9. Levitas, *Concept of Utopia*, 73.

10. Ibid., 74–77.

11. Ricoeur, *Lectures on Ideology and Utopia*.

12. See Mannheim, *Ideology and Utopia*.

13. For examples of revolutionary messianism in medieval Europe, the political messianism of the French Enlightenment, the results of utopian movements ending in radicalism and totalitarianism, see Cohn, *Pursuit of the Millennium*, and J. L. Talmon, *Origins of Totalitarian Democracy*. On the violent conflicts between the ruled and the ruling class, see Worsley, *Trumpet Shall Sound*, 225.

14. See More, *Utopia*.

15. See ibid. See also Hexter, *Vision of Politics*, 19–149.

16. More, *Utopia*, 135.

17. Quoted in Cort, *Christian Socialism*, 63, 64.

18. On the Greek parallel of utopian communism in Plato ("A City without the Household"), Cynic ("A Life without the Household"), and Stoic ("A World without Households"), see Dawson's careful analysis in *Cities of the Gods*.

19. See Dupré, *Philosophical Foundations of Marxism*.

20. See Hegel, *Hegels theologische Jugendschriften*.

21. Hegel, *Phenomenology of Mind*.

22. Hegel read the individualism of Christian morality in contrast to the Greek religions of political *polis* of cooperativeness and unity between religion and politics.

23. MacIntyre, *Marxism and Christianity*, 7–12.

24. Ibid., 13.

25. Löwith, *Meaning in History*, 192.

26. MacIntyre calls this "the stronger thesis" of Marxism, i.e., Marxism inherits some functions of Christianity. But MacIntyre argues that this thesis might be difficult to hold, since "its protagonists must be extremely selective in their attention to the phenomena." Thus MacIntyre advocates the "weaker thesis" that "Marxism inherited some of the functions of religion, without inheriting any of the content." See his discussion in MacIntyre, *Marxism and Christianity*, 5–6.

27. Marx, "Difference between the Democritean and Epicurean Philosophy of Nature," 1:97.

28. MacIntyre, *Marxism and Christianity*, 54.

29. Löwith, *Meaning in History*, 47.

30. Ibid., 49.

31. See Loubere, *Utopian Socialism*.

32. See Wittke, *Utopian Communist*.

33. Saint-Simon, *Selected Writings*, 103.

34. Saint-Simon, *Nouveau Christianisme*.

35. Meisner, *Marxism, Maoism, and Utopianism*, 8.

36. Geoghegan, *Utopianism and Marxism*, 27.

37. Levitas, *Concept of Utopia*, 57, the quote is that of Marx, "Critique of the Gotha Program," 3:23.

38. Meisner, *Marxism, Maoism, and Utopianism*, 12.

39. Marx and Engels believed that communism was "the real movement which abolishes the present state of things. The conditions of this movement result from the premises now in existence" (*German Ideology*, 26).

40. Marx and Engels, *Collected Works*, 5:246.

41. Thus Marx and Engels, for example, like the socially critical role of the utopian visions of More, Campanella, Saint-Simon, and Fourier because they "attack every principle of existing society. [And] they are . . . valuable materials for the enlightenment of the working class" (Marx and Engels, "Manifesto of the Communist Party," 1:121). See also Engels, "Socialism: Utopian and Scientific," in Marx and Engels, *Selected Works*, 2:108–10.

42. Marx and Engels, "Manifesto of the Communist Party," 1:121.

43. Marx and Engels, *German Ideology*, 49.

44. These are Engels's words describing the socialist utopianism with which he disagreed; see Engels, "Socialism: Utopian and Scientific," 2:109.

45. Engels, "Socialism: Utopian and Scientific," 2:111.

46. Meisner points out in his comparison of socialist utopianism and Marxist socialism: "In capitalism, the utopians saw only the social evils it perpetrated, not the socialist potentialities it offered. And in the proletariat they saw only the most exploited segment of society, not the potentially creative revolutionary class destined to be the bearer of the socialist future" (*Marxism, Maoism, and Utopianism*, 11).

47. Engels, *Peasant War in Germany*, 126.

48. Marx and Engels, "Holy Family," 4:84.

49. Lukes, "Marxism and Utopianism," 160.

50. Ibid., 154–55.

51. Marx, "Economic and Philosophical Manuscripts," 3:296. Emphasis his.

52. Marx, "Critique of the Gotha Program," 3:23.

53. Marx and Engels, "Manifesto of the Communist Party," 1:113.

54. Marx and Engels, *German Ideology*, 22.

55. See, e.g., Luke 4:16–21, which records the address of Jesus at the inauguration of his ministry to the poor, blind, and oppressed. The Old Testament prophetic traditions likewise sought social justice for the poor, the widows, and the weak. For additional evidence, see Exod. 22:21–24; Lev. 19:13, 18; Deut. 10:18–19; 24:19–22; Prov. 23:10–11; Isa. 3:16–24; 10:1–2; 58:3–11; Hos. 6:4–6; Amos 4:1–2; 5:21–24; Zech. 7:8–10; Matt. 25:31–46; Luke 10:25–37; Acts 2:44–45; 4:32–35; James 1:27; 2:2–6; 14–17; 5:1–6; 1 John 3:17–18.

56. MacIntyre, *Marxism and Christianity*, 5.

57. On Marxism as a cultural materialism, see also Williams, *Marxism and Literature*. I agree that Marxism needs the principle of hope.

58. Levitas is correct in pointing out the ambiguity of Bloch's term *noch nicht;* see his *Concept of Utopia*, 87–88.

59. Levitas, "Educated Hope," 66.

60. E. Bloch, *Principle of Hope*, 1:147.

61. Taken from Kellner, "Ernst Bloch, Utopia, and Ideology Critique," 84.

62. Moltmann, *Theology of Hope*.

63. See Metz, *Christianity and the Bourgeoisie;* idem, *Emergent Church*.

64. Gutiérrez, *Theology of Liberation*, 238.

65. Kellner, "Ernst Bloch, Utopia, and Ideology Critique," 81–82.

66. See Milbank, *Theology and Social Theory*, 206–55, where he accuses liberation theologies of subordinating theology to social science.

67. Marx and Engels, *German Ideology*, 1.

68. Marx and Engels, "Manifesto of the Communist Party," 1:134.

69. In contrast, God's revolutionary transformation always begins with an elect group of people who gradually witness to others about God's creative work in their lives. People are drawn to see the wonders of God's work. Their freedom is preserved, since they are not manipulated, coerced, or forced. See Lohfink, *Does God Need the Church*, 27.

70. Toynbee, *Study of History*, 400.

71. Cited in Lyall, *New Spring in China*, 154.

72. Löwith, *Meaning in History*, 46.

73. Ibid., 43–44. For a critique of Löwith, see Blumenberg, *Legitimacy of the Modern Age*. I still think that Löwith's analysis is correct.

74. Löwith, *Meaning in History*.

Chapter 4: The Meeting of Marxist and Chinese Views of History in Maoism

1. Mao's citation of "Either the east wind prevails over the west wind or the west wind prevails over the east wind" from Hong Lo Meng (Chuang, *Little Red Book and Current Chinese Language,* 39) was an applied interpretation within the modern context of Chinese nationalism against developed Western nations. Here I use the same imagery but argue that in Maoism a syncretic process is at work. The idea of syncretism is not unique to Mao, for people such as Kang Youwei had creatively combined Confucian *ren* with Western science.

2. The Legalist influence on Mao is evident in Mao's emphasis on "practice as the source, goal, and truth-criterion of theoretical knowledge" (Faricy, "Mao's Thought and Christian Belief," 55).

3. Cited in Meisner, *Marxism, Maoism, and Utopianism,* 165.

4. Ibid., 28–117, esp. 28–75. See also Engels, *Socialism: Utopian and Scientific.*

5. Schram, *Thought of Mao Tse-tung,* 19.

6. Snow, *Red Star over China,* 143.

7. Quoted in ibid., 129.

8. Cited in Bauer, *China and the Search for Happiness,* 345–46. Sun's speech was delivered on January 4, 1922.

9. Meisner, *Marxism, Maoism, and Utopianism,* 28–75. He summarizes the three departures of Maoism from Marxism: "First, Maoism rejects the Marxist premise that modern industrial capitalism is a necessary and progressive stage in historical development and a prerequisite for socialism. Second, Maoism denies the Marxist belief that the industrial proletariat is the bearer of the socialist future. Third, Maoism replaces the Marxist belief in objective laws of history with a voluntaristic faith in the consciousness and the moral potentialities of men as the decisive factor in sociohistorical development" (61).

10. The French Revolution (1789) resulted in the execution of seventeen thousand during the Reign of Terror; twenty-three thousand died in the chaotic situation. The Paris Commune closed all churches in Paris in 1793, mostly Catholic churches. The Cult of Reason was set up to counterattack the Christian religion.

11. Meisner, *Marxism, Maoism, and Utopianism,* 150.

12. Schurmann, *Ideology and Organization,* 510.

13. For documents published in the *Peking Review,* see ibid., 509 n. 5.

14. *People's Daily (Renmin Ribao),* September 3, 1965.

15. See Schram, *Thought of Mao Tse-tung,* 65. Mao's quotation can be found in Mao, "On Contradiction," 1:345.

16. Mao, "On the Ten Great Relationships," 5:284–307.

17. See Schram, *Thought of Mao Tse-tung,* 10.

18. Lin, *Quotations from Chairman Mao Tse-tung,* 1.

19. Ibid., foreword; see also Schram, ed., *Chairman Mao Talks to the People,* 280–81, idem, *Political Thought of Mao Tse-tung,* 56; Meisner, *Marxism, Maoism, and Utopianism,* 165–66.

20. Marx, *Capital,* 87. Similarly, Marx and Engels, *German Ideology,* 43: "The greatest division of material and mental labour is the separation of town and country. The antagonism between town and country begins with the transition from barbarism to civilization, from tribe to State, from locality to nation, and runs through the whole history of civilization to the present day."

21. Marx and Engels, "Manifesto of the Communist Party," 1:137.

22. Mao, "Analysis of the Classes in Chinese Society," 1:19.

23. See Mao, *Chinese Revolution* (reprinted in *Selected Works*, 2:305–34). Although Marx did not envision the ideal communist society as an industrialized and capitalistic one, he nevertheless saw industrialism and capitalism as necessary historical forces that would eventually usher in Marxist socialism. See Marx and Engels, "Manifesto of the Communist Party," 1:121.

24. Mao, *Chinese Revolution*, 22.

25. In February 1927, Mao issued a report to the Central Committee of the CCP regarding the investigation into the peasant movement in Hunan. Mao noted that "the privileges which the feudal landlords have enjoyed for thousands of years are shattered to pieces." See "Chinese Revolution," 2:307–8: "Although China is a great nation with a vast territory, an immense population, a long history, a rich revolutionary tradition, and a splendid historical heritage, she has remained sluggish in her economic, political, and cultural development since her transition from slave society to feudalism. The feudal system, beginning with the Chou and Chi'in dynasties, has lasted about three thousand years. . . . Since the Opium War of 1840, . . . imperialist penetration has hastened the disintegration of Chinese feudal society and introduced elements of capitalism, thereby transforming a feudal into a semifeudal society, and at the same time imposed their ruthless rule and reduced an independent China into a semicolonial and colonial China."

26. Mao, *Chinese Revolution*, 11–14.

27. Mao, "On Practice," 1:301.

28. As Meisner describes it: "recklessly utopian, wildly irrational, and wholly incongruous with presumably universal and necessary processes of modern economic and political development" (*Marxism, Maoism, and Utopianism,* x).

29. Wakeman, *History and Will*, 97–98.

30. This is the position of Chuang, *Little Red Book and Current Chinese Language;* and Ch'en, ed., *Mao Papers*, xiii–xxxi.

31. See Snow, *Red Star over China*, 127–28.

32. Rule, "Is Maoism Open to the Transcendent?" 35.

33. *China Reconstructs* 17, 1 (January 1968), 17, cited in Bauer, *China and the Search for Happiness*, 414. See the analysis of F. Wakeman, *History and Will*.

34. *China Reconstructs* 15, 10 (October 1966), 33, cited in Bauer, *China and the Search for Happiness*, 414.

35. Mao, "Study of Physical Education," 94.

36. D. Wilson, *Mao*, 59.

37. "Swimming" (May 1956), in Ch'en, *Mao and the Chinese Revolution*, 246.

38. Cited in Wakeman, *History and Will*, 91.

39. Mao, "Serve the People," 3:227–28.

40. Mao, "In Memory of Norman Bethune," 2:337–38.

41. Mao, "Foolish Old Man Who Removed the Mountains," 3:322.

42. Mao, quoted in Chai, ed., *Essential Works of Chinese Communism*, 163.

43. Mao, "Serve the People," 3:228.

44. *Wang Wen Cheng Gong Zhuan Shu* 21:5; see Henke, trans., *The Philosophy of Wang Yang-ming*, 362–64.

45. Guo Pu (276–324), *Classic of Mountains and Oceans* speaks of wandering immortals; see Bauer, *China and the Search for Happiness*, 181–83.

46. For an account of the Long March, see Ch'en, *Mao and the Chinese Revolution*, 185–200.

47. Bauer, *China and the Search for Happiness*, 231.

48. On the idea of violence, cruelty, and atrocity in Chinese traditions (secret societies and millenarian sects), see Shek, "Sectarian Eschatology and Violence," 87–109.

49. See Schram, *Thought of Mao Tse-tung*, 54.

50. Sun Zi, *Art of War,* ch. 6, par. 13. Sun Zi's statement that "people who do not lay down their arms will die by their arms" sounds like the pacificist saying of Jesus at the Garden of Gethsemane—"for all who draw the sword will die by the sword" (Matt. 26:52)—yet Sun Zi believed that, for the sake of economics, swift wars were necessary.

51. Mao, "Problems of Strategy in China's Revolutionary War," 1:239–49.

52. Ibid., 1:237.

53. Cited in Schram, *Political Thought of Mao Tse-tung,* 41.

54. Cited in ibid.

55. Cited in ibid., 40–41.

56. Bauer, *China and the Search for Happiness,* 390, translation of Payne, *Mao Tze-tung,* 41.

57. Cited in Schram, *Political Thought of Mao Tse-tung,* 18.

58. Mao, "Report of an Investigation," 1:25.

59. Schram, *Political Thought of Mao Tse-tung,* 203. See Mao, "Report of an Investigation," 1:56.

60. Mao, "Report of an Investigation," 1:23.

61. Mao, "Orientation of the Youth Movement," 2:242.

62. Mao, "On Coalition Government," 3:296. See also Mao, "Draw in Large Numbers of Intellectuals," 2:301.

63. See Bauer, *China and the Search for Happiness,* 392.

64. See Murphey, "Man and Nature in China," 313–33.

65. Mao, "Chinese Revolution," 2:306–7.

66. Ibid., 2:307.

67. Mao, "On the People's Democratic Dictatorship," 4:411–24.

68. Mao, "Remarks at the Spring Festival," 204. Mao also said, "If you read too many books, they petrify your mind in the end" (207).

69. Mao, "Speech at the Lushan Conference," 140. See also Hsiao Hsü-tung, *Mao Tse-tung and I Were Beggars,* which relates how Mao and Hsiao experienced the life of beggars as well as their discussion of Liu Bang. Mao regarded Liu Bang as a hero because he was the first commoner to become an emperor, but Hsiao regarded Liu as a tyrant.

70. The 1973 "Anti–Lin Biao, Anti-Confucius" campaign was Mao's call to the masses to criticize the counterrevolutionary and feudal aspects of Lin Biao. Lin was linked to Confucius because both of them symbolized for Mao strongholds of feudalism and power holders. The same campaign almost critiqued Zhou Enlai, the so-called Anti-Zhougong, because Zhou Enlai's politics involved the doctrine of the mean, a typical Confucian wisdom. But Mao foresaw disaster if Zhou were accused.

71. Bauer, *China and the Search for Happiness,* 32.

72. Mao called this "democratic centralism" in 1962; see his "Talk at Enlarged Work Conference," 36–39. The movie *Emperor and the Assassin* portrays the totalitarian reign of Qin Shihuangdi. Margolin describes the violence and atrocities during Mao's ("China," 463–546).

73. Schram, *Thought of Mao Tse-tung,* 69.

74. Schram, *Political Thought of Mao Tse-tung,* 56.

75. See ibid., 172–73.

76. The translation of Bauer, *China and the Search for Happiness,* 351.

77. *New Youth* (April 4, 1918): 307–8; quoted in Bauer, *China and the Search for Happiness,* 373.

78. Schram, *Thought of Mao Tse-tung,* 29.

79. Mao, "On New Democracy," 2:340.

80. Lo, *Romance of the Three Kingdoms,* 1.

81. Lin, "Informal Address at Politburo Meeting," cited in Ebon, *Lin Piao,* 255.

82. Mao, "Talk at Enlarged Work Conference," 39.

83. Mao, "Bombard the Bourgeois Headquarters."

84. Ibid. Lin Biao replaced Peng Dehuai. But the ambitious Lin Biao would encounter his own ill fate when he opposed Mao; his coup attempt failed, and he died in a plane crash trying to escape China (September 13, 1972). In the rightist accusation campaign, Liu Shaoqi was sacked and died without any memorial service. Only in Deng's era could some of the wrongly accused rightists have their honor and integrity restored.

85. Mao, "On Practice," 1:300.

86. Ibid., 1:300–301.

87. Ibid., 1:301.

88. Bauer, *China and the Search for Happiness*, 393.

89. Mao, "On Practice," 1:307–8.

90. Mao, "On Contradiction," 311.

91. Ibid., 312.

92. Ibid., 1:312–19.

93. Ibid., 313.

94. See Schram, *Thought of Mao Tse-tung*, 63.

95. See Starr, *Ideology and Culture*, 24–29; Schurmann, *Ideology and Organization*, 19–23.

96. Mao, "On the Ten Great Relationships," 61–83.

97. Mao, "On Contradictions," 1:343–45.

98. Taken from Bauer, *China and the Search for Happiness*, 377.

99. See the discussion by Schram, *Political Thought of Mao Tse-tung*, 98–101.

100. Mao, "Speech at the Supreme State Conference," 94.

101. "Sixty Work Methods (Draft): The General Office of the Central Committee of the Communist Party of China" (February 1958), cited in Wakeman, *History and Will*, 236.

102. Mao, "On the Correct Handling of Contradictions," 5:386.

103. Schram, *Thought of Mao Tse-tung*, 19.

104. Quoted in Ch'en, ed., *Mao Papers*, 145; originally in *People's Daily* (*Renmin Ribao*), August 30, 1967.

105. "Maxims for Revolutionaries—The 'Three Constantly Read Articles,'" *Peking Review* 6 (January 1967): 7–8. The three articles are entitled "In Memory of Norman Bethune" (1939), "Serve the People" (1944), and "The Foolish Old Man Who Removed the Mountains" (1945).

106. Mao, "Chinese Revolution," 2:321.

107. Meisner, *Marxism, Maoism, and Utopianism*, 127.

108. Mao, "On New Democracy," 2:339–84.

109. See Legge, *Four Books*, 1.

110. Mao, "The Foolish Old Man Who Removed the Mountains," 3:322.

111. Ibid.

112. Mao, "Bankruptcy of Idealist Conception of History," 4:454.

113. Graham, trans., *Book of Lieh-tzu*, 67–68.

114. Bauer, *China and the Search for Happiness*, 339.

115. Wakeman, *History and Will*, xi.

Chapter 5: The Meeting of Maoism and Christianity in Red China

1. Cary-Elwes, *China and the Cross*, 235.

2. Ibid., 259.

3. The change is most obvious in poetry, where the traditional Chinese poems had to observe strict rhythm, fixed numbers of words, and intonations. But in other genres, such

as novels and short narrative essays, modern Chinese is free from idiosyncratic patterns and has the creativity that is characteristic of the common people's use of language.

4. Bauer, *China and the Search for Happiness*, 387. He was to become a victim in August 1927, when it became known that he preferred to work with the world proletariat and did not like to rely on peasant revolution, since peasant uprisings were often brutal.

5. Chen Duxiu, "Ouhsiang pohailun" ("On the Destruction of Idols"), *New Youth* (May 12, 1918), cited in Charbonnier and Trivière, "New China," 1:94.

6. Quoted in Whyte, *Unfinished Encounter*, 150.

7. Whyte, *Unfinished Encounter*, 152.

8. To view Mao as a religious leader, see Smart, *Mao*, 83–94.

9. Fitzgerald, *Birth of Communist China*, 146.

10. Wallis, *China Miracle*, 73.

11. See Snow, *Long Revolution*, 219.

12. See Schram, ed., *Chairman Mao Talks to the People*, 220.

13. Ibid., 297.

14. All these heroic acts were evaluated in accordance with the thought of Mao and promoted proletarian feelings.

15. Berger, *Social Reality of Religion;* idem, *Sacred Canopy*.

16. Wakeman, *History and Will*, 19.

17. Mao, "Report of an Investigation," 1:23–24.

18. However, Edgar Snow, in his 1936 interview of Mao, denied the "ritual of hero-worship built up around him" but confirmed that "the role of his personality in the movement was clearly immense" (*Red Star over China*, 69).

19. Ch'en, *Mao and the Chinese Revolution*, 185–200.

20. Yonina Talmon says that "millenarism assumes that history has its *predetermined, underlying plan* which is being carried to its completion, and that this predestined *dénouement* is due in the near future" ("Millenarian Movements," 166). This is exactly what Mao believed and determined to do.

21. Mao, "On Practice," 1:308.

22. "Stood up" in the sense that China had gained independence and victory over imperialist foreign powers. Cf. Schram, *Thought of Mao Tse-tung*, 195.

23. Mao, *On New Democracy*, 43.

24. Meisner, *Marxism, Maoism, and Utopianism*, 164, quoting Mao Zedong, "Talks at the Chengtu Conference," 99–100.

25. The economic crisis was the result of the inefficient leadership of Mao and the Party as well as the militarization of mass workers. In the politicization of social campaigns throughout China, Mao had led the nation into a frenzy of illusions. The Maoist illusion was that socialism would be realized in the collectivation of agriculture and industrialization. Natural disaster was not the main cause of hunger and death. The hierarchical leadership could not allow the people to own the vision of the top leadership. People simply do what is ordered and become passive if no order is given. In contrast, the Jesus movement began with a small group of people and allowed them to share his vision, then gradually allowed this small group to expand as others were invited to come in and decide if they wished to join.

26. Mao, "Speech at the Lushan Conference," 138.

27. Ibid., 145.

28. Meisner, *Marxism, Maoism, and Utopianism*, 165–66; quoting Lin, *Quotations from Chairman Mao Tse-tung*, foreword.

29. Snow, *Long Revolution*, 68–69.

30. Ibid.

31. A popular poem reflects the belief that the paradise had arrived: "Ploughing without the bulls, Lighting without the oil; Milk could be lavishly drunk, Apples could be crushing one another."

32. Schurmann, *Ideology and Organization*, 71.

33. Ibid.

34. Snow, *Long Revolution*, 69.

35. Chuang, *Great Proletarian Cultural Revolution*, 30.

36. Rule, "Is Maoism Open to the Transcendent?" 34.

37. Schurmann, *Ideology and Organization*, 524. See Mannheim, *Ideology and Utopia*, 207, on the charismatic individual in utopian movements.

38. Meisner, *Marxism, Maoism, and Utopianism*, 169. Bloodworth writes of another incantation: "the nine planets revolve around the Red Sun—The Red Sun is Chairman Mao and his Thought" (*Messiah and the Mandarins*, 259).

39. Meisner, *Marxism, Maoism, and Utopianism*, 169–70.

40. See anonymous, " 'New Man' in China," 49.

41. See Joseph, Wong, and Zweig, eds., *New Perspectives on the Cultural Revolution*.

42. Snow, *Long Revolution*, 106.

43. Snow, "Conversation with Mao Tse-tung," 46.

44. Rule, "Is Maoism Open to the Transcendent?" 40.

45. Li, quoted and translated by Barmé, *In the Red*, 322.

46. See Edson, "Macedonia, II," 133; Jewett, *Thessalonian Correspondence*, 89–108; and Wanamaker, *Epistles to the Thessalonians*, 3–4.

47. Edson, "Macedonia, II," 127–33, citing Gaebler.

48. Ibid., 127.

49. Cf. Lyall, *God Reigns in China*, 126, who elaborates this point.

50. MacInnis, *Religious Policy and Practice*, 12: "The imperialist powers have never slackened their efforts to poison the minds of the Chinese people. This is their policy of cultural aggression. And it is carried out through missionary work." MacInnis explains how the Chinese Communist Party viewed Christianity.

51. Lyall, *God Reigns in China*, 126; cf. Jones, ed., *Documents of the Three-Self Movement*, 172.

52. Zhang, "Origin of the 'Three Self,' " 175–202.

53. Warren, ed., *To Apply the Gospel*, 26.

54. Beaver, ed., *To Advance the Gospel*, 37.

55. Baldwin, "Self-Support of the Native Church," 283–87; Talmage, "Should the Native Churches in China Be United," 429–33.

56. Lyall, *God Reigns in China*, 129.

57. G. Brown, *Christianity in the People's Republic of China*, 84–85. See also Jones, ed., *Documents of the Three-Self Movement*: "Message from Chinese Christians to Mission Boards Abroad" (14–18); "Church of Christ in China Report to Mission Boards Abroad" (24–25); "Methodist Patriotic Covenant" (26–27); and "Methods for Dealing with Christian Bodies" (27–28).

58. Cf. Ching, "Faith and Ideology," 24.

59. Gao, "Y. T. Wu," 351.

60. R. W. Lee III, "General Aspects of Chinese Communist Religious Policy," 162: "In the old China, says the Chinese Communist Party, religion had a two-fold purpose: to serve the ends of Chinese reactionaries and foreign imperialists. Now, religion has 'basically shaken off their influence,' and the government solicits the 'wholehearted cooperation' from religion in creating the new China. In the theoretical terms of Maoism, an 'antagonistic' contradiction has been basically transformed into a 'nonantagonistic' contradiction. The ideological difference between religion and 'scientific' Marxism-Leninism

is a contradiction among the people. Religion and the Chinese Communist Party can find a political basis of cooperation in building Socialism."

61. Freemantle, ed., *Papal Encyclicals in Their Historical Context*, 253.

62. Ibid., 255.

63. Jones, ed., *Documents of the Three-Self Movement*, 184–91; cf. G. Brown, *Christianity in the People's Republic of China*, 81.

64. G. Brown, *Christianity in the People's Republic of China*, 82.

65. By 1952, at least 400,000 Christians had signed it. Cf. ibid., 83.

66. *Tien Fung* 423 (July 7, 1954): 1; and 425–27 (September 3, 1954): 3–10.

67. G. Brown, *Christianity in the People's Republic of China*, 84; and Jones, ed., *Documents of the Three-Self Movement*, 177–86.

68. The full text of the document is published in *Tien Fung* 233–34 (September 1950): 146–47. Cf. Wickeri, *Seeking the Common Ground*, 127–33.

69. Jones, ed., *Documents of the Three-Self Movement*, 19–20.

70. MacInnis, *Religious Policy and Practice*, 99.

71. Ibid.

72. In 1954 the name was changed to the Protestant Three-Self Patriotic Movement for the sake of unity. Cf. Jones, ed., *Documents of the Three-Self Movement*, 4.

73. Lyall critically observes that the TSPM was not a spontaneous, free, independent body of the Chinese church but an organization created by the Communist Party to carry out Party policy. Lyall's point is that the late Wu Yao-tsung was pro-Communist and a serious student of Marxism.

74. Jones, ed., *Documents of the Three-Self Movement*, 19–21.

75. Lyall, *God Reigns in China*, 131; cf. Jones, ed., *Documents of the Three-Self Movement*, 184–91.

76. Patterson, *Christianity in Communist China*, 88–89.

77. It is a fairly written essay, but the religious and ideological assumptions of communism and Christianity are not mentioned at all. To Wu Christianity was more a sociopolitical reality than a personal faith commitment.

78. See Patterson, *Christianity in Communist China*, 58.

79. Ching, "Faith and Ideology," 26.

80. Ibid.

81. Ting, "Call for Clarity," 145–49.

82. For details, see G. Brown, *Christianity in the People's Republic of China*, 86–88.

83. On the theological views of the TSPM, see *China and the Church* (*Zhouggua Yu Jiaohui*) 3 (April–May 1986): 21–24; and 4 (June–July1986): 21–27.

84. On the Catholic and patriotic movements, see Whyte, *Unfinished Encounter*, 159–64, 170–71.

85. For more, see G. Brown, *Christianity in the People's Republic of China*, 76–77.

86. Tucker, *Philosophy and Myth in Karl Marx*, 105.

87. G. Brown, *Christianity in the People's Republic of China*, 76–77.

88. Feuerbach, *Essence of Christianity*, 195.

89. Ching, "Faith and Ideology," 18.

90. Feuerbach, *Essence of Christianity*, 226.

91. See Feuerbach, *Essence of Christianity*, 12–32; Marx, "Contribution to the Critique," 3:42.

92. See MacInnis, *Religious Policy and Practice*, 60.

93. Ibid., 35–89, here 61.

94. Cf. Jones, *Church in Communist China*.

95. Cf. *Time* magazine (January 8, 1951).

96. Dehoney, *Dragon and the Lamb*, 22.

97. *South China Morning Post,* cited in Patterson, *Christianity in Communist China,* 139.

98. Dehoney, *Dragon and the Lamb,* 47.

99. G. Brown, *Christianity in the People's Republic of China,* 125.

100. For detailed examples, see Jones, *Church in Communist China,* 74–77.

101. Quoted in Wallis, *China Miracle,* 65.

102. Hunder and Chan, *Protestantism in Contemporary China,* 1.

103. Wallis, *China Miracle,* 115.

104. Cited from Patterson, *Christianity in Communist China,* 12. George Patterson was a missionary to China. See also Hunter and Chan, *Protestantism in Contemporary China,* 76.

105. See Lyall, *New Spring in China;* idem, *Red Sky at Night.*

106. See, for example, Lyall, *Red Sky at Night,* 77–79. Likewise, W. H. Clark, *Church in China,* 185–87, has a section called "interaction between communism and Christianity" which does not deal with the question of eschatology; so also Wallis, *China Miracle;* Hayward, *Christians and China;* and Ting et al., eds., *Chinese Christians Speak Out.*

Chapter 6: Mao Meets Paul I

1. MacInnis, *Religious Policy and Practice in Communist China,* 60.

2. As early as the eighteenth century, merchants from the West brought opium into China through India despite incessant imperial bans. Opium was traded for silver. So much was traded that China almost went bankrupt. In 1729, when it was banned by the imperials for the first time, two hundred cases weighing 120 English pounds each were the registered amount imported. But by 1793, the amount increased to four thousand cases. By 1834 and during the following years, the conservative figure is no fewer than thirty thousand cases annually, i.e., approximately 3.6 million pounds. See Bauer, *China and the Search for Happiness,* 275.

3. Wallis, *China Miracle,* 25.

4. On the multiple causes of the First Opium War, see Roberts, *Modern China,* 31–34.

5. K. E. A. Gutzlaff joined the Netherlands Missionary Society in 1826. He left the Society and went to China in 1831. He was a man with vision and enthusiasm to reach the whole of China with the gospel of Christ. He adopted Chinese dress and spoke fluent Chinese, but his itinerant preaching often left converts unnurtured. His evangelistic literature left his converts detached from the community of believers.

6. Elijah C. Bridgeman and David Abeel were the first American missionaries to arrive in China, sent by the American Board of Commissioners for Foreign Missions in 1830.

7. Cary-Elwes, *China and the Cross,* 198–99.

8. Ibid., 199.

9. Milne hired Liang Fa (1789–?) to work as a printer. He was converted from Buddhism and baptized by Milne in 1816. Liang became the first Protestant Chinese clergy in 1827, and his nine-chapter gospel literature, *Good Words to Admonish the Age,* infused Hong Xiuquan to have an apocalyptic vision of national salvation in the Taiping Rebellion.

10. This is the title of Jonathan D. Spence's intriguing work on the Taiping Rebellion; see his *God's Chinese Son.*

11. Cheng, *Chinese Sources for the Taiping Rebellion,* 82.

12. Ibid., 83.

13. Cary-Elwes, *China and the Cross,* 193.

14. Bauer, *China and the Search for Happiness,* 286.

15. Ibid., 279.

16. Quoted in Bauer, *China and the Search for Happiness,* 279. For more on Marx's sharp analysis, see Torr, ed., *Marx on China 1853–1860.*

17. Cary-Elwes, *China and the Cross,* 221–22.

18. Whyte, *Unfinished Encounter,* 138.

19. Cary-Elwes, *China and the Cross,* 223.

20. Wanamaker, *Epistles to the Thessalonians,* 202.

21. Lyall, *New Spring in China,* 46.

22. Ibid.

23. Li Dazhao, a Marxist, supported the cooperation between the KMT and CCP, but after their separation Li sought refuge in the Soviet Russian embassy in Beijing in 1926. He was executed the following year when the warlord Chang Tso-lin attacked the embassy. See Bauer, *China and the Search for Happiness,* 376.

24. Whyte, *Unfinished Encounter,* 155.

25. Ibid., 167.

26. See Lyall, *New Spring in China,* 50.

27. Ting, "A Chinese Christian's View of the Atheist," 97.

28. Stauffer, ed., *Christian Occupation of China.* The Chinese name of the book literally means "China returns to the Lord," i.e., China believes in Christ.

29. Ting, "A Chinese Christian's View of the Atheist," 97.

30. See, however, the views of other scholars, such as Cort, *Christian Socialism,* who speaks of "Christian Socialism."

31. Yang, *Religion in Chinese Society,* 386.

32. Quoted in Lyall, *Red Sky at Night,* 64–65.

33. On Christian socialism in the biblical traditions, the fathers of the church, and the Middle Ages, and on its influence in Europe and the Western hemisphere, see Cort, *Christian Socialism.*

34. Lyall, *New Spring in China,* 68. His assessment is not precisely accurate and is unnecessarily critical: "Communist doctrine has established itself as a religion in China, then the Communist Party is the sacred priesthood or the incarnation of the leadership of the people whose programme will ultimately lead to 'a earthly Paradise'. But this, according to Mao, may take 'a thousand years' to attain. This new religion makes no pretence of democracy or free will." Lyall is mixing categories and confusing the contrast between Maoism and Christianity. It is better to use categories of self-designation and to bring out the differences and similarities.

35. Gao, "Y. T. Wu," 352.

36. This is the viewpoint of Lyall, *New Spring in China,* 153.

37. Ibid., 35–36.

38. Collected in Ting et al., eds., *Chinese Christians Speak Out,* 95–103; and Ting, *No Longer Strangers: Selected Writings of K. H. Ting,* 124–28.

39. Ting, "A Chinese Christian's View of the Atheist," 95–96.

40. Missionary accounts tend to tell stories of their own persecutions and expulsions from China, showing less interest in the concurrent suffering of Chinese Christians. Moreover, the missionary biases concerning the Chinese government and the TSPM, as well as their own religious arrogance, have not brought about an admission that though their motives are sincere, their sharing of the gospel is not without Western and imperialistic influence.

41. Needham, *Christian China,* taken from Lyall, *New Spring in China,* 133. We also see some positive assessment of Mao and his revolutions. During the Cultural Revolution, President Sukarno of Indonesia said: "If Mao fails, it will be the end of the era of great revolutions." President Bhutto of Pakistan said: "Men like Mao [Zedong] come once in a

century, perhaps once in a millennium. They capture the stage and write the pages of history with divine inspiration."

42. Ting, *No Longer Strangers,* 123.

43. Ting, "A Chinese Christian's View of the Atheist," 99–100.

44. The word *holy* is taken to mean the plentitude of power that evokes awe. In biblical apocalyptic eschatology, God as the Holy One transcends all yet "intrudes" all as God manifests his presence and glory. See R. Otto, *Idea of the Holy;* and Gammie, *Holiness in Israel.*

45. Jones, ed., *Documents of the Three-Self Movement,* 171.

46. Ibid., 172.

47. Ibid., 156.

48. Ibid., 19–20.

49. Nietzsche, *Will to Power,* 542–43; Milbank, *Theology and Social Theory,* 391; and Augustine, *City of God* 4.26.

50. Toole, *Waiting for Godot in Sarajevo,* 85–86.

51. Lohfink, *Does God Need the Church,* 118: "[The church] . . . is a network of communities spread over the whole earth and yet existing within non-Christian society, so that each person can freely choose whether to be a Christian or not; it is genuine community and yet not constructed on the model of pagan society, a true homeland and yet not a state."

52. Gager, *Kingdom and Community;* Meeks, *First Urban Christians.*

53. Judge, "Decrees of Caesar at Thessalonica," 1–7, here 3: "At the time of this edict (11 A.D.) Augustus was in his seventy-fourth year. He had already been in power fifty-five years, dogged by ill-health and rumors of death, and everyone's attention was concentrated upon the fascinating and unprecedented struggle that was pending."

54. *Parousia* does not simply mean return; it means the arrival, the presence, of a significant person such as a king, the arrival of Caesar or of any dignitary visiting a city. Out of the twenty-four occurrences of the word *parousia* in the New Testament, the Thessalonian correspondence has seven (1 Thess. 2:19; 3:13; 4:15; 5:23; 2 Thess. 2:1, 8, 9). See Moltmann, *Coming of God,* 25: "the language of the prophets and apostles has brought into the word [*parousia*] the messianic note of hope. The expectation of the *parousia* is an advent hope. For in the New Testament the past presence of Christ in the flesh, or the present presence of Christ in the Spirit, is never termed *parousia.* The word is kept exclusively for Christ's coming presence in glory."

55. Bruce, *1 and 2 Thessalonians,* 172. Outside the Pastorals, *epiphany* occurs only here (2 Thess. 2:8) in the New Testament.

56. Krentz, "1 Thessalonians," 16, following the suggestion of Milligan, *St. Paul's Epistles to the Thessalonians,* 145–48; Deissmann, *Light from the Ancient East,* 368–73.

57. The term *parousia* does not appear in pre-Christian apocalyptic literature; its technical usage, in a royal-political sense, referred to the arrival of a king or emperor. The fanfare accompanying such arrivals included acclamation, joyous celebration, and the wearing of bright clothing and crowns. See Oepke, "[*parousia, pareimi*]," 5:860; Rigaux, *Saint Paul, les Epitres aux Thessaloniciens,* 196–201.

58. Evans, "Eschatology and Ethics," 118.

59. See Josephus, *Ant.* 11.327; Best, *Commentary,* 199; Krentz, "1 Thessalonians," 16.

60. For the first inscription of *kyrios* (lord) referring to Emperor Nero, see Deissmann, *Light from the Ancient East,* 351; Rigaux, *Saint Paul, les Epitres aux Thessaloniciens,* 200.

61. Krentz, "1 Thessalonians," 16.

62. See Evans, "Eschatology and Ethics," xi–xii.

63. Robertson, *Origins of Christianity,* 210.

64. On the reconstruction, see Donfried, "Cults of Thessalonica," 342–52; and Jewett, *Thessalonian Correspondence*, 123–25.

65. Cf. Schrenk and Quell, *"Eklegomai,"* 4:144–76 for discussion of Israel's "chosenness" by God in both biblical and extrabiblical Jewish texts.

66. Meeks, *First Urban Christians*, 85.

67. E.g., Plato, *Rep.* 536c; Polybius, 6, 10, 9; Plato, *Laws* 802b. Cf. Coenen, "[*eklegomai*]," 1:536.

68. Burke, *Rhetoric of Motives*, 324–28.

69. Perelman, *Realm of Rhetoric*, 126.

70. Wuellner, "Argumentative Structure of 1 Thessalonians," 133.

71. Homer, *Od.* 10.231; 17.386; *Il.* 9.165; Xenophon, *Symp.* 1.7; Plutarch, *Per.* 7.5. In the Old Testament tradition, this divine calling implies claims on humans that "often lead to suffering for God's sake" (Coenen, "[*kaleo*]," 1:271–73, here 1:273). Cf. Exod. 3:4; 5:2; 2 Kings 1:3, 9.

72. Cf. Hughes, "Rhetoric of 1 Thessalonians," 101.

73. For "kingdom," see Schmidt, "[*basileia*]," 1:579. For "glory," see von Rad and Kittel, "[*dokeo*, etc.]," 2:232–55.

74. Cf. Jewett, *Thessalonian Correspondence*, 126.

75. See the aorist tense in 1 Thess. 4:7; 2 Thess. 2:14; Gal. 1:6; 1 Cor. 1:9. A variant reading of 1 Thess. 2:12 offers the aorist tense ("who called"), but the present tense has stronger evidence. Cf. Best, *Commentary*, 108.

76. Best, *Commentary*, 135; cf. 1 Thess. 3:4: "we told you . . . that we were to suffer affliction." Likewise, Bruce concludes, "persecution is a natural concomitant of Christian faith" (*1 and 2 Thessalonians*, 45).

77. Hock, *Social Context of Paul's Ministry*, 34–36.

78. For the eschatological understanding of this term, see Best, *Commentary*, 216.

79. Donfried, "Cults of Thessalonica," 344.

80. Peterson, "[*apantesis*]," 1:380–81; Oepke, "[*parousia, pareimi*]," 5:860. Also suggested by Milligan, *St. Paul's Epistles to the Thessalonians*, 145–48.

81. Donfried, "Cults of Thessalonica," 341.

82. Foerster observes that the imagery was used more and more in the first and second centuries (Foerster and Quell, "[*kyrios*, etc.]," 3:1054–58).

83. Radl, *Ankunft des Herrn*, 173–81.

84. Danker and Jewett, "Jesus As the Apocalyptic Benefactor," 492.

85. Jewett, *Thessalonian Correspondence*, 79–82.

86. Danker, *Benefactor*, 320–23. "The result of God's beneficent activity in producing believers who are people of exceptional character will enhance the reputation of Jesus, and the Thessalonians will in turn have their reputation enhanced in connection with the increased recognition accorded Jesus" (323).

87. Wolfhart Pannenberg has convincingly shown the cultural-religious worldview of apocalyptic theology, from which hope emerges as one knows the end of history. For adaptation of Pannenberg's view, see Yeo, "Revelation 5 in the Light of Pannenberg's Christology," 308–34. It is argued here that Pauline apocalyptic theology also has a similar symbolic worldview and function. See also Burke, *Rhetoric of Motives*, who says, "The depicting of a thing's *end* may be a dramatic way of identifying its *essence*. This Grammatical 'Thanatopsis' would be a narrative equivalent of the identification in terms of a thing's 'finishedness' we find in the Aristotelian 'entelechy' " (17).

88. See Yeo, "Rhetoric of Calling and Election Language in 1 Thessalonians."

89. Bauerschmidt, *Julian of Norwich*, 4. On the rise of liberalism in Christian theology that accepts the division of the church and the state, see Manent, *Intellectual History of Liberalism*.

Chapter 7: Mao Meets Paul II

1. Y. Talmon, "Millenarian Movements," 166.
2. Gager, *Kingdom and Community*, 21.
3. Cf. Meisner, *Marxism, Maoism, and Utopianism*, 159.
4. Wakeman, *History and Will*, 14.
5. Meisner, *Marxism, Maoism, and Utopianism*, 165.
6. Foreword to Lin, ed., *Quotations from Chairman Mao Tse-tung*.
7. Wakeman, *History and Will*, 13–14.
8. Chuang, *Little Red Book and Current Chinese Language*, 7–8.
9. What made the Cultural Revolution unbelievably chaotic was the division Mao had created between the masses and the Party leadership and Mao's deliberate admonition for the masses to attack the Party, its leadership, and its organization. That the antileft and antiright campaigns occurred one after another also indicated that Mao himself probably could not discern clearly at the moment what was right and what was wrong.
10. For more, see my work on the redaction of 1 Corinthians, *Rhetorical Interaction in 1 Corinthians 8 and 10*, 75–83; and Jewett, "Redaction of 1 Corinthians," 398–444.
11. Hays, *Moral Vision of the New Testament*.
12. The fact that biblical scholars seek to determine which letters in the New Testament are authentic letters written by the apostle Paul (e.g., Romans) or are pseudonymous letters (e.g., Titus) indicates that Paul's penned letters have greater authority in the matters of faith and life for believers.
13. Mao, *Chinese Revolution and the Chinese Communist Party*, 1.
14. Deng, "Report on the Revision of the Constitution," 1:200.
15. Shen, "Toward a Critique of Power in the New China," 110.
16. Ibid., 111.
17. Mao, "Some Questions Concerning Methods of Leadership," 3:119.
18. Cited in "Resolution on Questions Concerning People's Communes."
19. Malherbe, *Paul and the Thessalonians*, 17.
20. Ibid., 18.
21. Jewett, "Tenement Churches and Communal Meals in the Early Church," 23–43.
22. Ibid., 26.
23. Ibid., 32.
24. "Resolution on Questions Concerning People's Communes."
25. But not Zhou Enlai, who seemed to be able to support Mao in a capacity that would not pose any threat to Mao at all. See Yang, *Mao Zedong and Zhou Enlai*.
26. Mao, "On the Correct Handling of Contradictions," 5:384–421.
27. Hock's thesis about Paul using the workshop as a public sphere in which the gospel is shared with the working class is very plausible. See Hock, *Social Context of Paul's Ministry*, 38–41.
28. Jewett, "Tenement Churches and Communal Meals in the Early Church," 33.
29. The law has the protasis describing the negative behavior of some members refusing to work, and the apodosis prescribing the legal consequence of the behavior, "do not eat!" If the members have their meals in their individual homes, surely such refusal to work does not negatively affect the community resources, and the enforcement of such a penalty would be ineffective.
30. Jewett, "Tenement Churches and Communal Meals in the Early Church," 37.
31. Ibid., 41.
32. Aristotle identifies six different kinds of leadership: kingship and tyranny, aristocracy and oligarchy, timocracy and democracy. See Aristotle, *Nicomachean Ethics* 8.10–11.

33. These two styles are identified by D. Martin, who gives two broad categories (*Slavery As Salvation*, 88–100).

34. Milbank, *Theology and Social Theory*, 391.

35. Yoder, *Politics of Jesus*, 246.

36. Toole, *Waiting for Godot in Sarajevo*, 214.

37. Yoder, *Politics of Jesus*, 47.

38. "Organizational ideology [i]s *a systematic set of ideas with action consequences serving the purpose of creating and using organization*" (Schurmann, *Ideology and Organization*, 18; emphasis his). See also Reinhard Bendix's understanding of ideology as "a type of goal-orientation, a special aspect of the teleology that is characteristic of all human action" ("Age of Ideology," 297).

39. See, for example, the Party rules adopted at the Seventh Party Congress (April–June, 1945): "The Chinese Communist party takes the theories of Marxism-Leninism and the unified thought of the practice of the Chinese Revolution, the thought of Mao [Zedong], as the guideline for all of its actions." Marxism provided the worldview, and Leninism provided the organizational principles. See Schurmann, *Ideology and Organization*, xlix.

40. Schurmann, *Ideology and Organization*, xlix.

41. Ibid., xlii.

42. Mannheim, *Ideology and Utopia*, 5.

43. Danker, *Benefactor*, is essentially a source book of fifty-three pieces of Greco-Roman inscriptions that are related to the theme of benefaction (1–316).

44. Danker argues that "the language and themes of Graeco-Roman inscriptions that reflect the pervasive interest in the function of a benefactor offer a manageable hermeneutical control base for determining the meaning that an auditor or reader of literary documents is likely to have attached to certain formulations and thematic treatment" (ibid., 29.)

45. Ibid., 351. Danker writes, "That Paul construes their performance as the work of benefactors is clear from his opening thanksgiving, which . . . is perfectly understandable as an expression of appreciation for the *arete* (. . . virtue) that has been evidenced by the recipients (verse 2–3)."

46. The example Danker gives is the letter to the Ionian League where Eumenes II affirms himself to be "the common benefactor of the Greeks and had undertaken many great struggles against the barbarians" (ibid., 365). Danker observes that this *agon* motif is "used to describe heroic measures taken by those who endure challenges or hardships in behalf of others."

47. Ibid., 26.

48. Ibid., 321–22.

49. Ibid., 354–55.

50. See Yeo, "Rhetoric of the Election and Calling Language in 1 Thessalonians."

51. Danker and Jewett, "Jesus As the Apocalyptic Benefactor," 490.

52. Ibid., 486–98.

53. Meisner, *Marxism, Maoism and Utopianism*, 168.

54. Meisner calls this Maoist doctrine "the ideals of communism" (ibid., 123).

55. What kind of order is meant depends on the context. Philo refers to matter before creation as *ataktos* (*Op. Mund.* 22); Josephus uses *ataktos* in parallelism with *anomos*, "lawlessly" (*C. Ap.* 2.151), and he characterizes the retreat of an army as *ataktos* (*B.J.* 3.1113). In papyri, the word refers to lack of discipline (*P.Oxy.* 275). See also Spicq, "Les Thessaloniciens," 1–13; Delling, "[*tasso*, etc.]," 8:27–48.

56. See Dittmer, *Liu Shao-ch'i and the Chinese Cultural Revolution*.

57. Meisner, *Mao's China and After*, 336. Meisner also mentions Mao's deification act a month earlier in which he swam in the Yangtze River for a distance of nine miles in sixty-five minutes; the event was much publicized.

58. As early as 1939, Mao summed up "all the truths of Marxism in one sentence: 'To rebel is justified.' " In August 24, 1966, the *People's Daily (Renmin Ribao)* used this summation to encourage the Red Guards to rebel. See Mao, "Talk at Meeting of All Circles," 427–28).

59. Meisner, *Marxism, Maoism and Utopianism*, 167; see also Bloodworth, *Messiah and the Mandarins*, 201–53.

60. The army in Communist China comprised two groups: the People's Liberation Army and the civil militia (*minbing*). The former constituted the main defense force as well as economic and industrial administrators in civil society; the latter functioned in the commune system. Young cadres in New China played a major leadership role; without them Chinese Communists would not have had much success. The strength of young blood brought challenges to older leadership and thus maintained the authority flow and shift to more people rather than being centralized on a few individuals.

61. Schram, *Thought of Mao Tse-tung*, 11.

62. The term *Red Guard* traditionally refers to the armed Russian workers and soldiers who seized power in the Bolshevik Revolution of 1917.

63. Chuang, *Great Proletarian Cultural Revolution*, 10–11.

64. "False Christ," which appears in Mark 13:22, is a near synonym of antichrist.

65. Antiochus Epiphanes did not himself sit in the temple at Jerusalem but only had a pagan altar set up there (1 Macc. 1:36–40, 54, 59). Nor did Caligula sit in the temple; he only ordered a statue of himself to be erected there. Despite their actual and attempted desecration of the temple, these emperors do not provide fully adequate models for Paul's man of lawlessness.

66. Wanamaker, *Epistles to the Thessalonians*, 247.

67. The phrase *en pase dynamei* (with all power) indicates that the lawless one is accompanied by a manifestation of satanic power. *Dynamis* (power) is found in conjunction with *semeia* (signs or miracles) and *terata* (wonders; cf. Rom. 15:19; 2 Cor. 12:12). In Romans 15:19, the "power" is what works the miracles and wonders, but the parallelism between "power and signs and wonders" precludes this idea here. Undoubtedly signs and wonders are to be taken together, since these two terms are commonly juxtaposed in the Greek Bible to indicate miraculous activity (Exod. 7:3; Deut. 4:34; Isa. 8:18; Jer. 39:21 [Eng. 32:21]; John 4:48; Acts 2:43; 4:30; 5:12; 6:8; 7:36; Heb. 2:4). Paul does not underestimate the reality of the satanic miracles; hence he uses the adjectival genitive *pseudous* to label them as deceptive. See Bruce, *1 and 2 Thessalonians*, 173.

68. Schurmann, *Ideology and Organization*, 589.

69. Ibid.

70. Meisner, *Mao's China and After*, 371–72.

71. Feng, *Ten Years of Madness*.

72. Milligan, *St. Paul's Epistles to the Thessalonians*, 152–54; Frame, *Critical and Exegetical Commentary*, 197, idem, "[*Hoi Ataktoi*]," 194; Bruce, *1 and 2 Thessalonians*, 122; Best, *Commentary*, 230.

73. Jewett, *Thessalonian Correspondence*, 104. Cf. Spicq, "Les Thessaloniciens," 1–13.

74. Menken, "Paradise Regained," 277. On the order of the law of Moses, see Exod. 29:43; Lev. 18:4; Deut. 27:1; Philo, *Spec. Leg.* 1.296; 2.175; Josephus, *Ant.* 5.98; Mark 1:44; Acts 7:44; 22:10. On order of creation, see Job 38:12; Wis. 11.20; *T. Naph.* 2:8–9; Philo, *Cher.* 23; Josephus, *Ant.* 1.30; Acts 17:26.

75. Menken clarifies, "Josephus in his *Ant.* 1.51 refers to God's words in Gen. 3:14–19 by means of *prospixas*, 'having ordered'. Also elsewhere in early Jewish literature, the fact

that man has to work hard for his living is considered to be an order established by God after the Fall. Sir 7.15 speaks of 'toilsome labour and agriculture, created by the most High' " (ibid., 277–78.) See also *Life of Adam and Eve* 22; *Sib. Or.* 1.57–58.

Since Genesis 2:15–16 and 3:17–19 have been seen in the Jewish tradition to be God's imposition upon human beings to work in order to eat the fruit of their labor, it is likely that Paul's teaching in 2 Thess. 3:6–10 finds its source in this Jewish theology.

76. Menken, "Paradise Regained," 279.

77. *Tg. Pseudo-Jonathan and Fragmentary Tg.*; see Menken, "Paradise Regained," 279.

78. See, for example, *1 Enoch* 10:17–11:2; *Sib. Or.* 3.619–623; Luke 14:15–24; Rev. 7:16; 21:1–22:6; see Menken, "Paradise Regained," 285.

79. See Isa. 11:6–8; Hos. 2:18–20; *4 Ezra* 8:52.

80. Menken, "Paradise Regained," 285.

81. Morris, *First and Second Epistles to the Thessalonians*, 252; Marshall, *1 and 2 Thessalonians*, 219; and Best, *1 and 2 Thessalonians*, 176–78.

82. The reference to "those not working but being busybodies" suggests the problem caused by the *ataktoi*. The wording of 2 Thess. 3:16 ("the Lord of peace himself give you peace") also indicates that the church was going through disturbances caused by the *ataktoi* rebelling against Paul's ethics and his attitude toward work.

83. Paul's injunction "in the name of our Lord Jesus" was to ask working Christians "to keep away from a brother who is *ataktos*." This is a way of detaching oneself from the patron-client relationship and the possible abuse such a system would provide for the *ataktoi*. This is "the only way of relieving the patron of his obligation without the latter's refusal to provide food being seen as an act of enmity within the church" (Winter, "If a Man Does Not Wish to Work," 313).

84. The fact that Paul saw it necessary to work himself and not to burden anyone at Thessalonica may indicate that the majority poor were not to be burdened. Paul's autobiographical message is an imitation rhetoric that exhorts the *ataktoi* poor not to burden others. The *ataktoi* are most probably poor, since their refusal to work would not be a burden to anyone if they were rich. If they would work, they would be able to support themselves and the poorer believers in Jerusalem (2 Cor. 8:4). There were rich people as well, though not many, and mostly women, as literary sources indicate.

85. Scott, "Paul and Late-Jewish Eschatology," 135.

86. Evans, "Eschatology and Ethics," 190: "The Thessalonians grasped by faith the Gospel of love thereby guaranteeing for themselves a future. No matter that their future was called into question by persecution and a possible delay of the *Parousia*, the gospel of faith, hope, and love secured their future."

87. Ibid.

88. While the Synoptic tradition does not use the negative expression of "do not sleep," the positive expression of "being watchful" is found in Mark 13:34–35; Matt. 24:43; Luke 12:37, 39.

89. Evans, "Eschatology and Ethics," 189; emphasis his.

Chapter 8: Mao Meets Paul III

1. Schurmann, *Ideology and Organization*, 506.

2. Wakeman, *History and Will*, xi.

3. Mannheim, *Ideology and Utopia*, 192. See also the introduction chapter of this volume.

4. For example, just as in old times, when the peasantry gained revolutionary consciousness and victory through the land reform, later the proletariat would gain spiritual transformation through a class struggle against the Party authorities. In other words, the ruling class consolidated power, but only the masses in the class struggle could achieve

change through revolution and rebellion. Likewise, Schurmann says that, "We can now conclude that the primary purpose of the great ideological drama which culminated in the Cultural Revolution was to create a new generation of political leaders, not through a Party-guided ideological indoctrination but through a class struggle waged against those who controlled the Party" (*Ideology and Organization*, 518).

5. Bauer, *China and the Search for Happiness*, 397–98.

6. This is Mao's conversation with André Malraux, France's Minister of Culture; see Malraux, *Anti-Memoirs*, 373–74.

7. More, *Utopia*, 1.

8. Mumford, *Story of Utopias*, 1.

9. Mao, *Mao Zedong Sixiang Wansui*, 1:240.

10. See Bloch, *Principle of Hope*, 3:1316: "the ideal was related to the utopian function, which is overhauling and goal-oriented in each case. The utopian function, in the idea of craving that which is not to hand, indeed that which is not at hand, already gives to all the things it grasps the cachet of the wishful good, or, if what corresponds to the wishful good is objectively contained in the thing, it makes us receptive to it."

11. Mannheim, *Ideology and Utopia*, 236.

12. Ibid.

13. See, e.g., Gen. 1:17; 17:5; 1 Kings 9:3; Job 38:10; Pss. 33:7 [LXX 32:7]; 103:9 [LXX 104:9]; Isa. 26:1; Jer. 1:5. See Maurer, "[*Tithemi*, etc.]," 8:154.

14. On rhetoric as a movement of hope in a unifying whole, see Ong, *Rhetoric, Romance, and Technology*, 12–13.

15. Meisner, *Marxism, Maoism, and Utopianism*, 18.

16. Mao, "Chinese Revolution," 2:321.

17. In Ch'en, ed., *Mao Papers*, 145; originally in *People's Daily* (*Renmin Ribao*) (August 30, 1967).

18. Lin, ed., *Quotations from Chairman Mao Tse-tung*, section 22.

19. *Qodesh* means essentially (a) belonging to Yahweh (in the priestly tradition) as God sets the people apart for his purpose—thus people, Sabbath (Exod. 16:23), assembly (Exod. 12:16), heaven (Ps. 20:6), and Mount Zion (Ps. 2:6) are said to be holy; (b) participating in the ethical and moral holiness of God (in the prophetic tradition). Cf. Snaith, *Distinctive Ideas of the Old Testament*, 21–50.

20. Exod. 29:43; Lev. 19:2; 1 Sam 2:2; Pss. 18:30; 101:2, 6; and 1 Peter 1:15.

21. This does not necessarily imply the origin of Gnosticism in Thessalonica, because such dualistic belief was prevalent throughout the Greco-Roman world. Cf. Schweizer, "[*Pneuma*, etc.]," 6:390–91.

22. Schurmann explains the difference between Mao and Liu on transformation of humans (*Ideology and Organization*, 514–15): "Mao says, in effect, that correct thought can only come about through open struggle in the social arena. Liu, on the other hand, says that correct thought must be cultivated through struggle and persuasion within the confines of the Party. Mao, more confident than Liu in the forces of society, welcomes the upsurge from below, for in the struggles of that upsurge men will inevitably develop a true revolutionary consciousness. Liu . . . believes that such an upsurge can only be destructive. He believes that true revolutionary consciousness can only develop through ideologically and organizationally controlled thought reform."

23. Socialism treated inner opposition as more serious than outer enemies, so communism fought more fiercely against revisionism than against the democracy of the West. At the end of the 1973, the "anti–Lin Biao and anti-Confucius" campaign was launched, and whoever went against Maoism was charged in the same category. Liu was charged as a "capitalist roader" during the Cultural Revolution.

24. Han, *China in the Year 2001*, 185–86.

25. Schurmann, *Ideology and Organization*, 513.

26. Meisner, *Mao's China and After*, 210.

27. Chai, ed., *Essential Works of Chinese Communism*, 477.

28. Mao, "On the Protracted War," 2:224.

29. Mao, "Report of an Investigation," 1:28.

30. Mao, "Combat Liberalism," 2:31.

31. Whitehead, "Love and Animosity in the Ethic of Mao," 1:76.

32. E. J. Richard, *First and Second Thessalonians*, 124–25. See also Pearson, "1 Thessalonians 2:13–16," 79–91; D. Schmidt, "1 Thess. 2:13–16," 269–79. Because of the series of charges placed against Jews as persecutor of Jesus and his followers, many scholars read this section as an interpolation (see R. F. Collins, "A Propos the Integrity of 1 Thessalonians," 67–106). An alternate interpretation is to view this pericope in its literary and rhetorical intention. "Jews" in verse 14 does not denote *universal Jews* but a particular group of Jewish leaders who resisted Jesus' message, accused Jesus of breaking the laws, and drove him to the cross. Paul's intention is *not* to blame *all* the Jews for the death of Jesus! See Frank D. Gilliard's delineation of the misunderstanding of the "antisemitic comma" between 1 Thess. 2:14 and 15 and the restrictive participles as well as particular Jews referred to in the pericope ("Problem of the Antisemitic Comma," 481–502; idem, "Paul and the Killing of the Prophets," 259–70).

33. Wanamaker, *Epistles to the Thessalonians*, 118. See Lausberg, *Handbuch der Literarischen Rhetorik*, 187, 542–44.

34. This will be the same case with Revelation; see A. Y. Collins, "Vilification and Self-Definition," 314.

35. Faricy, "Mao's Thought and Christian Belief," 62.

36. Ibid., 62–63.

37. The group that responds to a utopian impulse is not necessarily the disprivileged, marginalized one. Even privileged intellectuals having dissonance in their expectations and understanding of reality could find a utopian movement appealing.

38. O'Leary, *Arguing the Apocalypse*, 34.

39. Lifton, *Revolutionary Immortality*, 20–21.

40. Ibid., 22.

41. Evans, "Eschatology and Ethics," 172.

42. Löwith, *Meaning in History*, 6.

Chapter 9: Millenarian Hope in the Post-Paul and Post-Mao Eras

1. Bauckham, "Time and Eternity" in *God Will Be All in All*, 20.

2. Hunter and Chan, *Protestantism in Contemporary China*, 3.

3. Ibid., 4.

4. See Sun, *Chinese Reassessment of Socialism*.

5. Barmé, *In the Red*, 320.

6. Ibid., 316–44, here 319.

7. Chang Zhengzhi's article, quoted and translated by Barmé, *In the Red*, 323.

8. Manuel and Manuel, *Utopian Thought in the Western World*, 811.

9. Moltmann, "Liberation of the Future," 277.

10. Ibid., 280.

11. Bauckham, "Time and Eternity" in *God Will Be All in All*, 172.

12. Hart, "Imagination for the Kingdom of God?" 63.

13. This group's latest tragedy occurred on March 22, 1997, when five disciples of the group were consumed in a propane fire in the French Canadian village of St. Casimir.

14. E. Richard, *AD 1000*.

15. Duby, *L'An Mil*, 9, quoted and trans. by Kumar, "Apocalypse, Millennium and Utopia Today," 200.

16. See the discussion of the ethos of 1000 and the debate over 1000 or 1033 in Gurevich, *Categories of Medieval Culture*, 113–22; Focillon, *The Year 1000*, 53–68.

17. See Moore and McGehee, eds., *Need for a Second Look at Jonestown*, 23–40, 53–59, 61–74, 91–114.

18. See *Sunday Morning Post Magazine* (Hong Kong) (June 18, 1995): 15.

19. Jewett, "Coming to Terms with the Doom Boom," 14.

20. Ibid.

21. Romans 12:17–21 speaks from the same vein of doing good for others while leaving judgment to God (cf. 2 Thess. 1:6 on the judgment theme).

22. See the comments on 2 Thess. 1 and 2 in chapter 8.

23. Evans, "Eschatology and Ethics," 139: "Hope was the theological quantity most lacking in Roman-Hellenism; hope was the quantity most in abundance in the Church at Thessalonica. Their hope was generated by Paul's preaching of Jesus Christ as Lord. Since hope spelled-out, defined, or systematized is eschatology, Paul's theology can be understood rightly only when we comprehend the basis of this hope."

24. Beker, *Paul the Apostle*, 18–19.

25. Krishan Kumar calls this "debased millenarianism." See Kumar, "Apocalypse, Millennium and Utopia Today," 214–16.

26. Ibid., 212.

27. Ibid., 219.

28. Ibid., 212.

29. Rowland, "Upon Whom the Ends of the Ages Have Come," 43.

30. Ibid., 56.

31. Kumar, "Apocalypse, Millennium and Utopia Today," 202. In a similar tone, Evan notes, concerning Paul's prophetic realism in Thessalonians: "The 'already' and 'not yet' of eschatology impinge upon the present moment, upon the 'now' of our present existence. 'Now' is the time of the Holy Spirit. 'Now' is the time of eschatological decision. 'Now' is the time when we are confronted with Jesus Christ and His past and future" (Evans, "Eschatology and Ethics," 168).

bibliography

Ackroyd, P. B. *Israel under Babylon and Persia.* London: Oxford University Press, 1970.

Anonymous, " 'New Man' in China: Myth or Reality?" In *Christianity and the New China,* 2 vols. South Pasadena, Calif.: Ecclesia, 1976. 2:45–52.

Appleby, Joyce, Lynn Hunt, and Margaret Jacob. *Telling the Truth about History.* New York: W. W. Norton, 1994.

Aristotle. *Nicomachean Ethics.* Translated by H. Rackham. New and rev. ed. London: W. Heinemann; Cambridge: Harvard University Press, 1939.

Augustine. *The City of God.* Translated by Demetrius B. Zema and Gerald G. Walsh, 3 vols. New York: Fathers of the Church, 1950–1954.

Aune, David. "The Apocalypse of John and the Problem of Genre." *Semeia* 36 (1986): 65–96.

Baldwin, S. L. "Self-Support of the Native Church." In *Records of the General Conference of the Protestant Missionaries of China Held at Shanghai, May 10–20, 1877,* 283–87. Shanghai: Presbyterian Mission Press, 1878.

Barmé, Geremie R. *In the Red: On Contemporary Chinese Culture.* New York: Columbia University Press, 1999.

Bauckham, Richard, ed. *God Will Be All in All: The Eschatology of Jürgen Moltmann.* Edinburgh: T. & T. Clark, 1999.

Bauer, Wolfgang. *China and the Search for Happiness: Recurring Themes in Four Thousand Years of Chinese Cultural History.* Translated by Michael Shaw. New York: Seabury, 1976.

Bauerschmidt, Frederick Christian. *Julian of Norwich and the Mystical Body Politic of Christ.* Notre Dame, Ind.: University of Notre Dame Press, 1999.

Beaver, R. Pierce, ed. *To Advance the Gospel: Selections from the Writings of Rufus Anderson.* Grand Rapids: Eerdmans, 1967.

Beker, J. Christian. *Paul the Apostle: The Triumph of God in Life and Thought.* Philadelphia: Fortress, 1980.

Bendix, Reinhard. "The Age of Ideology: Persistent and Changing." In *Ideology and Discontent,* edited by David E. Apter, 294–327. New York: Free Press, 1964.

Berger, Peter. *The Sacred Canopy.* New York: Doubleday, 1969.

——. *The Social Reality of Religion.* London: Faber, 1969.

Berger, Peter, and T. Luckmann, *The Social Construction of Reality: A Treatise in the Sociology of Knowledge.* Garden City, N.Y.: Doubleday, 1967.

Best, Ernest E. *A Commentary on the First and Second Epistles to the Thessalonians.* London: Adam & Charles Black, 1972.

Bloch, Ernst. *The Principle of Hope.* 3 vols. Cambridge, Mass.: MIT Press, 1986.

Bloodworth, Dennis. *The Messiah and the Mandarins: Mao Tsetung and the Ironies of Power.* New York: Atheneum, 1982.

Blumenberg, Hans. *The Legitimacy of the Modern Age.* Translated by Robert M. Wallace. Cambridge, Mass.: MIT Press, 1983.

Bodde, Derk. *Essays on Chinese Civilization.* Princeton, N.J.: Princeton University Press, 1981.

Brown, G. Thompson. *Christianity in the People's Republic of China.* Atlanta: John Knox, 1986.

Brown, Raymond E. *The Death of the Messiah.* 2 vols. New York: Doubleday, 1994.

Bruce, F. F. *1 and 2 Thessalonians.* Waco, Tex.: Word, 1982.

Burke, Kenneth. *A Rhetoric of Motives.* Berkeley: University of California Press, 1969.

Burridge, Kenelm. *New Heaven, New Earth: A Study of Millenarian Activities.* New York: Schocken, 1969.

Capra, Fritjof. *The Tao of Physics: An Exploration of the Parallels between Modern Physics and Eastern Mysticism.* Boston: Shambhala, 1991.

Cary-Elwes, Columba. *China and the Cross: Studies in Missionary History.* London: Longmans, 1957.

Casey, Maurice. *From Jewish Prophet to Gentile God: The Origins and Development of New Testament Christology.* Louisville: Westminster John Knox, 1991.

——. *Son of Man: The Interpretation and Influence of Daniel 7.* London: SPCK, 1979.

Chai, Winberg, ed. *Essential Works of Chinese Communism.* New York: Bantam, 1972.

Charbonnier, Jean and Léon Trivière. "The New China and the History of Salvation." In *Christianity and the New China,* 2 vols. South Pasadena, Calif.: Ecclesia, 1976. 1:87–112

Ch'en, Jerome, ed. *Mao Papers: Anthology and Bibliography.* London and New York: Oxford University Press, 1970.

——. *Mao and the Chinese Revolution.* London: Oxford University Press, 1965.

Cheng, J. Chester. *Chinese Sources for the Taiping Rebellion in China 1850–1864.* Hong Kong: Hong Kong University Press, 1963.

Ching, Julia. "Faith and Ideology in the Light of the New China." *Christianity and the New China,* 2 vols. South Pasadena, Calif.: Ecclesia, 1976. 1:15–36.

Chuang, H. C. *The Great Proletarian Cultural Revolution*. Berkeley: Center for Chinese Studies, University of California, 1967.

———. *The Little Red Book and Current Chinese Language*. Berkeley: Center for Chinese Studies, 1968.

Clark, William H. *The Church in China: Its Vitality; Its Future?* New York: Council Press, 1969.

Coenen, L. "[*eklegomai*]." *New International Dictionary of New Testament Theology*, edited by C. Brown, 4. vols. Grand Rapids: Zondervan, 1975–1985. 1:536–43.

———, "[*kaleo*]." *New International Dictionary of New Testament Theology*, edited by C. Brown, 4. vols. Grand Rapids: Zondervan, 1975–1985. 1:271–76.

Cohn, Norman. *The Pursuit of the Millennium*. New York: Oxford University Press, 1970.

Collins, Adela Yarbro. *Cosmology and Eschatology in Jewish and Christian Apocalypticism*. New York: E. J. Brill, 1996.

———. *Crisis and Catharsis*. Philadelphia: Westminster, 1984.

———. "Vilification and Self-Definition in the Book of Revelation." *Harvard Theological Review* 79 (1986): 308–20.

———. ed. *Early Christian Apocalypticism: Genre and Social Setting*. Semeia 36 (1986).

Collins, John J. "Introduction: Towards the Morphology of a Genre." *Semeia* 14 (1979): 1–20.

Collins, Raymond F. "A Propos the Integrity of 1 Thessalonians." *Ephemerides theologicae lovanienses* 55 (1979): 67–106.

———. *Studies on the First Letter to the Thessalonians*. Leuven: Leuven University Press, 1984.

———. ed. *The Thessalonian Correspondence*. Leuven: Leuven University Press, 1990.

Cone, James. *A Black Theology of Liberation*. Philadelphia: Lippincott, 1970.

The Constitution of the People's Republic of China. Beijing: Foreign Languages Press, 1982.

Cook, Stephen L. *Prophecy and Apocalypticism: The Postexilic Social Setting*. Minneapolis: Augsburg, 1995.

Cort, John C. *Christian Socialism: An Informal History*. Maryknoll, N.Y.: Orbis, 1988.

Cullmann, O. *Christ and Time: The Primitive Christian Conception of Time and History*. Translated by Floyd V. Filson. Philadelphia: Westminster, 1975.

Danker, F. W. *Benefactor: Epigraphic Study of a Graeco-Roman and New Testament Semantic Field*. St. Louis: Clayton, 1982.

Danker, F. W., and R. Jewett. "Jesus As the Apocalyptic Benefactor in Second Thessalonians." In *The Thessalonian Correspondence*, edited by Raymond F. Collins, 486–98. Leuven: Leuven University Press, 1990.

Dawson, Doyne. *Cities of the Gods: Communist Utopias in Greek Thought.* New York: Oxford University Press, 1992.

Dehoney, W. *The Dragon and the Lamb.* Nashville: Broadman, 1988.

Deissmann, Adolf. *Light from the Ancient East.* Grand Rapids: Baker, 1978.

Delling, G. "[*tasso*, etc.]." In *Theological Dictionary of the New Testament,* edited by Gerhard Kittel, Gerhard Friedrich, and Geoffrey W. Bromiley, and translated by Geoffrey W. Bromiley, 10 vols. Grand Rapids: Eerdmans, 1964–1976. 8:27–48.

Deng Xiaoping. "Report on the Revision of the Constitution of the Communist Party of China." Delivered at the Eighth National Congress of the CCP, September 16, 1956. In *Eighth National Congress of the Communist Party of China,* vol 1. Peking: Foreign Languages Press, 1956.

Dittmer, Lowell. *Liu Shao-ch'i and the Chinese Cultural Revolution: The Politics of Mass Criticism.* Berkeley and Los Angeles: University of California Press, 1974.

Donfried, Karl Paul. "The Cults of Thessalonica and the Thessalonian Correspondence." *New Testament Studies* 31 (1985): 336–56.

Dubs, Homer H, trans. *The Works of Hsüntze.* London: A. Probsthain, 1928.

Duby, Georges. *L'An Mil.* Paris: Julliard, 1980.

Duling, Dennis C. "Millennialism." In *The Social Sciences and New Testament Interpretation,* edited by Richard L. Rohrbaugh, 183–205. Peabody, Mass.: Hendrickson, 1996.

———. *The New Testament: Proclamation and Parenesis, Myth and History.* Fort Worth: Harcourt Brace College, 1994.

Dupré, Louis. *The Philosophical Foundations of Marxism.* New York: Harcourt, Brace & World, 1966.

Edson, Charles. "Macedonia, II. State Cults in Thessalonica." *Harvard Studies in Classical Philology* 51 (1940): 127–36.

Eliade, M. *The Myth of the Eternal Return,* or *Cosmos and History.* Princeton, N.J.: Princeton Unviersity Press, 1971.

Engels, Frederick. *The Peasant War in Germany.* New York: International, 1934.

———. *Socialism: Utopian and Scientific.* Translated by Edward Aveling. Chicago: Charles H. Kerr, 1941.

Erasmus, Charles J. *In Search of the Common Good: Utopian Experiments Past and Future.* New York: Free Press, 1977.

Evans, Robert. "Eschatology and Ethics: A Study of Thessalonica and Paul's Letters to the Thessalonians." Ph.D. diss., University of Basel, 1967.

Fang, Thomé H. "The World and the Individual in Chinese Metaphysics." In *The Chinese Mind: Essentials of Chinese Philosophy and Culture,* edited by Charles A. Moore, 238–63. Honolulu: University Press of Hawaii, 1967.

Fannon, P. "The Apocalypse." *Scripture* 14/26 (1962): 33–43.

Faricy, Robert. "Mao's Thought and Christian Belief." In *The New China: A Catholic Response,* ed. Michael Chu, 44–80. New York: Paulist, 1977.

Feng Jicai (Chi-t'sai). *Ten Years of Madness: Oral Histories of China's Cultural Revolution*. San Francisco: China Books, 1996.

Feuerback, Ludwig. *The Essence of Christianity*. Trans. George Eliot. New York: Harper & Brothers, 1957.

Finger, Thomas N. *Christian Theology: An Eschatological Approach*, vol. 1. Nashville: Thomas Nelson, 1985.

Fitzgerald, C. P. *The Birth of Communist China*. Baltimore: Penguin, 1964.

Focillon, Henri. *The Year 1000*. Translated by F. D. Wieck. New York: Harper & Row, 1969.

Foerster, W. and G. Quell. "[*kyrios*, etc.]." In *Theological Dictionary of the New Testament*, edited by Gerhard Kittel, Gerhard Friedrich, and Geoffrey W. Bromiley, and translated by Geoffrey W. Bromiley, 10 vols. Grand Rapids: Eerdmans, 1964–1976. 3:1039–98.

Ford, Lewis S. "God As the Subjectivity of the Future." *Encounter* 41 (1980): 287–92.

Frame, James E. *A Critical and Exegetical Commentary on the Epistles of St. Paul to the Thessalonians*. New York: Scribners, 1912.

———. "[*Hoi ataktoi*] (I Thess. 5.14)." In *Essays in Modern Theology and Related Subjects: Gathered and Published As a Testimonial to Charles A. Briggs*, 189–206. New York: Charles Scribner's, 1911.

Freemantle, A., ed. *The Papal Encyclicals in Their Historical Context*. New York: Putnam, 1956.

Fung Yu-lan. *A History of Chinese Philosophy*. 2 vols. Princeton, N.J.: Princeton University Press, 1952–1953.

———. *A Short History of Chinese Philosophy*. Edited by Derk Bodde. New York: Macmillan, 1948.

Gager, John G. *Kingdom and Community: The Social World of Early Christianity*. Englewood Cliffs, N.J.: Prentice-Hall, 1975.

Gammie, John. *Holiness in Israel*. Minneapolis: Fortress, 1989.

Geertz, Clifford. *The Interpretation of Culture: Selected Essays*. New York: Basic Books, 1973.

Geoghegan, Vincent. *Utopianism and Marxism*. London and New York: Methuen, 1987.

Gilliard, Frank D. "Paul and the Killing of the Prophets in 1 Thess. 2:15." *Novum Testamentum* 36 (1994): 259–70.

———. "The Problem of the Antisemitic Comma between 1 Thessalonians 2:14 and 15." *New Testament Studies* 35 (1989): 481–502.

Graham, A. C., trans. *The Book of Lieh-tzu*. London: J. Murray, 1960.

Guan Zi, "Emperor versus His Officers." In Liang Qichao, *History of Chinese Political Thought During the Early Tsin Period*, 116–29. Taipei: Cheng-wen, 1968.

Gurevich, A. J. *Categories of Medieval Culture*. Translated by G. L. Campbell. London and Boston: Routledge & Kegan Paul, 1985.

Gutiérrez, Gustavo. *Theology of Liberation: History, Politics, and Salvation*. Maryknoll, N.Y.: Orbis, 1973.

Han Suyin. *China in the Year 2001*. New York: Basic Books, 1967.

Hanson, Paul D. *The Dawn of Apocalyptic*. Philadelphia: Fortress, 1975.

Hanson, Paul D., et al., "Apocalypses and Apocalypticism." In *Anchor Bible Dictionary*, edited by D. N. Freedman, 6 vols. New York: Doubleday, 1992. 1:279–92.

Harrison, J. F. C. "Millennium and Utopia." In *Utopia*, edited by Peter Alexander and Roger Gill, 61–66. London: Duckworth, 1984.

Hart, Trevor. "Imagination for the Kingdom of God?" In *God Will Be All in All: The Eschatology of Jürgen Moltmann*, edited by Richard Bauckham, 49–76. Edinburgh: T. & T. Clark, 1999.

Hays, Richard. *The Moral Vision of the New Testament*: *A Contemporary Introduction to New Testament Ethics*. New York: HarperSanFrancisco, 1996.

Hayward, V. *Christians and China*. Belfast: Christian Journals, 1974.

Hegel, G. W. F. *Hegels theologische Jugendschriften*. Edited by Herman Nohl. Tübingen: Frankfurt, 1907.

———. *Phenomenology of Mind*. Translated by J. B. Baillie. New York: Humanities, 1966.

Hellholm, David. "The Problem of Apocalyptic Genre and the Apocalypse of John." *Semeia* 36 (1986): 13–64.

Hemberg, Bengt. *Die Kabiren*. Uppsala: Almqvist & Wiksell, 1950.

Henke, Frederick G., trans. *The Philosophy of Wang Yang-ming*. Chicago: Open Court Publishing, 1916.

Hexter, J. H. *The Vision of Politics on the Eve of the Reformation: More, Machiavelli, and Seyssel*. London: Allen Lane, 1973.

Hock, Ronald F. *The Social Context of Paul's Ministry: Tentmaking and Apostleship*. Philadelphia: Fortress, 1980.

Holmberg, B. *Paul and Power: The Structure of Authority in the Primitive Church as Reflected in the Pauline Epistles*. Philadelphia: Fortress, 1980.

Homer. *Iliad*. Translated by A. T. Murray. London: W. Heinemann; New York: G. P. Putnam's Sons, 1930.

———. *Odyssey*. Translated by A. T. Murray. Cambridge: Harvard University Press, 1960.

Horsley, Richard. *Jesus and the Spiral of Violence: Popular Jewish Resistance in Roman Palestine*. Minneapolis: Fortress, 1993.

Horsley, Richard, and John S. Hanson. *Bandits, Prophets and Messiahs: Popular Movements of the Time of Jesus*. Minneapolis: Winston, 1985.

Hsiao Hsü-tung (Siao-yü). *Mao Tse-tung and I Were Beggars*. Syracuse: Syracuse University Press, 1959.

Hughes, Frank W. "The Rhetoric of 1 Thessalonians." In *The Thessalonian Correspondence*, edited by Raymond F. Collins, 94–116. Leuven: Leuven University Press, 1990.

Hunter, Alan, and Kim-Kwong Chan. *Protestantism in Contemporary China.* Cambridge: Cambridge University Press, 1993.

Jacobs, Dan N., and Hans H. Baerwald, eds. *Chinese Communism: Selected Documents.* New York: Harper & Row, 1963.

Jameson, Fredrick. *The Political Unconscious: Narrative As a Socially Symbolic Act.* Ithaca: Cornell University Press, 1982.

Jensen, Lionel. *Manufacturing Confucianism: Chinese Tradition and Universal Civilization.* Durham, N.C.: Duke University Press, 1997.

Jewett, Robert. "Coming to Terms with the Doom Boom." *Quarterly Review* 4 (Fall 1984): 14–15.

———. "A Matrix of Grace: The Theology of 2 Thessalonians As a Pauline Letter." In *Pauline Theology.* Vol. 1: *Thessalonians, Philippians, Galatians, Philemon,* edited by Jouette M. Bassler, 63–70. Minneapolis: Fortress, 1991.

———. "The Redaction of 1 Corinthians and the Trajectory of the Pauline School." *Journal of the American Academy of Religion Supplement* 46 (1978): 398–444.

———. "Tenement Churches and Communal Meals in the Early Church: The Implications of a Form-Critical Analysis of 2 Thessalonians 3:10." *Biblical Research* 38 (1993): 22–43.

———. *The Thessalonian Correspondence: Pauline Rhetoric and Millenarian Piety.* Philadelphia: Fortress, 1986.

Johnson, Luke Timothy. "The Humanity of Jesus. What's at Stake in the Quest for the Historical Jesus?" In *The Jesus Controversy: Perspectives in Conflict,* edited by John Dominic Crossan, Luke Timothy Johnson, and Werner H. Kelber, 48–74. Harrisburg, Pa.: Trinity Press International, 1999.

Jones, C. *The Church in Communist China: A Protestant Appraisal.* New York: Friendship Press, 1962.

Jones, Francis P., ed. *Documents of the Three-Self Movement: Source Materials for the Study of the Protestant Church in Communist China.* New York: National Council of the Churches of Christ, 1963.

Joseph, William A., Christine P. W. Wong, and David Zweig, eds. *New Perspectives on the Cultural Revolution.* Cambridge: Harvard University Press, 1991.

Josephus, Flavius. *Works.* Translated by H. St. J. Thackeray et al. 10 vols. Cambridge: Harvard University Press; London: W. Heinemann, 1926–1976.

Judge, E. A. "The Decrees of Caesar at Thessalonica." *Reformed Theological Review* 30 (1971): 1–17.

Käsemann, Ernst. "The Beginnings of Christian Theology." In *New Testament Questions of Today,* translated by W. J. Montague, 82–107. Philadelphia: Fortress, 1969.

Kaylor, R. David. *Jesus the Prophet: His Vision of the Kingdom on Earth.* Louisville: Westminster John Knox, 1994.

Kellner, Douglas. "Ernst Bloch, Utopia, and Ideology Critique." In *Not Yet: Reconsidering Ernst Bloch,* edited by Jamie Owen Daniel and Tom Moylan, 80–95. London: Verso, 1997.

———. "Ideology, Marxism, and Advanced Capitalism." *Socialist Review* 42 (1978): 37–41.

Khang Yu-Wei [Kang Youwei]. *Ta Thung Shu: The One-World Philosophy of Khang Yu-Wei.* Abridged translation by L. G. Thompson. London: Faber & Faber, 1958.

Krentz, Edgar. "1 Thessalonians: A Document of Roman Hellenism." Unpublished Society of Biblical Literature seminar paper. New York City, November 1979.

———. "Traditions Held Fast: Theology and Fidelity in 2 Thessalonians." In *The Thessalonian Correspondence,* edited by Raymond F. Collins, 505–15. Leuven: Leuven University Press, 1990.

Kumar, Krishan. "Apocalypse, Millennium and Utopia Today." In *Apocalypse Theory and the Ends of the World,* edited by Malcolm Bull, 200–26. Oxford: Blackwell, 1995.

———. *Utopia and Anti-utopia in Modern Times.* Oxford: Basil Blackwell, 1987.

———. *Utopianism.* Minneapolis: University of Minnesota Press, 1991.

La Barre, Weston. *The Ghost Dance: Origins of Religion.* Garden City, N.Y.: Doubleday, 1970.

Lanternari, Vittorio. *The Religions of the Oppressed.* Translated by L. Sergio. New York: Knopf, 1963.

Lausberg, H. *Handbuch der literarischen Rhetorik.* Munich: Hueber, 1973.

Lee, Jung Young. "Search for a Theological Paradigm: An Asian-American Journey." *Quarterly Review* (Spring 1989): 36–47.

———. *The Theology of Change: A Christian Concept of God in an Eastern Perspective.* Maryknoll, N.Y.: Orbis, 1979.

Lee, Rensselaer W., III. "General Aspects of Chinese Communist Religious Policy, with Soviet Comparisons." *China Quarterly* 19 (July–Sept 1964): 161–73.

Legge, James, trans. *The Chinese Classics: With a Translation, Critical and Exegetical Notes, Prolegomena and Copious Indexes.* 5 vols. Reprint. Hong Kong: Hong Kong University Press, 1960.

———, trans. *The Four Books.* Taipei: Wen-hua shu-chü, 1960.

———, trans. *Tao Te Ching and the Writings of Chuang Tzu.* New ed. Taipei: Wen-hua shu-chü, 1963.

Levitas, Ruth. *The Concept of Utopia.* Syracuse, N.Y.: Syracuse University Press, 1990.

———. "Educated Hope: Ernst Bloch on Abstract and Concrete Utopia." In *Not Yet: Reconsidering Ernst Bloch,* edited by Jamie Owen Daniel and Tom Moylan, 65–79. London: Verso, 1997.

Liao, W. K., trans. *The Complete Works of Han Fei Tzu.* 2 vols. London: A Probsthain, 1939.

Lifton, Robert Jay. *Revolutionary Immortality: Mao Tse-tung and the Chinese Cultural Revolution*. New York: Vintage, 1968.

Lin Biao, "Informal Address at Politburo Meeting" (May 18, 1966). Cited in Marton Ebon, *Lin Piao: The Life and Writings of China's New Ruler*. New York: Stein & Day, 1970.

———, ed. *Quotations from Chairman Mao Tse-tung*. 2d ed. Peking: Foreign Languages Press, 1966.

Lo Kuan-chung. *Romance of the Three Kingdoms*. Translated by C. H. Brewitt-Taylor. Shanghai: Kelly & Walsh, 1929.

Lohfink, Gerhard. *Does God Need the Church? Toward a Theology of the People of God*. Collegeville, Minn.: Liturgical, 1999.

———. *Jesus and Community: The Social Dimension of Christian Faith*. Philadelphia: Fortress, 1984.

Loubere, Leo. *Utopian Socialism: Its History since 1800*. Cambridge: Schenkman, 1974.

Löwith, Karl. *Meaning in History: The Theological Implications of the Philosophy of History*. Chicago: University of Chicago Press, 1949.

Lukes, Steven. "Marxism and Utopianism." In *Utopia*, edited by Peter Alexander and Roger Gill, 153–67. London: Duckworth, 1984.

Lyall, Leslie. *God Reigns in China*. London: Hodder & Stoughton, 1985.

———. *New Spring in China? A Christian Appraisal*. London: Hodder & Stoughton, 1979.

———. *Red Sky at Night: Communism Confronts Christianity in China*. London: Hodder & Stoughton, 1969.

MacInnis, Donald E. *Religious Policy and Practice in Communist China: A Documentary History*. New York: Macmillan, 1972.

MacIntyre, Alasdair. *Marxism and Christianity*. New York: Schocken, 1968.

Malherbe, Abraham J. *Paul and the Thessalonians: The Philosophic Tradition of Pastoral Care*. Philadelphia: Fortress, 1987.

Malraux, Andre. *Anti-Memoirs*. New York: Holt, Rinehart & Winston, 1968.

Manent, Pierre. *An Intellectual History of Liberalism*. Translated by Rebecca Balinski. Princeton, N.J.: Princeton University Press, 1994.

Mannheim, Karl. *Ideology and Utopia: An Introduction to the Sociology of Knowledge*. Translated by Louis Wirth and Edward Shils. New York: Harcourt, Brace, and Co., 1949.

Manuel, Frank E., ed. *Utopias and Utopian Thought*. Boston: Beacon, 1967.

Manuel, Frank E., and Fritzie P. Manuel. *Utopian Thought in the Western World*. Cambridge: Harvard University Press, 1979.

Mao Zedong. "Analysis of the Classes in Chinese Society" (March 1926). In *Selected Works of Mao Tse-tung*. 5 vols. Peking: Foreign Languages Press, 1975. 1:13–21

———. "Bankruptcy of Idealist Conception of History" (September 1949). In *Selected Works of Mao Tse-tung.* 5 vols. Peking: Foreign Languages Press, 1975. 4:451–59.

———. "Be a True Revolutionary" (June 1950). In *Selected Works of Mao Tse-tung.* 5 vols. Peking: Foreign Languages Press, 1975. 5:37–40.

———. "Bombard the Bourgeois Headquarters." *Peking Review* 33 (August 5, 1966): 9.

———. "The Chinese People Have Stood Up!" (September 1949). In *Selected Works of Mao Tse-tung.* 5 vols. Peking: Foreign Languages Press, 1975. 5:15–18.

———. *The Chinese Revolution and the Chinese Communist Party.* Peking: Foreign Languages Press, 1954. Also published as "The Chinese Revolution and the Chinese Communist Party" (December 1939). In *Selected Works of Mao Tse-tung.* 5 vols. Peking: Foreign Languages Press, 1975. 2:305–34.

———. "Combat Liberalism" (September 1937). In *Selected Works of Mao Tse-tung.* 5 vols. Peking: Foreign Languages Press, 1975. 2:31–35.

———. "Draw in Large Numbers of Intellectuals" (December 1939). In *Selected Works of Mao Tse-tung.* 5 vols. Peking: Foreign Languages Press, 1975. 2:301–3.

———. "The Foolish Old Man Who Removed the Mountains" (June 1945). In *Selected Works of Mao Tse-tung.* 5 vols. Peking: Foreign Languages Press, 1975. 3:321–24.

———. "In Memory of Norman Bethune" (December 1939). In *Selected Works of Mao Tse-tung.* 5 vols. Peking: Foreign Languages Press, 1975. 2:337–38.

———. "Manifesto of the Chinese People's Liberation Army" (October 1947). In *Selected Works of Mao Tse-tung.* 5 vols. Peking: Foreign Languages Press, 1975. 4:147–53.

———. *Mao Zedong Sixiang Wansui (Long Live the Thought of Mao Tse-tung).* 2 vols. Tapiei: n.p., 1967–1969.

———. "On Coalition Government" (April 1945). In *Selected Works of Mao Tse-tung.* 5 vols. Peking: Foreign Languages Press, 1975. 3:255–320.

———. "On Contradiction" (June 1945). In *Selected Works of Mao Tse-tung.* 5 vols. Peking: Foreign Languages Press, 1975. 1:311–47.

———. *On New Democracy.* Peking: Foreign Languages Press, 1954. Also published as "On New Democracy" (January 1940). In *Selected Works of Mao Tse-tung.* 5 vols. Peking: Foreign Languages Press, 1975. 2:339–84.

———. "On Practice" (July 1937). In *Selected Works of Mao Tse-tung.* 5 vols. Peking: Foreign Languages Press, 1975. 1:295–309.

———. "On the Correct Handling of Contradictions among the People" (February 1957). In *Selected Works of Mao Tse-tung.* 5 vols. Peking: Foreign Languages Press, 1975. 5:384–421.

———. "On the People's Democratic Dictatorship" (June 1949). In *Selected Works of Mao Tse-tung.* 5 vols. Peking: Foreign Languages Press, 1975. 4:411–24.

————. "On the Protracted War" (May 1938). In *Selected Works of Mao Tse-tung.* 5 vols. Peking: Foreign Languages Press, 1975. 2:113–94.

————. "On the Ten Great Relationships." In *Chairman Mao Talks to the People,* edited by Stuart Schram, 61–83. New York: Pantheon, 1974. Full text of "On the Ten Great Relationships" (April 1956) in *Selected Works of Mao Tse-tung.* 5 vols. Peking: Foreign Languages Press, 1975. 5:284–307.

————. "The Orientation of the Youth Movement" (May 1939). In *Selected Works of Mao Tse-tung.* 5 vols. Peking: Foreign Languages Press, 1975. 2:241–49.

————. "Problems of Strategy in China's Revolutionary War" (December 1936). In *Selected Works of Mao Tse-tung.* 5 vols. Peking: Foreign Languages Press, 1975. 1:179–253.

————. "Remarks at the Spring Festival" (February 1964; summary record). In *Chairman Mao Talks to the People,* edited by Stuart Schram, 197–211. New York: Pantheon, 1974.

————. "Report of an Investigation into the Peasant Movement in Hunan" (March 1927). In *Selected Works of Mao Tse-tung.* 5 vols. Peking: Foreign Languages Press, 1975. 1:23–59.

————. *The Sayings of Chairman Mao.* Peking: General Political Department of the People's Liberation Army, 1966.

————. *Selected Readings from the Works of Mao Tsetung.* Beijing: Foreign Languages Press, 1971.

————. "Serve the People" (September 1944). In *Selected Works of Mao Tse-tung.* 5 vols. Peking: Foreign Languages Press, 1975. 3:227–28.

————. "Some Questions Concerning Methods of Leadership" (June 1943). In *Selected Works of Mao Tse-tung.* 5 vols. Peking: Foreign Languages Press, 1975. 3:117–22.

————. "Speech at the Lushan Conference" (July 1959). In *Chairman Mao Talks to the People,* edited by Stuart Schram, 130–46. New York: Pantheon, 1974.

————. "Speech at the Supreme State Conference" (January 1958; excerpt). In *Chairman Mao Talks to the People,* edited by Stuart Schram, 91–95. New York: Pantheon, 1974.

————. "A Study of Physical Education." In Stuart Schram, *The Political Thought of Mao,* rev. and enlarged ed., 94–102. New York: Praeger, 1969.

————. "Talk at the Chengtu Conference" (March 10, 1958). In *Chairman Mao Talks to the People,* edited by Stuart Schram, 96–124. New York: Pantheon, 1974.

————. "Talk at Enlarged Work Conference" (January 30, 1962). In *Mao Papers: Anthology and Bibliography,* edited by Jerome Ch'en, 36–39. London: Oxford University Press, 1970.

————. "Talk at Meeting of All Circles in Yenan Celebrating the Sixtieth Birthday of Stalin" (December 21, 1939). In Stuart Schram, *The Political Thought of Mao,* rev. and enlarged ed., 427–28. New York: Praeger, 1969.

Margolin, Jean-Louis. "China: A Long March into Night." In *The Black Book of Communism: Crimes, Terror, Repression,* edited by Stéphane Courtois et al., translated by Jonathan Murphy et al., 463–546. Cambridge: Harvard University Press, 1999.

Marshall, I. H. *1 and 2 Thessalonians*. London: Marshall, Morgan & Scott, 1983.

Martin, D. *Slavery As Salvation: The Metaphor of Slavery in Pauline Christianity*. New Haven, Conn.: Yale University Press, 1990.

Marx, Karl. *Capital: A Critique of Political Economy*. Translated by Samuel Moore and Edward Aveling. New York: Modern Library, 1906.

———. "Contribution to the Critique of Hegel's Philosophy of Right." In Karl Marx and Friedrich Engels, *Collected Works*. Translated by Richard Dixon et al. 48 vols. to date. London: Lawrence & Wishart, 1975–. 3:3–129

———. "Critique of the Gotha Program." In Karl Marx and Friedrich Engels, *Selected Works of Karl Marx and Frederick Engels*. 2 vols. Moscow: Foreign Languages Publishing, 1951. 2:9–30.

———. "The Difference between the Democritean and Epicurean Philosophy of Nature." In Karl Marx and Friedrich Engels, *Collected Works*. Translated by Richard Dixon et al. 48 vols. to date. London: Lawrence & Wishart, 1975–. 1:25–108.

———. "Economic and Philosophical Manuscripts." In Karl Marx and Friedrich Engels, *Collected Works*. Translated by Richard Dixon et al. 48 vols. to date. London: Lawrence & Wishart, 1975–. 3:229–348.

Marx, Karl and Friedrich Engels. *The German Ideology*. New York: International, 1960.

———. "The Holy Family." Or "Critique of Critical Criticism." In Karl Marx and Friedrich Engels, *Collected Works*. Translated by Richard Dixon et al. 48 vols. to date. London: Lawrence & Wishart, 1975–. 4:5–211.

———. "Manifesto of the Communist Party." In Karl Marx and Friedrich Engels, *Selected Works of Karl Marx and Frederick Engels*. 2 vols. Moscow: Foreign Languages Publishing, 1951. 1:98–137.

Matlock, R. B. *Unveiling the Apocalyptic Paul: Paul's Interpreters and the Rhetoric of Criticism*. Sheffield: Sheffield Academic Press, 1996.

Maurer, C. "[*Tithemi*, etc.]." In *Theological Dictionary of the New Testament*, edited by Gerhard Kittel, Gerhard Friedrich, and Geoffrey W. Bromiley, and translated by Geoffrey W. Bromiley, 10 vols. Grand Rapids: Eerdmans, 1964–1976. 8:154–60.

Meeks, W. *First Urban Christians: The Social World of the Apostle Paul*. New Haven, Conn.: Yale University Press, 1983.

Meisner, Maurice. *Mao's China: A History of the People's Republic*. New York: Free Press, 1977.

———. *Mao's China and After: A History of the People's Republic*. Rev. and expanded ed. of *Mao's China*. New York: Free Press, 1986.

———. *Marxism, Maoism and Utopianism. Eight Essays*. Madison: University of Wisconsin Press, 1982. Translated into Chinese and published in 1991 by the Chinese Communist Central Documentary Research Department.

Menken, M. J. J. "Paradise Regained or Still Lost? Eschatology and Disorderly Behaviour in 2 Thessalonians." *New Testament Studies* 38 (1993): 271–89.

Metz, Johannes. *Christianity and the Bourgeoisie.* New York: Seabury, 1979.

———. *The Emergent Church: The Future of Christianity in a Post-Bourgeois World.* Translated by Peter Mann. New York: Crossroad, 1981.

Milbank, John. *Theology and Social Theory: Beyond Secular Reason.* Oxford: Basil Blackwell, 1990.

Milligan, George. *St. Paul's Epistles to the Thessalonians.* New York: Macmillan, n.d.

Moltmann, Jürgen. *The Coming of God: Christology Eschatology.* Translated by M. Kohl. London: SCM, 1996.

———. "Hope and Reality: Contradiction and Correspondence." In *God Will Be All in All: The Eschatology of Jürgen Moltmann,* edited by Richard Bauckham, 77–85. Edinburgh: T. & T. Clark, 1999.

———. "The Liberation of the Future and Its Anticipations in History." In *God Will Be All in All: The Eschatology of Jürgen Moltmann,* edited by Richard Bauckham, 265–89. Edinburgh: T. & T. Clark, 1999.

———. *Theology of Hope: On the Ground and the Implications of a Christian Eschatology.* Translated by James W. Leitch. New York: Harper & Row, 1967.

———. *The Way of Jesus Christ: Christology in Messianic Dimensions.* Translated by M. Kohl. London: SCM, 1990.

Moore, Rebecca, and Fielding M. McGehee III, eds., *The Need for a Second Look at Jonestown.* Lewiston: Edwin Mellen Press, 1989.

More, Thomas. *Utopia.* New York: Appleton-Century-Crofts, 1949.

Morgan, A. E. *Nowhere Was Somewhere: How History Makes Utopias and How Utopias Make History.* Chapel Hill: University of North Carolina Press, 1946.

Morris, Leon. *The First and Second Epistles to the Thessalonians.* Grand Rapids: Eerdmans, 1991.

Mumford, Lewis. *The Story of Utopias.* New York: Viking, 1962.

Murphey, Rhoads. "Man and Nature in China." *Modern Asian Studies* 1 (January 1967): 313–33.

Needham, Joseph. *Christian China.* Colombo: Logos, 1967.

———. "Human Laws and Laws of Nature in China and the West." *Journal of the History of Ideas* 12 (1951): 3–30, 194–230.

Nietzsche, Friedrich. *The Will to Power.* Translated by Walter Kaufmann and R. J. Hollingdale. New York: Random House, 1967.

Nisbet, R. *History of the Idea of Progress.* New York: Basic Books, 1980.

Oepke, A. "[*Parousia, pareimi*]." In *Theological Dictionary of the New Testament,* edited by Gerhard Kittel, Gerhard Friedrich, and Geoffrey W. Bromiley, and translated by Geoffrey W. Bromiley, 10 vols. Grand Rapids: Eerdmans, 1964–1976. 5:858–71.

O'Leary, Stephen. *Arguing the Apocalypse.* New York: Oxford University Press, 1994.

Olson, Theodore. *Millennialism, Utopianism, and Progress.* Toronto: University of Toronto Press, 1982.

Ong, Walter J. *Rhetoric, Romance, and Technology.* London: Cornell University Press, 1971.

Otto, Rudolf. *The Idea of the Holy.* Translated by John W. Harvey. New York: Oxford University Press, 1950.

Overholt, *Prophecy in Cross-Cultural Perspective: A Sourcebook for Biblical Researchers.* Atlanta: Scholars Press, 1986.

Pannenberg, Wolfhart. *Jesus: God and Man.* Philadelphia: Westminster, 1968.

———. *Theology and the Kingdom of God.* Philadelphia: Westminster, 1969.

Patterson, George N. *Christianity in Communist China.* Waco, Tex.: Word, 1969.

Payne, Robert. *Mao Tze-tung.* New York: Weybright & Talley, 1965.

Pearson, B. "1 Thessalonians 2:13–16: A Deutero-Pauline Interpolation." *Harvard Theological Review* 64 (1971): 79–91.

Perelman, Chaïm. *The Realm of Rhetoric.* Notre Dame, Ind.: University of Notre Dame Press, 1982.

Peterson, E. "[*Apantesis*]." In *Theological Dictionary of the New Testament,* edited by Gerhard Kittel, Gerhard Friedrich, and Geoffrey W. Bromiley, and translated by Geoffrey W. Bromiley, 10 vols. Grand Rapids: Eerdmans, 1964–1976. 1:380–81.

Philo of Alexandria. *Philo.* Translated by F. H. Colson and G. H. Whitaker. 10 vols. London: Heinemann; New York: Putnam, 1929–1962.

Plutarch. *Moralia.* Cambridge: Harvard University Press; London: Heineman, 1959–1976.

Rad, Gerhard von. *Das Formgeschichtliche Problem des Hexateuchs.* Stuttgart: W. Kohlhammer, 1938.

Rad, Gerhard von, and G. Kittel, "[*Dokeo,* etc.]," In *Theological Dictionary of the New Testament,* edited by Gerhard Kittel, Gerhard Friedrich, and Geoffrey W. Bromiley, and translated by Geoffrey W. Bromiley, 10 vols. Grand Rapids: Eerdmans, 1964–1976. 2:232–55

Radl, W. *Ankunft des Herrn.* Frankfurt A. M.: Peter D. Lang, 1981.

Rasmusson, Arne. *The Church As Polis: From Political Theology to Theological Politics As Exemplified by Jürgen Moltmann and Stanley Hauerwas.* Notre Dame, Ind.: University of Notre Dame Press, 1995.

"Resolution on Questions Concerning People's Communes" (1958). *Sixth Plenary Session of the Eighth Central Committee of the CCP, 10 Dec 1958.* Peking: New China News Agency, 1958.

Richard, E. J. *First and Second Thessalonians.* Collegeville, Minn.: Liturgical, 1995.

Richard, Erdoes. *AD 1000: Living on the Brink of Apocalypse.* New York: Harper & Row, 1989.

Ricoeur, Paul. *Figuring the Sacred: Religion, Narrative, and Imagination.* Translated by David Pellauer. Edited by Mark I. Wallace. Minneapolis: Fortress, 1995.

———. *Lectures on Ideology and Utopia.* New York: Columbia University Press, 1986.

Rigaux, Beda. *Saint Paul, les Epitres aux Thessaloniciens.* Paris: J. Gabalda, 1956.

Roberts, J. A. G. *Modern China: An Illustrated History.* Phoenix Mill, England: Sutton, 1998.

Robertson, Archibald. *The Origins of Christianity.* London: Lawrence & Wishart, 1953.

Roth, Wolfgang. *Isaiah.* Atlanta: John Knox, 1988.

Rowland, Christopher. " 'Upon Whom the Ends of the Ages Have Come': Apocalyptic and the Interpretation of the New Testament." In Malcolm Bull, *Apocalypse Theory and the Ends of the World,* 38–57. Oxford: Blackwell, 1995.

Ruether, Rosemary. *Sexism and God-Talk.* Boston: Beacon, 1983.

Rule, Paul. "Is Maoism Open to the Transcendent?" In *The New China: A Catholic Response,* edited by Michael Chu, 25–43. New York: Paulist, 1977.

Russell, D. S. *Apocalyptic: Ancient and Modern.* London: SCM, 1978.

Saint-Simon, Henri. *Nouveau Christianisme.* Paris: Bureau de Globe, 1832.

———. *Selected Writings.* Edited by Keith Taylor. New York: Holmes & Meier, 1975.

Sanders, E. P. *The Historical Figure of Jesus.* London: Penguin, 1993.

———. *Jesus and Judaism.* Philadelphia: Fortress, 1985.

Sauter, Gerhard. *What Dare We Hope? Reconsidering Eschatology.* Harrisburg, Pa.: Trinity Press International, 1999.

Schmidt, D. "1 Thess. 2:13–16: Linguistic Evidence for an Interpolation." *Journal of Biblical Literature* 102 (1983): 269–79.

Schmidt, K. L. "[*Basileia*]." In *Theological Dictionary of the New Testament,* edited by Gerhard Kittel, Gerhard Friedrich, and Geoffrey W. Bromiley, and translated by Geoffrey W. Bromiley, 10 vols. Grand Rapids: Eerdmans, 1964–1976. 1:574–93.

Schram, Stuart R. *Mao Tse-tung.* New York: Simon & Schuster, 1967.

———. *The Political Thought of Mao Tse-tung.* Rev. and enlarged ed. New York: Praeger, 1969.

———. *The Thought of Mao Tse-Tung.* Cambridge, Britain: Cambridge University Press, 1989.

———, ed. *Chairman Mao Talks to the People.* New York: Pantheon, 1974. Also published as Schram, ed. *Mao Tse-tung Unrehearsed: Talks and Letters, 1956–1971.* Harmondsworth: Penguin, 1974.

Schrenk, G., and G. Quell. "[*Eklegomai*]." In *Theological Dictionary of the New Testament,* edited by Gerhard Kittel, Gerhard Friedrich, and Geoffrey W. Bromiley, and translated by Geoffrey W. Bromiley, 10 vols. Grand Rapids: Eerdmans, 1964–1976. 4:144–76.

Schurmann, Franz. *Ideology and Organization in Communist China*. 2d enlarged ed. Berkeley and Los Angeles: University of California Press, 1968.

Schüssler Fiorenza, E. *The Book of Revelation, Justice and Judgment*. Philadelphia: Fortress, 1985.

Schwartz, Benjamin I. *Communism and China: Ideology in Flux*. Cambridge: Harvard University Press, 1968.

Schweitzer, Albert. *The Quest of Historical Jesus: A Critical Study of Its Progress from Reimarus to Wrede*. New York: Macmillan, 1964.

Schweizer, E. "[*Pneuma*, etc.]." In *Theological Dictionary of the New Testament*, edited by Gerhard Kittel, Gerhard Friedrich, and Geoffrey W. Bromiley, and translated by Geoffrey W. Bromiley, 10 vols. Grand Rapids: Eerdmans, 1964–1976. 6:389–455.

Scott, J. Julius. "Paul and Late-Jewish Eschatology—A Case Study, 1 Thess. 4:13–18 and 2 Thess. 2:1–12." *Journal of the Evangelical Theological Society* 15 (1972): 133–43.

Shek, Richard. "Sectarian Eschatology and Violence." In *Violence in China: Essays in Culture and Counterculture*, edited by Jonathan N. Lipman and Stevan Harrell, 87–109. New York: State University of New York Press, 1990.

Shen, Philip. "Toward a Critique of Power in the New China." In *Christianity and New China*, 2 vols. South Pasadena, Calif.: Ecclesia, 1976. 2:109–12.

Smart, Ninian. *Mao*. Glasgow: Fontana-Collins, 1974.

Smith, A. *Comfort One Another: Reconstructing the Rhetoric and Audience of 1 Thessalonians*. Louisville: Westminster John Knox, 1995.

Snaith, Norman H. *The Distinctive Ideas of the Old Testament*. New York: Schocken, 1964.

Snow, Edgar. "A Conversation with Mao Tse-tung." *Life Magazine* (April 30, 1971): 46.

———. *The Long Revolution*. New York: Random House, 1972.

———. *Red Star over China*. New York: Random House, 1938.

Spence, Jonathan D. *God's Chinese Son: The Taiping Heavenly Kingdom of Hong Xiuquan*. New York: W. W. Norton, 1996.

Spicq, C. "Les Thessaloniciens 'inquiets' Etainet Ils Des Paresseux?" *Studia Theologia* 10 (1956): 1–13.

Starr, John Bryan. *Ideology and Culture*. New York: Harper & Row, 1973.

Stauffer, M. T., ed. *The Christian Occupation of China*. Shanghai: China Continuation Committee, 1922.

Steinmetz, David C. "The Superiority of Pre-critical Exegesis." In *The Theological Interpretation of Scripture*, edited by Stephen E. Fowl, 26–38. Cambridge: Blackwell, 1997.

Sun, Yan. *The Chinese Reassessment of Socialism, 1976–1992*. Princeton, N.J.: Princeton University Press, 1995.

Sun Zi (Sun Tzu). *The Art of War*. Translated by Samuel B. Griffith. Oxford: Clarendon, 1963.

Talmage, J. V. N. "Should the Native Churches in China Be United Ecclesiastically and Independent of Foreign Churches and Societies?" *Records of the General Conference of the Protestant Missionaries of China Held at Shanghai, May 10–20, 1877,* 429–33. Shanghai: Presbyterian Mission Press, 1878.

Talmon, J. L. *The Origins of Totalitarian Democracy.* New York: Praeger, 1965.

Talmon, Y. "Millenarian Movements." *Archives Europeennes de Sociologie* 7 (1966): 159–200.

Theissen, Gerd. *The Gospels in Context: Social and Political History in the Synoptic Tradition.* Minneapolis: Augsburg Fortress, 1991.

———. *The Shadow of the Galilean: The Quest of the Historical Jesus in Narrative Form.* Philadelphia: Fortress, 1987.

Thiselton, Anthony C. *New Horizons in Hermeneutics.* Grand Rapids: Zondervan, 1992.

Thompson, Laurence, trans. *Ta T'ung Shu: The One-World Philosophy of K'ang Yu-wei.* London: Allen & Unwin, 1958.

Ting, K. H. "A Call for Clarity: Fourteen Points from Christians in the People's Republic of China to Christians Abroad." *China Notes* 19 (Winter 1980–1981): 145–49.

———. "A Chinese Christian's View of the Atheist," In *Chinese Christians Speak Out—Addresses and Sermons,* edited by K. H. Ting et al., 95–103. Beijing: New World, 1984.

———. *No Longer Strangers: Selected Writings of K. H. Ting.* Edited by Raymond L. Whitehead. Maryknoll, N.Y.: Orbis, 1989.

Ting, K. H., et al., eds. *Chinese Christians Speak Out—Addresses and Sermons.* Beijing: New World, 1984.

Toole, David. *Waiting for Godot in Sarajevo: Theological Reflections on Nihilism, Tragedy, and Apocalypse.* Boulder, Colo.: Westview, 1998.

Torr, Dona, ed. *Marx on China, 1853–1860: Articles from the New York Daily Tribune.* London: Lawrence & Wishart, 1951.

Toynbee, Arnold. *A Study of History.* New York: Oxford University Press, 1947.

Tucker, Robert C. *Philosophy and Myth in Karl Marx.* Cambridge: Cambridge University Press, 1972.

Van der Watt, J. G. "The Use of ZAW in 1 Thessalonians: A Comparison with ZAW/ZWH in the Gospel of John." In *The Thessalonian Correspondence,* edited by Raymond F. Collins, 356–69. Leuven: Leuven University Press, 1990.

Wakeman, F. *History and Will.* Berkeley and Los Angeles: University of California Press, 1973.

Waley, Arthur, trans. *The Way and Its Power: A Study of the Tao te ching and Its Place in Chinese Thought.* London: Allen & Unwin, 1934.

Wallis, Arthur. *China Miracle: A Voice to the Church in the West.* Eastbourne: Kingsway, 1985.

Wanamaker, C. A. "Apocalypticism at Thessalonica." *Neotestamentica* 21 (1987): 1–10.

————. *The Epistles to the Thessalonians: A Commentary on the Greek Text*. Grand Rapids: Eerdmans, 1990.

Wang Pi. *Commentary on the* Lao Tzu. Translated by Ariane Rump. Honolulu: The University Press of Hawaii, 1979.

Warren, M. A. C., ed. *To Apply the Gospel: Selections from the Writings of Henry Venn*. Grand Rapids: Eerdmans, 1971.

Weiss, Johannes. *Jesus' Proclamation of the Kingdom of God*. Philadelphia: Fortress, 1971.

Wells, H. G. *A Modern Utopia*. Lincoln: University of Nebraska Press, 1967.

Wengst, Klaus. *Pax Romana and the Peace of Jesus Christ*. Translated by John Bowden. Philadelphia: Fortress, 1987.

Whitehead, Alfred North. *Process and Reality*. Corrected ed. New York: Free Press, 1978.

Whitehead, Raymond. "Love and Animosity in the Ethic of Mao." In *Christianity and the New China*, 2 vols. South Pasadena, Calif.: Ecclesia, 1976. 1:71–85.

Whyte, Bob. *Unfinished Encounter: China and Christianity*. Glasgow: William Collins Sons, 1988.

Wickeri, Philip L. *Seeking the Common Ground: Protestant Christianity, the Three-Self Movement, and China's United Front*. Maryknoll, N.Y.: Orbis, 1988.

Williams, Raymond. *Marxism and Literature*. Oxford: Oxford University Press, 1977.

Wilson, Bryan R. *Magic and the Millennium: A Sociological Study of Religious Movements of Protest among Tribal and Third-World Peoples*. London: Heinemann, 1973.

Wilson, Dick, *Mao, The People's Emperor*. London: Hutchinson, 1979.

————, ed. *Mao Tse-tung in the Scales of History*. Cambridge: Cambridge University Press, 1977.

Winter, Bruce. "'If a Man Does Not Wish to Work . . .': A Cultural and Historical Setting for 2 Thessalonians 3:6–16." *Tyndale Bulletin* 40 (1989): 303–15.

Witherington, Ben, III. *The Jesus Quest: The Third Search for the Jew of Nazareth*. Downers Grove, Ill.: InterVarsity Press, 1995.

Wittke, Carl. *The Utopian Communist: A Biography of Wilhelm Weitling*. Baton Rouge: Louisiana State University Press, 1950.

Worsley, Peter. *The Trumpet Shall Sound: A Study of "Cargo" Cults in Melanesia*. 2d augmented ed. New York: Schocken, 1968.

Wuellner, W. "The Argumentative Structure of 1 Thessalonians As Paradoxical Encomium." In *The Thessalonian Correspondence*, edited by Raymond F. Collins, 117–36. Leuven: Leuven University Press, 1990.

Yang, C. K. *Religion in Chinese Society*. Berkeley and Los Angeles: University of California Press, 1961.

Yang Pik Chuang. *Mao Zedong and Zhou Enlai*. Taipei: One Bridge, 1999.

Yeo Khiok-khng. "Paul's Eschatology and Mao's Utopianism—A Clash of Ideology." *Asia Journal of Theology* 13 (1999): 375–86.

————. "A Political Reading of Paul's Eschatology in 1 and 2 Thessalonians." *Asia Journal of Theology* 12 (1998): 77–88.

————. "Revelation 5 in the Light of Pannenberg's Christology: Christ the End of History and the Hope of the Suffering." *Asia Journal of Theology* 8 (1994): 308–34.

————. "The Rhetoric of Calling and Election Language in 1 Thessalonians." Paper read at Rhetorical Conference, Florence, August 1–5, 1998; to be published in the conference collection of essays by Sheffield Academic Press.

————. *Rhetorical Interaction in 1 Corinthians 8 and 10: A Formal Analysis and Its Preliminary Implication for a Chinese, Cross-Cultural Hermeneutics.* Leiden: E. J. Brill, 1995.

————. "A Rhetorical Study of Acts 17:22–31: What Has Jerusalem to Do with Athens and Beijing?" *Jian Dao: A Journal of Bible and Theology* 1 (1994): 75–107.

————. "The Rise of Three-Self Patriotic Movement (TSPM): Chinese Christianity in Light of Communist Ideology in New China." *Asia Journal of Theology* 6 (1992): 1–14.

————. *What Has Jerusalem to Do with Beijing? Biblical Interpretation from a Chinese Perspective.* Harrisburg, Pa.: Trinity Press International, 1998.

————. "The 'Yin and Yang' of God (Exod. 3:14) and Humanity (Gen. 1:27)." *Zeitschrift für Religions und Geistesgeschichte* 46 (1994): 319–32.

Yoder, John Howard. *The Original Revolution: Essays on Christian Pacifism.* Scottdale: Herald, 1972.

————. *The Politics of Jesus: Vicit Agnus Noster.* Grand Rapids: Eerdmans, 1994.

Zhang, Richard X. Y. "The Origin of the 'Three Self.'" *Jian Dao* 5 (1996): 175–202.

scripture index

subject index